First World War
and Army of Occupation
War Diary
France, Belgium and Germany

46 DIVISION
137 Infantry Brigade
South Staffordshire Regiment
1/6th Battalion (Territorial Force)
1 February 1915 - 31 May 1919

WO95/2687/1

The Naval & Military Press Ltd
www.nmarchive.com
Published in association with The National Archives

Published by

The Naval & Military Press Ltd

Unit 10 Ridgewood Industrial Park,

Uckfield, East Sussex,

TN22 5QE England

Tel: +44 (0) 1825 749494

www.naval-military-press.com

www.nmarchive.com

This diary has been reprinted in facsimile from the original. Any imperfections are inevitably reproduced and the quality may fall short of modern type and cartographic standards.

© Crown Copyright
Images reproduced by permission of The National Archives, London, England, 2015.

Contents

Document type	Place/Title	Date From	Date To
Heading	WO95/2687/1 1/6 Battalion Smith Staffordshire Regiment.		
Heading	46th Division 137th Infy Bde 1-6th Bn Sth Staffs Feb 1915-May 1919		
Heading	N.M. Div. 1st Staffordshire Brigadier 1/6th South Staffordshire Regt. Vol I		
War Diary	Saffron Walden.	01/02/1915	18/02/1915
War Diary	Halliquebury Park	19/02/1915	19/02/1915
War Diary	Saffron Walden	20/02/1915	28/02/1915
Heading	137th Inf. Bde. 46th Div. Battn. Disembarked Havre From England 3/5.3.15. War Diary 1/6th Battn. The South Staffordshire Regiment. March 1915		
War Diary	Saffron Walden	01/03/1915	01/03/1915
War Diary	Southampton	02/03/1915	02/03/1915
War Diary	Havre	03/03/1915	06/03/1915
War Diary	Noordpeene	07/03/1915	08/03/1915
War Diary	Barre.	09/03/1915	10/03/1915
War Diary	Sailly	11/03/1915	16/03/1915
War Diary	Steent-Je	17/03/1915	17/03/1915
War Diary	Fletre	18/03/1915	19/03/1915
War Diary	Armentieres	20/03/1915	23/03/1915
War Diary	Fletre	24/03/1915	31/03/1915
Heading	137th Inf. Bde. 46th Div. War Diary 1/6th Battn. The South Staffordshire Regiment. April 1915		
War Diary	Bailleul	01/04/1915	01/04/1915
War Diary	Bulford Camp	02/04/1915	05/04/1915
War Diary	Wulverghem	06/04/1915	10/04/1915
War Diary	Bulford Camp	11/04/1915	13/04/1915
War Diary	Wulverghem	14/04/1915	18/04/1915
War Diary	Bulford Camp	19/04/1915	22/04/1915
War Diary	Wulverghem	23/04/1915	26/04/1915
War Diary	Bulford Camp	27/04/1915	30/04/1915
Heading	137th Inf. Bde. 46th Div. War Diary 1/6th Battn. The South Staffordshire Regiment. May 1915		
War Diary	Wulverghem	01/05/1915	04/05/1915
War Diary	Bulford Camp	05/05/1915	08/05/1915
War Diary	Wulverghem	09/05/1915	12/05/1915
War Diary	Bulford Camp	13/05/1915	16/05/1915
War Diary	Wulverghem	17/05/1915	20/05/1915
War Diary	Bulford Camp	21/05/1915	23/05/1915
War Diary	Wulverghem	24/05/1915	28/05/1915
War Diary	Bulford Camp	29/05/1915	31/05/1915
Heading	137th Inf. Bde. 46th Div. War Diary 1/6th Battn. The South Staffordshire Regiment. June 1915		
War Diary	Bulford Camp	01/06/1915	01/06/1915
War Diary	Wuloerghem	02/06/1915	05/06/1915
War Diary	Bulford Camp	06/06/1915	09/06/1915
War Diary	Wulverghem	10/06/1915	12/06/1915
War Diary	Bulford Camp	13/06/1915	15/06/1915
War Diary	Wulverghem	16/06/1915	19/06/1915

War Diary	Bulford Camp	20/06/1915	25/06/1915
War Diary	Duderdom	26/06/1915	30/06/1915
Heading	137th Inf. Bde. 46th Div. War Diary 1/6th Battn. The South Staffordshire Regiment. July 1915		
War Diary	Ouderdom	01/07/1915	04/07/1915
War Diary	Zillebeke	05/07/1915	11/07/1915
War Diary	Ouderdom	12/07/1915	18/07/1915
War Diary	Hill 60	19/07/1915	22/07/1915
War Diary	Zillebeke	23/07/1915	27/07/1915
War Diary	Hill 60	27/07/1915	31/07/1915
Heading	137th Inf. Bde. 46th Div. War Diary 1/6th Battn. The South Staffordshire Regiment. August 1915		
War Diary	Hill 60	01/08/1915	02/08/1915
War Diary	J Camp	03/08/1915	03/08/1915
War Diary	Ouderdom	03/08/1915	09/08/1915
War Diary	Hill 60	10/08/1915	16/08/1915
War Diary	Zillebeke	17/08/1915	22/08/1915
War Diary	Hill 60	23/08/1915	30/08/1915
War Diary	J Huts	31/08/1915	31/08/1915
Heading	137th Inf. Bde. 46th Div. War Diary 1/6th Battn. The South Staffordshire Regiment. September 1915		
War Diary	J Huts	01/09/1915	01/09/1915
War Diary	Canada Huts	02/09/1915	06/09/1915
War Diary	Hill 60	07/09/1915	12/09/1915
War Diary	Zillebeke	13/09/1915	17/09/1915
War Diary	Hill 60	18/09/1915	25/09/1915
War Diary	Canada Huts.	26/09/1915	30/09/1915
Heading	137th Inf. Bde. 46th Div. War Diary 1/6th Battn. The South Staffordshire Regiment. October 1915		
War Diary	Canada Huts.	01/10/1915	01/10/1915
War Diary	Robecq	02/10/1915	05/10/1915
War Diary	Vaudricourt	06/10/1915	11/10/1915
War Diary	Vermelles.	12/10/1915	15/10/1915
War Diary	Vaudricourt	16/10/1915	18/10/1915
War Diary	Vaudricourt & Allouagne.	19/10/1915	19/10/1915
War Diary	Allouagne.	20/10/1915	24/10/1915
War Diary	Fouquereuil.	25/10/1915	31/10/1915
Heading	137th Inf. Bde. 46th Div. War Diary 1/6th Battn. The South Staffordshire Regiment. November 1915		
War Diary	Fouquereuil.	01/11/1915	04/11/1915
War Diary	Lestrem.	05/11/1915	09/11/1915
War Diary	Croix Barbee.	10/11/1915	30/11/1915
Heading	137th Inf. Bde.46th Div. War Diary 1/6th Battn. The South Staffordshire Regiment. December 1915		
War Diary	Croix Barbee.	01/12/1915	04/12/1915
War Diary	Pacaut.	05/12/1915	18/12/1915
War Diary	Le Pont A Balque.	19/12/1915	25/12/1915
War Diary	Train.	26/12/1915	27/12/1915
War Diary	Marseilles.	28/12/1915	31/12/1915
Heading	1/6th Sth Staffs Jan Vol XII		
War Diary	Marseilles. France	01/01/1916	07/01/1916
War Diary	Alexandria Egypt.	08/01/1916	10/01/1916
War Diary	Shallufa.	11/01/1916	31/01/1916
War Diary	Alexandria.	01/02/1916	16/02/1916
War Diary	Vauchelles	17/02/1916	20/02/1916
War Diary	Beaumetz.	21/02/1916	25/02/1916

War Diary	Autheux. Beaumetz.	26/02/1916	29/02/1916
Heading	1/6 S. Stafford Regt Vol XIV		
War Diary	Autheux	01/03/1916	15/04/1916
War Diary	Neuville St Vaast.	16/03/1916	09/04/1916
War Diary	Ecoivres	10/04/1916	14/04/1916
War Diary	Neuville St Vaast.	15/04/1916	20/04/1916
War Diary	Monchy Breton.	21/04/1916	03/05/1916
War Diary	Ivergny.	04/05/1916	04/05/1916
War Diary	St Amand.	05/05/1916	05/05/1916
War Diary	Fonque-Villiers.	06/05/1916	19/05/1916
War Diary	Sus-St-Leger.	20/05/1916	10/06/1916
War Diary	Humbercamp	11/06/1916	16/06/1916
War Diary	Fonque-Villers.	17/06/1916	18/06/1916
War Diary	Sus-St-Leger	19/06/1916	22/06/1916
War Diary	Souastre.	23/06/1916	30/06/1916
Miscellaneous	G.S.46th Division July 1916 South Staffs June 1916 War History M.S.S. (Wire Reports)		
Miscellaneous	The Grange Broseley. Shropshire.	10/08/1926	10/08/1926
Miscellaneous	The Grange Broseley. Shropshire.	06/08/1926	06/08/1926
Miscellaneous			
Miscellaneous	Order Of Battle Of XIV Res. Corps.		
Miscellaneous	Order Of Battle 52nd Reconstituted Division		
Miscellaneous	Artillery 52nd Division		
Miscellaneous	Lieutenant-General Von Stein. (Commanding XIV Reserve Corps).		
Miscellaneous	Enemy Work on Sector from Sunken Road (K.17.a.b.) to left of Sector held by the 48th Division (References are from VIII Corps Summary during the month of April 1916		
Miscellaneous	Trench Mortars		
Miscellaneous	Active Hostile Batteries N.B. All respected By Div. Art. unless otherwise stated		
Miscellaneous	Gommecourt.		
Miscellaneous	Order Of Battle Of XIV Res. Corps.		
Miscellaneous	Order Of Battle 52nd Reconstitued		
Miscellaneous	Artillery 52nd Division		
Miscellaneous	Lieutenant-General Von Stein.		
Miscellaneous	Enemy work on Sector from Sunken Road (K.17.A.o.) to the left of Sector held by the 48th Division on (References are from VIII Corps Summary during the month of April 1916)		
Miscellaneous	Trench Mortars		
Miscellaneous	Active Hostile Batteries N.B. All Reported by Div.Art. Unless Otherwise Stated		
Miscellaneous	Gommecourt.		
Map			
Miscellaneous	137th Infantry Brigade Instructions.	24/06/1916	24/06/1916
Diagram etc	Diagram of German Troops on Front Serre-Gommecourt		
Miscellaneous	Service Instructions.		
Miscellaneous	Notes On The Ground In The Neighbourhood Of Gommecourt.		
Miscellaneous	Points Which Influenced The Attack On Gommecourt.		
Miscellaneous	Wire Report Patrol.	26/06/1916	26/06/1916
Miscellaneous	Copy.		
Miscellaneous	Copy.	28/06/1916	28/06/1916

Type	Description	From	To
Miscellaneous	Copy. Situation Report.	27/06/1916	27/06/1916
Miscellaneous	Copy. Patrol.	27/06/1916	27/06/1916
Miscellaneous	Wire Patrol. Report. 4th Leic. Regt.	27/06/1916	27/06/1916
Miscellaneous	Copy. Wire Patrol Report. 5th N.S.Reg.	27/06/1916	27/06/1916
Miscellaneous	To 46th Divn., Repeat C.R.A.		
Miscellaneous	Gap Practically Untouched.		
Miscellaneous	To:- 137th Infantry Bde. Herewith Original Reports On Condition Of Enemy Wire.	26/06/1916	26/06/1916
War Diary	Souastre	01/07/1916	01/07/1916
War Diary	Fonque Villers	01/07/1916	01/07/1916
War Diary	St. Amand	02/07/1916	03/07/1916
War Diary	Berles.	04/07/1916	27/07/1916
War Diary	Bailleulmont.	28/07/1916	31/07/1916
Miscellaneous	Casualties For Month Of July 1916		
Miscellaneous	War Diary of 1/6th South Staff Regt For The Month Of August 1916 Vol 19		
Miscellaneous	1/6 & Stafford Regt Feb Vol XIII		
War Diary	Bailleul-Mont.	01/08/1916	02/08/1916
War Diary	Berles-Au-Bois.	03/08/1916	22/08/1916
War Diary	Bailleul-Mont.	23/08/1916	29/08/1916
War Diary	Berdes-Au-Bois.	30/08/1916	31/08/1916
Miscellaneous	Total Casualties For Month Of August 1916		
War Diary	Berles-Au-Bois.	01/09/1916	09/09/1916
War Diary	Berles-Au-Bois	10/09/1916	15/09/1916
War Diary	Bailleulmont.	16/09/1916	21/09/1916
War Diary	Berles-Au-Bois.	22/09/1916	30/09/1916
Miscellaneous	Total Casualties For Month Of September 1916		
War Diary	Berles-Au-Bois.	01/10/1916	09/10/1916
War Diary	Bailleul-Mont.	10/10/1916	15/10/1916
War Diary	Berles-Au-Bois.	16/10/1916	28/10/1916
Miscellaneous	Coullemont.	29/10/1916	29/10/1916
War Diary	Lucheux.	30/10/1916	31/10/1916
Miscellaneous	Copies Issued To:-		
Operation(al) Order(s)	Operation Order No 11 by Lieut: Colonel F.J. Trump. Commanding 1/6th Btn South Staffordshire Regiment.	18/10/1916	18/10/1916
Miscellaneous	Sequence Of Events.	27/10/1916	27/10/1916
Miscellaneous			
Miscellaneous	To:- G.O.C. 137th Infantry Brigade.	27/10/1916	27/10/1916
War Diary	Bonnieres.	01/11/1916	03/11/1916
War Diary	Yvrencheux.	04/11/1916	11/11/1916
War Diary	Argenvilliers.	12/11/1916	22/11/1916
War Diary	Cramont-Les-Masures.	23/11/1916	23/11/1916
War Diary	Noeux.	24/11/1916	25/11/1916
War Diary	Le Souich.	26/11/1916	06/12/1916
War Diary	Pommier	07/12/1916	10/12/1916
War Diary	Bienvillers	11/12/1916	15/12/1916
War Diary	St Amand.	16/12/1916	19/12/1916
War Diary	Bienvillers	20/12/1916	23/12/1916
War Diary	Pommier.	24/12/1916	31/12/1916
Miscellaneous	Total Casualties For Month Of December 1916		
War Diary	St Amand	01/01/1917	02/01/1917
War Diary	Bienvillers	03/01/1917	07/01/1917
War Diary	Pommier	07/01/1917	11/01/1917
War Diary	Bienvillers	12/01/1917	16/01/1917
War Diary	St Amand.	17/01/1917	20/01/1917
War Diary	Bienvillers-Au-Bois.	21/01/1917	24/01/1917

Type	Description	Start	End
War Diary	Pommier.	25/01/1917	28/01/1917
War Diary	Bienvillers Au-Bois.	29/01/1917	31/01/1917
Miscellaneous	Total Casualties For Month Of January 1917		
War Diary	St Amand.	01/02/1917	02/02/1917
War Diary	Pommier	03/02/1917	06/02/1917
War Diary	Berles-Au Bois	07/02/1917	15/02/1917
War Diary	Pommier.	16/02/1917	18/02/1917
War Diary	Berles-Au-Bois.	19/02/1917	28/02/1917
War Diary	Pommier	01/03/1917	02/03/1917
War Diary	Berles-Au-Bois.	03/03/1917	05/03/1917
War Diary	Pommier	06/03/1917	11/03/1917
War Diary	Bayencourt	12/03/1917	13/03/1917
War Diary	Biez Wood	14/03/1917	14/03/1917
War Diary	Bayencourt	15/03/1917	18/03/1917
War Diary	Hannescamps	19/03/1917	23/03/1917
War Diary	Bus-En-Artois	24/03/1917	24/03/1917
War Diary	Contay	25/03/1917	25/03/1917
War Diary	Bertangles	26/03/1917	26/03/1917
War Diary	Dury.	27/03/1917	29/03/1917
War Diary	Lespresses	30/03/1917	31/03/1917
War Diary	Auchy-Au-Bois	01/04/1917	12/04/1917
War Diary	Bethune	13/04/1917	18/04/1917
War Diary	Lievin	18/04/1917	24/04/1917
War Diary	Fains-En Gohelle	25/04/1917	30/04/1917
Operation(al) Order(s)	Operation Order No. 1. By Major R. Evans, Commanding, 1/6th Battalion South Staffordshire Regiment.	08/04/1917	08/04/1917
Operation(al) Order(s)	Battalion Operation Orders No. 2 By Major R. Evans Commanding 1/6th Battalion South Staffordshire Regiment.	11/04/1917	11/04/1917
Operation(al) Order(s)	Operation Order No. 4 By Major R. Evans Commanding, 1/6th Battalion South Staffordshire Regt.	18/04/1917	18/04/1917
Operation(al) Order(s)	Operation Order No. 5 By Major R. Evans Commanding, 1/6th Battalion South Staffordshire Regt.	19/04/1917	19/04/1917
Operation(al) Order(s)	Operation Order No. 6 By Major R. Evans Commanding, 1/6th Battalion South Staffordshire Regt.	23/04/1917	23/04/1917
Operation(al) Order(s)	Operation Order No. 9 By Major R. Evans Commanding, 1/6th Battalion South Staffordshire Regt.	29/04/1917	29/04/1917
War Diary	Red Mill. Angres.	01/05/1917	08/05/1917
War Diary	Angres.	09/05/1917	12/05/1917
War Diary	Sains-En-Gohelle.	13/05/1917	19/05/1917
War Diary	Petit Loos.	20/05/1917	22/05/1917
War Diary	In Front of Lens.	23/05/1917	25/05/1917
War Diary	Petit Loos.	26/05/1917	27/05/1917
War Diary	Elvaston Castle	28/05/1917	31/05/1917
Miscellaneous	Appendix To War Diary. May 1917. 1/6th Btn. S. Staffs Rgt.	28/05/1917	28/05/1917
Operation(al) Order(s)	Operation Order No 10 By Lieutenant Colonel F.J Trump D.S.O. Commanding In The Battalion South Staffordshire Regiment	03/05/1917	03/05/1917
Operation(al) Order(s)	Operation Order No 11		
Operation(al) Order(s)	Operation Orders No 12	11/05/1917	11/05/1917
Operation(al) Order(s)	Operation Order No 13 By Lieutenant Colonel F.J. Trump D.S.O. Commanding, 1/6th Battalion South Staffordshire Regiment.	18/05/1917	18/05/1917

Type	Description	Date From	Date To
Operation(al) Order(s)	Operation Orders No 14 By Lieutenant Colonel F.J. Trump. D.S.O. Commanding. 1/6th Battalion South Staffordshire Regiment.	18/05/1917	18/05/1917
Operation(al) Order(s)	Operation Order No. 15. By Lieut Colonel F.J. Trump D.S.O. Commanding, 1/6th Battalion South Staffordshire Regiment.	22/05/1917	22/05/1917
Operation(al) Order(s)	Operation Order No. 16. By Lieut Colonel F.J. Trump D.S.O. Commanding, 1/6th Battalion South Staffordshire Regiment.	23/05/1917	23/05/1917
Operation(al) Order(s)	Operation Order No. 18. By Lieut Colonel F.J. Trump D.S.O. Commanding, 1/6th Battalion South Staffordshire Regiment.	27/05/1917	27/05/1917
Operation(al) Order(s)	Operation Order No. 19. By Lieut Colonel F.J. Trump D.S.O. Commanding, 1/6th Battalion South Staffordshire Regiment.	30/05/1917	30/05/1917
War Diary	Cite St Pierre	01/06/1917	15/06/1917
War Diary	Bouvigny Boyeffles	16/06/1917	22/06/1917
War Diary	Calonne	23/06/1917	23/06/1917
War Diary	Lievin	24/06/1917	25/06/1917
War Diary	Bully Grenay	26/06/1917	27/06/1917
War Diary	Lievin.	28/06/1917	30/06/1917
Operation(al) Order(s)	Operation Order No 20	03/06/1917	03/06/1917
Operation(al) Order(s)	Operation Orders No. 21	06/06/1917	06/06/1917
Operation(al) Order(s)	Operation Orders No 22. By Lieutenant-Colonel F.J. Trump. D.S.O. Commanding 1/6th Battalion South Staffordshire Regt.	07/06/1917	07/06/1917
Operation(al) Order(s)	Operation Order No 24. By Lieutenant-Colonel F.J.Trump.D.S.O. Commanding. 1/6th Btn South Staffs Regiment.	11/06/1917	11/06/1917
Miscellaneous	Operation Orders No. 25		
Operation(al) Order(s)	Operation Orders No 27 by Lieutenant Colonel F.J. Trumps D.S.O. Commanding 1/6th Battn South Staffordshire Regiment.	23/06/1917	23/06/1917
Operation(al) Order(s)	Operation Orders No 28. by Lieutenant Colonel F.J. Trumps D.S.O. Commanding 1/6th Battn. South Staffordshire Regiment	24/06/1917	24/06/1917
Operation(al) Order(s)	Warning Order No 01 By Lieut Colonel F.J Trump D.S.O. Commanding 1/6th Battn South Staffordshire Regiment.	23/06/1917	23/06/1917
Operation(al) Order(s)	Operation Order No 29.By Lieutenant Colonel F.J.Trump D.S.O. Commanding, 1/6th Battalion South Staffordshire Regiment.	25/06/1917	25/06/1917
Operation(al) Order(s)	Operation Orders No 30.by Lieut Colonel F.J. Trump D.S.O. Commanding, 1/6th Battalion. South Staffordshire Regiment.	27/06/1917	27/06/1917
Operation(al) Order(s)	Operation Order No 31.By Lieut Colonel F.J. Trump D.S.O. Commanding, 1/6th Battalion South Staffordshire Regiment.	27/06/1917	27/06/1917
War Diary	Lievin	01/07/1917	02/07/1917
War Diary	Burbure.	03/07/1917	25/07/1917
War Diary	Fouquieres	26/07/1917	26/07/1917
War Diary	Labourse	27/07/1917	31/07/1917
Miscellaneous	List of Prizes Won at Divisional Rifle Meeting.		
Operation(al) Order(s)	Operation Order No 32 by Lieutenant-Colonel F.J. Trump. D.S.O. Commanding 1/6th Btn South Staffordshire Rgt.	24/07/1917	24/07/1917

Operation(al) Order(s)	Operation Order No 33 by Lieutenant-Colonel F.J. Trump. D.S.O. Commanding 1/6th Btn South Staffordshire Rgt.	26/07/1917	26/07/1917
War Diary	Labourse	01/08/1917	03/08/1917
War Diary	Trenches S.W. Of Hulluch	04/08/1917	07/08/1917
War Diary	Mazingarbe	08/08/1917	11/08/1917
War Diary	Trenches S.W. Of Hulluch	12/08/1917	14/08/1917
War Diary	Noeux-Les-Mines.	15/08/1917	17/08/1917
War Diary	Trenches S.W. Of Hulluch	18/08/1917	21/08/1917
War Diary	Mazingarbe	22/08/1917	25/08/1917
War Diary	Trenches S.W. Of Hulluch.	26/08/1917	29/08/1917
War Diary	Mazingarbe	29/08/1917	31/08/1917
Operation(al) Order(s)	Operation Order No 33 by Lieutenant-Colonel F.J. Trump. D.S.O. Commanding 1/6th Battalion South Staffordshire Regiment.	01/08/1917	01/08/1917
Operation(al) Order(s)	Operation Order No 34 by Lieutenant-Colonel F.J. Trump. D.S.O. Commanding 1/6th Battalion South Staffordshire Regiment.	06/08/1917	06/08/1917
Operation(al) Order(s)	Operation Order No 35.By Lieutenant-Colonel F.J.Trump. D.S.O. Commanding 1/6th Battalion South Staffordshire Regiment.	10/08/1917	10/08/1917
Operation(al) Order(s)	Operation Order No 36. By Lieutenant-Colonel F.J. Trump. D.S.O. Commanding 1/6th Battalion South Staffordshire Regiment.	13/08/1917	13/08/1917
Operation(al) Order(s)	Operation Orders No 37. 1/6th Battalion South Staffordshire Regiment.		
Operation(al) Order(s)	Operation Order No. 38. 1/6th Battalion. South Staffordshire Regiment.	20/08/1917	20/08/1917
Operation(al) Order(s)	Operation Order No. 39. 1/6th Battalion South Staffordshire Regiment.	24/08/1917	24/08/1917
Miscellaneous	1/6th Battalion South Staffordshire Regt. Code Issued In Conjunction With Operation Order No 39	24/08/1917	24/08/1917
Operation(al) Order(s)	Operation Order No 40. 1/6th Battalion South Staffordshire Regiment.	24/08/1917	24/08/1917
Operation(al) Order(s)	Operation Order No 41,1/6th Battalion South Staffordshire Regiment.	25/08/1917	25/08/1917
Miscellaneous	Appendix "A"	26/09/1917	26/09/1917
Miscellaneous	Order By B/e Raid 1/6th Battn South Staff Regiment. Appendix "B"	26/08/1917	26/08/1917
Operation(al) Order(s)	Operation Order No 12 1/6th South Staffordshire Regiment	27/08/1917	27/08/1917
Operation(al) Order(s)	Operation Order No 43 1/6th Btn South Staffordshire Regiment	29/08/1917	29/08/1917
War Diary	Mazingarbe	01/09/1917	18/09/1917
War Diary	Verquin.	19/09/1917	23/09/1917
War Diary	Noyelles	24/09/1917	24/09/1917
War Diary	Trenches S.W. Of Hulluch	25/09/1917	28/09/1917
War Diary	Mazingarbe	29/09/1917	30/09/1917
Operation(al) Order(s)	Operation Order No 44 1/6th Battalion South Staffordshire Regiment.	17/09/1917	17/09/1917
Operation(al) Order(s)	Operation Order No 45. 1/6th Btn South Staffordshire Regiment.		
Operation(al) Order(s)	Operation Order No 46 1/6th	27/09/1917	27/09/1917
War Diary	Mazingarbe Hulluch.	01/10/1917	06/10/1917
War Diary	Verquin.	07/10/1917	09/10/1917
War Diary	Hulluch.	10/10/1917	15/10/1917

War Diary	Mazing-Arbe.	15/10/1917	17/10/1917
War Diary	Hulluch	18/10/1917	22/10/1917
War Diary	Verquin	23/10/1917	26/10/1917
War Diary	Hulluch	27/10/1917	30/10/1917
War Diary	Mazing-Arbe.	31/10/1917	31/10/1917
Operation(al) Order(s)	Operation Order No 47. 1/6th Btn South Staffordshire Regiment.	01/10/1917	01/10/1917
Operation(al) Order(s)	Operation Order No 48. 1/6th Btn South Staffordshire Regiment.	05/10/1917	05/10/1917
Operation(al) Order(s)	Operation Order No 49. 1/6th Battalion South Staffordshire Regiment.	09/10/1917	09/10/1917
Operation(al) Order(s)	Operation Order No 50. 1/6th Batt South Staffordshire Regiment.	13/10/1917	13/10/1917
Operation(al) Order(s)	Operation Order No 51. 1/6th Battn South Staffordshire Regiment.	13/10/1917	13/10/1917
Operation(al) Order(s)	Operation Order No 52. 1/6th Battalion South Staffordshire Regiment.	17/10/1917	17/10/1917
Operation(al) Order(s)	Operation Order No 53. 1/6th Battn South Staffordshire Regiment.	21/10/1917	21/10/1917
Operation(al) Order(s)	Operation Order No 54. 1/6th Battalion South Staffordshire Regiment.	25/10/1917	25/10/1917
Operation(al) Order(s)	Operation Order No 55. 1/6th Battalion South Staffordshire Regiment.	29/10/1917	29/10/1917
Heading	War Diary of 1/6th Btn South Staffordshire Regiment. From 1st November 1917 To 30th November 1917		
War Diary	Mazingarbe	01/11/1917	03/11/1917
War Diary	Hulluch.	04/11/1917	07/11/1917
War Diary	Verquin.	08/11/1917	11/11/1917
War Diary	Hulluch.	12/11/1917	15/11/1917
War Diary	Mazingarbe	16/11/1917	19/11/1917
War Diary	Hulluch.	20/11/1917	23/11/1917
War Diary	Verquin	24/11/1917	27/11/1917
War Diary	Hulluch.	28/11/1917	30/11/1917
Operation(al) Order(s)	Operation Orders No 57. 1/6th Btn South Staffordshire Regiment.	02/11/1917	02/11/1917
Operation(al) Order(s)	Operation Order No. 58. 1/6th Btn South Staffordshire Regiment.	06/11/1917	06/11/1917
Operation(al) Order(s)	Operation Order No. 59. 1/6th Battalion South Staffordshire Regiment.	10/11/1917	10/11/1917
Miscellaneous			
Operation(al) Order(s)	Operation Order No. 60. 1/6th Battn South Staffordshire Regiment.	14/11/1917	14/11/1917
Operation(al) Order(s)	Operation Order No. 61, 1/6th Battalion South Staffordshire Regiment.	18/11/1917	18/11/1917
Operation(al) Order(s)	Operation Order No. 62. 1/6th Battalion South Staffordshire Regiment.	22/11/1917	22/11/1917
Operation(al) Order(s)	Operation Order No. 63. 16th Battalion South Staffordshire Regiment.	26/11/1917	26/11/1917
Operation(al) Order(s)	Operation Order No. 54. 1/6th Battalion South Staffordshire Regt.	30/11/1917	30/11/1917
Heading	War Diary. 1/6th Btn. South Staffordshire Regiment. From:- 1st December 1917 To 31st December 1917		
War Diary	Hulluch	01/12/1917	01/12/1917
War Diary	Noyelles	02/12/1917	04/12/1917
War Diary	Hulluch	05/12/1917	08/12/1917
War Diary	Noeux-Les-Mines.	09/12/1917	13/12/1917

War Diary	Hulluch.		14/12/1917	17/12/1917
War Diary	Noyelles.		18/12/1917	21/12/1917
War Diary	Hulluch.		22/12/1917	25/12/1917
War Diary	Noeux-Les-Mines.		26/12/1917	29/12/1917
War Diary	Hulluch.		30/12/1917	31/12/1917
Operation(al) Order(s)	Operation Orders No 65. 1/6th Battalion South Staffordshire Regiment.		04/12/1917	04/12/1917
Operation(al) Order(s)	Operation Orders No 66. 1/6th Battalion South Staffordshire Regiment.		08/12/1917	08/12/1917
Operation(al) Order(s)	Operation Orders No 67. 1/6th Battalion South Staffordshire Regiment.		12/12/1917	12/12/1917
Operation(al) Order(s)	Operation Orders No 68. 1/6th Btn South Staffordshire Regiment.		16/12/1917	16/12/1917
Operation(al) Order(s)	Operation Orders No 69. 1/6th Btn South Staffordshire Regiment.		20/12/1917	20/12/1917
Operation(al) Order(s)	Operation Orders No 70. 1/6th Btn South Staffordshire Regiment.		24/12/1917	24/12/1917
Operation(al) Order(s)	Operation Orders No 71. 1/6th Btn South Staffordshire Regiment.		28/12/1917	28/12/1917
Heading	War Diary. 1/6th Btn South Staffordshire Regiment. From 1st January To 31st January 1916			
Heading	Hulluch		01/01/1918	01/01/1918
War Diary	Mazin-Garbe.		02/01/1918	06/01/1918
War Diary	Hulluch		07/01/1918	10/01/1918
War Diary	Mines.		11/01/1918	14/01/1918
War Diary	Hulluch		15/01/1918	18/01/1918
War Diary	Mazingarbe		19/01/1918	22/01/1918
War Diary	Hulluch		23/01/1918	24/01/1918
War Diary	Vaudri-Court		25/01/1918	31/01/1918
Operation(al) Order(s)	Operation Order No 72. 1/6th Btn South Staffordshire Regiment.		01/01/1918	01/01/1918
Operation(al) Order(s)	Operation Order No 73. 1/6th Btn South Staffordshire Regiment.		05/01/1918	05/01/1918
Operation(al) Order(s)	Operation Order No 74. 1/6th Btn South Staffordshire Regiment.		06/01/1917	06/01/1917
Operation(al) Order(s)	Operation Order No 75. 1/6th Btn South Staffordshire Regiment.		13/01/1918	13/01/1918
Operation(al) Order(s)	Operation Order No 76. 1/6th Battalion South Staffordshire Regiment.		18/01/1918	18/01/1918
Operation(al) Order(s)	Operation Order No 77. 1/6th Battalion South Staffordshire Regiment		21/01/1918	21/01/1918
Operation(al) Order(s)	Operation Order No 78. 1/6th Battalion South Staffordshire Regiment		23/01/1918	23/01/1918
Heading	War Diary 1/6th Battalion. South Staffordshire Regt. From 1st February To 28th February.		01/02/1918	01/02/1918
War Diary	Vaudricourt		01/02/1918	09/02/1918
War Diary	Burbure		10/02/1918	10/02/1918
War Diary	Fontaine-Lez-Boulans		11/02/1918	28/02/1918
Operation(al) Order(s)	Operation Orders No 80. 1/6th Battalion South Staffordshire Regiment.		28/02/1918	28/02/1918
Heading	War Diary 1st To 31st. March 1918 Vol 38			
War Diary	Fontaine-Lez-Boulans		01/03/1918	01/03/1918
War Diary	Auchy-Au-Bois.		02/03/1918	02/03/1918
War Diary	La Miquellerie.		05/03/1918	05/03/1918
War Diary	Beuvry.		06/03/1918	06/03/1918
War Diary	Annequin		09/03/1918	09/03/1918

War Diary	Cuinchy	10/03/1918	13/03/1918
War Diary	Annequin.	14/03/1918	17/03/1918
War Diary	Cuinchy	18/03/1918	21/03/1918
War Diary	Annequin	22/03/1918	24/03/1918
War Diary	Cambrin	25/03/1918	25/03/1918
War Diary	Le Preol.	26/03/1918	27/03/1918
War Diary	Souchez	28/03/1918	28/03/1918
War Diary	Lens	29/03/1918	31/03/1918
Operation(al) Order(s)	Operation Order No 82. 1/6th Battalion South Staffordshire Regiment.	04/03/1918	04/03/1918
Operation(al) Order(s)	Operation Order No 83. 1/6th Btn South Staffordshire Regt.	05/03/1918	05/03/1918
Operation(al) Order(s)	Operation Order No 84. 1/6th Btn South Staffordshire Regt.	08/03/1918	08/03/1918
Operation(al) Order(s)	Operation Order No 85. 1/6th Btn South Staffordshire Regiment.	12/03/1918	12/03/1918
Operation(al) Order(s)	Operation Order No 86. 1/6th Btn South Staffordshire Regt.	14/03/1918	14/03/1918
Operation(al) Order(s)	Operation Order No 87. 1/6th Btn South Staffordshire Regt.	16/03/1918	16/03/1918
Operation(al) Order(s)	Operation Order No 88. 1/6th Btn South Staffordshire Regt.	20/03/1918	20/03/1918
Operation(al) Order(s)	Operation Order No 89. 1/6th Btn South Staffordshire Regiment.	20/03/1918	20/03/1918
Operation(al) Order(s)	Operation Order No 90. 1/6th Btn South Staffordshire Regt.	27/03/1918	27/03/1918
Operation(al) Order(s)	Operation Order No 89. 1/6th Btn South Staffordshire Regiment.	25/03/1918	25/03/1918
Heading	137th Brigade. 36th Division. 1/6th Battalion South Staffordshire Regiment April 1918		
War Diary	Lens.	01/04/1918	01/04/1918
War Diary	Lievin.	02/04/1918	03/04/1918
War Diary	Lens.	04/04/1918	07/04/1918
War Diary	Lievin.	08/04/1918	09/04/1918
War Diary	Lens.	10/04/1918	11/04/1918
War Diary	Fosseio.	12/04/1918	12/04/1918
War Diary	Divion.	13/04/1918	17/04/1918
War Diary	Hallicourt.	18/04/1918	24/04/1918
War Diary	Loisne	25/04/1918	30/04/1918
Operation(al) Order(s)	Operation Order No 93. 1/6th Btn South Staffordshire Regiment.	06/04/1918	06/04/1918
Operation(al) Order(s)	Operation Order No 94. 1/6th Btn South Staffordshire Regiment.	08/04/1918	08/04/1918
Operation(al) Order(s)	Operation Order No 95. 1/6th Btn South Staffordshire Regiment.	12/04/1918	12/04/1918
Heading	War Diary. 1/6th Btn South Staffordshire Regiment. From 1st May 1918 To 31st May 1918. Pages 155 To 157. Vol 40		
War Diary	Gorre	01/05/1918	02/05/1918
War Diary	Vaudricourt Wood.	03/05/1918	06/05/1918
War Diary	Essars	07/05/1918	14/05/1918
War Diary	Verquin.	15/05/1918	17/05/1918
War Diary	Gorre.	18/05/1918	22/05/1918
War Diary	Verquin.	23/05/1918	24/05/1918
War Diary	Essars.	25/05/1918	31/05/1918

Operation(al) Order(s)	Operation Order No 98. 1/6th Btn South Staffordshire Regt.	06/05/1918	06/05/1918
Operation(al) Order(s)	Operation Order No 99. 1/6th Btn South Staffs Regiment.	09/05/1918	09/05/1918
Operation(al) Order(s)	Operation Order No 100. 1/6th Btn South Staffordshire Regt.	11/05/1918	11/05/1918
Operation(al) Order(s)	Operation Order No 101. 1/6th Btn South Staffs Regiment.	14/05/1918	14/05/1918
Operation(al) Order(s)	Operation Order No 101A. 1/6th Btn South Staffs Regiment.	17/05/1918	17/05/1918
Operation(al) Order(s)	Operation Order No 101B. 1/6th Btn South Staffs Regiment.	19/05/1918	19/05/1918
Operation(al) Order(s)	Operation Order No 102. 1/6th Btn South Staffs Regiment.	22/05/1918	22/05/1918
Operation(al) Order(s)	Operation Order No 102A. 1/6th Btn South Staffs Regiment.	25/05/1918	25/05/1918
Heading	War Diary. 1/6th Btn South Staffordshire Regiment. From:- 1st To 30th June 1918. Pages. 158 To 160. Vol 41		
War Diary	Essars.	01/06/1918	03/06/1918
War Diary	Vaudri-Court	04/06/1918	10/06/1918
War Diary	Gorre.	11/06/1918	15/06/1918
War Diary	Vaudri-Court.	16/06/1918	19/06/1918
War Diary	Esars.	20/06/1918	27/06/1918
War Diary	Verquin.	28/06/1918	30/06/1918
Miscellaneous	Total Casualties During Month Of June 1918	02/07/1918	02/07/1918
Operation(al) Order(s)	Operation Order No 103. 1/6th Btn South Staffordshire Regiment.	02/06/1918	02/06/1918
Operation(al) Order(s)	1/6th Btn South Staffordshire Regt. Operation Order No 105		
Operation(al) Order(s)	Operation Order No 104. 1/6th Btn South Staffs Regiment.	07/06/1918	07/06/1918
Operation(al) Order(s)	1/6th Battalion South Staffordshire Regiment. Operation Orders No 106	10/06/1918	10/06/1918
Operation(al) Order(s)	1/6th Battalion South Staffordshire Regiment. Operation Orders No 107	13/06/1918	13/06/1918
Operation(al) Order(s)	1/6th Battalion South Staffordshire Regiment. Operation Orders No 108	15/06/1918	15/06/1918
Operation(al) Order(s)	Operation Order No 108. 1/6th Battalion South Staffordshire Rgt.	19/06/1918	19/06/1918
Operation(al) Order(s)	1/6th Battalion South Staffordshire Rgt. Operation Orders No 109	21/06/1918	21/06/1918
Operation(al) Order(s)	1/6th Battalion South Staffordshire Rgt. Operation Orders No 110	24/06/1918	24/06/1918
Operation(al) Order(s)	1/6th Battalion South Staffordshire Regt. Operation Order No 111		
Heading	War Diary. 1/6th Btn South Staffordshire Regt. From 1-7-1918. To 31-7-1918. Sheets 160/162		
War Diary	Gorre.	01/07/1918	09/07/1918
War Diary	Vaudricourt	10/07/1918	15/07/1918
War Diary	Essars.	16/07/1918	20/07/1918
War Diary	Gorre.	21/07/1918	27/07/1918
War Diary	Vaudricourt Wood.	28/07/1918	01/08/1918
Operation(al) Order(s)	Operation Order No 112. 1/6th Btn South Staffordshire Rgt.	01/07/1918	01/07/1918

Operation(al) Order(s)	1/6th Btn South Staffordshire Rgt. Operation Order No 112A	04/07/1918	04/07/1918
Operation(al) Order(s)	1/6th Btn South Staffordshire Rgt. Operation Order No 113	06/07/1918	06/07/1918
Operation(al) Order(s)	1/6th Btn South Staffordshire Rgt. Operation Order No 114	09/07/1918	09/07/1918
Operation(al) Order(s)	Operation Orders No 115. 1/6th Btn South Staffordshire Rgt.	15/07/1918	15/07/1918
Operation(al) Order(s)	1/6th Btn South Staffordshire Rgt. Operation Order No 117	18/07/1918	18/07/1918
Operation(al) Order(s)	1/6th Btn South Staffs Regt Operation Order No 118	21/07/1918	21/07/1918
Heading	War Diary. 1/6th Btn South Staffordshire Regiment. From:- 1st August 1918. To:- 31st August 1918. Sheets. 165 To 170		
War Diary	Vaudricourt Wood	01/08/1918	02/08/1918
War Diary	Essars	03/08/1918	14/08/1918
War Diary	Verquin	15/08/1918	20/08/1918
War Diary	Essars	21/08/1918	22/08/1918
Operation(al) Order(s)	Operation Order No 121. 1/6th Btn South Staffs Regiment.	01/08/1918	01/08/1918
Operation(al) Order(s)	1/6th Btn South Staffs Regiment. Operation Order No. 122	04/08/1918	04/08/1918
Operation(al) Order(s)	1/6th Btn South Staffs Regiment. Operation Order No 125	10/08/1918	10/08/1918
Operation(al) Order(s)	1/6th Btn South Staffs Regiment. Operation Order No 126	13/08/1918	13/08/1918
Operation(al) Order(s)	Operation Order No 124. 1/6th Btn South Staffs Regiment.	20/08/1918	20/08/1918
Operation(al) Order(s)	1/6th Btn South Staffs Regiment. Operation Order No. 128	25/08/1918	25/08/1918
War Diary	Essars.	01/09/1918	01/09/1918
War Diary	Vaudricourt Wood.	02/09/1918	05/09/1918
War Diary	Allouagne.	06/09/1918	12/09/1918
War Diary	Heilly.	13/09/1918	19/09/1918
War Diary	Vraignes.	20/09/1918	21/09/1918
War Diary	Leverguier	22/09/1918	24/09/1918
War Diary	Jeancourt.	25/09/1918	29/09/1918
War Diary	Bellenglise	30/09/1918	30/09/1918
Operation(al) Order(s)	1/6th South Staffs Regt. Operation Order No 131	01/09/1918	01/09/1918
Operation(al) Order(s)	Operation Order No. 132 1/6th Bn. South Staffordshire Regiment.	19/09/1918	19/09/1918
Operation(al) Order(s)	Operation Order No. 134 1/6th Btn. South Staffordshire Regiment.	20/09/1918	20/09/1918
Operation(al) Order(s)	Operation Order No. 135 1/6 South Staffordshire Regt.	23/09/1918	23/09/1918
Operation(al) Order(s)	Operation Order No. 136 1/6th South Staffordshire Regt.	24/09/1918	24/09/1918
Operation(al) Order(s)	Operation Order No 137. 1/6th Btn South Staffordshire Regt.	17/09/1918	17/09/1918
War Diary		01/10/1918	31/10/1918
War Diary	Bohain.	01/11/1918	14/11/1918
War Diary	Preux Au Bois.	15/11/1918	08/12/1918
War Diary	Busigny	09/12/1918	16/12/1918
War Diary	Fresnoy Le Grand	16/12/1918	20/01/1919
War Diary	Fresnoy	21/01/1919	31/01/1919
War Diary	Fresnoy Le-Grand	01/03/1919	04/03/1919
War Diary	Troisvilles.	05/04/1919	30/04/1919

War Diary 01/05/1919 31/05/1919

WO/95/2687/1

1/6 Battalion South Staffordshire Regiment

46TH DIVISION
137TH INFY BDE

1-6TH BN STH STAFFS
FEB   MAY
MAR 1915 - APR 1919

Box 25 11/137/46

N.M. Div.
1st Staffordshire Brigade   121/4634

1/6th South Staffordshire Regt.
Vol I 1 – 28.2.15

16th Essex Staff Regt

Army Form C. 2118.

WAR DIARY
or
INTELLIGENCE SUMMARY.
(Erase heading not required.)

Instructions regarding War Diaries and Intelligence Summaries are contained in F. S. Regs., Part II. and the Staff Manual respectively. Title pages will be prepared in manuscript.

Hour, Date, Place	Summary of Events and Information	Remarks and references to Appendices
1915 Feb. 1st Monday — Saffron Walden	Two Companies firing on miniature ranges. Remainder of Battalion, Company and Platoon Drill etc. One company night digging.	
Feb. 2nd Tuesday — Saffron Walden	One Company firing on miniature Range. One Company digging. Remainder of Battalion, Company and Platoon Drill etc.	
Feb. 3rd Wednesday — "	7 Officers and 325 men to Hutton for musketry.	
Feb. 4th Thursday — "	Musketry — Drill	

1/6th South Staff Regt.

Army Form C. 2118.

WAR DIARY
or
INTELLIGENCE SUMMARY.
(Erase heading not required.)

Instructions regarding War Diaries and Intelligence Summaries are contained in F.S. Regs., Part II. and the Staff Manual respectively. Title pages will be prepared in manuscript.

Hour, Date, Place	Summary of Events and Information	Remarks and references to Appendices
1915.		
5th Feb. Friday	Saffron Walden — Musketry — Drill	
6th Feb. Saturday	" — Musketry — Drill	
7th Feb. Sunday	" — Sunday	
8th Feb. Monday	" — Musketry on 30 yards and Miniature Ranges — Drill. Digging by night.	
9th Feb. Tuesday	" — Musketry on 30 yards and Miniature Ranges — Drill. Digging by night.	

1/6th L. Staff. Regt.

Army Form C. 2118.

WAR DIARY
or
INTELLIGENCE SUMMARY.
(Erase heading not required.)

Instructions regarding War Diaries and Intelligence Summaries are contained in F. S. Regs., Part II. and the Staff Manual respectively. Title pages will be prepared in manuscript.

Hour, Date, Place	Summary of Events and Information	Remarks and references to Appendices
1915. Oct. 10th Wednesday	Saffron Walden. Brigade Route March. Digging by night.	
" 11th Thursday	" Musketry on miniature and 30 yards Ranges. – Sort Drill Digging by night.	
" 12th Friday	" Musketry – Recruits. Conference by O.C., N.M.D. at Bishop's Stortford.	
" 13th Saturday	" Musketry – Recruits Bath: Transport Entraining practice.	
" 14th Sunday	" Sunday.	

1/6th South Staff. Regt.

Army Form C. 2118.

WAR DIARY
or
INTELLIGENCE SUMMARY.
(Erase heading not required.)

Instructions regarding War Diaries and Intelligence Summaries are contained in F. S. Regs., Part II. and the Staff Manual respectively. Title pages will be prepared in manuscript.

Hour, Date, Place	Summary of Events and Information	Remarks and references to Appendices
1915.		
Feb. 15 Saffron Walden.	12 Officers & 518 returned from Luton. Recruits, musketry at Audley End and miniature Ranges. night outpost exercises owing to snow.	
" 16th "	Company attack in morning and afternoon. Inspection of equipment. Battalion conference.	
" 17th "	Inspection by C.O., N.M.D. Lecture by some officer.	
" 18th "	Drilling in trenches during the morning. Battalion Drill etc. during the afternoon.	

1/6th S. Staff Regt

5

Army Form C. 2118.

WAR DIARY
or
INTELLIGENCE SUMMARY.
(Erase heading not required.)

Instructions regarding War Diaries and Intelligence Summaries are contained in F. S. Regs., Part II. and the Staff Manual respectively. Title pages will be prepared in manuscript.

Hour, Date, Place	Summary of Events and Information	Remarks and references to Appendices
1915 Feb. 19th Friday, Hellingbury Park	Inspection by H.M. King George V	
" 20th Saturday, Gifford Wotton	Company's disposal of Company Commanders for interior economy	
" 21st Sunday	Sunday	
Feb. 22nd Monday	Inspection of equipment, Company and Platoon Drill.	
" 23rd Tuesday	Kit and equipment inspection	
" 24th Wednesday	Route march under Company arrangements	

North Bn South Staff Rgt

Army Form C. 2118.

WAR DIARY
or
INTELLIGENCE SUMMARY.

(Erase heading not required.)

Hour, Date, Place		Summary of Events and Information	Remarks and references to Appendices
1915			
Feb. 25 Thursday	Saffron Walden	Issue and inspection of new equipments etc.	
Feb. 26 Friday	"	Inspection by G.O.C. Staffs Infantry Brigade.	
Feb. 27 Saturday	"	Completion of equipments etc preparatory to embarkation.	
Feb. 28 Sunday	"	Sunday.	F. Swinnan Lt-Col Comman 1/6 S Staff Regt

137th Inf.Bde.
46th Div.

Battn. disembarked
Havre from England
3/5.3.15.

WAR DIARY

1/6th BATTN. THE SOUTH STAFFORDSHIRE REGIMENT.

M A R C H

1 9 1 5

Army Form C. 2118.

WAR DIARY
or
INTELLIGENCE SUMMARY.
(Erase heading not required.)

March 1 Staff RFA

Instructions regarding War Diaries and Intelligence Summaries are contained in F. S. Regs., Part II. and the Staff Manual respectively. Title pages will be prepared in manuscript.

1915

Hour, Date, Place	Summary of Events and Information	Remarks and references to Appendices
March 1st Monday. Saffron Walden.	Batts. entrained at Audley End for Southampton & on arrival there proceeded as follows:— ½ Batts. to the Rest Camp ½ Batts. to billets in the Town.	
March 2nd Tuesday. Southampton	½ Batts. embarked for Havre S.S. "Jupiter" ½ Batts. remained at Southampton.	

1/6th Oxford & Bucks Regt.

WAR DIARY
or
INTELLIGENCE SUMMARY
(Erase heading not required.)

Army Form C. 2118.
(2)

Instructions regarding War Diaries and Intelligence Summaries are contained in F. S. Regs., Part II. and the Staff Manual respectively. Title pages will be prepared in manuscript.

Hour, Date, Place		Summary of Events and Information	Remarks and references to Appendices
March 3rd Wednesday	Havre	6 Bn arrived Havre. 2 Platoons then proceeded to Hard Leene as an advance party of the remainder of the 6 Bn proceeded to Ibo to Rest Camp Havre. Issuing & fitting of warm clothing.	
March 4th Thursday	Havre		
March 5th Friday	Havre	Remainder of Battn arrived at Havre from Southampton & joined the 1st 6 Bn at the Rest Camp. Havre.	
March 6th Saturday	Havre	Battalion entrained for Hondspeene.	
March 7th Sunday	Hondspeene	Battalion arrived at Hondspeene.	
March 8th Monday	Hondspeene	Companies at disposal of Coy Commanders. G.O.C. delivered a lecture to Officers & Coy Sgt Majors	
March 9th Tuesday	Bavre	Battalion marched from Hondspeene to Bavre.	

WAR DIARY
or
INTELLIGENCE SUMMARY.

(Erase heading not required.)

Army Form C. 2118.

1/4th West Riff Regt

Instructions regarding War Diaries and Intelligence Summaries are contained in F. S. Regs., Part II. and the Staff Manual respectively. Title pages will be prepared in manuscript.

Hour, Date, Place	Summary of Events and Information	Remarks and references to Appendices
1915		
March 10th. Bonne. Wednesday.	Companies at disposal of Company Commanders	
March 11th. Sailly Thursday.	Been ordered to Sailly & took up billets at Rue de Lepp.	
March 12th. Sailly Friday.	Companies at disposal of Company Commanders	
March 13th. Sailly Saturday.	Companies at disposal of Company Commanders	
March 14th. Sailly Sunday.	Sunday	
March 15th. Sailly Monday.	Standing by awaiting orders.	
March 16th. Steenje Tuesday.	Battalion marched to STEENTJE.	
March 17th. Wednesday. Steenje	Companies at disposal of Company Commanders	

Army Form C. 2118.

WAR DIARY
or
INTELLIGENCE SUMMARY.
(Erase heading not required.)

1st South Staff Regt

Instructions regarding War Diaries and Intelligence Summaries are contained in F. S. Regs., Part II. and the Staff Manual respectively. Title pages will be prepared in manuscript.

Hour, Date, Place	Summary of Events and Information	Remarks and references to Appendices
1915		
March 18th Flêtre Thursday	Batt. marched to Flêtre.	
March 19th Friday Flêtre	Companies at different company headquarters.	
March 20th Saturday Armentières	The Battalion marched to Armentières.	
March 21st Sunday. Armentières	Sunday.	
March 22nd	"A" & "C" Companies went into trenches held by 1st North Staff Regt & 3rd Rifle Brigade.	
Tuesday Armentières		
March 23rd	"B" Company relieved "A" Coy in 3rd Rifle Brigade trenches	
Tuesday Armentières	"C" Company returned from trenches.	
March 24th Wednesday	"A" and "C" Companies at disposal of Company Commanders. "B" Company returned from the trenches	

Army Form C. 2118.

10

WAR DIARY
or
INTELLIGENCE SUMMARY.
(Erase heading not required.)

6th ——— Staff Page

Instructions regarding War Diaries and Intelligence Summaries are contained in F.S. Regs., Part II. and the Staff Manual respectively. Title pages will be prepared in manuscript.

Hour, Date, Place	Summary of Events and Information	Remarks and references to Appendices
1915		
March 25th Festre Thursday.	The Battn. returned to Festre.	
March 26th Festre Friday.	Companies at disposal of Company Commanders for the purpose of washing clothing. 1 Officer & 40 men were attached to the 4th Lincoln & Leicester Brigade for instruction in the trenches.	
March 27th Festre Saturday	Companies at disposal of Company Commanders.	
March 28th Festre Sunday	Sunday.	
March 29th Festre Monday.	Battalion engaged digging Trenches. Two Companies in the morning & two Companies in the afternoon.	
March 30th Festre Tuesday	Two Companies engaged in Grenade throwing practice in the morning in trenches dug on the 29th & two Companies in the afternoon ditto.	

Army Form C. 2118.

6th Lovat Scouts Regt.

WAR DIARY
or
INTELLIGENCE SUMMARY.
(Erase heading not required.)

Instructions regarding War Diaries and Intelligence Summaries are contained in F.S. Regs., Part II. and the Staff Manual respectively. Title pages will be prepared in manuscript.

Hour, Date, Place	Summary of Events and Information	Remarks and references to Appendices
March 31st. Flêtre. Wednesday.	Continue again handed at trenches for construction of hurdles & wire entanglements	

T. Swinnon
Lt Colonel
Commanding 1/6th Lovat Scouts Regt.

137th Inf.Bde.
46th Div.

WAR DIARY

1/6th BATTN. THE SOUTH STAFFORDSHIRE REGIMENT.

A P R I L

1 9 1 5

Army Form C. 2118.

(12)

WAR DIARY
or
INTELLIGENCE SUMMARY.

(Erase heading not required.)

10th Rich Staff Regt

Instructions regarding War Diaries and Intelligence
Summaries are contained in F.S. Regs., Part II.
and the Staff Manual respectively. Title pages
will be prepared in manuscript.

Hour, Date, Place	Summary of Events and Information	Remarks and references to Appendices
1915		
April 1st. Bailleul. Thursday.	The Battalion marched to Bailleul.	
April 2nd. Bulford Camp. Friday.	The Battalion marched to Bulford Camp & took over the camp from the 5th Lond Staff Regt.	
April 3rd. Bulford Camp. Saturday.	Companies at disposal of Company Commanders for musketry exercises & physical drill.	
April 4th. Bulford Camp. Sunday.	Sunday.	
April 5th. Bulford Camp. Monday.	Companies at disposal of Company Commanders for musketry & physical exercises	
April 6th. Westoutre Tuesday.	Batln marched to Westoutre and took over trenches from the 5th Rth Lond. Staff Regt.	
April 7th. Westoutre Wednesday.	Situation quiet.	
April 8th. Westoutre Thursday.	Situation quiet, artillery quiet	

6th South Staff Regt.

WAR DIARY
or
INTELLIGENCE SUMMARY.
(Erase heading not required.)

Army Form C. 2118.
(13)

Hour, Date, Place	Summary of Events and Information	Remarks and references to Appendices
1915		
April 9th. Wulverghem. Friday	Situation quiet, enemy placed 2 shells 300 yds north of X Sugar.	
April 10th. Wulverghem. Saturday	Situation quiet, enemy artillery opened at 5:20 pm on trenches A4 and A5, damage done slight. Our artillery opened in return and obtained direct hits in enemys trenches. Battalion was relieved by 5th South Staff Regt and marched to Rest Camp. Some casualties during tour of duty:- Killed 5. Wounded 7.	
April 11th. Bulford Camp. Sunday	Sunday.	
April 12th. Bulford Camp. Monday	Distval Company Commanders to clearing clothing, rifles and ammunition. Inspection by Commanding Officer.	
April 13th. Bulford Camp. Tuesday	A speech of Company Commanders to normal 30 yds Range allotted for practice.	

Army Form C. 2118.

6th South Staff

1915

WAR DIARY
or
INTELLIGENCE SUMMARY.
(Erase heading not required.)

Hour, Date, Place	Summary of Events and Information	Remarks and references to Appendices
April 14th Wulverghem Wednesday	Companies at disposal of Company Commanders until evening.	
April 15th Wulverghem Thursday	Battalion relieved 5th Lincs. Staff. Regt. in trenches.	
April 16th Wulverghem Friday	Situation quiet.	
April 17th Wulverghem Saturday	Situation quiet, artillery quiet.	
April 18th Wulverghem Sunday	Situation quiet. Enemy shelled B.9. 10 A.R. trenches in the afternoon; no damage done. Battn. relieved by 5th South Staff Regt. Took over barracks. Three wounded.	
April 19th Belford Monday. Camp	Disposal Company Commanders. Cleaning of clothes, equipment and rifles, ammunition etc.	
April 20th Belford Tuesday. Camp	Disposal Company Commanders for Company Drills etc. Inspection of "B" Company by Brigadier General. Inspection of horses by B.G. Commanding.	

Forms/C. 2118/10

Army Form C. 2118.

WAR DIARY
or
INTELLIGENCE SUMMARY.
(Erase heading not required.)

Old Bruch Staff

1915

15

Instructions regarding War Diaries and Intelligence Summaries are contained in F.S. Regs., Part II. and the Staff Manual respectively. Title pages will be prepared in manuscript.

Hour, Date, Place	Summary of Events and Information	Remarks and references to Appendices
April 21st Wednesday	Bulford Camp	"A" Company engaged in digging. Remainder of Battn. at disposal of Company Commanders for physical drill etc.
April 22nd Thursday	Bulford Camp	Proposed Company Commanders entrenchments in erecting wire entanglements. Obtaining equipment and rifles etc. Battalion relieved 5th South Staffs Regt in the trenches.
April 23rd Friday	Bulverghem	Situation quiet. Enemy artillery active.
April 24th Saturday	Bulverghem	Situation quiet.
April 25th Sunday	Bulverghem	Situation quiet.
April 26th Monday	Bulverghem	Situation quiet. Enemy's artillery shelled Bulford huts, no damage done. Battn relieved by 5th South Staffs Regt and returned to Bulford.
April 27th Tuesday	Bulford Camp	Disposal of Company Commanders for cleaning of clothes, equipment and ammunition etc.

Army Form C. 2118.

6th Dorset Staff Regt.

1915

WAR DIARY
or
INTELLIGENCE SUMMARY.
(Erase heading not required.)

Instructions regarding War Diaries and Intelligence Summaries are contained in F.S. Regs., Part II. and the Staff Manual respectively. Title pages will be prepared in manuscript.

No.

Hour, Date, Place	Summary of Events and Information	Remarks and references to Appendices
April 28th Wednesday Bulford Camp.	Battalion engaged in digging G.H.Q trench. 3 Companies each working for period of 3 hours.	
April 29th Thursday Bulford Camp.	Battalions engaged in digging G.H.Q trench. 3 Companies each working for period of 3 hours.	
April 30th Friday Bulford Camp.	Working party of 250 NCO's & men engaged in completing G.H.Q trenches. Remainder of Btn. on issue of company commanders for cleaning equipment, rifles, ammunition. Cleaning up of camp etc. Battalion relieved 5th Btn Dorset Staff Regt in trenches.	

T.F.Wadman Lieut. Colonel
Commanding 6th Dorset Staff Regiment

137th Inf.Bde.
46th Div.

WAR DIARY

1/6th BATTN. THE SOUTH STAFFORDSHIRE REGIMENT.

M A Y

1 9 1 5.

Army Form C. 2118.

WAR DIARY
or
INTELLIGENCE SUMMARY.

(Erase heading not required.)

Oxb. Smith Staff

Instructions regarding War Diaries and Intelligence Summaries are contained in F.S. Regs., Part II. and the Staff Manual respectively. Title pages will be prepared in manuscript.

17

Hour, Date, Place	Summary of Events and Information	Remarks and references to Appendices
1915		
May 1st. Bulverghem. Saturday	Situation quiet.	
May 2nd. Bulverghem. Sunday.	Situation quiet.	
May 3rd. Bulverghem. Monday	Situation quiet.	
May 4th. Bulverghem. Tuesday.	Situation quiet. Battalion relieved by 5th Dorset Regt in the trenches. Total casualties during tour:- Killed 4. (other ranks) Died of wounds 1. Wounded 8.	
May 5th. Belford Schezang Camp.	Companies at disposal of Company Commanders for cleaning of equipment, ammunition & clothing. 1 Officer accidentally killed. 2 OR wounded.	
May 6th. Belford Thursday Camp.	Companies at disposal of Company Commanders for musketry exercises, Company Drill etc.	

Army Form C. 2118.

18

WAR DIARY
or
INTELLIGENCE SUMMARY.
(Erase heading not required.)

W. Londn Staff

Instructions regarding War Diaries and Intelligence Summaries are contained in F.S. Regs., Part II. and the Staff Manual respectively. Title pages will be prepared in manuscript.

Hour, Date, Place	Summary of Events and Information	Remarks and references to Appendices
1915		
May 7th. Friday Bedford Camp	Companies of draped of bngy any kommanders for instruction in the the of habs musketry, exercises, cleaning arms, ammunition and equipment	
May 8th. Saturday Reylford Camp	Battalion relieved 5th Dorset Staff Regt in the trenches.	
May 9th Sunday Kulverghem	Situation quiet	
May 10th Monday Kulverghem	Situation quiet	
May 11th Kulverghem Tuesday	Situation quiet	
May 12th Kulverghem Wednesday	Situation quiet Battn relieved by 5th Dorset Staff Regt. in the trenches. Total casualties during tour:- Officers - nil. Other ranks - 1 Killed & 4 Wounded	

Army Form C. 2118.

WAR DIARY
or
INTELLIGENCE SUMMARY.
(Erase heading not required.)

6th South Staff Regt.

Instructions regarding War Diaries and Intelligence Summaries are contained in F.S. Regs., Part II. and the Staff Manual respectively. Title pages will be prepared in manuscript.

Hour, Date, Place	Summary of Events and Information	Remarks and references to Appendices
1915		
May 13th. Rulford Camp. Thursday.	Disposal of Company Commanders for cleaning arms, ammunition, equipment and clothing.	
May 14th. Rulford Camp. Friday.	Disposal of Company Commanders for instruction in the use of bombs. Company drill etc.	
May 15th. Rulford Camp. Saturday.	Disposal of Company Commanders for instruction in the erection of wire entanglements. Company drill etc.	
May 16th. Rulford Camp. Sunday.	Battalion relieved 5th South Staff Regt in the trenches.	
May 17th. Wulverghem. Monday.	Situation quiet.	
May 18th. Wulverghem. Tuesday.	Situation quiet.	
May 19th. Wulverghem. Wednesday.	Situation quiet.	
May 20th. Wulverghem. Thursday.	Situation quiet. Battalion relieved by the 5th South Staff Regt in the trenches. Total casualties during tour:- (Other ranks) Killed 1, Wounded 7.	

Army Form C. 2118.

WAR DIARY
or
INTELLIGENCE SUMMARY.
(Erase heading not required.)

6th South Staff Regt.

Instructions regarding War Diaries and Intelligence Summaries are contained in F. S. Regs., Part II. and the Staff Manual respectively. Title pages will be prepared in manuscript.

1915

Hour, Date, Place	Summary of Events and Information	Remarks and references to Appendices
May 21st Bulford Camp. Friday.	Companies at disposal of Company Commanders for cleaning of equipment, arms, ammunition & clothing.	
May 22nd. Bulford Camp. Saturday.	At disposal of Company Commanders for instruction in the erection of Wire entanglement, use of Bombs. Inspection of clothing, equipment, arms, ammunition and rifles.	
May 23rd. Bulford Camp. Sunday.	Sunday	
May 24th. Wulverghem. Monday. Bulford.	Cleaning ammunition, equipment. Inspection of 5 Co. by Capt. Cox. Bn. relieved Y & L Staffs in the trenches.	
May 25th Wulverghem Tuesday.	Situation quiet	
May 26th Wulverghem Wednesday.	Situation quiet	
May 27th Wulverghem Thursday.	Situation quiet	
May 28th Wulverghem Friday.	Situation quiet. Bn. relieved by 5th N Staffs in the trenches. Total casualties for week:— 1 killed 5 wounded (other ranks)	

(9 29 6) W 3322—1107 100,000 10/13 H W V Forms/C. 2118/10.

Army Form C. 2118.

21

WAR DIARY
or
INTELLIGENCE SUMMARY.
(Erase heading not required.)

6th South Staff

Instructions regarding War Diaries and Intelligence Summaries are contained in F.S. Regs., Part II. and the Staff Manual respectively. Title pages will be prepared in manuscript.

Hour, Date, Place	Summary of Events and Information	Remarks and references to Appendices
1915 May 29th Belford Saturday camp	Cleaning of ammunition, equipment etc.	
May 30th Belford Sunday camp	Sunday.	
May 31st Belford Monday camp	Disposal of Company Commanders, musketry. Company drill, cleaning of ammunition, arms etc. Inspection of Regiments by Commanding Officer.	

T. Swinnerton
Lt Colonel
Commanding 6th South Staff Regiment

31-5-15.

137th Inf.Bde.
46th Div.

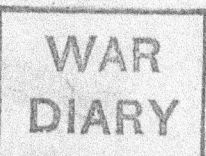

1/6th BATTN. THE SOUTH STAFFORDSHIRE REGIMENT.

J U N E

1 9 1 5

Army Form C. 2118.

22

WAR DIARY
or
INTELLIGENCE SUMMARY.
(Erase heading not required.)

6th South Staff Regt

Instructions regarding War Diaries and Intelligence Summaries are contained in F.S. Regs., Part II. and the Staff Manual respectively. Title pages will be prepared in manuscript.

1915/

Hour, Date, Place	Summary of Events and Information	Remarks and references to Appendices
June 1st Belfort Camp Tuesday	Disposal of Company Commanders for cleaning arms ammunition etc. Been relieved 5th B. Suck Staff in the trenches one company 3rd R. Bde attached.	
June 2nd Wulverghem Wednesday	Situation quiet	
June 3rd Wulverghem Thursday	do	
June 4th Wulverghem Friday	do	
June 5th Saturday	do	
	Battalion relieved by 5th Lanc Staff in the trenches. 8th Rifle Bde Company returned to own Battalion casualties (OR) 1 Killed & 6 wounded.	
June 6th Belfort Camp Sunday	Sunday	
June 7th Belfort Camp Monday	Disposal of Company Commanders for cleaning of arms ammunition clothing etc.	

WAR DIARY or INTELLIGENCE SUMMARY.

(Erase heading not required.)

6th Bn: Cameron Staff Regt.

Army Form C. 2118.
23

Instructions regarding War Diaries and Intelligence Summaries are contained in F.S. Regs., Part II. and the Staff Manual respectively. Title pages will be prepared in manuscript.

1915.

Hour, Date, Place	Summary of Events and Information	Remarks and references to Appendices
June 8th. Bulford Tuesday Camp.	Cleaning arms ammunition and equipment. Bayonet Drill. Rapid loading & aiming. Inspection of respirators.	
June 9th. Bulford Wednesday Camp	Battalion relieved 5th Camn Staff in the trenches at 8:30 pm	
June 10th. Kruisenghem Thursday	Situation quiet	
June 11th. Bulverghem Friday	Fire continually should by enemy, no damage done.	
June 12th Bulverghem Saturday	Situation quiet. Later relieved by 5th Camn Staff in trenches. Having the howr "D" Company type Brigade was attached for instruction. Total casualties for tour:— Officer: Capt Kyllock Killed in action 11-6-1915. 1 man Killed and 9 wounded.	
June 13th. Bulford Sunday Camp.	Cleaning clothing, arms, ammunition, equipment etc. Habiats inspected by Commanding Officer	

6th Lonsdale Staff Regt.

WAR DIARY
or
INTELLIGENCE SUMMARY.
(Erase heading not required.)

Army Form C. 2118.
24

Hour, Date, Place	Summary of Events and Information	Remarks and references to Appendices
1915		
June 17th Thursday Bulford Camp.	Cleaning arms ammunition etc Inspection of boots. Inspection of Smoke Helmets and respirators	
June 15th Tuesday Bulford Camp.	Battalion relieved 5th Lonsdale Staff Regt in the trenches.	
June 16th Wednesday Wulverghem	Situation quiet	
June 17th Thursday Wulverghem	ditto.	
June 18th Friday Wulverghem	ditto.	
June 19th Saturday Wulverghem	ditto. Battn. was relieved by 5th Lonsd. Staff Regt. Total casualties for tour: 2 men wounded	
June 20th Sunday Bulford Camp	Sunday	
June 21st Monday Bulford Camp	Cleaning clothing arms ammunition. Inspection smoke helmets and respirators	

Army Form C. 2118.

WAR DIARY
or
INTELLIGENCE SUMMARY.
(Erase heading not required.)

6th South Staffs

Instructions regarding War Diaries and Intelligence Summaries are contained in F.S. Regs., Part II. and the Staff Manual respectively. Title pages will be prepared in manuscript.

25

1915

Hour, Date, Place	Summary of Events and Information	Remarks and references to Appendices
June 22nd. Bulford Tuesday. Camp.	Cleaning arms, ammunition, equipment	
June 23rd. Bulford Wednesday Camp	Route march.	
June 24th. Bulford Thursday. Camp.	Route march.	
June 25th. Bulford Friday Camp	Battalion marched to find billeting area.	
June 26th. Ouderdom Saturday	Cleaning arms and ammunition etc	
June 27th Ouderdom Sunday	Sunday	
June 28th Ouderdom Monday.	Running drill. Bayonet fighting etc.	
June 29th. Ouderdom Tuesday	Route march. Bayonet fighting	
June 30th. Ouderdom Wednesday.	Route march. Bayonet fighting etc.	

Army Form C. 2118.

WAR DIARY
or
INTELLIGENCE SUMMARY.

(Erase heading not required.)

6th Donset Staff

1915.

26.

Hour, Date, Place	Summary of Events and Information	Remarks and references to Appendices
June 1915.	An inspection by the Commanding Officer was held daily of Smoke Helmets and Respirators. E. N. Colman Capt + adjt R. F. Colmer Comdg 6th Donset Staff Regt.	

137th Inf.Bde.
46th Div.

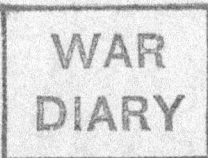

1/6th BATTN. THE SOUTH STAFFORDSHIRE REGIMENT.

J U L Y

1 9 1 5

1915 4th Somerset L.I.

Army Form C. 2118.

27.

WAR DIARY
or
INTELLIGENCE SUMMARY.
(Erase heading not required.)

Hour, Date, Place	Summary of Events and Information	Remarks and references to Appendices
July 1st Ouderdom Thursday	Training exercises. Wet bayonet fighting	
July 2nd Ouderdom Friday	ditto	
July 3rd Ouderdom Saturday	ditto	
July 4th Ouderdom Sunday	Sunday.	
July 5th ZILLEBEKE Monday	The Battalion relieved the 4th Bn Leicester Regiment in the trenches at Zillebeke. (13 Officers)	
July 6th Zillebeke Tuesday	Situation quiet except for artillery duels.	
July 7th do Wednesday	ditto	
July 8th do Thursday	ditto	
July 9th do Friday	ditto	

Army Form C. 2118.

WAR DIARY
or
INTELLIGENCE SUMMARY.
(Erase heading not required.)

28.

Instructions regarding War Diaries and Intelligence Summaries are contained in F.S. Regs., Part II. and the Staff Manual respectively. Title pages will be prepared in manuscript.

Hour, Date, Place	Summary of Events and Information	Remarks and references to Appendices
1915		
July 10th Saturday Zillebeke	Situation quiet.	
July 11th Sunday Zillebeke	Situation quiet. Battn relieved by 6th Sherwood Foresters in the trenches (3920 Bde) Total casualties: 3 men killed 18 wounded	
July 12th Monday Ouderdom	Cleaning arms, ammunition, clothing etc.	
July 13th Tuesday Ouderdom	Working party 700 men found	
July 14th Wednesday Ouderdom	Cleaning arms, ammunition, clothing etc.	
July 15th Thursday Ouderdom	Working party 600 men furnished	
July 16th Friday Ouderdom	Cleaning arms, ammunition, clothing etc.	
July 17th Saturday Ouderdom	Working party 600 men furnished	

Army Form C. 2118.

WAR DIARY
or
INTELLIGENCE SUMMARY.
(Erase heading not required.)

1st Lincoln Staff

Instructions regarding War Diaries and Intelligence
Summaries are contained in F.S. Regs., Part II.
and the Staff Manual respectively. Title pages
will be prepared in manuscript.

1915

Hour, Date, Place		Summary of Events and Information	Remarks and references to Appendices
July 18 Sunday	Ouderdom	Sunday	
July 19 Monday	Hill 60	Batts relieved 1/4th Lincoln Regt in the trenches	
July 20 Tuesday	Hill 60	Situation quiet except for artillery duels	
July 21 Wednesday	Hill 60	do	
July 22 Thursday	Hill 60	do	
July 23/27 Friday to Tuesday	Zillebeke	Batts relieved in trenches by 5th North Staff Regiment and proceeded to dugouts at Zillebeke. Battalion in Brigade Reserve.	
July 27 Tuesday	Hill 60	Battalion relieved 5th North Staff Regt in the trenches on night of 27th July, 1915	
July 28 Wednesday	Hill 60	Situation quiet except for artillery duels.	
July 29 Thursday	Hill 60	ditto.	

6th North Staff Regt.

Army Form C. 2118.

30.

WAR DIARY
or
INTELLIGENCE SUMMARY.
(Erase heading not required.)

Instructions regarding War Diaries and Intelligence Summaries are contained in F. S. Regs., Part II. and the Staff Manual respectively. Title pages will be prepared in manuscript.

Hour, Date, Place	Summary of Events and Information	Remarks and references to Appendices
1915		
July 30 Dieppe Friday	Situation quiet except for Artillery duels.	
July 31 Dieppe Saturday	ditto.	
	Casualties for period: 2 Officers wounded. 4 men killed. 1 man died of wounds. 35 men wounded.	
	E. N. Collison Capt & adjt North Staff Regt.	
	Commdg 1/6th Bn North Staff Regt.	
31-7-15.		

137th Inf.Bde.
46th Div.

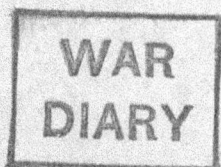

1/6th BATTN. THE SOUTH STAFFORDSHIRE REGIMENT.

A U G U S T

1 9 1 5

6th South Staff Regt.

WAR DIARY
or
INTELLIGENCE SUMMARY.
(Erase heading not required.)

Army Form C. 2118.

31

1915

Hour, Date, Place		Summary of Events and Information	Remarks and references to Appendices
August 1. Tuesday	Hill 60	Situation quiet except for Artillery duels.	
August 2. Monday	Hill 60	Battalion relieved by 5th South Staff Regt. in the trenches.	
August 3. Tuesday	Z Camp Ouderdom	Cleaning arms, ammunition, equipments.	
August 4. Wednesday	do.	Platoon and arms drill. Bayonet fighting.	
August 5. Thursday	do	Rapid loading, Bayonet fighting etc.	
August 6. Friday	do.	Route march.	
August 7. Saturday	do.	Route march. Bayonet fighting. Rapid loading.	
August 8. Sunday	do	Sunday.	

WAR DIARY
or
INTELLIGENCE SUMMARY.
(Erase heading not required.)

1st Batt. Staff Regt.

Army Form C. 2118.

32

Hour, Date, Place	Summary of Events and Information	Remarks and references to Appendices
1915		
August 9th Monday Oudenden	Battalion moved into Dugouts at Kruisstraat continuing as Divisional Reserve.	
August 10th Hill 60. Tuesday	Relieved the 1/5th Hants Staff Regt in the trenches at Hill 60.	
August 11th Hill 60 Wednesday	Situation quiet.	
August 12th Hill 60 Thursday	ditto.	
August 13th Hill 60 Friday	ditto.	
August 14th Hill 60 Saturday	ditto	
August 15th Hill 60 Sunday	ditto.	
August 16th Monday Hill 60	ditto	

Army Form C. 2118.

33

WAR DIARY
or
INTELLIGENCE SUMMARY.
(Erase heading not required.)

1st Lincoln Staff Regt

Instructions regarding War Diaries and Intelligence Summaries are contained in F. S. Regs., Part II. and the Staff Manual respectively. Title pages will be prepared in manuscript.

1915

Hour, Date, Place	Summary of Events and Information	Remarks and references to Appendices
August 19th Zillebeke Thursday	Battalion relieved in the trenches by the 1/5th Hants Staff Regt and went into Railway Dugouts, Zillebeke as Brigade Reserve.	
August 18th Zillebeke Wednesday	Supplying parties fatigue parties.	
August 19th Thursday Zillebeke	ditto	
August 20th Friday Zillebeke	ditto	
August 21st Saturday Zillebeke	ditto	
August 22nd Sunday Zillebeke	ditto	
August 23rd Monday Hill 60	The Bn relieved the 1/5 th North Staff Regt in the trenches	
August 24th Tuesday Hill 60	Situation quiet.	

WAR DIARY or INTELLIGENCE SUMMARY

Army Form C. 2118.

Hour, Date, Place	Summary of Events and Information	Remarks and references to Appendices
August 25th Hill 60 Wednesday.	Right of 24/25th August 1915 5th Lincolns reported hearing sound of working underneath end of trench apparently the matter was immediately reported to the 175th Coy R.E. who on investigation concurred with opinion of the 5th Lincolns. The Engineers at once took the matter in hand and at 3 am commenced boring and the intention of firing the CAMOUFLET. This was done at 7.30 am 25.8.15.	
August 26th Thursday Hill 60	At 12.53 am 26.8.15; according to miners R.E. hearing Company exploded a mine 10 ft 12 feet below the bottom of the crater made by the Camouflet fired on the 25.8.15 with the result that the crater was enlarged and the R.E. Officer reported that nothing could possibly be left undiscovered or alive.	
August 27th Friday Hill 60.	At 7.15 am 175th mining Company reported hearing sound of a truck being moved or doing a gallery in front of the listening post in N mine. It was decided to bore and fire a charge. This was done and the mine was fired at 10.50 am and the Engineers reported that it was successful.	

Army Form C. 2118.

35.

WAR DIARY
or
INTELLIGENCE SUMMARY.
(Erase heading not required.)

North Lancs Regt.

Instructions regarding War Diaries and Intelligence Summaries are contained in F.S. Regs., Part II. and the Staff Manual respectively. Title pages will be prepared in manuscript.

1915

Hour, Date, Place	Summary of Events and Information	Remarks and references to Appendices
August 28th Hill 60. Saturday	Situation quiet except for occasional artillery duels	
August 29th Hill 60. Sunday	Situation quiet, very little shelling by enemy batteries or our own.	
August 30th Hill 60. Monday	Situation quiet. Battalion relieved in the trenches by 115th North Staffs Regt. and proceeded to G.H.Q. Huts as Divisional Reserve.	
August 31st G.H.Q. Huts. Tuesday	Cleaning of arms and ammunition, clothing &c. Total casualties for the month. Officers killed 11, wounded 22, died of wounds 3. Other ranks killed, wounded &c.	

T. Swainson Lt Colonel
Commandg 115th North Staffs Regt.

137th Inf.Bde.
46th Div.

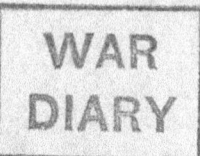

1/6th BATTN. THE SOUTH STAFFORDSHIRE REGIMENT.

S E P T E M B E R

1 9 1 5

Army Form C. 2118.

6th South Staff Regt.

WAR DIARY
or
INTELLIGENCE SUMMARY.
(Erase heading not required.)

1915

Hour, Date, Place	Summary of Events and Information	Remarks and references to Appendices
September 1st. Wednesday. S.Kils	Bayonet fighting, Company drill etc.	
September 2nd. Thursday. Bomada Kils	Battalion moved into new billeting area and took over Kamadan Kils.	
September 3rd. Friday. do.	(Working parties found for R.E. Coys.) Remained away to hold weather and found on the 4th instead	
September 4th. Saturday. do.		
September 5th. Sunday. do	Working parties for R.E. Companies.	
September 6th. Monday. do	Battalion relieved 5th North Staff Regiment in the trenches.	
September 7th. Hill 60. Tuesday	Situation quiet.	

Army Form C. 2118.

37/

WAR DIARY
or
INTELLIGENCE SUMMARY.
(Erase heading not required.)

Instructions regarding War Diaries and Intelligence Summaries are contained in F. S. Regs., Part II. and the Staff Manual respectively. Title pages will be prepared in manuscript.

Hour, Date, Place	Summary of Events and Information	Remarks and references to Appendices
September 8th Hill 60 Wednesday	Situation quiet except for slight bombardment of enemys trenches by our Heavy Artillery.	
September 9th Hill 60 Thursday	Situation quiet during morning, but during the afternoon enemy heavily bombarded the wood situated at the rear of our trenches. Our artillery bombarded enemys trenches in front of trench 40 with good result.	
September 10th Hill 60 Friday	Situation quiet. Our field artillery destroyed enemys observation post on Hill 60	
September 11th Hill 60 Saturday	13/9th Bn. having taken over armament to Bomb after Garrisons left at midnight 10/11th without success owing to Pr.dr.Rokes leading man. Our howitzers bombarded enemys trenches from 12.30pm until 2.30pm. Situation quiet.	
September 12th Hill 60 Sunday		

(9 29 6) W 3332—1307 100,000 10/13 H W V Forms/C. 2118/10.

WAR DIARY
or
INTELLIGENCE SUMMARY.

(Erase heading not required.)

Army Form C. 2118.

38.

Hour, Date, Place	Summary of Events and Information	Remarks and references to Appendices
September 12. Hill 60. Sunday. (continued)	At 5pm 12-9-'15, the Engineers fired a mine in front of 39. The result was a small crater about 15ft. in diameter and about 20 yards in front of trench 39. The Battalion was relieved in the trenches by the 15th North Staffs Regt. and went into Brigade Reserve, Railway Dugouts, Zillebeke.	
September 13. Zillebeke. Monday.	Situation quiet.	
September 14. Zillebeke. Tuesday.	ditto.	
September 15. Zillebeke. Wednesday.	ditto.	
September 16. Zillebeke. Thursday.	ditto.	

Army Form C. 2118.

39

WAR DIARY
or
INTELLIGENCE SUMMARY.
(Erase heading not required.)

Instructions regarding War Diaries and Intelligence Summaries are contained in F.S. Regs., Part II. and the Staff Manual respectively. Title pages will be prepared in manuscript.

Hour, Date, Place	Summary of Events and Information	Remarks and references to Appendices
September 17. Zillebeke. Friday.	Situation quiet except for considerable artillery fire by own Batteries during the morning.	
September 18. Hill 60 Saturday	The Battalion relieved the 1/5th North Staff Regt in the trenches	
September 19. Hill 60. Sunday.	Situation quiet.	
September 20. Hill 60. Monday	Situation quiet.	
September 21. Hill 60. Tuesday	Situation quiet. 175th Coy R.E. blew up a mine at 2.00pm from No 9 Left Offside 39 Left, and surface was fell broken.	
September 22. Hill 60 Wednesday	Situation quiet except for slight artillery duels.	

Army Form C. 2118.

WAR DIARY
or
INTELLIGENCE SUMMARY.
(Erase heading not required.)

Instructions regarding War Diaries and Intelligence Summaries are contained in F. S. Regs., Part II. and the Staff Manual respectively. Title pages will be prepared in manuscript.

Hour, Date, Place	Summary of Events and Information	Remarks and references to Appendices
September 23. Hill 60. Thursday	Situation quiet, except for artillery duels.	
September 24. Hill 60. Friday	Situation quiet.	
September 25. Hill 60. Saturday	Situation active, 15th Artillery firing continuously on to enemys observation posts on Hill 60. Enemy dropped eight heavy shells on to own trenches. Batn relieved in trenches. Staff Regt. in the trenches.	
September 26. Braham Huts. Sunday	Sunday.	
September 27. do Monday	Cleaning rifles, equipment etc.	

Army Form C. 2118.

WAR DIARY
or
INTELLIGENCE SUMMARY.
(Erase heading not required.)

Instructions regarding War Diaries and Intelligence Summaries are contained in F.S. Regs., Part II. and the Staff Manual respectively. Title pages will be prepared in manuscript.

Hour, Date, Place	Summary of Events and Information	Remarks and references to Appendices
September 28. Canada Tuesday. Huts.	Digging tanks for R.E. Companies.	41
September 29 Wednesday	to leaving at Quincey.	
September 30 Thursday.	Route march by Companies. Bombardier during march:- Captain D.J. Lackey killed. 8 Other ranks killed 11 " " wounded.	

T. Iwardieum
Lt Colonel
Commanding 110th Down Staff Regt.

137th Inf.Bde.
46th Div.

WAR DIARY

1/6th BATTN. THE SOUTH STAFFORDSHIRE REGIMENT.

O C T O B E R

1 9 1 5

Army Form C. 2118.

WAR DIARY
or
INTELLIGENCE SUMMARY.

(Erase heading not required.)

1/6th Battn South Staffs Rgt.

Instructions regarding War Diaries and Intelligence Summaries are contained in F.S. Regs., Part II. and the Staff Manual respectively. Title pages will be prepared in manuscript.

1915 Hour, Date, Place		Summary of Events and Information	Remarks and references to Appendices
October 1st. Friday.	CANADA HUTS.	Bayonet fighting, Company drill etc.	
October 2nd. Saturday.	ROBECQ.	Battalion marched to APEELE, and entrained for FOUQUEREUIL, from there marching to ROBECQ.	
October 3rd. Sunday.	ROBECQ.	S U N D A Y.	
October 4th. Monday.	ROBECQ.	Rapid marching and doubling. Physical drill, Bayonet fighting. Instruction in Bomb throwing.	
October 5th. Tuesday.	ROBECQ.	ditto	
October 6th. Wednesday.	VAUDRICOURT.	The Battn marched to Vaudricourt, and took up billets in the Colliery buildings.	
October 7th. Thursday.	do	Rapid marching and doubling. Battalion route march. Instruction in bomb throwing. Bayonet Fighting.	
October 8th. Friday.	do	Rapid marching and doubling. Special instruction in bomb throwing. Rapid loading. Battalion route march.	
October 9th. Saturday.	do	ditto.	

Army Form C. 2118.

WAR DIARY (43).
or
INTELLIGENCE SUMMARY.

(Erase heading not required.)

1/6th Battn South Staffs Regt.

Instructions regarding War Diaries and Intelligence Summaries are contained in F.S. Regs., Part II. and the Staff Manual respectively. Title pages will be prepared in manuscript.

1915. Hour, Date, Place	Summary of Events and Information	Remarks and references to Appendices
October 10th. Sunday. VAUDRICOURT.	Instruction as to blocking up Communication Trenches. Arms drill and muscle exercises. Cleaning arms and ammunition. Signalling instruction. Inspection of Iron rations.	
October 11th. do Monday.	Battalion Bombing parties paraded under Bomb officer for special instruction. Machine Guns tested. Practising advancing over open ground in fighting kit. Rapid loading and muscle exercises.	
October 12th. Tuesday. VERMELLES.	The Battalion marched into assembly trenches North East of VERMELLES.	
October 13th. Wednesday. VERMELLES.	The 46th (North Midland) Division having been ordered to capture the HOHENZOLLERN REDOUBT and FOSSE No 8, the 137th Infantry Brigade carrying out the right attack, the Battalion was formed as follows - "A" & "C" Companies in the front line of assembly trenches, and with two Companies of the 1/6th North Staffs Regt formed the 3rd line, and were ordered to follow the 2nd line at 200 paces distance, and carry R.E. materials, the other two Companies "B" & "D", with 2 Companies 1/6th North Staffs Regiment forming the fourth line, and ordered to at once follow the third line, and occupy DUMP trench on the frontage allotted to the Brigade. The attack was covered by a two hours Artillery bombardment commencing at 12 n●on, gas was used at 1p.m. also smoke shells which at times completely hid the points of attack. Enemy Machine Guns were heard ranging on our assembly trenches at 1-30p.m. & 1-45p.m, which was notified to Brigade Headquarters.	

WAR DIARY (44)
or
INTELLIGENCE SUMMARY.

(Erase heading not required.)

Army Form C. 2118.

1/6th Battn South Staffs Regiment.

Instructions regarding War Diaries and Intelligence Summaries are contained in F.S. Regs., Part II. and the Staff Manual respectively. Title pages will be prepared in manuscript.

1915.	Hour, Date, Place	Summary of Events and Information	Remarks and references to Appendices
Continued. October 13th. Wednesday. and	VERMELLES.	Having received no message that our front line had not been able to advance, and not being able to see their position for smoke, the two Companies forming the third line followed the second line and suffered very heavy casualties. The fourth line then advanced, and also suffered from Machine Gun fire, from the direction of SOUTH FACE. All that remained of the 3rd line reached our fire trench between point 87 & 89 to assist the 5th South Staffs Regt to hold that portion until this Battalion	
October 14th. Thursday.	VERMELLES.	was ordered to retire at noon on the 14th. The remainder of the fourth line trench and when reinforcements were called for, were sent up to support the fire trench.	
October 14th.	do	The Battalion was relieved in the trenches by the Guards, and billeted for the night at SAILLY la BOURSE.	
October 15th. Friday.	VERMELLES.	The Battalion returned to its former billets at the Colliery buildings, VAUDRICOURT.	
October 16th. Saturday. October 17th. Sunday.	VAUDRICOURT. do	Cleaning clothing equipment, clothing etc. Inspection by G.O.C. Commanding 46th (N.M.) Division. S U N D A Y.	
October 18th. Monday.	VAUDRICOURT.	Bombing, bayonet fighting, rapid loading etc.	
October 19th. Tuesday.	VAUDRICOURT & ALLOUAGNE.	The Battalion marched to ALLOUAGNE. Bombing and bayonet fighting.	

Army Form C. 2118.

WAR DIARY (45)
or
INTELLIGENCE SUMMARY.

(Erase heading not required.)

6th Battn South Staffs Regt.

Instructions regarding War Diaries and Intelligence Summaries are contained in F. S. Regs., Part II. and the Staff Manual respectively. Title pages will be prepared in manuscript.

1915.	Hour, Date, Place	Summary of Events and Information	Remarks and references to Appendices
October 20th. Wednesday.	ALLOUAGNE.	Bombing, bayonet fighting, muscle exercises. Inspection of smoke helmets.	
October 21st. Thursday.	ALLOUAGNE.	Rapid marching. Bombing instruction. Bayonet fighting.	
October 22nd. Friday.	ALLOUAGNE.	Bombing instruction. Throwing of bombs. Musketry. Bayonet fighting.	
October 23rd. Saturday.	ALLOUAGNE.	Instruction in use of bombs. Route march. Bayonet fighting.	
October 24th. Sunday.	ALLOUAGNE.	S U N D A Y. Inspection by Brigadier General E.Feetham. Commdg 137th Infantry Brigade.	

Army Form C. 2118.

WAR DIARY
or
INTELLIGENCE SUMMARY. (46)

(Erase heading not required.)

1/6th Battn South Staffs Regt.

Instructions regarding War Diaries and Intelligence Summaries are contained in F. S. Regs., Part II. and the Staff Manual respectively. Title pages will be prepared in manuscript.

Hour, Date, Place		Summary of Events and Information	Remarks and references to Appendices
1915.			
October 25th. Monday.	FOUQUEREUIL.	The Battalion marched to FOUQUEREUIL and took up billets in the Hutments there.	
October 26th. Tuesday.	do.	Instruction in the use of bombs, and throwing of bombs. Bayonet Fighting. Rapid loading and muscle exercises.	
October 27th. Wednesday.	do	Running drill. Parties engaged in the movement of huts to fresh ground.	
October 28th. Thursday.	do	One Composite Company paraded for King's Inspection. Parties engaged in the movement of huts to fresh ground.	
October 29th. Friday.	do	Instruction in the use of bombs, and bomb throwing. Bayonet Fighting. Route march by Companies. 3 officers 110 other ranks engaged as working party at LABOURSE.	
October 30th. Saturday.	do	ditto Instruction in the use of bombs. Formation of bombing parties. Bomb throwing. Bayonet fighting. Route march by Companies.	
October 31st. Sunday.	do	S U N D A Y. Total casualties for month:- Officers Killed. 5. " Wounded. 14. O. Ranks. Killed. 35. " Died wounds. 5.	

Army Form C. 2118.

1/6th Battn South Staffs Regt.

WAR DIARY
or
INTELLIGENCE SUMMARY.

(Erase heading not required.) (47)

Instructions regarding War Diaries and Intelligence Summaries are contained in F.S. Regs., Part II. and the Staff Manual respectively. Title pages will be prepared in manuscript.

Place	Date	Hour	Summary of Events and Information	Remarks and references to Appendices
	1915. OCTOBER.		Casualties for month (continued).	
			Other ranks. Wounded. 239	
			" Missing. 105.	
			Total casualties. OFFICERS. 19	
			OTHER RANKS. 384	
			F. W. Law Major.	
			Commanding 1/6th Btn South Staffordshire Regiment	
			2-11-1915.	

137th Inf.Bde.
46th Div.

WAR DIARY

1/6th BATTN. THE SOUTH STAFFORDSHIRE REGIMENT.

N O V E M B E R

1 9 1 5

Army Form C. 2118.

WAR DIARY (48)
or
INTELLIGENCE SUMMARY.
(Erase heading not required.)

1/6th Battn South Staffs Regt.

Instructions regarding War Diaries and Intelligence Summaries are contained in F.S. Regs., Part II. and the Staff Manual respectively. Title pages will be prepared in manuscript.

Hour, Date, Place		Summary of Events and Information	Remarks and references to Appendices
1915.			
November 1st. Monday.	FOUQUEREUIL.	Instruction in bombthrowing. Bayonet Fighting. Route March.	
November 2nd. Tuesday.	do	do	
November 3rd. Wednesday.	do	Platoon Drill. Grouping Practice. Bayonet Fighting. Route March.	
November 4th. Thursday.	do	do	
November 5th. Friday.	LESTREM.	The Battn marched to LESTREM and took up billets there.	
November 6th. Saturday.	do	Bomb throwing. Formation of bombing parties. Platoon Drill. Bayonet Fighting.	
November 7th. Sunday.	do	S U N D A Y.	
November 8th. Monday.	do	Bayonet Fighting. Bomb throwing etc. Six officers visited trenches occupied by SIRHIND BRIGADE.	
November 9th. Tuesday.	do	Rapid marching and doubling. Bomb throwing. Bayonet Fgt. etc	

Army Form C. 2118.

WAR DIARY
or
INTELLIGENCE SUMMARY.

1/6th Btn S. Staffs Rgt. (49)

(Erase heading not required.)

Instructions regarding War Diaries and Intelligence Summaries are contained in F.S. Regs., Part II. and the Staff Manual respectively. Title pages will be prepared in manuscript.

1915 Hour, Date, Place		Summary of Events and Information	Remarks and references to Appendices
November 10th. Wednesday.	CROIX BARBEE.	The Battn marched to CROIX BARBEE, and took up billets there as Brigade Reserve.	
November 11th. Thursday.	do	Lectures given to troops on care of arms. Inspection of kits. Lecture by Medical Officer on sanitation and cleanliness.	
November 12th. Friday.	do	ditto	
November 13th. Saturday.	do	The Battalion relieved the 4th Kings Liverpool Regt in the trenches, to the right of NEUVE CHAPELLE.	
November 14th. Sunday.	do	Quiet day.	
November 15th. Monday.	do	" "	
November 16th. Tuesday.	do	" "	
November 17th. Wednesday.	do	Battalion relieved in the trenches by 5th Btn Lincolnshire Regiment, and proceeded into Brigade Reserve at Croix Barbee.	
November 18th. Thursday.	do	Cleaning equipment, side arms etc.	

Army Form C. 2118.

WAR DIARY (50)
or
INTELLIGENCE SUMMARY.
(Erase heading not required.)

1/6th Battn South Staffs Regt.

Instructions regarding War Diaries and Intelligence Summaries are contained in F.S. Regs., Part II. and the Staff Manual respectively. Title pages will be prepared in manuscript.

1915. Hour, Date, Place		Summary of Events and Information	Remarks and references to Appendices
November 19th. Friday.	CROIX BARBEE.	Bathing. Inspection of kits. Cleaning up billets and surroundings.	
November 20th. Saturday.	do	The Battn relieved the 5th Lincon Regt in the trenches.	
November 21st. Sunday.	do	Fairly quiet day. Little shelling during afternoon.	
November 22nd. Monday.	do	ditto	
November 23rd. Tuesday.	do	Battn relieved in the trenches by the 1/6th North Staffs Regiment.	
November 24th. Wednesday.	do	Cleaning equipment etc.	
November 25th. Thursday.	do	Lectures by Company Commanders.	
November 26th. Friday.	do	Battn relieved the 1/6th North Staffs Regt in the trenches	
November 27th. Saturday.	do	Quiet day.	
November 28th. Sunday.	do	do	
November 29th. Monday.	do	do	

(9 29 6) W 3332—1107 100,000 10/15 H W V Forms/C. 2118/10

1/6th Battn South Staffs Regiment.

Army Form C. 2118.

WAR DIARY
or
INTELLIGENCE SUMMARY.
(*Erase heading not required.*)

(51)

Instructions regarding War Diaries and Intelligence Summaries are contained in F.S. Regs., Part II. and the Staff Manual respectively. Title pages will be prepared in manuscript.

Hour, Date, Place	Summary of Events and Information	Remarks and references to Appendices
1915.		

November 30th. Tuesday. CROIX BARBEE.	Cleaning equipment etc.
	
	TOTAL CASUALTIES FOR MONTH:-
	    Killed one. (O.R.)
	    Died of wounds. one. (O.R.)
	    Wounded. nine. (O.R.)
	
	Captain Clifford Howl accidentally wounded. 3-11-15.
	
	                Milner. Lieutenant.
	    For Officer Commanding 1/6th Battn South Staffs Regt.	

137th Inf.Bde.
46th Div.

WAR DIARY

1/6th BATTN. THE SOUTH STAFFORDSHIRE REGIMENT.

D E C E M B E R

1 9 1 5

Army Form C. 2118.

1/6th Battn South Staffs Regiment.

WAR DIARY (52)
or
INTELLIGENCE SUMMARY.

(Erase heading not required.)

Instructions regarding War Diaries and Intelligence Summaries are contained in F.S. Regs., Part II. and the Staff Manual respectively. Title pages will be prepared in manuscript.

1915. Hour, Date, Place		Summary of Events and Information	Remarks and references to Appendices
December 1st. Wednesday.	CROIX BARBEE.	As much indoor training carried out as possible. All men of the Battalion bathed.	
December 2nd. Thursday.	do	The Battalion relieved the 1/6th North Staffs Rgt in the Trenches.	
December 3rd. Friday.	do	All quiet on our front.	
December 4th. Saturday.	do	The Battalion was relieved in the trenches by the 7th King's Own Royal L.Rgt, 56th Brigade,19th Division, and proceeded to Rest Billets at Croix Barbee.	
December 5th. Sunday.	PACAUT.	The Battalion marched to PACAUT, and took billets there.	
December 6th. Monday.	do	Inspection of clothing and kits. " " arms and ammunition. Lectures on "Duties on Board ship", by Company Commanders.	
December 7th. Tuesday.	do	Inspection of Companies by Commanding Officer. Inspection of Battalion by the G.O.C. 46th Division.	
December 8th. Wednesday.	do	Inspection of Platoons by Platoon Commanders. Drill in Guard mounting. Route March by Companies. Lectures to Platoons on "Care of arms & ammunition".	
December 9th. Thursday.	do	The morning was devoted to the cleaning of equipment & clothing. Route March.	
December 10th. Friday.	do	Drill in Guard Mounting. Route march by Companies. Lectures to Platoons on "Duties in Barracks" & Extended Order Drill.	

1/6th South Staffs Regiment.

Army Form C. 2118.

WAR DIARY (53)
or
INTELLIGENCE SUMMARY.
(Erase heading not required.)

Instructions regarding War Diaries and Intelligence Summaries are contained in F.S. Regs., Part II. and the Staff Manual respectively. Title pages will be prepared in manuscript.

1915. Hour, Date, Place		Summary of Events and Information	Remarks and references to Appendices
December 11th. Saturday.	PACAUT.	Platoon Drill under the Regimental Sgt Major. Route march. All subaltern officers and senior N.C.O's lectured by Regt Sgt Major on "Barrack Discipline". Company Drill.	
December 12th. Sunday.	do	S U N D A Y.	
December 13th. Monday.	do	Platoon Drill. Company Drill. Route march. Lectures by regimental Sgt major.	
December 14th. Tuesday.	do	A Composite Company sent to Divisional training School at CALONNE for training purposes, and ret'd same night. Brigadier General inspected No 4 Platoon in full marching order, and was also present at a lecture to No 10 Platoon on "EXTENDED ORDER".	
December 15th. Wednesday.	do	Platoon Drill, and Guard Mounting. Route March. Company drill. Lectures to platoons on "ADVANCE GUARDS".	
December 16th. Thursday.	do	do. training.Lectures to platoons on "REAR GUARDS"	
December 17th. Friday.	do	Battalion inspected by Commanding Officer. Company Drill. Lectures to Companies on "COMPANY IN ATTACK".	
December 18th. Saturday.	do	Platoon Drill. Inspection of rifles. Drill in Guards & Guard mounting. Lectures by Company Commanders on "COMPANY IN DEFENCE".	

Army Form C. 2118.

WAR DIARY (54)
or
INTELLIGENCE SUMMARY.

1/9th Battn South Staffs Regt.

(Erase heading not required.)

Instructions regarding War Diaries and Intelligence Summaries are contained in F.S. Regs., Part II. and the Staff Manual respectively. Title pages will be prepared in manuscript.

1915. Hour, Date, Place		Summary of Events and Information	Remarks and references to Appendices
December 19th. Sunday.	LE PONT A BALQUE.	The Battalion marched to le Pont a Balque and took up billets there.	
December 20th. Monday.	do.	Company & Platoon Drill. Lectures to Platoons on "Duties on board ship". Arms drill under Section Commanders.	
December 21st. Tuesday.	do	Company & Platoon Drill. Lecture on "OUTPOSTS BY NIGHT". Drill in Guard Mounting. Arms Drill. Route March.	
December 22nd. Wednesday.	do	Company & Platoon Drill. Guards & Guard Mounting. Lecture by the Adjutant to all Subaltern Offs. Lectures to Coys on "DUTIES OF SENTRY GROUPS IN AN OUTPOST LINE".	
December 23rd. Thursday.	do	Route march.	
		Company & Platoon Drill. Guards & Guard Mounting. Saluting Drill. N.C.O's paraded under Regt Sgt Major for Instruction.	
December 24th. Friday.	do		
December 25th. Saturday.	do	Observed by Battn as XMAS DAY in view of entrainment on December 25th 1915.	
Dec: 26th & 27th. Sunday & Monday.	TRAIN.	THE BATTN ENTRAINED AT BERGUETTE STATION AT 3-40 p.m. These days were spent in travelling, the Battn arriving at MARSEILLES at 9p.m. 27th December 1915 & proceeded to SANTI CAMP.	
December 28th. Tuesday.	MARSEILLES.	Drill in Guards & Guard Mounting. Platoon Drill. Route March. Lecture to Coys "PATROLS FROM AN OUTPOST LINE".	

1/6th Btn South Staffs Regt. (55).

Army Form C. 2118.

WAR DIARY
or
INTELLIGENCE SUMMARY.
(Erase heading not required.)

Instructions regarding War Diaries and Intelligence Summaries are contained in F.S. Regs. Part II. and the Staff Manual respectively. Title pages will be prepared in manuscript.

Hour, Date, Place	Summary of Events and Information	Remarks and references to Appendices
1915.		
December 29th. Wednesday. MARSEILLES.	Drill in Guards & Guard Mounting. Inspection of rifles by Armourer Q.M. Sgt. Lecture to Coys on "DUTIES ON BOARD SHIP". Machine Gun Instruction. Signalling Instruction. Bugle Practise.	
December 30th. Thursday. do	Rapid Loading & Aiming. Route march. Lecture to Coys on "FIRE CONTROL".	
December 31st. Friday. do	ditto.	
	Total Casualties for month.	
	5 other ranks wounded.	

R.C. Piper-Cobb
Alfred ffrench

Lieut: Colonel.
Commanding 1/6th Btn South Staffordshire Regiment.

31-12-1915.

Q12

Army Form C. 2118.

WAR DIARY (56)
or
INTELLIGENCE SUMMARY.
(Erase heading not required.)

1/6th Btn South Staffs Regt.

Instructions regarding War Diaries and Intelligence Summaries are contained in F.S. Regs., Part II. and the Staff Manual respectively. Title pages will be prepared in manuscript.

1916. Hour, Date, Place	Summary of Events and Information	Remarks and references to Appendices
January 1st. MARSEILLES. Saturday. FRANCE.	Battalion held in readiness to embark.	
January 2nd. do Sunday.	The Battalion embarked at Mole "D" MARSEILLES on board H.M.S. "MAGNIFICENT", together with 1/5th South Staffs Regt, 1/1st & 1/2nd Field Coys R.E. 46th N.M. Division.	
January 3rd to January 7th.	AT SEA.	
January 8th. ALEXANDRIA. Saturday. EGYPT.	Ship entered ALEXANDRIA HARBOUR and anchored for the night.	
January 9th. do Sunday.	First portion of the Battalion entrained for SHALLUFA STATION at 11p.m.	
January 10th. do Monday.	Remainder of Battalion entrained for SHALLUFA STATION at 2am.10-1-1916, arriving there at 1 p.m. Crossing the SUEZ CANAL and camping on the EAST BANK.	
January 11th. SHALLUFA. Tuesday.	Day spent in bringing remainder of baggage and rations across the SUEZ CANAL from SHALLUFA STATION.	
January 12th. do Wednesday.	Physical Drill. Company Drill. Inspection of arms & ammunition. Lecture to Coys on "CUSTOMS OF THE COUNTRY".	
January 13th. do Thursday.	Entire Battalion engaged upon fatigue work in connection with the arrival at station of remainder of Brigade.	

Army Form C. 2118

WAR DIARY (57)
or
INTELLIGENCE SUMMARY
(Erase heading not required.)

1916. 1/6th Btn South Staffs Rgt.

Instructions regarding War Diaries and Intelligence Summaries are contained in F.S. Regs., Part II. and the Staff Manual respectively. Title Pages will be prepared in manuscript.

Place	Date	Hour	Summary of Events and Information	Remarks and references to Appendices
SHALLUFA.	14-1-1916.		Physical Exercise. Drill by Platoons. Lectures to Coys on "DUTIES OF PICQUET IN OUTPOST LINE".	
do	15-1-1916.		Extended order drill. Fire Control. Rapid Loading. Company Drill. Drill in Guards & Guard Mounting.	
do	16-1-1916.		Drill by Platoons. Extended Order drill. Fire Control. Rapid Loading. Company Drill. Drill in Guards & Guard Mounting.	
do	17-1-1916.		137th I.Brigade less 1/5th S.Staffs Rgt assembled at 8a.m. for a manoeuvre parade, returning at 3p.m. Brig: General Commanding 137th I.Bde inspected the Battn at drill. Company drill etc performed afterwards.	
do	18-1-1916.		Kit Inspection. Drill by Platoons. Company Drill. Btn Drill.	
do	19-1-1916.		Physical Exercises. Squad Drill. Battn Drill. Bayonet Fighting. Lecture to Coys on "Extended order drill".	
do	20-1-1916.		Physical Exercises. Squad Drill. Battn Drill. Bayonet Fighting. Lecture to Coys on "Extended order drill".	
do	21-1-1916.		Physical Exercises. Squad Drill. Platoon Drill. Battn Drill. Company Drill. Lecture to Coys on "Fire control & Fire Discipline". Lecture to Officers on the Compass.	
do	22-1-1916.		Physical Exercises. Guards & Sentries duties. Platoon Drill. Company Drill. Battn Drill. Lecture to Coys on "Outposts".	
do	23-1-1916.		SUNDAY.	
do	24-1-1916.		Physical Exercises. Platoon Drill. Company Drill. Battn Drill. Judging Distance. Fire control and Fire Discipline. Night marching for officers by Compass.	
do	25-1-1916.		(Musketry Instruction.) Inspection Tests.	

Army Form C. 2118

WAR DIARY
or
INTELLIGENCE SUMMARY

(Erase heading not required.)

Instructions regarding War Diaries and Intelligence Summaries are contained in F. S. Regs., Part II. and the Staff Manual respectively. Title Pages will be prepared in manuscript.

Place	Date	Hour	Summary of Events and Information	Remarks and references to Appendices
SHALLUFA.	26-1-1916.		The Battalion proceeded into the Desert to No 3 Post, 61½° N.E. of SHALLUFA, true bearing, and proceeded to construct this Post. Trenches were dug, and revetting and wiring were commenced.	
do	27-1-1916.		Work on No 3 Post continued.	
do	28-1-1916.		The Battalion was ordered to return to former camp, arriving there at 4p.m.	
do	29-1-1916.		Battalion in attack. Fire control. Fire direction. Judging distance.	
do	30-1-1916.		The Battalion entrained at SHALLUFA STATION at 8 a.m. for ALEXANDRIA, detraining at SIDI GABA STATION at 6p.m. and then proceeded to SIDI BISHR CAMP, encamping there.	
do	31-1-1916.		All tents repitched and camp put in order.	

R.C. Piper, Capt.
Adjutant for Lieut: Colonel.
Commanding 1/6th Battn South Staffs Regiment.

4-2-1916.

Army Form C. 2118

WAR DIARY or INTELLIGENCE SUMMARY (59)

(Erase heading not required.)

1/6th Battn South Staffs Regt.

Instructions regarding War Diaries and Intelligence Summaries are contained in F.S. Regs., Part II. and the Staff Manual respectively. Title Pages will be prepared in manuscript.

Q 13

Place	Date	Hour	Summary of Events and Information	Remarks and references to Appendices
ALEXANDRIA.	1-2-1916.		Platoon Drill. Company Drill. Bathing for whole Battalion.	
"	2-2-1916.		ditto	
"	3-2-1916.		Inspection by G.O.C.137th Infantry Brigade.	
"	4-2-1916.		Day spent in issuing and fitting of equipment etc, and clearing of Camp prior to moving.	
	5-2-1916.		Battalion entrained at SIDI BISHR tram station for the Docks, embarking on H.T. "Transylvania" at 10 a.m. together with the remainder of the 137th Infantry Brigade.	
	6-2-1916 to 9-2-1916.		AT SEA.	
	10-2-1916		Ship arrived in MARSEILLES HARBOUR, FRANCE at 1 p.m.	
	11-2-1916.		Troops did not disembark.	
	12-2-1916.		Battalion disembarked at 8-15a.m. and entrained at AREUC Station at 10 a.m.	
	13-2-1916.		Journey continued.	
	14-2-1916.		Battalion detrained at 10 a.m. at LONG PRE Station, and marched to VAUCHELLES, taking up billets there.	
	15-2-1916.		Route march during morning by Companies. Company and platoon drill in the afternoon.	
	16-2-1916.		Bayonet Fighting. Route march. Lectures to Companies. Company and platoon drill.	

Army Form C. 2118

WAR DIARY (60)
or
INTELLIGENCE SUMMARY
(Erase heading not required.)

1/6th Batt'n South Staffs Regiment.

Instructions regarding War Diaries and Intelligence Summaries are contained in F. S. Regs., Part II. and the Staff Manual respectively. Title Pages will be prepared in manuscript.

Place	Date	Hour	Summary of Events and Information	Remarks and references to Appendices
VAUCHELLES	17-2-1916.		Running Drill. Route march. Practice in bomb-throwing. Bayonet fighting. Instn given to Lewis Machine Gun Section undergoing formation.	
"	18-2-1916.		Lecture to N.C.O's by Regt Sgt Major.	
"	19-2-1916.		Extended order drill. Physical exercises. Bayonet fighting. Bomb throwing practice. Lecture to N.C.O's on "Company in attack" by Adjutant.	
"	20-2-1916.		Physical exercises. Bayonet fighting. Judging distance. Route march by Companies. Fire control & Fire discipline. Lecture to N.C.O's on "Fire discipline and control".	
"	20-2-1916.		S U N D A Y.	
BEAUMETZ.	21-2-1916.		The Battalion moved into new billets at BEAUMETZ, arriving there at 2p.m.	
"	22-2-1916.		Instruction carried out on range. Trained bombers put through a refresher course at trenches. Companies at disposal of Company Commanders for Company and Platoon Drill.	
"	23-2-1916.		Bayonet fighting. Route march by Companies. Trained bombers continued refresher course. Snipers practiced on Range. Judging distance. Fire control. Fire discipline. Lecture to Companies on "C.D.S.307. C.D.S.312". Lewis M.G. instruction continued.	
"	24-2-1916.		Programme for 23rd repeated.	
"	25-2-1916.		" " " "	

1875 W: W593/826 1,000,000 4/15 J.B.C. & A. A.D.S.S./Forms/C.2118.

Army Form C. 2118

WAR DIARY or INTELLIGENCE SUMMARY

1/6th Battn South Staffs Regt.

(Erase heading not required.)

Instructions regarding War Diaries and Intelligence Summaries are contained in F. S. Regs., Part II. and the Staff Manual respectively. Title Pages will be prepared in manuscript.

Place	Date	Hour	Summary of Events and Information	Remarks and references to Appendices
BEAUDREZ.	26-2-1916.		Physical exercises. Bayonet fighting. Route march. Judging distance. Fire direction and control. Rapid loading.	
	27-2-1916.		Bomb throwing instruction. Lectures on bombs to Coys. Bad weather interfered with programme of work, which could not be carried out.	
	28-2-1916.		Physical exercises. Route march by Companies. Bayonet fighting. Platoon drill.	
AUTHEUX.	29-2-1916.		The Battalion moved into fresh billets at AUTHEUX, arriving there at 1 p.m.	

29-2-1916.

F. J. Laws Lieut: Colonel.

Commanding 1/6th Battn South Staffordshire Regt.

46

1/6 S. Stafford Regt
Vol XIV

Army Form C. 2118

WAR DIARY (62)
or
INTELLIGENCE SUMMARY

(Erase heading not required.)

1/6th Battn South Staffs Regiment.

Instructions regarding War Diaries and Intelligence Summaries are contained in F.S. Regs., Part II. and the Staff Manual respectively. Title Pages will be prepared in manuscript.

Q14

Place	Date	Hour	Summary of Events and Information	Remarks and references to Appendices
AUTHEUX	1-3-1916.		Battalion Training:- Rapid Loading.Fire Direction & Control. Route march by Companies. Bayonet Fighting. Bomb Practice.	
	2-3-1916.		Battalion Training:- Judging Distance.Fire Direction & Control.Bayonet Fighting. Platoon Drill. Route March by Companies.	
	3-3-1916.		Battalion Drill. Battalion Training:- Musketry on Range. Battalion Drill.	
	4-4-1916.		Battalion Training:- Bayonet Fighting.Fire Direction & Control.Judging Distance. Musketry on Range. Battalion Drill.	
	5-4-1916.		S U N D A Y.	
	6-4-1916.		Battalion marched to New billets at REBREUVIETTE.	
	7-4-1916.		Medical Inspection of Battalion. Lectures by Platoon Commanders.	
	8-4-1916.		Battalion marched to New billets at Houvin.	
	9-4-1916.		Battalion marched to New billets at MAIZIERES.	
	10-4-1916.		Battalion Training in billets.	
	11-4-1916.		Battalion march to New billets at MONT ST ELOY. Advance party proceeded to Trenches at NEUVILLE ST VAAST.	
	12-4-1916.		Machine Gunners,Bombers,Signallers proceeded to Trenches.	
	13-4-1916.		Battalion relieved the 50th French Regiment in the Trenches at NEUVILLE ST VAAST. Relief reported complete Midnight 13/14-3-1916.	
	14-4-1916.		Quiet day.	
	15-4-1916.		Quiet day.	

1875 W. W593/826 1,000,000 4/15 J.B.C. & A. A.D.S.S./Forms/C. 2118.

Army Form C. 2118

WAR DIARY (63)
or
INTELLIGENCE SUMMARY
(Erase heading not required.)

1/6th Battn South Staffs Regt.

Instructions regarding War Diaries and Intelligence Summaries are contained in F. S. Regs., Part II. and the Staff Manual respectively. Title Pages. will be prepared in manuscript.

Place	Date	Hour	Summary of Events and Information	Remarks and references to Appendices
NEUVILLE ST VAAST.	16-4-1916.		Quiet day.	
	17-4-1916.		Quiet day except for a little bombing which ceased when we replied vigorously.	
	18-4-1916.		Quiet day.	
	19-4-1916.		Enemy directed many rifle grenades against Y Listening Post. a little R.E. Shelling by enemy over Parallel 8 & at VAAST. Battalion relieved in the Trenches by 1/5th South Staffs Regt. and went into Divisional Reserve at ECOIVRES.	
	20-4-1916.		Working parties found for Hutments etc.	
	21-4-1916.		ditto	
	22-4-1916.		ditto.	
	23-4-1916.		ditto	
	24-3-1916.		ditto.	
	25-3-1916.		The Battalion relieved the 1/5th South Staffs Regt in the Trenches. Relief reported complete 11-15p.m.	
	26-3-1916.		Quiet day on our front. Our Field Guns shelled trenches beyond B6. Heavy Bombing and M.T. Fire in the sector on our right.	
	27-3-1916.		Very quiet day, until 10p.m. when enemy commenced heavy fire with mortars, Field Guns, rifle grenades and Machine Guns on ground between O63 and OS3.O64 and OR64. This ceased upon vigorous action of our Field Guns. Enemy trench mortars fired intermittently single bombs during the night.	
	28-3-1916.		Enemy fired eleven heavy trench bombs which fell behind O65 AND O64 between 6 a.m. and noon.	

1875 Wt. W393/826 1,000,000 4/15 J.B.C. & A. A.D.S.S./Forms/C. 2118.

Army Form C. 2118

WAR DIARY
or
INTELLIGENCE SUMMARY

(Erase heading not required.)

1/6th Battn South Staffs Regt.

Instructions regarding War Diaries and Intelligence Summaries are contained in F.S. Regs., Part II. and the Staff Manual respectively. Title Pages will be prepared in manuscript.

Place	Date	Hour	Summary of Events and Information	Remarks and references to Appendices
	29-3-1916.		Enemy shelled our trenches heavily from 2p.m. to 2-20 p.m. using Howitzers and H.E, concentrating upon O64,O64,O63,O64 with H.E. and the ground between these trenches with Howitzers. Our artillery barrage operated very quickly. At 6-50 p.m. last night we sprang a mine which formed a crater on left of B4. The whole was occupied and partly consolidated. Our artillery support followed promptupon the explosion, and was excellent in effect. The enemy severely bombarded FAYENNE TRENCH and O63,O64,O63,O64 with H.E. His Howitzers damaged BOYOU DES ONDRS and DENNIS LAROCHE. Intermittent artillery fire continued till 8p.m. and from that time the situation was quiet, and the work of repairing and consolidating was pressed on.	
	30-3-1916.		Quiet day. Battalion relieved by 1/5th Btn South Staffs Regt in the trenches, and went into Brigade Reserve in billets at ANNVILLE & VAASE.	
	31-3-1916.		In Brigade Reserve. Total casualties for month:-. 2/Lieutenant C.H.Pearson. Killed.18-3-1916. Lieutenant G.H. Smith. Died of wounds.29-3-1916. Lieutenant T.H. Highfield-Jones.Wounded.16-3-1916. Captain H.A. Page.Slightly wounded.(At duty)18-3-1916. 2/Lieutenant J.P.Miller.Wounded. 30-3-1916. 3 Other ranks. Killed. 15 Other ranks. Wounded. (2 slightly remaining at duty).	

Major.

For O.C.1/6th S.Staffs Rgt.

Army Form C. 2118

WAR DIARY or INTELLIGENCE SUMMARY

(Erase heading not required.)

1/5th Batn. South Staffs Regt.

Instructions regarding War Diaries and Intelligence Summaries are contained in F. S. Regs, Part II. and the Staff Manual respectively. Title Pages will be prepared in manuscript.

Place	Date	Hour	Summary of Events and Information	Remarks and references to Appendices
NEUVILLE ST VAAST	1-4-16.		In Brigade Reserve.	
do	2-4-16.		ditto	
do	3-4-16.		ditto	
do	4-4-16.		Battalion relieved the 1/5th Batn South Staffs Regt. in the trenches, relief being reported complete at 8-35pm.	
do	5-4-16.		Quiet day. Enemy fired a few shells over OS3.OS65 and POUQUER this morning from 10-30 a.m. to 11-30a.m.	
do	6-4-16.		Quiet day.	
do	7-4-16.		Quiet day.	
do	8-4-16.		Quiet day. Seven kites observed in a chain over Sector on our right.	
do	9-4-16.		Quiet day. Our heavy and Field Artillery active opposite O64. Some reply from enemy's Field Guns. Battalion relieved in the trenches by the 1/5th Btn South Staffs Regiment.	
ECOIVRES	10-4-16.		In Divisional Reserve.	
do	11-4-16.		ditto	
do	12-4-16.		ditto	
do	13-4-16.		ditto	
do	14-4-16.		ditto	

Q15

Army Form C. 2118

WAR DIARY
or
INTELLIGENCE SUMMARY
(Erase heading not required.)

1/6th South Staffs Regt.

Instructions regarding War Diaries and Intelligence Summaries are contained in F. S. Regs., Part II. and the Staff Manual respectively. Title Pages will be prepared in manuscript.

Place	Date	Hour	Summary of Events and Information	Remarks and references to Appendices
ABUVILLE ST VAAST	15-4-16.		Battalion relieved the 1/5th Battn South Staffs regiment in the trenches. Relief reported complete 11-15p.m.	
do	16-4-16.		Artillery activity from dawn till noon by enemy howitzers and field guns against fire and support trenches. Also O63 and O63 bombarded with light aerial torpedoes. Artillery active on both sides between 6p.m. & 7p.m. our artillery bombarding the enemy trenches. About midnight two mines were exploded on our left, followed by a heavy bombardment.	
do	17-4-16.		Quiet day.	
do	18-4-16.		At 6-55p.m. the enemy blew in left side of Y Listening Post, but no activity followed. And we occupied & consolidated the new lip of the Crater, known as B5. Otherwise a quiet day.	
do	19-4-16.		From 10-30p.m. to 11-30 p.m. our artillery bombarded the enemy's position opposite the left of the Divisional Sector. Some artillery reply from enemy. Otherwise a quiet day.	
do	20-4-16.		Enemy bombarded the trenches on our left at 6-30p.m. Weakening for 3/4 of an hour. Otherwise a quiet day.	
MONCHI BRETON	21-4-16.		The Battalion was relieved in the trenches by the 8th Border Regt, 75 Bde, 25th Division, and proceeded to MONCHY BRETON, the 46th Division being ordered to rest.	
do	22-4-16.		Battalion resting.	

Army Form C. 2118

WAR DIARY or INTELLIGENCE SUMMARY
(Erase heading not required.)

1/6th Battn South Staffs Regiment.

Instructions regarding War Diaries and Intelligence Summaries are contained in F. S. Regs., Part II. and the Staff Manual respectively. Title Pages will be prepared in manuscript.

Place	Date	Hour	Summary of Events and Information	Remarks and references to Appendices
LUXURY BRETON	23-4-16.		Easter Day.	
do	24-4-16.		Cleaning of clothing and equipment.	
	25-4-16.		ditto	
	26-4-16.		"B" Company inspected by Brigadier General Connac 137th Bde. Lecture by Commanding Officer to Officers, C.S.Majors and Platoon Sergeants on Bayonet sighting. Inspection of clothing by Quartermaster. Battalion Training.	
	27-4-16.		Physical Drill. Squad Drill. Platoon Drill. Bayonet sighting. Lecture and instruction by Adjutant to N.C.O's on Guards and Guard Mounting.	
	28-4-16.		ditto.	
	29-4-16.		Physical Drill. Platoon Drill. Bayonet sighting. Rifle Exercises.	
	30-4-16.		SUNDAY.	
			Total casualties for month:- 5 other ranks killed.
2 " " died of wounds.
1 " " missing.
10 " " wounded.
6 " " wounded but still at duty.	

Lieut: Colonel.
Commanding 1/6th Battn South Staffordshire Regiment.

Army Form C. 2118.

WAR DIARY or INTELLIGENCE SUMMARY.

(Erase heading not required.)

1/6th Battn South Staffs Regiment. (67)

Instructions regarding War Diaries and Intelligence Summaries are contained in F.S. Regs., Part II. and the Staff Manual respectively. Title pages will be prepared in manuscript.

Place	Date	Hour	Summary of Events and Information	Remarks and references to Appendices
MONCHY BRETON.	1-5-1916.		Battalion Training.	
"	2-5-1916.		ditto	
"	3-5-1916.		ditto	
IVERGNY.	4-5-1916.		The Battalion marched to IVERGNY.	
ST AMAND.	5-5-1916.		The Battalion marched to ST AMAND.	
FONQUE-VILLIERS.	6-5-1916.		"A" & "B" Coys proceeded to FONQUEVILLIERS & took over F.G.H.J. Works, Fort Dick, Junction Keep & La Haie Farm. "C" & "D" Coys occupied dugouts etc in FONQUEVILLIERS.	
"	7-5-1916.		In Brigade Reserve.	
"	8-5-1916.		ditto	
"	9-5-1916.		ditto	
"	10-5-1916.		ditto	
"	11-5-1916.		ditto	
"	12-5-1916.		The Battalion relieved the 1/5th Battn North Staffs Regt in the Centre Sector.	
"	13-5-1916.		An anti-aircraft gun was brought up into action about 12 midnight midday by the enemy. Previously from 8-30 a.m. to noon Machine Gun & Rifle fire had only been used by the enemy against our aeroplanes.	
"	14-5-1916.		Quiet day.	
"	15-5-1916.		Quiet day. At 2-45p.m. some 12 trench mortars and a few whizzbangs were fired between Post 9a and Trench 50. At 4-0 p.m. 30 bombs in a period of 10 minutes were thrown in the vicinity of the head of F3 Communication Trench.	

T2134. Wt. W708-776. 500000. 4/15. Sir J.C. & S.

1/6th Battn South Staffs Regt.

WAR DIARY (68)
or
INTELLIGENCE SUMMARY.

Army Form C. 2118.

Instructions regarding War Diaries and Intelligence Summaries are contained in F. S. Regs. Part II. and the Staff Manual respectively. Title pages will be prepared in manuscript.

(Erase heading not required.)

Place	Date	Hour	Summary of Events and Information	Remarks and references to Appendices
FONQUE-VILLERS.	16-5-1916.		At 12-30 a.m. the enemy opened sudden bombardment with heavy and light artillery,Lachrymatory shells and trench mortars on the Village & Wood,a fair percentage of shells and mortars bursting short and over our front line between Posts 7 & 11. This heavy bombardment lasted until 1-30 a.m. when things quietened down and a few intermittent shells were sent over until 2-15 a.m. when all was quiet. During the heavy bombardment the enemy fired a number of shrapnel shells bursting high over "No Man's Land", and they also during this period fired an unusual number of flare lights,all falling short and lighting up their own front wire. The sentry in No 7 Post reports that after the bombardment, Flare lights were sent up from the trench at the edge of the wood and bombs were thrown into their front line trench, and it is assumed that the enemy evacuated their front line during the bombardment. A trench mortar position was located from Post 8. 150° magnetic bearing,and was noted by the F.O.O.	
do	17-5-1916.	4 a.m. & 8-30 a.m.	German Biplane of a large type observed over our lines at 4 a.m. & 8-30 a.m. A new anti-aircraft devise by the enemy was seen yesterday evening. Small incendiary bombs were seen passing through the air,17 shells being in the air at one time. This new devise seems most effective against aircraft flying at low altitudes. The gun is very mobile. A sentry reported that at 4 a.m. seeing two heads appear above the parapet(enemy) as if inquisitive as to their new surroundings. One was an old man with grey beard. A small enemy party,most probably a working party was dispersed by Lewis Gun fire from No 2 Post. Some casualties are believed to have been caused as shouts were heard.	

Army Form C. 2118.

WAR DIARY (69)
or
INTELLIGENCE SUMMARY.
(Erase heading not required.)

1/6th Battn South Staffs Regt.

Instructions regarding War Diaries and Intelligence Summaries are contained in F.S. Regs, Part II. and the Staff Manual respectively. Title pages will be prepared in manuscript.

Place	Date	Hour	Summary of Events and Information	Remarks and references to Appendices
FONQUE-VILLIERS.	18-5-1916.		1 Officer & 2 N.C.O's went out from No 5 Trench at 12-45a.m. to the Sugar Factory on the GOMMECOURT ROAD, in order to ascertain whether the enemy were in the factory. The enemy appear to have a new Machine Gun, similar to our Lewis Gun, the rate of fire being identical. Quiet day.	
"	19-5-1916.		Quiet day. Battalion relieved by the 6th Battn Notts & Derby Regt, 139th Brigade, 46th Division, in the trenches. Relief reported complete 1-15 a.m. 20-5-16. The Battalion then proceeded to HUMBERCAMP to rest billets.	
SUS-ST-LEGER.	20-5-1916.		The Battalion marched to SUS-ST-LEGER.	
"	21-5-1916.		Resting.	
"	22-5-1916.		Battalion training.	
"	23-5-1916.		Battalion training.	
"	24-5-1916.		Battalion engaged as a working party at LUCHEUX FOREST.	
"	25-5-1916.		" " " " " "	
"	26-5-1916.		Battalion practiced "The Attack".	
"	27-5-1916.		" engaged as a working party at LUCHEUX FOREST.	
"	28-5-1916.		Route march.	
"	29-5-1916.		Battalion engaged as a working party at LUCHEUX FOREST.	
"	30-5-1916.		Battalion practiced "The Attack"	

Army Form C. 2118.

1/6th Battn South Staffs Regt.

WAR DIARY
or
INTELLIGENCE SUMMARY.
(Erase heading not required.)

Instructions regarding War Diaries and Intelligence Summaries are contained in F. S. Regs., Part II. and the Staff Manual respectively. Title pages will be prepared in manuscript.

Place	Date	Hour	Summary of Events and Information	Remarks and references to Appendices
Sus-St-LEGER.	31-5-1916.		The Battalion was engaged as a working party at LUCHEUX FOREST.	
			Total casualties for month:-	
			Other ranks killed. 3	
			" " wounded. 4	
			" " " but still at duty. 2	
			[signature] Major.	
			Commanding 1/6th Battn South Staffordshire Regiment.	
			2-6-1916.	

Army Form C. 2118.

WAR DIARY or **INTELLIGENCE SUMMARY**

1/6th Battn South Staffs Regt. (38)

(Erase heading not required.)

Instructions regarding War Diaries and Intelligence Summaries are contained in F.S. Regs., Part II. and the Staff Manual respectively. Title pages will be prepared in manuscript.

1/6 S Stafford Regt

46

Q 17

Place	Date	Hour	Summary of Events and Information	Remarks and references to Appendices
SUS-ST-LEGER	1-6-1916.		Battalion practised "The attack".	
	2-6-1916.		ditto	
	3-6-1916.		Battalion at disposal of Company Commanders for interior economy.	
	4-6-1916.		S U N D A Y.	
	5-6-1916.		Battalion practised "The attack".	
	6-6-1916.		Battalion practised Bayonet Fighting. Physical exercises. The Battalion marched to HUMBERCAMP.	
	7-6-1916.		Battalion engaged as working party.	
	8-6-1916.		ditto	
	9-6-1916.		ditto	
HUMBERCAMP	10-6-1916.		ditto	
	11-6-1916.		ditto	
	12-6-1916.		ditto	
	13-6-1916.		ditto	
	14-6-1916.		ditto	
	15-6-1916.		ditto	
	16-6-1916.		Battalion relieved the 1/5th Leicester Regiment in the trenches, Right Sector, FONQUEVILLERS.	

Army Form C. 2118.

1/6th Battn South Staffs Regiment.   (39)

WAR DIARY
or
INTELLIGENCE SUMMARY.
(Erase heading not required.)

Instructions regarding War Diaries and Intelligence Summaries are contained in F.S. Regs., Part II. and the Staff Manual respectively. Title pages will be prepared in manuscript.

Place	Date	Hour	Summary of Events and Information	Remarks and references to Appendices
FONQUE-VILLERS.	17-6-1916.		Quiet day.	
"	18-6-1916.		Quiet day. Battalion was relieved in the trenches by the 1/5th Leicester Regiment, and proceeded to old billets at SUS-ST-LEGER arriving there at 6-30 a.m.	
SUS-ST-LEGER.	19-6-1916.		Cleaning of clothing and equipment.	
"	20-6-1916.		The Battalion practised "The attack".	
"	21-6-1916.		Battalion at disposal of Company Commanders for interior economy.	
"	22-6-1916.		Battalion marched to SOUASTRE.	
SOUASTRE.	23-6-1916.		Working parties found for the trenches at FONQUEVILLERS.	
"	24-6-1916.		ditto.	
"	25-6-1916.		~~Only~~ ditto	
"	26-6-1916.		Bathing. Working parties found for trenches at FONQUEVILLERS	
"	27-6-1916.		Bathing. ditto	
"	28-6-1916.		Bathing. ditto	
"	29-6-1916.		Operations to be carried out on 29-6-1916 cancelled. See War Diary for 1-7-1916.	
"	30-6-1916.		The Battalion proceeded to the trenches at FONQUEVILLERS at 8-45 p.m.	

T2134. Wt. W708-776. 500000. 4/15. Sir J.C. & S.

Army Form C. 2118.

1/6th Battn South Staffs Regiment.   WAR DIARY   (40)
or
INTELLIGENCE SUMMARY.
(Erase heading not required.)

TOTAL CASUALTIES FOR THE MONTH:-

Other ranks.   Killed.   5
    "   Wounded.   27
    "   Wounded & at duty. -
    "   Died of wounds.   2

R e P for, Captain Adjutant.

M Lieut: Colonel.

Commanding 1/6th Battn South Staffordshire Regiment.

G.S. 46ᵗʰ Division July 1916

South Staffs. June 1916

War History

M.S.S. (Wire Reports etc)

Sonnecampt

Sent by. C. Ashford
(Late) Capt. 1/6 S. Staffs. Rgt.

POTTS & POTTS,
SOLICITORS.
FREDK H. POTTS.
CYRIL A. POTTS.
ALSO AT MUCH WENLOCK.

The Grange
Broseley.
Shropshire,
10th Augt 1926

Dear Major Becke, 46th Divn attack on Gommecourt.

Thank you for your letter of yesterday's date. By all means place the documents I sent you with the permanent records – I do not want them back.

In case they are of interest, I enclose 2 air photographs of our front of attack, taken 26/6/16 and 9/11/16 respectively. A comparison of these shows the effect of the barrage. No. 8 L 1343 also gives a good idea of the wire and some indication of the direction of enemy artillery fire.

Both photographs show our jumping off trenches, which were actually nothing but death traps. The old sugar factory ruins are shown on 8 L 382, and a corner of the village of Gommecourt, from which came heavy machine gun fire.

The communication trenches to our forward trench were supposed to be Russian saps & invisible !

Yours very truly
C. Ashford.

P.A.
with
46 Divn G.S.
July 1916
AFB

POTTS & POTTS,
SOLICITORS.
FRED. H. POTTS.
CYRIL A. POTTS.
ALSO AT MUCH WENLOCK.

The Grange
Broseley,
Shropshire.
6th August 1926

Ref. 16/543.

Dear Sir,

As you may remember, I sent you a few notes on the 46th Divisional attack on Gommecourt, about three years ago, & promised to send you certain documents relating thereto. These documents have been in other hands & I have only just received them back. Some, I am afraid, have been mislaid and all are probably too late to be of use to you. However, I am enclosing a selection, in case they are of use.

I am sending copies of patrol reports which prove that the wire was not properly cut & can send you most of the originals, if you would like them. I may point out that even the gaps reported clear were partially repaired, or filled with loose wire from time to time. I also think the instructions support my view that the assault troops were too heavily laden.

Yours faithfully,
C. Ashford
(late) Capt. 1/6 S. Staffs Regt.

ORDER OF BATTLE of XIV RES. CORPS.

Corps Commander - Lieut-General von STEIN.
Head-Quarters - BAPAUME.

52nd Division.	26th Res. Division.	28th Res. Division
Gen. von BORIES.	Lt-Gen. Fr. v. SODEN.	Gen. d. Inf. v. PAVEL.

CORPS TROOPS

6th Battery (2nd Mortar Battalion) 1st Foot Artillery Regiment recruited in KONIGSBERG.
8th Battery 10th Foot Artillery Regiment recruited in STRASBURG.
Elements of Bavarian Pioneer Regiment.
Field Company 2nd Battalion 14th Pioneers.   } recruited in XIV Corps
32nd Flying Squadron.   } area (KARLSRUHE).
XIV Reserve Corps Bridging Train.
XIV Reserve Corps Telegraph & Telephone Detachments.
Columns, Trains, etc.

NOTE BY THE FRENCH ON HEAVY ARTILLERY ON THIS FRONT IN JUNE.

XIV Reserve Corps - 4 Batteries of 15 cm
52nd Division   - 2, or possibly 3 Batteries of 15 cm.
52nd Division   - 1, or 2 Batteries of 12 cm.
One Battery of 21 cm.
One armoured train with heavy Naval Gun stated to have fired from MIRAUMONT.

ORDER OF BATTLE - 52nd RECONSTITUTED DIVISION
Commander - Lieut-General von BORIS.

Headquarters BIHUCOURT   (P.S.6.1.1916).
              BAPAUME   (P.S.26.11.1915).
              ABLAINZEVILLE (P.S.24.12.1915).

104th INFANTRY BRIGADE
Commander - Major-General von SCHUSSLER.
Headquarters - ABLAINZEVILLE Chateau.

No. of Regiment	Bttns	Line held	Supports	Rest Billets	Commanders	District from which recruited	Remarks
170th	3	South of MONCHY - BIENVILLERS Road to Gommecourt - FONQUEVILLERS Rd.	2nd Bn. has 1 Coy in support in 2nd line trenches.	1st Bn. BUCQUOY 2nd Bn. ABLAINZE- VILLE. 3rd Bn. —do— (P.S.24.12.15). (BUCQUOY) (P.S.6.1.1916).	Major ILENFELD (H.Q. in BUCQUOY)	BADEN	2nd. Bn.holds from HOMCHY to just N. HANNESCAMPS — FSS Road, with 2 Coys. resting at ABLAINZ- VILLE. The other 2 Bttns relieve one another in the Southern of the Sector.
169th	3	E.28.b.50.35. to SUNKEN ROAD.	3 Coys in GOMMECOURT. 1 Coy. in RETTEMCY FM.	BUCQUOY	Col. BERTHOLDT H.Q. in BUCQUOY.	BADEN	
66th	3	SUNKEN ROAD to 400 N. of SERRE MAILLY — x MAILLET Rd. K.29.d.1.9.	1 Coy. in K.24.00. 1 Bn in PUISIEUX.	ACHIET—le—PETIT	Major von STICKLER. H.Q. ACHIET- le—PETIT.	PRUSSIA	Bn. H.Q. S.E. co of STAR WOOD.

ARTILLERY 52nd DIVISION

Artillery Regt.&c.	No. of Btys.	No. of Guns	Reference to Pages. (1) French Book. (2) German Fuzes.	Maximum Range	Weight of Shell.	Date of Model of Gun.
103rd F.A.R.	6, of 4 guns.	24 (7.7 cm)	(1) Page 6. (2) PP36,62,70.	5350 m.time. 8400 m.percussion.	6.8 Kilos.	1896.
104th F.A.R.	6, of 4 guns.	24 (7.7 cm)	(1) Page 6. (2) PP.36,62,70.	5350 m.time, 8400 m.percussion	6.8 Kilos	
52. Foot A. Bn. 239th Foot A.Bty.	2 1.	? 8. ? 3 (15 cm)	(1) P. 29. (2) P. 42.	8300 m.	40. 5. Kilos.	1913.

Divisional Troops. Recruiting District.

2 Sqns. 16th Ulans   Salzwedel

52nd Cyclist Co.

103rd & 104th
Pioneer Coys.

Lieutenant-General VON STEIN. (Commanding XIV Reserve Corps).

Born	1856 (60 years old)
First Commission	1875
1st Lieutenant	1885
Captain	1890
Major	1896
Lieut.-Colonel	1902
Colonel	1905
Major-General	1910
Lieut- General	1912

General VON STEIN belonged to the Field Artillery. As a Major-General he held the appointment of "Oberquartiormeister" (head of a section of the General Staff at the War Ministry), and when promoted Lieutenant-General in 1912, obtained command of the 41st Division (XX Corps).

While still a Lieutenant-General he was appointed in 1915 to command the XIV Reserve Corps.

Lieut-Colonel RUSSELL (M.A.BERLIN) made the following notes about General VON STEIN in 1911:-

"Considered one of the most brilliant of the younger Generals in the German Army. Would without doubt be Oberquartiermeister to one of the armies in war. He has been referred to as a possible successor to the present Chief of the General Staff, General of Infantry von MOLTKE. He gives the impression at once of a man of soldier like qualities and of exceptionally keen intelligence. Of very active habits.

As an instance of the high esteem in which he is held, it may be mentioned that this Officer was specially appointed to be Chief of the Staff to Prince Frederick LEOPOLD of Prussia, who was commander of the Red side on the Imperial Manoeuvres this year, so as to counterbalance what was considered the somewhat overwhelming qualities of the commander of the other side, Field Marshall Freiherr von der GOLTZ"

Lieutenant- General Graf VON SODEN. (Commanding 26th Reserve Divn. XIV R)

Born,	(?) 1869 (now 47 years old)
First Commission	1888
1st Lieutenant	1895
Captain	1901
Major	1906
Lieut-Colonel	1912
Colonel	1914
Major-General	
Lieut-General	

General Graf VON SODEN is, exclusive of Royal Princes, the youngest Divisional Commander in the German Army. He is more of a courtier than a soldier, as he was formerly a A.D.C. to the Kaiser, and officer-in-waiting to H.R.H.Prince OSKAR of PRUSSIA.

Before the war he was only a Lieutenant-Colonel, and he doubtless owes his rapid promotion since then to royal influence.

(over)

General der Infanterie VON PAWEL. (Commanding 28th Reserve Divn. XIV R.)

      General VON PAWEL was promoted Major General in 1914, but had retired from active command before the war. He was Commandant of the Training Camp at SENNE, near PADERBORN.

Lieutenant-General VON BORRIES. (Commanding 52nd Division - attached XIV Res. Copps.)

    Born,
    First Commission   1871
    1st Lieutenant   1881
    Captain   1887
    Major   1895
    Lieutenant-Col   1902
    Colonel   1905
    Maj-General   1909
    Lieut-General   1911.

      Before the war, General von BORRIES was Commamdant at ALTONA, and G.O.C. Troops at HAMBURG and WANDSBEK.
      He belongs to the Infantry.

Enemy work on Sector from SUNKEN ROAD (K.17.a.5.) to the left of Sector held by the 48th Division (References are from VIII Corps Summary during the month of April 1916).

TRENCHES.

Sq. on 1/10,000	Remarks.	Date of VIII Corps. Summary.
K.3.d.9.5.	Short new piece.	April 1st
K.11.c.65.70.	Front line being strengthened.	" 2nd
K.5.d.4.9. to) K.6.c.5.0.)	Work ~~progressing~~ continues	" 3rd
K.3.c.28.84/66 to E.28.b.15/65.) (a) K.4.d.7.5.) E.28.c.84.66.) E.28.b.15.05.	Work progressing. (also parallel trench running N.at LOUVIERE FARM)	" 3rd
	Large quantities of fine sand thrown up in front.	" 5th
K.4.d.8.5.	Good deal of work going on.	" 6th
(a) K.4.d.7.5./ K.11.b.	Considerable new work	" 7th
K.11.a.45/55	Large amount of earth thrown up.	" 7th
E.28.d.20/76.to) E.28.b.85/25.)	Work continues.	" 8th
E.28.b.15/10	(Communication trench) Work proceeding	" 10th
E.28.b.2.8./ E.28.b.5.1.	2nd Line trench (work going on).	" 10th
K.11.d.8.4) K.5.b.2.2.)	Earth thrown up.	" 10th
K.11.c.6.7.	"	" 11th
K.11.a.1.8.	Work done (timber and iron seen).	" 11th
K.4.d.6.3.- 8.5.		" 12th
K.11.a.8.9.) K.5.c.6.1.)	Work going on	" 12th
K.4.a.03.15. to K.3.b.87.02.	New trench in wire.	" 12th
F.26.a.2.0.) F.26.c.5.8.) E.30.b.3.d.) E.30.d.5.8.) K.5.c.59/12)	Trenches being cleared	" 13th
K.5.c.2.8.) K.4.d.)	Trenches being baled	" 13th
K.5.c.27.44.) K.5.c.3.5.) K.4.d.6.3.) F.26.c.50.85) F.26.c.8.6.) E.28.d.55.85) E.30.b.3.4.)	Work done.	" 14th
E.28.d.15.75.	New trench dug parallel to fire trench. (from communication trench)	" 14th
K.3.d.85.85.	Communication trench deepened.	" 15th
E.28.d.2.7.	New trench 20 yards long.	" 15th
L.14.a.k.4.b.32.	Work going on.	" 17th.
K.4.a.4.9.) K.3.d.80.86) K.3.d.76.82)	Sandbags and girders used.	" 17th
E.30.b.2.8.	Work on trenches running N.E.	" 17th
K.4.b.6.2. (b)	Fresh Chalk	" 18th
K.12.a.55/95 - K.12.a.05/33.	This communication trench has been continued to K.11.d.5.8.	" 18th

Sq. on 1/10,000	Remarks.	Dated of VIII Corps Summary.	
K.4.b.6.2. (b)	Chalk has increased.	April	19th
K.11.c.7.6.)			
K.11.a.K.5.c.)	Working party	"	20th
K.4.d.	Parapet being levelled	"	20th
L.7.c. (c)	Trenches here being reconstructed (loopholes observed)	"	20th
K.3.d.65.70.)			
K.3.b.00.13.)	Much activity in these front line trenches	"	20th
E.29.b.4.8.)			
E.29.b.1.3.)			
L.7.c. (c)	Working party	"	21st
K.3. and K.4.(d)	Parallelogram continually being strengthened.	"	22nd
K.12.b.3.0.	Working party dispersed by fire but continually reappeared.	"	23rd.
L.7.c.9.1. (c)	100 men entered trench with working materials - from Rossignol	"	23rd
L.7.c.6.1.	Fresh earth visible	"	23rd
K.3.d. (d)	(Parallelogram) 1st and 2nd line trenches being deepened.	"	23rd
E.28.d./E.28.b.7.1.	Large party (2nd line trench)	"	23rd
K.3.d.7.7.	Short communication trench from GOMMECOURT PARK to front line.	"	24th
K.4.a.and c.	Fresh chalk at 2nd line trench	"	24th
E.28.d.35.90)			
E.28.d.1.8.)	Fresh chalk and earth	"	24th
E.28.d.38.90)			
E.28.b.48.10.)	Repaired.	"	24th
E.30.d.90.95 to E.30.d.7.7.	New trench being repaired.	"	25th
L.13.b.4.0. to 2.4.	Freshly dug out.	"	25th
E.30.b.4.5.	Working party	"	26th
K.11.c.6.7.	Baling	"	26th
L.31.d.30.10.	Communication trench joined to that at L.31.c.35.35.	"	26th
K.4.b.7.0.		"	27th
K.12.d.7.4.	Shallow trench across road	"	27th
L.7.c.5.4./K.12.b.5.7.	Communication trench	"	27th
L.7.a.15.45.)			
L.7.c.00.94.)	Working party	"	28th
E.28.d.,E.30.d.	W.P. Communication Trench	"	28th
K.17.b.	Working Party	"	28th

TRENCH MORTARS		MACHINE GUNS	
Position	Remarks	Position	Remarks
E.23.c.5.1.		E.28.b.7.5.	
E.23.c.80.35.		E.28.b.5.3.	
E.28.b.75.05.		E.28.b.2.1.	
E.28.b.80.25.		E.28.c.6.5.	Suspected
E.28.b.5.2.		E.28.c.5.0.	
E.28.b.95.20.		E.28.c.40.25.	
E.28.c.40.25.		E.28.c.70.50.	Suspected
E.28.c.8.4.		E.28.c.80.64.	
E.28.c.6.1.		E.28.d.05.75.	
E.28.c.70.65.		E.28.d.3.6.	
E.28.c.5.0.		E.28.d.10.95.	Suspected
E.28.c.8.0.		E.28.d.8.6.	
E.28.c.80.35.		E.28.d.5.4.	
E.28.c.70.35.		E.29.b.1.3.	
E.28.d.2.5.			
E.28.d.0.4.		K.3.b.90.05.	
E.28.d.3.6.	Under construction	K.3.d.8.6.	
E.28.d.10.95.	Suspected	K.3.d.7.3. (?)	
E.28.d.8.6.		K.3.d.7.0.80.	
E.28.d.5.4.		K.3.d.7.5.	
E.28.d.10.35.		K.4.a.30.85.	
		K.4.a.4.9.	
K.3.b.90.05.		K.4.a.2.5.	
K.3.d.80.80		K.4.a.1.2.	Suspected
K.4.b.15.75.	Suspected.	K.4.a.3.7.	
K.4.a.4.3.		K.4.a.03.15.	
K.4.a.35.10.		K.4.c.9.4.	
K.4.a.1.1.		K.4.d.25.47.	
K.4.c.9.5.		K.4.d.4.4.	
K.4.c.60.80.		K.4.d.0.5.	
K.4.c.4.7.		K.4.d.5.3.	
K.4.d.7.5.		K.4.d.8.2.	
K.4.d.3.6.		K.5.c.25.26.	
K.4.d.55.25.		K.11.a.4.1.	
K.4.c.20.90.		K.11.a.3.5.	
K.11.a.6.5.		K.11.a.30.92.	
K.11.c.9.8.		K.11.a.2.8.	
		K.11.a.4.1.	

ACTIVE HOSTILE BATTERIES

N.B. All reported by Div.Art. unless otherwise stated

Position	Calibre	Remarks	
E.24.c.60.10	77.mm	Doubtful.	(KITE COPSE)
E.30.a.05.80	"		(PIGEON WOOD)
E.30.d.60.60.	"		(RETTEMOY Fm)
F.14.	105 mm		(? Quesnoy Fm)
F.19.c.84.30.	77 mm		(ESARTS)
F.19.d.38.59.	105.mm		"
F.19.d.30.06.	77 mm		"
F.21.b.	105 mm	Doubtful	
F.25.a.97.67	77 mm		(ESSARTS)
F.26.d.45.51.	150 mm		(? BUCQUOY)
K.6.a.	105 mm	Doubtful	
K.6.b.70.60	77 mm		(BIEZ WOOD)
K.c.b.90.60	150 mm		" "
K.6.b.90.65	150 mm		" " Confirmed in 4th Army list
K.12.b.30.70	77 mm		(ROSSIGNOL WOOD)
K.12.b.55.55.	105.mm	Doubtful	" "
K.12.b.80.30	150 mm		" "
K.12.a.60.95.	?		" "
K.18.b.30.02.	77 mm		(LA LOUVIERE FME.)
K.18.d.27.85.	"		" "
K.12.c.90.99.	"		(ROSSIGNOL WOOD)
L.1.a.87.40.	150 mm		(BIEZ WOOD)
L.1.a.	77 mm		" "
L.1.a.	105 mm		" "
L.1.b.40.50	How	Confirmed in 4th Army List	
L.1.b.12.36	L65 or 150 mm		(BIEZ WOOD)
L.7.a.60.20	77 mm		
L.7.a.33.23	"		
L.7.a.70.20	? 105 mm		
L.7.c.25.52	?		
L.8.a.55.25	105 mm		(FORK WOOD)
L.8.a.26.94	150 mm	Doubtful	
L.8.b.	77 mm		
L.8.d.	"		
L.8.d.45.36	105 mm		" "
L.8.d.10.45	150 mm		" "
L.8.d.20.40	150 mm		" "
L.8.d.40.40. or) L.8.b.30.10)	150 mm		
L.9.a.60.27	150.mm		
L.9.c.80.20	77 mm		
L.13.d.17.54	"		(BOX WOOD)
L.14.a.72.27.	"		(N.PUISIEUX)
L.14.a.40.10.	"		" "
L.14.c.20.20	"		(W. PUISIEUX)
L.14.c.50.92	105 mm		" "
L.14.d.80.18	77 mm		(E. PUISIEUX)
L.15.c.	105 mm		" "

GOMMECOURT.

TROOPS IN SECTOR

169th Regiment   1 Battalion in front Line.
                 1   "   in support in 2nd line.
                 1   "   in reserve (BUCQUOY). P.26.11.15.

Prisoner stated they spend 14 days in the trenches, none in reserve, and 7 days in BUCQUOY. When they go into the trenches half the Company remain behind to dig.   P.16.10.15.

The French stated that the 169th Regt. had generally two battalions in front line and one at BUCQUOY.

Ten days in front line and six days in support close up to trenches in GOMMECOURT.   P.23.3.16.

AIR PHOTOGRAPHS OF SECTOR.

No.	Date	Place.	No.	Date.	Place.
L/31	20.2.16.	BUCQUOY	L/513	8.4.16.	N. of BUCQUOY
L/70	5.3.16.	W. of FONQUEVILLERS	L/514	"	E.N.E. of ESSARTS
L/77	5.3.16.	E. of "	L/515	"	ESSARTS
M/1	5.3.16.	S. of HANNESCAMPS	L/516	"	E. of ESSARTS
M/18	7.3.16.	E. of FONQUEVILLERS	L/520	"	ESSARTS
L/271	25.3.16.	S. of ESSARTS	L/521	"	N.W. of ABLAINZEVILLE.
L/272	25.3.16	E. of GOMMECOURT			
L/394	1.4.16.	E. of FONQUEVILLERS	L/517	"	S.E. of QUESNOY FARM
L/405	1.4.16.	N.W. of ESSARTS			
L/406	1.4.16.	W. of ESSARTS	8.L.5.	21.4.16.	PIGEON WOOD
L/409	1.4.16.	W. of ESSARTS	6	"	GOMMECOURT
L/444	2.4.16.	E. of Fonquevillers	8	"	GOMMECOURT WOOD
L/446	"	W. of ESSARTS	10	"	Pigeon Wood
L/448	"	BRAYELLE Fme.	11	"	KITE COPSE
L/469	3.4.16	S.W. of ESSARTS	13	"	S. of GOMMECOURT
L/468	"	E. of ESSARTS	14	"	behind Gommecourt Wood
L/479	"	N. of GOMMECOURT			
L/480	"	S.E. of ESSARTS	23.M.31	25.4.16	N. of BUCQUOY
L/482	"	N.E. of GOMMECOURT	32	"	S.E. of AYETTE
L/483	"	N.E. of GOMMECOURT	33	"	ESSARTS
L/484	"	W. of ESSARTS	34	"	ESSARTS
L/486	"	S.W. of ESSARTS	36	"	ABLAINZEVILLE
L/487	"	N.E. of GOMMECOURT	37	"	N. of BUCQUOY
L/488	"	S. of ESSARTS	38	"	W. of ABLAINZEVILLE
L/510	8.4.16	S.E. of Quesnoy Fme			
L/511	8.4.16	E.N.E. of ESSARTS	39	"	BUCQUOY
L/512	"	ESSARTS	40	"	E. of BUCQUOY
			41	"	BOIS de LOGEAST
			42	"	E. of BUCQUOY
			43	"	S. of ABLAINZEVILLE
			93	29.4.16	E. of ESSARTS
			79	"	N. of ABLAINZEVILLE.

REST BILLETS

1 Battn. of 169th Regt. rests in BUCQUOY.   P.26.11.15.
1 " occupies 2nd line trenches   P.16.10.15.
Rest Billets 169th Regt. in BUCQUOY. P. 170th Regt. 5.1.16.

TROOPS/

TROOPS IN SUPPORT

103rd, 104th Field Arty. Regts. were seen in BUCQUOY. P.26.11.15.
Prisoner saw men of either the 185th or 188th Regt.
    in BUCQUOY   P. "
1 Battn. 169th Regt. holds 2nd line
Dug-outs for 1 company are in RETTEMOY FARM   P.16.10.15.
About the end of November 55th Landwehr Bde. Essarts
    Bn. were in BUCQUOY   P.5.1.16
52nd, 104th Fd. Artillery Regts. seen in
    ABLAINZEVILLE and BAPAUME.   P. 170th Regt. 5. 1. 16.
Trenches on the W. edge of BUCQUOY have wire 80 yards
    deep and very strongly constructed.   P.23.3.16
Prisoner confirms presence of 104th Field Arty, and
    has seen men wearing No.52.   P. "

ROADS AND TRACKS USED

Supplies come up by road from BUCQUOY to ESSARTS and then turn to the left to GOMMECOURT. Reliefs use the road skirting N. side of BOIS de BIEZ.   P.16.10.15
    Reliefs use the BUCQUOY - ESSARTS Road   P.26.11.15
    In case of bombardment communication trenches are used
from ESSARTS.   P.23.3.16

SUPPLY DUMPS

Supplies come up by BUCQUOY - ESSARTS - GOMMECOURT Road. The wagons stop just short of GOMMECOURT. Railhead ACHIET-le-GRAND.
                                                                                     P.23.3.16

AMMUNITION DEPOTS, BOMB STORES, ETC.

R.E. Dump at   BUCQUOY F.27.d.7.0 is connected to ACHIET by a small steel railway.   P.23.3.16

HEADQUARTERS, COMMAND POSTS, ETC.

H.Q. 169th Regt. Bucquoy at L.3.d.6.½.   P.26.11.15
Battalion H.Q. between S.E. corner of GOMMECOURT PARK
    and the village.
Possibly a Battalion H.Q. in RETTEMOY FARM.
Two Bn. H.Q. in BUCQUOY, one L.3.a.5.6. and one F.27.d.7.4.
                                                                                 P.23.3.16
Company H.Q. in front line E.28.d.0.7.   P.

WIRE

Prisoner stated front line wire is 50/60 metres wide. There is a narrow path through the wire on each platoon front. Second line trenches   close   behind first line has wire in front of it and more wire behind again. There is no wire in GOMMECOURT
                                            Village   P.26.11.15
New wire was put up in GOMMECOURT WOOD.   W.S.29.9.15
" " " " " " " " " ")
" " " " " " E.28.d.19, K.11.c.55)   " 6.10.15.
" " " " " " K.3.d.79 - K.3.d.77   "29.12.15.
" " " " " " E.28.c.96   " "
Wire about E.28.c.52 - K.4.a.28 is about 60 paces
wide. It is weak in front but strong near German
parapet.   29.12.15.
Wire strengthened S.W. corner GOMMECOURT PARK, K.4.a.28, front line E.28.b.   W.S.20.12.15.
Wire strengthened at K.3.d.78 and K.3.d.91, support line L.7.c. - L.13.a. K.4.d.24 West of road and parallel to Wood, K.3.d.56 and K.4.d.43.   W.S.13.1.16.
Work on wire. K.3.d.7.6, K.4.c. & d., K.4.a.00.20 (and bomb-proof screen); opposite FONQUEVILLERS.   W.s.20.2.16.

                                                                                  New wire/

35.K.11.a.18

New wire. K.4.d.30.45; K.11.a.~~18~~; K.3.b.81;
    K.3.d.66.   W.S.20.2.16.
Work on wire. K.4.a.36; E.28.d.0.9; K.4.c.24; K.3.d.65."28.2.16
Wire strengthened. K.3.d.57, K.3.d.64.   " 6.3.16

MACHINE GUNS
  One Machine Gun to every 150 yards of front.   P.16.10.15

E.28.b.7.5. - W.S.20.10.15.   Emplacements
K.4.d.2.5.) - W.S.6.10.15.   Suspected K.3.d.44)
E.28.b.10.7)   K.4.a.38)
E.30.a.22 Under construction.   "   E.28.c.4) W.S.20.1.16
    W.S.6.10.15.20.10.15.   "   E.28.d.18)
E.28.b.33 -)   "   E.28.d.1598)
E.30.a.03   )
E.28.b.51   )   "   E.28.c.50 - W.S.20.2.16
  (2 guns)) W.S.13.10.15. Located   K.3.b.72 - W.S.30.1.16
K.4.a.36   )   "
E.28.d.19   )   "   K.11.d.41 -   "   "
E.28.d.47   )   "   K.11.a.41 -   "   6.2.16
  (2 guns))   "   K.5.c.2526   "   "
              "   E.28.b.75)
E.30.a.05   )   "   K.11.a.3150)
E.28.b.21   ) W.S.20.10.15.   "   K.4.d.2547) W.S.13.2.16
E.28.c.80.65)   "   K.11.a.3092)
K.4.a.02   )   "   K.4.a.3085)

E.2.8.d.49)   A.A. E.28.b.95.65 - W.S.13.3.16.
E.28   ) W.S.30.10.15.
E.28.b.20.05)   MACHINE GUNS

K.4.d.38 -   W.S.6.11.15. N.W.corner of GOMMECOURT WOOD
K.11.a.34 (Susp)   "   E.29.a.2075)
E.29.a.3550   "   E.28.b.54   ) W.S.20.3.16.
E.28.d.11 (Susp) 20.11.15.
E.29.a.29   W.S.13.12.15. Trench Mortars.
E.28.b.19   "   13.1.15. K.3.d.78 - W.S.6.1.16.
              E.28.d.2575 - W.S. 13.1.16]
Rifle Battery. E.28.d.36 - W.S. 13.2.16.

GENERAL
  Prisoner stated that trenches are paved and at least 11 feet deep.
Second line close behind the front line. It is wired. P.26.11.15.
  Railway from ACHIET-le-GRAND to BOIS de LOGEAST to BUCQUOY.
                        W.S. 6.2.16.
  Railway suspected from BUCQUOY to ABLAINZEVILLE. W.S.13.2.16.
  Train of 3 trucks going from BUCQUOY to PUISIEUX. W.S.13.2.16.
  " going from PUISIEUX to BUCQUOY 9th Feb.   "   "
  French inhabitants remain in villages as follows:
    BUCQUOY 150;
    ABLAINZEVILLE, COURCELLES, ACHIET-le-GRAND, ACHIET-le-PETIT,
    ERVILLERS, in large numbers.

ORDER OF BATTLE of XIV RES. CORPS.

Corps Commander - Lieut-General von STEIN.
Head-Quarters - BAPAUME.

52nd Division.	26th Res. Division.	28th Res. Division
Gen. von BORIES.	Lt-Gen. Fr. v. SOEDEN.	Gen. d. Inf. v. PAVEL.

CORPS TROOPS

6th Battery (2nd Mortar Battalion) 1st Foot Artillery Regiment recruited in KONIGSBERG.
8th Battery 10th Foot Artillery Regiment recruited in STRASSBURG.
Elements of Bavarian Pioneer Regiment.
Field Company 2nd Battalion 14th Pioneers.   } recruited in XIV Corps
32nd Flying Squadron.   } area (KARLSRUHE).
XIV Reserve Corps Bridging Train.
XIV Reserve Corps Telegraph & Telephone Detachments.
Columns, Trains, etc.

NOTE BY THE FRENCH ON HEAVY ARTILLERY ON THIS FRONT IN JUNE.

XIV Reserve Corps - 4 Batteries of 15 cm
52nd Division   - 2, or possibly 3 Batteries of 15 cm.
52nd Division   - 1, or 2 Batteries of 12 cm.
One Battery of 21 cm.
One armoured train with heavy Naval Gun stated to have fired from MIRAUMONT.

ORDER OF BATTLE → 52nd RECONSTITUTED DIVISION
Commander - Lieut-General von BORIS.

Headquarters - BIHUCOURT (P.S.6.1.1916).
BAPAUME (P.S.26.11.1915).
ABLAINZEVILLE (P.S.24.12.1915).

104th INFANTRY BRIGADE
Commander - Major-General von SCHUSSLER.
Headquarters - ABLAINZEVILLE Chateau.

Regiment	No. of Bttns	Line held	Supports	Rest Billets	Commanders	District from which recruited	Remarks
170th	3	South of MONCHY → BIENVILLERS Road to Gommecourt - FONQUEVILLERS Rd.	2nd Bn. has 1 Coy. in support in 2nd line trenches.	1st Bn. BUCQUOY 2nd Bn. ABLAINZE-VILLE -do- (P.S.24.12.15). 3rd Bn. (BUCQUOY) (P.S.6.1.1916).	Major ILLENFELD (H.Q. in BUCQUOY)	BADEN	2nd Bn. holds from MONCHY to just N. HANNESCAMPS Road, with 2 Coys. resting at ABLAINZ-VILLE. The other 2 Bttns relieve one another in the southern of the sector.
169th	3	E.28.b.5C.35. to SUNKEN ROAD.	3 Coys in GOMMECOURT. 1 Coy. in ROTTEMOY FM.	BUCQUOY	Col. BERTHOLDT H.Q. in BUCQUOY.	BADEN	
66th	3	SUNKEN ROAD to 400 N. of SERRE MAILLY K.24.00. MAILLET Rd. K.29.d.1.9.	1 Coy. in K.24.00. 1 Bn in PUISIEUX.	ACHITT-le-PETIT	Major von STICKLER. H.Q. ACHITT-le-PETIT.	PRUSSIA	Bn. H.Q. S. E. of STAR WOOD.

ARTILLERY 52nd DIVISION

Artillery Regt.&c.	No. of Btys.	No. of Guns	Reference to Pages. (1) French Book. (2) German Fuzes.	Maximum Range	Weight of Shell.	Date of Model of Gun.
103rd F.A.R.	6, of 4 guns.	24 (7.7 cm)	(1) Page 6. (2) PP35, 62, 70.	5350 m. time. 8400 m. percussion.	6.8 Kilos.	1896.
104th F.A.R.	6, of 4 guns.	24 (7.7 cm)	(1) Page 6. (2) PP.35, 62, 70.	5350 m. time. 8400 m. percussion	6.8 Kilos	
52. Foot A. Bn. 239th Foot A.Bty.	2 1.	? 8. ? 3 (15 cm)	(1) P. 29. (2) P. 42.	8300 m.	40.5. Kilos.	1913.

Divisional Troops.   Recruiting District.

2 Sqns. 16th Ulans   Salzwedel

52nd Cyclist Co.

103rd & 104th
Pioneer Coys.

Lieutenant-General VON STEIN. (Commanding XIV Reserve Corps).

Born	1856 (60 years old)
First Commission	1875
1st Lieutenant	1885
Captain	1890
Major	1896
Lieut.-Colonel	1902
Colonel	1905
Major-General	1910
Lieut-General	1912

General VON STEIN belonged to the Field Artillery. As a Major-General he held the appointment of "Oberquartiormeister" (head of a section of the General Staff at the War Ministry), and when promoted Lieutenant-General in 1912, obtained command of the 41st Division (XX Corps).

While still a Lieutenant-General he was appointed in 1915 to command the XIV Reserve Corps.

Lieut-Colonel RUSSELL (M.A.BERLIN) made the following notes about General VON STEIN in 1911:-

"Considered one of the most brilliant of the younger Generals in the German Army. Would without doubt be Oberquartiermeister to one of the armies in war. He has been referred to as a possible successor to the present Chief of the General Staff, General of Infantry von MOLTKE. He gives the impression at once of a man of soldier like qualities and of exceptionally keen intelligence. Of very active habits.

As an instance of the high esteem in which he is held, it may be mentioned that this Officer was specially appointed to be Chief of the Staff to Prince Frederick LEOPOLD of Prussia, who was commander of the Red side on the Imperial Manoeuvres this year, so as to counterbalance what was considered the somewhat overwhelming qualities of the commander of the other side, Field Marshall Freiherr von der GOLTZ"

Lieutenant-General Graf VON SODEN. (Commanding 26th Reserve Divn. XLV R)

Born,	(?)	1869 (now 47 years old)
First Commission		1888
1st Lieutenant		1895
Captain		1901
Major		1906
Lieut-Colonel		1912
Colonel		1914
Major-General		
Lieut-General		

General Graf VON SODEN is, exclusive of Royal Princes, the youngest Divisional Commander in the German Army. He is more of a courtier than a soldier, as he was formerly a A.D.C. to the Kaiser, and officer-in-waiting to H.R.H.Prince OSKAR of PRUSSIA.

Before the war he was only a Lieutenant-Colonel, and he doubtless owes his rapid promotion since then to royal influence.

(over)

General der Infanterie VON PAWEL. (Commanding 28th Reserve Divn.
XIV R.)

General VON PAWEL was promoted Major General in 1914, but had retired from active command before the war. He was Commandant of the Training Camp at SENNE, near PADERBORN.

Lieutenant- General VON BORRIES. (Commanding 52nd Division –
attached XIV Res. Corps.)

Born,	
First Commission	1871
1st Lieutenant	1881
Captain	1887
Major	1895
Lieutenant-Col	1902
Colonel	1905
Maj-General	1909
Lieut-General	1911.

Before the war, General von BORRIES was Commandant at ALTONA, and G.O.C. Troops at HAMBURG and WANDSBEK.
He belongs to the Infantry.

Enemy work on Sector from SUNKEN ROAD (K.17.a.8.) to the left of Sector held by the 48th Division (References are from VIII Corps Summary during the month of April 1916).

TRENCHES.

Sq. on 1/10,000	Remarks.	Date of VIII Corps Summary.
K.3.d.9.5.	Short new piece.	April 1st
K.11.c.65.70.	Front line being strengthened.	" 2nd
K.5.a.4.9. to)		
K.6.c.3.0.)	Work ~~progressing~~ continues	" 3rd
K.3.c.28.84/66)		
to E.28.b.15/05.)		
(a) K.4.d.7.5.)		
E.28.c.84.66.)	Work progressing.	" 3rd
E.28.b.15.05.	(also parallel trench running N.at LOUVIERE FARM)	
	Large quantities of fine sand thrown up in front.	" 5th
K.4.d.8.5.	Good deal of work going on.	" 6th
(a) K.4.d.7.5./		
K.11.b.	Considerable new work	" 7th
K.11.a.45/55	Large amount of earth thrown up.	" 7th
E.28.d.20/76.to)		
E.28.b.85/25.)	Work continues.	" 8th
E.28.b.15/10	(Communication trench) Work proceeding	" 10th
E.28.b.2.8./		
E.28.b.5.1.	2nd Line trench (work going on).	" 10th
K.11.d.8.4)		
K.5.b.2.2.)	Earth thrown up.	" 10th
K.11.c.6.7.	"	" 11th
K.11.a.1.8.	Work done (timber and iron seen).	" 11th
K.4.d.6.3.- 8.5.		" 12th
K.11.a.8.9.)		
K.5.c.6.1.)	Work going on	" 12th
K.4.a.03.15.		
to K.3.b.87.02.	New trench in wire.	" 12th
F.26.a.2.0.)		
F.26.c.5.8.)		
E.30.b.3.d.)	Trenches being cleared	" 13th
E.30.a.5.8.)		
K.5.c.59/12)		
K.5.c.2.8.)		
K.4.a.	Trenches being baled	" 13th
K.5.c.27.44.)		
K.5.c.3.5.)		
K.4.d.6.3.)		
F.26.c.50.85)	Work done.	" 14th
F.26.c.8.6.)		
E.28.d.55.85)		
E.30.b.3.4.)		
E.28.d.15.75.	New trench dug parallel to fire trench. (from communication trench)	" 14th
K.3.d.85.85.	Communication trench deepened.	" 15th
E.28.d.2.7.	New trench 20 yards long.	" 15th
L.14.a.k.4.b.32.	Work going on.	" 17th.
K.4.a.4.9.)		
K.3.d.80.86)	Sandbags and girders used.	" 17th
K.3.d.76.82)		
E.30.b.2.8.	Work on trenches running N.E.	" 17th
K.4.b.6.2. (b)	Fresh Chalk	" 18th
K.12.a.55/95 -	This communication trench has been	
K.12.a.05/33.	continued to K.11.d.5.8.	" 18th

Sq. on 1/10,000	Remarks.	Dated of VIII Corps Summary.
K.4.b.6.2. (b)	Chalk has increased.	April 19th
K.11.c.7.6.)	Working party	" 20th
K.11.a.K.5.c.)	Parapet being levelled	" 20th
K.4.d. (c)	Trenches here being reconstructed (loopholes observed)	" 20th
L.7.c.		
K.3.a.65.70.)		
K.3.b.00.13.)	Much activity in these front line trenches	" 20th
E.28.b.4.8.)		
E.29.b.1.3.)		
L.7.c. (c)	Working party	" 21st
K.3. and K.4.(d)	Parallelogram continually being strengthened.	" 22nd
K.12. b.3.0.	Working party dispersed by fire but continually reappeared.	" 23rd.
L.7.c.9.1. (c)	100 men entered trench with working materials - from Rossignol	" 23rd
L.7.c.6.1.	Fresh earth visible	" 23rd
K.3.d. (d)	(Parallelogram) 1st and 2nd line trenches being deepened.	2. 23rd
E.28.d./E.28.b.7.1.	Large party (2nd line trench)	" 23rd
K.3.a.7.7.	Short communication trench from GOMMECOURT PARK to front line.	" 24th
K.4.a.and c.	Fresh chalk at 2nd line trench E.	" 24th
E.28.d.35.90)		
E.28.d.1.8.)	Fresh chalk and earth	" 24th
E.28.d.38.90)		
E.28.b.48.10.)	Repaired.	" 24th
E.30.a.90.95 to E.30.a.7.7.	New trench being repaired.	" 25th
L.13.b.4.0. to 2.4.	Freshly dug out.	" 25th
E.30.b.4.5.	Working party	" 26th
K.11.c.6.7.	Baling	" 26th
L.31.d.30.10.	Communication trench joined to that at L.31.c.35.35.	" 26th
K.4.b.7.0.		" 27th
K.12.d.7.4.	Shallow trench across road	" 27th
L.7.c.5.4./K.12.b.5.7.	Communication trench	" 27th
L.7.a.15.45.)		
L.7.c.00.94.)	Working party	" 28th
E.28.d.,E.30.d.	W.P. Communication Trench	" 28th
K.17.b.	Working Party	" 28th

TRENCH MORTARS		MACHINE GUNS	
Position	Remarks	Position	Remarks
E.23.c.5.1.		E.28.b.7.5.	
E.23.c.80.35.		E.28.b.5.3.	
E.28.b.75.05.		E.28.b.2.1.	
E.28.b.80.25.		E.28.c.6.5.	Suspected
E.28.b.5.2.		E.28.c.5.0.	
E.28.b.95.20.		E.28.c.40.25.	
E.28.c.40.25.		E.28.c.70.50.	Suspected
E.28.c.8.4.		E.28.c.80.64.	
E.28.c.6.1.		E.28.d.05.75.	
E.28.c.70.65.		E.28.d.3.6.	
E.28.c.5.0.		E.28.d.10.95.	Suspected
E.28.c.8.0.		E.28.d.8.6.	
E.28.c.80.35.		E.28.d.5.4.	
E.28.c.70.35.		E.29.b.1.3.	
E.28.d.2.5.			
E.28.d.0.4.		K.3.b.90.05.	
E.28.d.3.6.	Under construction	K.3.d.8.6.	
E.28.d.10.95.	Suspected	K.3.d.7.3. (?)	
E.28.d.8.6.		K.3.d.7.0.80.	
E.28.d.5.4.		K.3.d.7.5.	
E.28.d.10.35.		K.4.a.30.85.	
		K.4.a.4.9.	
K.3.b.90.05.		K.4.a.2.5.	
K.3.d.80.80		K.4.a.1.2.	Suspected
K.4.b.15.75.	Suspected.	K.4.a.3.7.	
K.4.a.4.3.		K.4.a.03.15.	
K.4.a.35.10.		K.4.c.9.4.	
K.4.a.1.1.		K.4.d.25.47.	
K.4.c.9.5.		K.4.d.4.4.	
K.4.c.60.80.		K.4.d.0.5.	
K.4.c.4.7.		K.4.d.5.3.	
K.4.d.7.5.		K.4.d.8.2.	
K.4.d.3.6.		K.5.c.25.26.	
K.4.d.55.25.		K.11.a.4.1.	
K.4.c.20.90.		K.11.a.3.5.	
K.11.a.6.5.		K.11.a.30.22.	
K.11.c.9.8.		K.11.a.2.8.	
		K.11.a.4.1.	

ACTIVE HOSTILE BATTERIES

N.B. All reported by Div.Art. unless otherwise stated

Position	Calibre	Remarks	
E.24.c.60.10	77.mm	Doubtful.	(KITE COPSE)
E.30.a.05.80	"		(PIGEON WOOD)
E.30.d.60.60.	"		(REFFEMCY Fm)
F.14.	105 mm		(? Quesnoy Fm)
F.19.c.84.80.	77 mm		(ESSARTS)
F.19.d.38.59.	105.mm		"
F.19.d.30.06.	77 mm		"
F.21.b.	105 mm	Doubtful	
F.25.a.97.67	77 mm		(ESSARTS) ?
F.26.d.45.51.	150 mm		(? BUCQUOY)
K.6.a.	105 mm	Doubtful	
K.6.b.70.60	77 mm		(BIEZ WOOD)
K.6.b.90.60	150 mm		" "
K.6.b.90.65	150 mm		" " Confirmed in 4th Army list
K.12.b.30.70	77 mm		(ROSSIGNOL WOOD)
K.12.b.55.55.	105.mm	Doubtful	" "
K.12.b.80.30	150 mm	"	" "
K.12.a.60.95.	?	"	" "
K.18.b.30.02.	77 mm		(LA LOUVIERE FME.)
K.18.d.27.85.	"		" " "
K.12.c.90.99.	"		(ROSSIGNOL WOOD)
L.1.a.87.40.	150 mm		(BIEZ WOOD)
L.1.a.	77 mm		" "
L.1.a.	105 mm		" "
L.1.b.40.50	How	Confirmed in 4th Army List	
L.1.b.12.36	105 or 150 mm		(BIEZ WOOD)
L.7.a.60.20	77 mm		
L.7.a.33.23	"		
L.7.a.70.20 ?	155 mm		
L.7.c.25.52	?		
L.8.a.55.25	105 mm		(FORK WOOD)
L.8.a.26.94	150 mm	Doubtful	
L.8.b.	77 mm		
L.8.d.	"		
L.8.d.45.36	105 mm		" "
L.8.d.10.45	150 mm		" "
L.8.d.20.40	150 mm		" "
L.8.d.40.40. or) L.8.b.30.10)	150 mm		
L.9.a.60.27	150.mm		
L.9.c.80.20	77 mm		
L.13.c.17.54	"		(BOX WOOD)
L.14.a.72.27.	"		(N.PUISIEUX)
L.14.a.40.10.	"		" "
L.14.c.20.20	"		(W. PUISIEUX)
L.14.c.50.92	105 mm		" "
L.14.d.80.18	77 mm		(E. PUISIEUX)
L.15.c.	105 mm		" "

GOMMECOURT.

TROOPS IN SECTOR

169th Regiment   1 Battalion in fron Line.
                    1   "   in support in 2nd line.
                    1   "   in reserve (BUCQUOY). P.26.11.15.

Prisoner stated they spend 14 days in the trenches, none in reserve, and 7 days in BUCQUOY.   When they go into the trenches half the Company remain behind to dig.   P.16.10.15

The French stated that the 169th Regt. has generally two battalions in front line and one at BUCQUOY.

Ten days in front line and six days in support close up to trenches in GOMMECOURT.   P.23.3.16.

AIR PHOTOGRAPHS OF SECTOR.

No.	Date	Place.	No.	Date.	Place.
L/31	20.2.16.	BUCQUOY	L/513	8.4.16.	N. of BUCQUOY
L/70	5.3.16.	W.of FONQUEVILLERS	L/514	"	E.N.E. of ESSARTS
L/77	5.3.16.	E.of "	L/515	"	ESSARTS
M/1	5.3.16.	S. of HANNESCAMPS	L/516	"	E. of ESSARTS
M/18	7.3.16.	E.of FONQUEVILLERS	L/520	"	ESSARTS
L/271	25.3.16.	S.of ESSARTS	L/521	"	N.W. of ABLAINZEVILLE.
L/272	25.3.16	E.of GOMMECOURT			
L/394	1.4.16.	E.ofFONQUEVILLERS	L/517	"	S.E.of QUESNOY FARM
L/405	1.4.16.	N.W. of ESSARTS			
L/406	1.4.16.	W. of ESSARTS	8.L.5.	21.4.16.	PIGEON WOOD
L/409	1.4.16.	W. of ESSARTS	6	"	GOMMECOURT
L/444	2.4.16.	E. ofFonquevillers	8	"	GOMMECOURT WOOD
L/446	"	W. of ESSARTS	10	"	Pigeon Wood
L/448	"	BRAYELLE Fme.	11	"	KITE COPSE
L/469	3.4.16	S.W.of ESSARTS	13	"	S.of GOMMECOURT
L/468	"	E. of ESSARTS	14	"	behind GommeCourt Wood
L/479	"	N.of GOMMECOURT			
L/480	"	S.E. of ESSARTS	23.M.31	25.4.16	N. of BUCQUOY
L/482	"	N.E. of GOMMECOURT	32	"	S.E. of AYETTE
L/483	"	N.E. of GOMMECOURT	33	"	ESSARTS
L/484	"	E. of ESSARTS	34	"	ESSARTS
L/486	"	S.W. of ESSARTS	36	"	ABLAINZEVILLE
L/487	"	N.E. of GOMMECOURT	37	"	N. of BUCQUOY
L/488	"	S. of ESSARTS	38	"	W. of ABLAINZEVILLE
L/510	8.4.16	S.E. of Quesnoy Fme			
L/511	8.4.16	E.N.E. of ESSARTS	39	"	BUCQUOY
L/512	"	ESSARTS	40	"	E. of BUCQUOY
			41	"	BOIS de LOGEAST
			42	"	E. of BUCQUOY
			43	"	S. of ABLAINZEVILLE
			93	29.4.16	E. of ESSARTS
			79	"	N. of ABLAINZEVILLE.

REST BILLETS

1 Battn. of 169th Regt. rests in BUCQUOY.   P.26.11.15.
1   "   occupies 2nd line trenches   P.16.10.15.
Rest Billets 169th Regt. in BUCQUOY. P. 170th Regt.   5.1.16.

TROOPS/

TROOPS IN SUPPORT

103rd, 104th Field Arty. Regts. were seen in BUCQUOY.   P.26.11.15.
Prisoner saw men of either the 185th or 188th Regt.
    in BUCQUOY   P. "
1 Battn. 169th Regt. holds 2nd line
Dug-outs for 1 company are in RETTEMOY FARM   P.16.10.15.
About the end of November 55th Landwehr Bde. Essarts
    Bn. were in BUCQUOY   P.5.1.16
52nd, 104th Fd. Artillery Regts. seen in
    ABLAINZEVILLE and BAPAUME.   P. 170th Regt. 5.1.16.
Trenches on the W. edge of BUCQUOY have wire 80 yards
    deep and very strongly constructed.   P.23.3.16
Prisoner confirms presence of 104th Field Arty, and
    has seen men wearing No.52.   P. "

ROADS AND TRACKS USED

Supplies come up by road from BUCQUOY to ESSARTS and then turn to the left to GOMMECOURT. Reliefs use the road skirting N. side of BOIS de BIEZ.   P.16.10.15
    Reliefs use the BUCQUOY - ESSARTS Road   P.26.11.15
    In case of bombardment communication trenches are used from ESSARTS.   P.23.3.16

SUPPLY DUMPS

Supplies come up by BUCQUOY - ESSARTS - GOMMECOURT Road. The wagons stop just short of GOMMECOURT. Railhead ACHIET-le-GRAND.
     P.23.3.16

AMMUNITION DEPOTS, BOMB STORES, ETC.

R.E. Dump at   BUCQUOY F.27.d.7.0 is connected to ACHIET by a small steel railway.   P.23.3.16

HEADQUARTERS, COMMAND POSTS, ETC.

H.Q. 169th Regt. Bucquoy at L.3.d.6.½.   P.26.11.15
Battalion H.Q. between S.E. corner of GOMMECOURT PARK
    and the village.
Possibly a Battalion H.Q. in RETTEMOY FARM.
Two Bn. H.Q. in BUCQUOY, one L.3.a.5.6. and one F.27.d.7.4.
     P.23.3.16
Company H.Q. in front line E.28.d.0.7.   P.

WIRE

Prisoner stated front line wire is 50/60 metres wide. There is a narrow path through the wire on each platoon front. Second line trenches   close   behind first line has wire in front of it and more wire behind again.   There is no wire in GOMMECOURT
     Village   P.26.11.15
New wire was put up in GOMMECOURT WOOD.   W.S.29.9.15
" " " " " " " ")
" " " " " " " E.28.d.19, K.11.c.55)   " 6.10.15.
" " " " " " " K.3.d.79 - K.3.d.77   "29.12.15.
" " " " " " " E.28.c.96   " "
Wire about E.28.c.52 - K.4.a.28 is about 60 paces wide. It is weak in front but strong near German parapet.   29.12.15.
Wire strengthened S.W. corner GOMMECOURT PARK, K.4.a.28, front line E.28.b.   W.S.20.12.15.
Wire strengthened at K.3.d.78 and K.3.d.91, support line L.7.c. - L.13.a. K.4.d.24 West of road and parallel to Wood, K.3.d.56 and K.4.d.43.   W.S.13.1.16.
Work on wire. K.3.d.7.6, K.4.c. & d., K.4.a.00.20 (and bomb-proof screen); opposite FONQUEVILLERS.   W.S.20.2.16.

        New wire/

K.11.a.35

New wire. K.4.d.30.45; K.11.a.18; K.3.b.81;
    K.3.a.66.   W.S.20.2.16.
Work on wire. K.4.a.36; E.28.d.0.9; K.4.c.24; K.3.d.65. "28.2.16
Wire strengthened. K.3.a.57, K.3.d.64.   " 6.3.16

MACHINE GUNS
    One Machine Gun to every 150 yards of front.   P.16.10.15

E.28.b.7.5. - W.S.20.10.15.   Emplacements
K.4.a.2.5.) - W.S.6.10.15.   Suspected K.3.d.44)
E.28.b.10.7)   K.4.a.38)
E.30.a.22 Under construction.   "   E.28.c.4) W.S.20.1.16
        W.S.6.10.15.20.10.15.   "   E.28.d.18)
E.28.b.33 -)   "   E.28.d.1598)
E.30.a.03   )
E.28.b.51   )   "   E.28.c.50 - W.S.20.2.16
  (2 guns)) W.S.13.10.15.   Located K.3.b.72 - W.S.30.1.16
K.4.a.36   )   "
E.28.d.19   )   "   K.11.d.41 -   "   "
E.28.d.47   )   "   K.11.a.41 -   " 6.2.16
  (2 guns))   "   K.5.c.2526   "   "
                                  "   E.28.b.75)
E.30.a.05   )   "   K.11.a.3150)
E.28.b.21   ) W.S.20.10.15.   "   K.4.d.2547) W.S.13.2.16
E.28.c.80.65)   "   K.11.a.3092)
K.4.a.02   )   "   K.4.a.3085)

E.28.d.49   )   A.A. E.28.b.95.65 - W.S.13.3.16.
E.28   ) W.S.30.10.15.
E.28.b.20.05)   MACHINE GUNS

K.4.d.38 -   W.S.6.11.15. N.W.corner of GOMMECOURT WOOD
K.11.a.34 (Susp)   "   E.29.a.2075)
E.29.a.3550   "   E.28.b.54   ) W.S.20.3.16.
E.28.d.11 (Susp) 20.11.15.
E.29.a.29   W.S.13.12.15. Trench Mortars.
E.28.b.19   " 13.1.15. K.3.d.78 - W.S.6.1.16.
                          E.28.d.2575 - W.S. 13.1.16
Rifle Battery. E.28.d.36 - W.S. 13.2.16.

GENERAL
    Prisoner stated that trenches are paved and at least 11 feet deep.
Second line close behind the front line. It is wired. P.26.11.15.
    Railway from ACHIET-le-GRAND to BOIS de LOGEAST to BUCQUOY.
                                                             W.S. 6.2.16.
    Railway suspected from BUCQUOY to ABLAINZEVILLE.   W.S.13.2.16.
    Train of 3 trucks going from BUCQUOY to PUISIEUX. W.S.13.2.16.
    " going from PUISIEUX to BUCQUOY 9th Feb.   " " "
    French inhabitants remain in villages as follows:
        BUCQUOY 150;
        ABLAINZEVILLE, COURCELLES, ACHIET-le-GRAND, ACHIET-le-PETIT,
ERVILLERS, in large numbers.

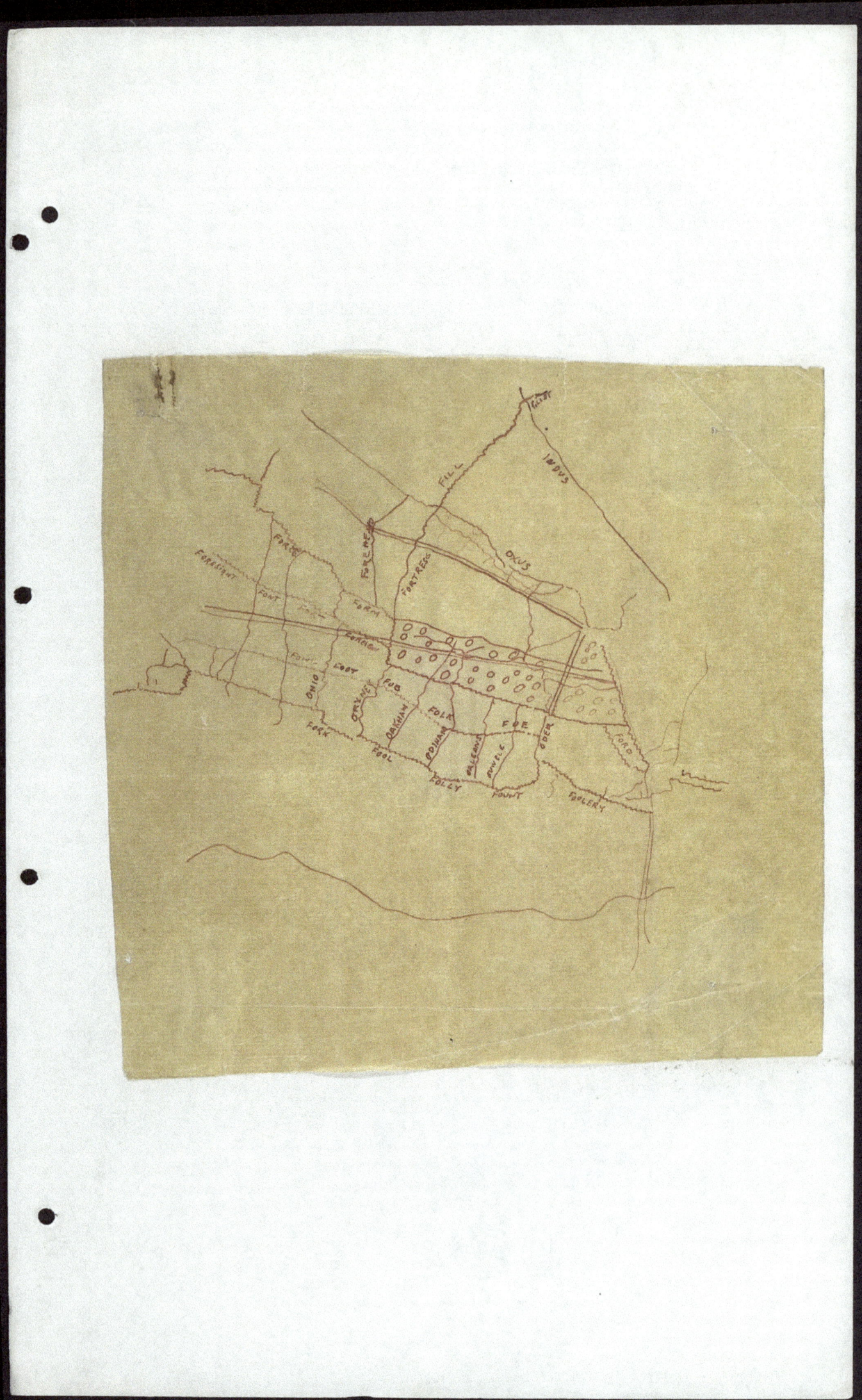

COPY.

SECRET.   Copy No. 42.

137th INFANTRY BRIGADE INSTRUCTIONS.

24. 6. 16.

Reference Map of GOMMECOURT 1/5,000 Edition 2. and sketches A & B attached.

1. (a) The 56th and 46th Divisions will attack the enemy's positions about GOMMECOURT with a view to cutting off the enemy's salient about GOMMECOURT village.

   (b) The right of the 46th Division will be on the FONQUEVILLERS-GOMMECOURT Road.

   (c) The left of the 56th Division will be directed on the junction of FILLET and INDUS trenches at K.5.a.73.82.

2. OBJECTIVE OF DIVISION

   ### First Objective

   The first objective of the 46th Division will be a defensive flank from our original front line at E.28.c.2.7. along the road to E.28.d.4.2., thence along OXUS trench to its junction with FORTRESS trench, thence along FORTRESS and the Northern edge of GOMMECOURT WOOD to E.29.a.0.2. The line will thence run along the enemy's new third line to its Junction with OUSE trench at E.29.a.6.6., thence along OUSE trench to the enemy's second line, along this line to E.29.a.5.9., and back through the little 'Z' to our original front line.

   ### Second Objective

   A junction with the 56th Division will be made by clearing FILL trench. This operation is timed to commence half an hour after the assault is launched, the 56th Division at the same time clearing FILLET trench.

   ### Third Objective.

   When the above position has been consolidated, and a junction made with the 56th Division, the clearing of GOMMECOURT village by 46th Division from North and 56th Division from South will commence. This is timed to begin 3 hours after the assault, and at that time, the Heavy Artillery will lift off GOMMECOURT village, keeping on, however, on the PARK. The 137th Infantry Brigade will push grenade parties into the village with this object, three hours after the assault commences..

3. ALLOTMENT OF TROOPS.

   The attack will be carried out by the 137th and 139th Brigades, each on a two battalion front.

   137th Infantry Brigade with 1/5th Leicester Regt and 1/2nd Field Coy R.E., attached on the Right, on a front of 700 yards.

   139th Infantry Brigade with 2/1st Field Coy R.E. attached, on the Left, on a front of 520 yards.

   138th Infantry Brigade (less 1 Battalion) and 1/1st Field

2.

Co. R.E. in Divisional Reserve West of FONQUEVILLERS.

1st Monmouth Regt will be constructing Russian saps forward from British front line to enemy's front line, Sap No. 1 to E.28.d.02.85, and Sap No. 2 to E.28.b.25.27.

2 other Saps are being constructed on front of 139th Brigade.

The 2 Cos working Nos 1 and 2 Saps will receive orders when to open the saps from Headquarters, 137th Infantry Brigade.

Dividing line between Brigades - STAFFORD AVENUE inclusive to both Brigades as a "down" communication trench, to the point where it reaches the CALVAIRE ROAD. Thence the dividing line runs through road junction in E.21.d.22. to Western Edge of FONQUEVILLERS, keeping North of, and parallel to, LINCOLN LANE.

4. DISTRIBUTION OF TROOPS FOR ATTACK.

Previous to the advance, 137th Infantry Brigade and attached troops will be distributed as indicated in Sketch B.

(a) Personnel of special Coy R.E. with 4" Stokes Mortars will be with their guns in emplacements dug off the retrenchment.

(b) 4 Officers and 140 O.R. of 138th Infantry Brigade will be employed in smoke duties in the new front line trench, and will be subsequently formed into carrying parties. (see para 17).

(c) The Sector of the 46th Division front to the South of the 137th Infantry Brigade will be held by troops detailed by G.O.C., 138th Brigade, and will be under his direct command.

(d) Artillery -46th Divisional Artillery with the assistance of the VIIth Corps Heavy Artillery will support the attack.

The Artillery under the C.R.A. 46th Division is grouped as follows :-

RIGHT GROUP.

Lt-Col. J.TONGE,C.M.G. 230th & 233rd - 137th Inf. Bde.
Bdes R.F.A.

LEFT GROUP.

Lt-Col. Sir HILL CHILDE, 231st & 232nd - 139th Inf.Bde.
Bart,M.V.C.,D.S.O.   Bdes R.F.A.

(e) Trench Mortars.

One Battery of Heavy and three Batteries of Medium Trench Mortars will support the attack, for position, vide Sketch A.

5. PRELIMINARY BOMBARDMENT.

The preliminary bombardment will extend over five days, to be known as U.V.W.X.Y. days. The date of U day will be notified later.

6. ATTACK OF 139th INFANTRY BRIGADE.

Objective The enemy's new trench from the N.W.corner of GOMMECOURT WOOD to its junction with CUSE Communication trench at E.29.a.6.6, thence along this communication trench to the enemy's second line, and through the little 'Z' to our original front line.
The clearing of the trench along the N edge of GOMMECOURT WOOD to the N.E. corner of the Wood, and the blocking of FORM and FOREHEAD trenches is allotted to this Brigade.
Strong Points should be consolidated at - E.29 a.5.5 E.29.a.6.6., and the little 'Z', special attention being paid to covering the front of FILL and FILLET trenches by machine guns fire.
The enemy's new trench between GOMMECOURT and PIGEON Woods, lies over a ridge. It is therefore possible that uncut wire will be found in front of this trench. It has therefore been arranged to keep up the bombardment against this line for 20 minutes after the hour of assault. The first advance of the 139th Inf. Bde. will, therefore, not go beyond the enemy's second line, but bombing parties up the communication trenches and patrols should go on as far as our artillery will allow. The assault of this line will take place 20 minutes after the first assault. If possible, this will be above ground, covered by machine gun fire from the N.Edge of GOMMECOURT WOOD. If, on the other hand, this is found to be impossible, the trench should be taken by bombing attacks up the communication trenches from the enemy's second line, and northwards from GOMMECOURT WOOD, great care being paid to assisting these bombing attacks with Lewis guns.

(b) OBJECTIVE of 137th INFANTRY BRIGADE.

The objective of the 137th Infantry Brigade will be from Cross roads at E.28.d.40.40.15. to junction of OXUS and FILL trenches at E.29.2.5.5. A right defensive flank will be formed from our front line at E.28.c.2.7. along the road to E.28.d.40.15.

6th South -GOMMECOURT ROAD inclusive to point E.28.d.
           40.15 to E.29.c.0.35 inclusive.

6th North - E.29.c.0.35.exclusive to trench junction
            E.29.c.5.5 inclusive, and the clearing of

FILL trench up to its junction with INDUS trench, and blocking the latter to the East.

Dividing line with 139th Brigade - From a point in British front line at E.28.a.9.9. to E.28.b.60.45 - E.28.b.90.15 to E.29.a.1.0, thence along FORTRESS trench (inclusive to 137th Brigade) to E.29.c.5.5.

7. PLAN OF ATTACK.

137th Brigade - The 137th Brigade will attack simultaneously with the 139th Brigade.

The attack will be covered by smoke. The smoke will be turned on 5 minutes before the assault, and will continue for one hour, but with the density decreased 10 minutes after the assault. (vide Appendix N.)

The 137th Brigade will attack from the following front :-

RIGHT - (6th South) on the GOMMECOURT ROAD inclusive, where it cuts our front line at 28.c.2.7.

LEFT - (6th North) at point 28.a.9.9. S of STAFFORD AVENUE.

The dividing line between battalions will be LEICESTER STREET in its entirety inclusive to the 6th North.

The dividing line forwards between Battalion will be from a point in the British front line at E.28.a.5.3., through E.28.d.05.98, E.28.d.42.75, E.28.d.65.60., E.29.c.00.35.

The Infantry attack will be carried out in successive waves.

If our new front line is wired, it will be removed on Y/Z night. Gaps in the wire between the old front line and the new front line will be cut, and as many communication trenches as possible made before Y/Z night.

Each wave will deploy in the new front line before advancing from it to the assault. At "zero" hour, the first wave will advance from the new front line.

All echelons in rear will commence to move forward simultaneously at zero - 4 minutes, in accordance with instructions contained in Appendix B.

As soon as OXUS Trench is reached, the C.O. 6th North will launch a bombing attack along FILL trench southwards from E.29.c.5.5. The 56th Division will be bombing up FILLET trench from K.5.a.6.2.

The 6th North will not proceed further south than the

junction of FILL and INDUS at K.5.a.72.80.

The 6th South and 6th North must be prepared to attack up communication trenches leading up to GOMMECOURT WOOD by bombing attacks, in case the attack is held up by uncut wire in front of the Wood. These attacks must, in this case, be assisted by bombers from either flank as soon as the third line is reached.

The right defensive flank will be consolidated under command of Lieut-Colonel R.R.RAYMER D.S.O., 1/5th South Staffs Regt, and strong points will be established as detailed in Appendix F.

A C.T. will be dug by 2 platoons, 1/5th Leicester Regt from E.28.c.30.75 to enemy's line to the 2nd C in FOOLERY. This trench will be organised as a defensive flank - vide 9th wave, Appendix B.

The 6th South will hold OXUS trench from E.28.d.40.15 to E.29.c.00.35 inclusive.

6th North will hold OXUS trench from E.29.c.00.35 exclusive to junction of OXUS and FILL trenches at E.29.c.5.5. inclusive.

The 6th North will be responsible for the consolidation of FILL trench, including the junction of OXUS and FILL.

The 5th North will be responsible for the consolidation of FORTRESS trench from the junction of OSUX and FILL exclusive, to the North west corner of GOMMECOURT WOOD.

Bombing Parties (of 5th North advancing with 3rd wave) will clear FILL trench to its junction with INDUS inclusive.

Strong Points will be established as follows :-

No.	Position	To be constructed by
1	E.28.d.45.15.	5th South
2	E.28.d.45.40.	6th South
3	E.28.d.55.55	6th South
4	E.28.d.75.75	5th North
5	E.28.b.95.10	5th North
6	E.29.a.05.05	5th North
7	E.29.c.42.76	5th North
8	E.29.c.5.5	6th North
9	E.29.c.60.18	6th North
10	K.5.a.70.82	6th North

Those in GOMMECOURT WOOD will be connected as soon as

possible by a continuous fire trench.

The strong point at E.28.d.45.40 will be sited so as to bring effective flanking machine gun fire to bear along the edges of the Wood to N.E. and S.E.

In the first place, Lewis guns, and later, Machine guns and Stokes Mortars, will be utilised to assist in the defence of these posts.

8. FURTHER OBJECTIVES

The clearing of FILL trench will commence 30 minutes after the first assault. A junction with the 56th Division will be ensured at the junction of INDUS and FILL trenches.

The clearing of GOMMECOURT villages will be undertaken by the 5th South 3 hours after the assualt is launched. This will be done by sending parties southwards into the village.

The 56th Division will, at the same time, bomb up into the village from the South. During this time, the Heavy Artillery will keep up fire on GOMMECOURT PARK.

9. BOMBING, BLOCKING AND CLEARING Composition of, and roles alloted to Bombing, Blocking and Clearing Parties are detailed in Appendix A.

10. 137th MACHINE GUN COY

For plan of action of 137th Machine Gun Coy, vide Appendix D.

11. 137th T.M. BATTERY

For plan of action of 137th T.M. Battery vide Appendix E.

12. SNIPERS

The 4 best snipers per battalion, with telescopic sights, will accompany Battalion Headquarters in the advance. They will be detailed to assist in covering the consolidation of the most important strong points.
All other telescopic sights will be sent to the Transport Lines on "Y" day.

13. TRENCH MORTAR PERSONNEL

The trained personnel serving with Battalions will be attached to the O.C., 137th T.M.Battery from 2 p.m. on W. day. to act as Carriers. They will be made up to five from each battalion, with untrained men if short of that number. Only 20% of the T.M.Battery personnel, including attached man, will carry rifles. All will carry 2 Mills grenades.

14. WATCHES

Watches will be synchronised daily at midnight, 8.a.m. and 4.p.m.

15. EQUIPMENT

Infantry will be equipped as follows:-

No packs or greatcoats.
Waterproof sheet
200 rounds S.A.A. per man.
4 sandbags per man.
2 Mills grenades per man.
Reserve Rations.
2 Gas helmets per man.
Waterbottle filled.
Havresack ration.

150 wire breakers and 150 wire cutters will be carried per battalion. The majority will be issued to the first and second waves, but a small proportion will be issued to subsequent waves. Wire breakers and wire cutters will be fixed on the rifles.

If the sun is shining, vigilant periscopes will be fixed on bayonets of six men per platoon to assist the Contest Patrol Aeroplane in following and progress.

16. S.A.A.

Each N.C.O. and man who normally carries 120 rds (leather) or 150 rds (web equipment), will be made up to 200 rounds on the evening before the attack.

Bombers as detailed in Appendix "A".

Others will carry 50 rounds more that the normal allowance.

Battalion Reserves (320 boxes)

320 boxes in 8 S.A.A. Stores at intervals in the Retrenchment.

Brigade Reserves (376 boxes)

(a) 50 boxes at dugout off NOTTINGHAM ST at E.27.b.95.08.
    50   "   "   "   "   BURTON ST at E.28.a.4.5

(b) 140 boxes at E.27.b.8.6 in dugouts off DERBY DYKE.

(c) 136 boxes in CRYPT off DERBY DYKE and NOTTINGHAM ST –
                Entrances at E.27.b.40.55.

17. VERY LIGHTS

At Battn Headquarters 6th South and 6th North:-

500 – 1"
250 – 1½"

All Very Pistols will be stored at their original Battn Headquarters, and will not be taken forward to the assualt.

18. COMMUNICATIONS

For instructions re Signals vide Appendix H.

19½. DEPOTS OF STORES

For position of stores vide Sketch A.

The following storekeepers will be provided:-

A T

Bde Reserve. S.A.A. – off DERBY DYKE   1 N.C.O. & 1 man
            About E.27.b.95.08   5th North.

Bde Bomb Reserve S.A.A.	– off DERBY DYKE About E.27.b.95.08	1 N.C.O. & 1 man Bde Bomb Officer to detail
" Reserve. Rations	E.27.a.05 and the SHRINE (E.27.a.8.8)	1 N.C.O. & 1 man 5th North.
" " Water) Bombs)	E.27.b.95.08.	1 N.C.O. & 1 man 5th South.
" " Water	Left E.28.a.25.60 in Support Line.	1 man 5th North.
Stokes Ammunition	E.27.b.95.10) E.28.a.4.5)	137th Trench Mortar Battery.

Brigade Reserve R.E. Dump is at Billet 93 (E.27.a.25.20)

20. COMMUNICATION TRENCHES AND CONTROL

　1. NOTTINGHAM ST & LEICESTER ST will be "up" trenches and DERBY DYKE & LINCOLN LANE "down" trenches (vide sketch). STAFFORD AVENUE (for evacuation only)

　2. Traffic control posts will be established on U day at the following points. 1 N.C.O. and 2 men will be posted at each:-

　　NOTTINGHAM ST – 5th South – E.28.c.2.9., E.27.b.4.6.

　　DERBY DYKE   – 5th   "   – E.28.a.2.1., E.27.b.20.85.

　　LEICESTER ST – 5th North – E.28.a.4.2., E.28.a.15.45.

　　X LINCOLN LANE –5th   "   – E.28.a.55.55., E.27.b.65.90.

　　X 1 N.C.O. and 3 men to supervise both LINCOLN LANE and LEICESTER STREET.

　3. They will regulate traffic, and ensure no "up" traffic goes up a "down" trench and vice versa
Each N.C.O. or man of a Control Post will wear a red band on the left upper arm.

21. SUPPLIES

　Rations.

　　(1) Each soldier will carry (a) Iron Ration

　　　　　　　　　　　　　　　(b) Unexpended portion of day's rations.

　　　　　　　　　　　　　　　(c) Bread and bacon ration in havresack.

　In addition:-

　　(2) 2 days Brigade Reserve will be stored under Brigade arrangements, In the event of Battns not being able to draw rations according to normal routine, these will be issued under Brigade arrangements.

　　(3) Arrangements will be made by units to issue hot pea soup or coffee to all ranks two hours before "Zero". A special ration will be issued of soup or coffee.

　　(4) Bread and bacon will be demanded by units in

sufficient time to allow of the bacon being
boiled, when cold sandwiches will be made up
into parcels, and issued to the men the night before
the action.

22. WATER All water bottles filled. This is a reserve supply,
and should not be used until absolutely necessary.

23. CARRYING PARTIES

The O.C. 5th Leicester Regt will detail the following
carrying parties:-

A. 1 platoon - to carry bombs from Bde Reserve at E.27.b.
8.6. to the British front line at the top of LINCOLN
Lane and LEICESTER STREET.

B. 1 platoon - to carry bombs from the top of LINCOLN
LANE and LEICESTER STREET to form Bomb Stores at
E.28.d.30.95 and E.28.d.25.60.
On the 2nd journey to carry S.A.A. to same dumps
from BURTON STREET E.28.a.5.6.

C. 2 platoons - to carry R.E. material from the Front
Trench Stores to the R.E. Stores., which they will
form at E.28.d.45.80. and E.28.b.75.05.
Having emptied forward stores, they will carry from
Bde Reserve Store at E.27.a.30.15.

D. 1 platoon - to carry 3" Stokes Mortar ammunition from
BURTON STREET (E.28.a.4.5 and from E.27.b.95.15) to
F in FOUNT. Battery carriers will carry on from
this point.

E. 1 platoon - to carry water from Bde Reserve at E.27.b.
8.6. to F of FOLLY E.28.d.3.3.

Two of the personnel of the 137th T.M. Battery will be
attached to this party as liaison orderlies with the
Battery. They will also carry.

These parties will all draw stores for the first journey
before taking up their position of assembly.

24. MEDICAL

Medical Aid Posts will be established as follows:-

DERBY DYKE   5th South.
LINCOLN LANE 5th North.

All Medical Officers and Stretcher Bearers with shut
stretchers, will advance when Battalion Headquarters
goes forward, and will establish Aid Posts in the
enemy trenches at the most convenient points. They
will evacuate stretcher cases down DERBY DYKE and
Stafford AVENUE. LINCOLN LANE being reserved for
walking cases.

During the bombardment, U to Y days, the 5th South and
5th North Aid Posts will be in FONQUEVILLERS.

FONQUEVILLERS   Advanced Dressing Station.
E.27.a.0.5.
E.21.a.9.0

GAUDIEMPRE   Main Dressing Station

The following trenches are "down" trenches, and will be
used for evacuation.

DERBY DYKE Down.
LINCOLN LANE. Evacuation of walking cases.
STAFFORD AVENUE. Evacuation only
PILL TRENCH running W.N.W. through E.20.c., E.19.d and b., will be used for evacuation only.

25. PRISONERS

Prisoners will be sent back under escort of slightly wounded men if possible, down DERBY DYKE.

LINCOLN LANE may be used as far as E.27.b.65.90., thence to DERBY DYKE at E.27.b.5.8., to E.27.a.50.95., where prisoners will be handed over to a detachment of the North Irish Horse. Infantry escorts will not proceed Westward beyond this point.

For instructions re prisoners vide Appendix I.

26. DOCUMENTS

Regimental officers will not carry on their person any documents, copies of orders or plans, which might be of use to the enemy in the event of their falling into his hands.

27. VETERINARY

An Advanced Veterinary Collecting Station will be at D.8.b. Central (Map 57D 1/40,000) on ST AMAND-GAUDIEMERE Road.

All seriously wounded and other animals belonging to units in front of Advanced Collecting Station will be sent by the Units to that collecting Station. All cases from units in rear of the above mentioned station will be sent to the Headquarters of the Mobile Veterinary Section at GRINCOURT.

N.C.O's and men on arrival with wounded and other sick horses and mules at the Advanced Collecting Station, or Headquarters of M.V.S., will hand the animals over to the Veterinary personnel, and return forthwith to their units.

28. OFFICERS

Not more than 20 Company officers per Battalion will be in the attack. Of the remainder, those who are not specially employed under Brigade arrangements will remain at the Transport Lines.

The 2nd in command of each battalion will remain at the original Battalion Headquarters and await orders from Brigade Headquarters.

29. SALVAGE The 137th Inf. Bde Salvage section under the general direction of the O.C. 46th Divl Salvage Section, will be responsible for clearing the battlefield in the Brigade Sector as far back as the western edge of FONQUEVILLERS. The position of dumps will be notified later.

Disposal of Greatcoats - Greatcoats will be stored in the trenches under Company arrangements on night of Y/Z.

Disposal of Packs. - By X/Y night, packs will have been worked back to the transport lines at LA BAZEQUE FARM in the empty transport returning from FONQUEVILLERS.

30. WOUNDED - Unwounded fighting men will not assist wounded men to the rear.

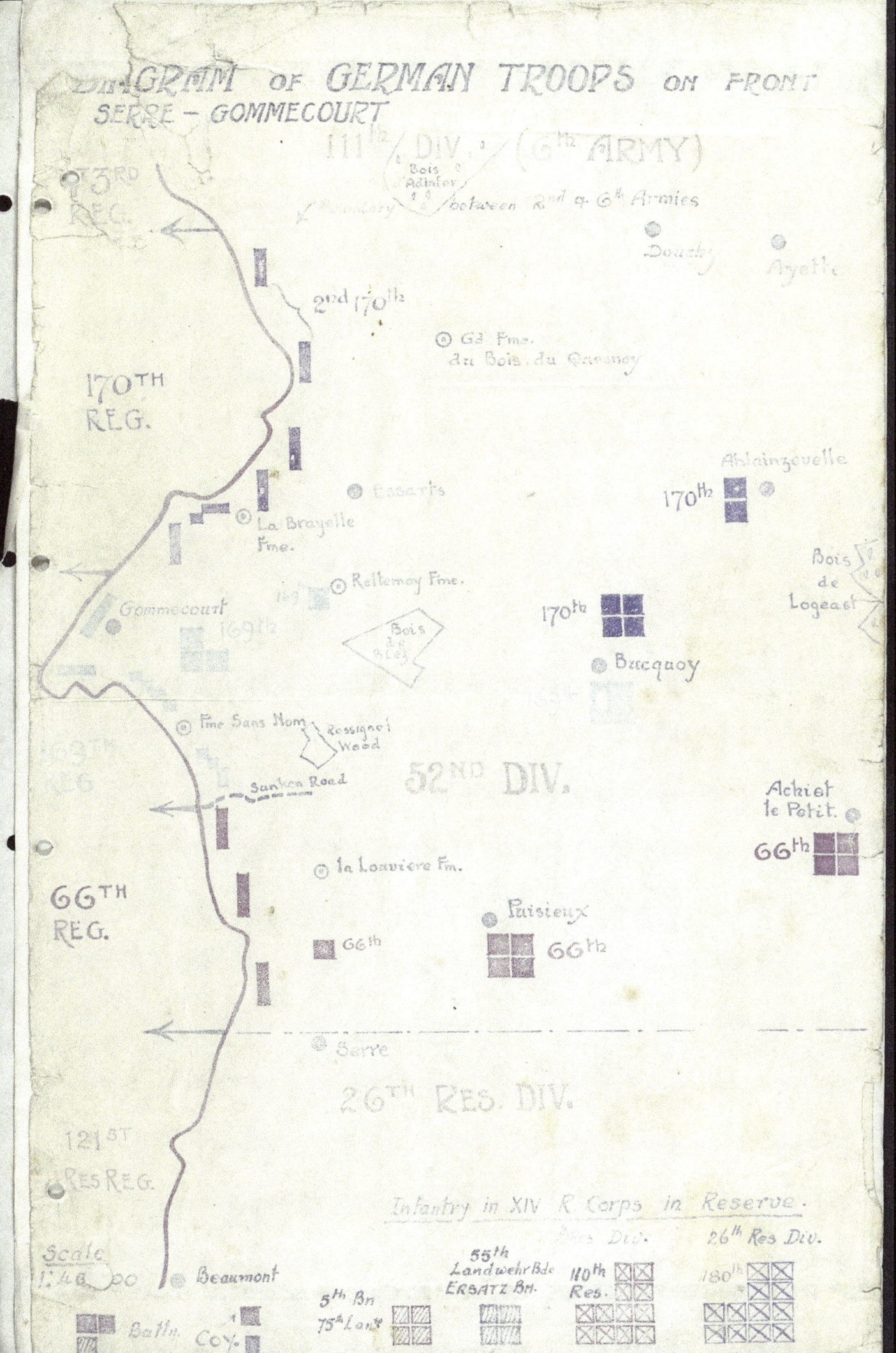

COPY.

No. of Message ... 5 ....

Service Instructions.

   PRIORITY   N U B

To 137 Brigade.

Situation normal aaa Wind still aaa Our Patrols met no hostile patrols aaa Inspecting our wire between about 49 Y and 50 Y three rifles and three helmets all British were found aaa No identification mark on them aaa addr 56 Divn reptd 143 and 137 Bdes

From   N U B

To   RN

REPORT ON WIRE aaa Right Company 39-40 Can find no gaps on his front aaa Left Company 41-42 practically no wire left around K 4a 20.64 but it is impossible to see if there is any close to edge of Park aaa At K 4a 10.43 there appears to be a path intentionally left through wire nearest to our trenches No wire against edge of Park can be seen aaa Wire looks very thin around K 4a 20.74 and K 4a 15.59 aaa It is impossible to say that there is no very low trip wire even at K 4a 10.43 aaa Telescopes and binoculars were used by both Companies.

From 5th South Staffs.   7.45 p.m.

                       J.LAMOND, Capt aaa

1.

COPY.
2.

Service Instructions

Priority of 3 addresses Q.J.
    137 Bde.

To :- 137 Bde.

Situation Germans very quiet Wind nil aaa Patrol 10 strong left our left Coy at 11 p.m. to search the German wire between F IR and F I T aaa The Germans wire remains uncut and has an average depth of 40 yards consisting of chevaux or frise and it is in good order aaa The sapheads in FIT were manned aaa A Patrol of 1 Officer 2 N.C.Os and 20 men left our left centre Coy at 11 p.m. but failed to reach German wire owing to the Artillery not lifting till 11.10 p.m. and also owing to the light caused by the constant firing of the guns aaa No hostile patrols were met aaa Patrol from our right centre Coy went out at 11 p.m. but was interfered with by M.G. fire and burst of enemy shelling aaa Opposite W 47 and 48 the wire for 50 yards N of 16 poplars is blown to bits aaa Opposite W 49 and 50 about 200 yards of wire was examined and is fairly well cut but requires more clearing in places aaa No repairing was being done aaa Addrd 56 Divn and reptd 137 and 143 Bdes.

From   N U B

COPY.
Service Instructions :- 5 South.
Handed in at   R N A
TO   D Z A

Enemy has shown very little activity all night aaa Some

Some trench mortar and machine gun fire and a few salvoes shrapnel aaa Patrols out as directed and strong posts aaa Two D Z A 1 and two D Z A 2 found dead aaa Several rifles brought in also equipment and helmets aaa Two casualties among D Z A 3 salvage party aaa Handed over to Major Whiston at 1.20 a.m. aaa Wire patrols at 2.0 a.m.

From :- Lt Col Raymer
        3.15 a.m.

COPY.

NOTES ON THE GROUND IN THE NEIGHBOURHOOD OF GOMMECOURT.

In general, the ground is undulating, and well wooded, in patches. Otherwise it is open.

It rises, gradually, from Fonquevilliers to our front line. It then dips down, into no-man's land, rises slightly to the enemy front line, and then, in a gentle sweep to the neighbourhood of Buquoy.

On the left of the sunken road, there is an old sugar factory. It is in the form of a roughly rectangular trench, about 50 yards square, and was overgrown with nettles. Old boilers &c were scattered about the ground. The enemy trenches, in front of the village, were about 200 yards distant here, but the distance increased to 400 or 500 yards further to our left. In front of the sugar factory, the ground fell away sharply.

This depression extended to the left for about 100 yards, making dead ground, in which there were thick bands of wire. The wire, in places, was 40 or 50 yards thick.

On the left of the Staffordshire front of attack, the ground was comparatively level, sloping gently towards the enemy lines, with no dead ground. The wire here, was utterly destroyed. The enemy front line, for the most part, followed a scrubby hedge, and was elevated on a bank, about 5 feet high.

There was dead ground behind Gommecourt Wood, otherwise

observation was good, right up to Buquoy.

Most of the ground behind our lines, was under observation from the enemy, except that portion which lay immediately behind Fonquevilliers. Our view was obstructed by the Wood and Park, so that only the houses on the extreme edge of the village were visible, and the ground immediately behind these was hidden from us. The first objectives were visible, but the final line which we were to hold was not. We had a good idea of the position and strength of the enemy defences, but anticipated trouble in the wood and village. Except for these, there was nothing in the way of a natural obstacle which was likely to cause us trouble, and, had the wire been cut, we would probably have succeeded, though our losses must have been heavy.

NOTE.

Prior to the attack, the enemy was very quiet, and appeared to do little registration. Most of his shooting was confined to counter-battery work. During the attack, most of the artillery fire came from our left front.....probably, from Adinfer Wood. Machine gun fire came from the edge of the village and from points immediately behind his front line. There was little, or no rifle fire.

Just before zero hour, our barrage was exceptionally intense, and, had the infantry followed it up, immediately, they would probably have met with no opposition.

During the actual attack, there was little or nothing to be seen. Men vanished into the smoke cloud, and, as that cleared, everything was obscured by the smoke of the bursting shells. On our left, the Sherwoods had penetrated into the ~~egd e~ t~~ edge of the wood, and we heard them bombing for a considerable time, before they were finally overcome, It was impossible to reach them. At two p.m. a further attack was ordered, but, owing to the impossibility of reorganizing after wuch heavy losses, the idea was abandoned. It is very doubtful if it could have met with any success.

In the afternoon, a report came, I think from the 56th Div. that the enemy was massing behind Gommecourt Park. I was sent by the Brigadier, to climb a tall tree, from which a good view could be obtained. There was not a man in sight, except our own dead. It was a wonderful sight. The whole of the battlefield was spread out before me. The bombardment had mown down the trees in Park and Wood and the whole country was visible for miles. It seemed strange to think that that desert was teeming with men who had barred our way. The bombardment of Gommecourt Park had been particularly effective and the enemy, finding it untenable, came across and surrendered to the 56th Division. The village, also, was very well pounded by our heavies.

The condition of our trenches added tremendously to the

horrors.   Wounded and dead sank beneath the mud, and one stumbled against them in walking.

The same night we were relieved, and the men slept in a switch line in front of Souastre. After that, we took over a quiet piece of line between Monchy au Bois and Ransart

COPY.

POINTS WHICH INFLUENCED THE ATTACK ON GOMMECOURT.

(1). There was no secrecy about the preparations. The enemy must have known our intentions a long while before the attack took place. This was probably intentional.

(2). Too much reliance was placed on the preliminary bombardment. This was less effective than was expected.

(3). The trenches were rendered nearly impassable by a heavy storm two days before the action. In addition to the difficulties this caused, it necessitated ceaseless work for the men who were already dropping with fatigue, and who ought to have been resting.

(4). The wire was tremendously thick, and owing to the formation of the ground, could not be cut by field gun fire. This applies, particularly, to the wire on the 6th Battn. S.S.& front.

See patrol reports.

There was an interval between the lifting of the barrage and the assault, which gave the enemy time to get his machine guns into action.

(6). The smoke screen, in my opinion, was a handicap. The wire was only cut, at intervals, and in narrow gaps, and, owing to the smoke, the men could not find them, except in small parties who entered the enemy front line and were cut up.

1.

(7). The men had too much weight to carry, and were impeded by material.

(8). The consolidating parties were too far forward. They blocked the trenches which were already difficult to pass along, and prevented the succeeding waves advancing. The trenches were, everywhere, at least, knee deep in mud and were badly knocked about by the enemy barrage.

(9). The enemy artillery was much stronger than was expected and was very accurate. This caused a certain amount of disorganization in our trenches.

(10). The fact that the attack was postponed for two days was a great additional strain on the nerves of the men.

(11). I say, emphatically, as I said at the enquiry, that the failure of the attack was, in no way, the fault of the men, who did everything possible under the circumstances.

(Signed) C. ASHFORD.

I have seen it suggested,* that the attacking troops ought to have advanced in the open instead of by means of communication trenches. In my opinion this would have made no difference on the 5．S.Staffs front. Owing to the intensity of the enemy barrage (artillery & machine gun) it is doubtful if sufficient men would have survived to be effective. The ground also was very badly cut up. C.A.

* ("Sir Douglas Haig's Command")

COPY.

June 26/16.

WIRE REPORT PATROL.

I went out from the head of No. 1 Sap with one man at 2.15 a.m.. I proceeded to point E.28.d.0.8 on the enemy wire. There is a lane 30 yards wide, and the wire is clear up to the few last feet, which is a low tangle. This still requires shelling by the artillery. This was observed from a point slightly to the right of the gap by the light of an ~~evening~~ enemy Very light. I then moved along wire to left intending to visit wire at point E.28.b.1.1 but owing to dawn I had to return before reacing my object. As I went to the left I noticed a great deal of damage had been done to the first line of wire. I returned at 3.20 a.m. to head of No. 1 Sap.

D.G.JARVIS-JONES,
2/Lieut.

SECRET.

Herewith Wire Reports.
From 5 North,

G.A.WILSON,
Capt & Adjt

REPORT ON ENEMY WIRE CUT.

I went out at 12.45 p.m. from No. 1 Sap along the advanced trench to examine the enemy wire between the 're-entrant' and the F in FOLLY and I report as follows :-

1. There is a gap of 45 yds in the enemy wire in front of the re-entrant. Working from right to left I saw that on the

extreme right of the re-entrant was very thick uncut wire - then a clear gap of 30 yds but for two big bunches of tangle at places shown on sketch map. There was a little loose tangle (quite low) at the nearer edge of the enemy parapet. then came a row of iron stakes running at right angles to the British trench and there were trails of wire from these stakes. Then came a clear gap of 15 yards before getting to the thick wire again.

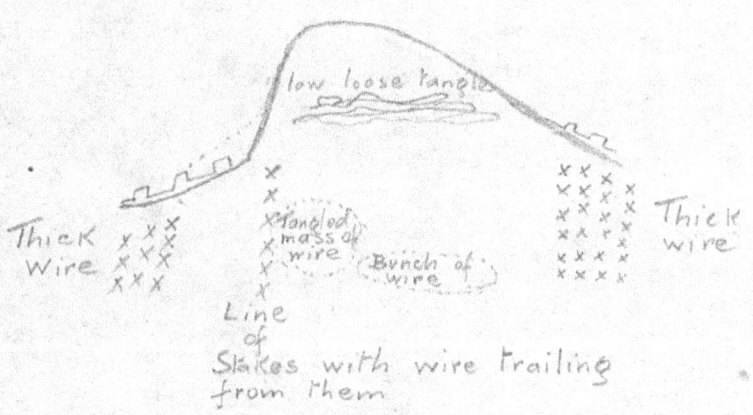

The parapet at the re-entrant is very badly damaged. I beg to suggest that infantry could enter at this gap if provided with mats to put over low wire.

No. 2. There is a gap in the enemy wire in front of the place where the new German communication trench meets T in FOUNT. There is a gap here of 30 yards in length and through to the parapet Except for six feet of sound wire. In this gap the stakes in front have all been rooted out and very little low trails of wire remain. If the remaining six feet of wire were cut it would make a very good clear gap.

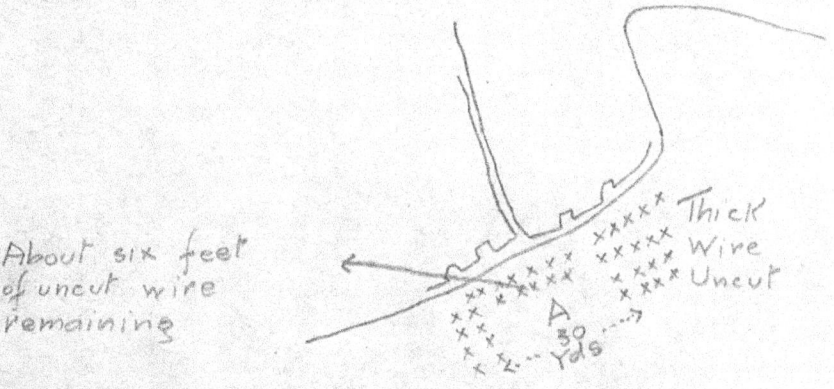

About six feet of uncut wire remaining

The Artillery have cleared the space marked A and have knocked the German parapet in a great deal, but have missed the six feet of wire nearest the parapet.
No. 3.   There is a gap in the enemy wire at about the F in Folly.   This gap is difficult to view as it lies in a dip.   The gap is about 30 yards in length.

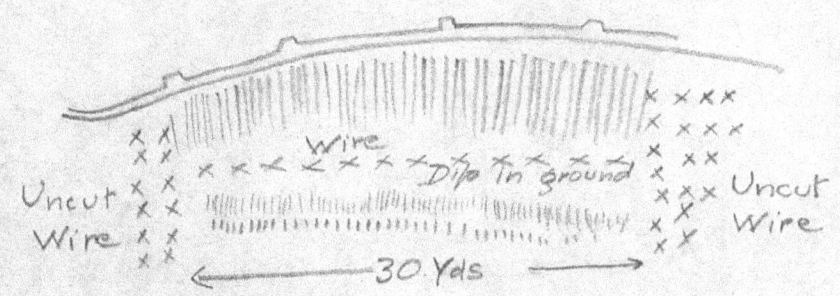

At this gap the Artillery has smashed the enemy's parapet and it has covered most of the wire near the parapet with earth.   Then comes about 8 feet of wire (in a slight dip) which is still in good condition and requires shelling.   Then nearer the British line is a little loose trailing wire which has been left after the shelling. If the wire in the dip were cut the gap would be easily passable for infantry.

I returned by Gap˟ at 2.15 p.m.

                (Signed) D.G.JARVIS-JONES,
                                2/Lt.
˟ Through our wire   5th N.Staffs Regt.

COPY.

WIRE REPORT.

Enemy wire from E.28 C 55.45 to E.28 C 95.70 same as stated in 4 a.m. report.

Wire on this frontage requires further cutting <u>especially</u> from E.28 C 55.45 to E.28 C 80.60 i.e. from Gommecourt Road for about 115 yds left (N.E.) of it.

Remainder of wire is cut down but lies on ground with no lanes through it.

                R.B.MELLARD,
                      2/Lt.

2 p.m. 26/6/16.

COPY.   REPORT ON ENEMY'S WIRE.

From the F in FOLLY of our Brigade left.

This afternoon I have made careful observation from our advance trench from No. 2 Sap working left also from the O.P. in LINCOLN LANE. From the latter it is quite impossible to observe the advance wire which is in dead ground, also the wire which is close to the enemy's parapet as there is some 10 ft. in depth concealed almost all the way along this Sector which is not smashed; also very little damage is done to the first line of wire which is also in dead ground.

A gap is being cut at E 28 B 5.5 4.5
"   "   "   "   E 28 B 4. 4

these are by no means finished - refer above remarks.

                2/Lt L.HOLMAN,
                    5 N.S.R.

COPY.

Left half of sector E 28 B 5.5 to E 28 B o 1.

The double line of wire which can be seen well to our left also runs at the foot of a slope which faces the enemy. This wire cannot be observed from our front line and consequently has not been fired on by our artillery. As stated in my former report trench mortars are essential and tomorrow I shall endeavour to direct X Battery's fire on this wire. Veri lights are fired on this piece of dead ground from the front and flanks, the enemy apparently wanting to keep us away from it.

At intervals on my right I heard a slight rattling of wire. This I put down to the patrol on my right. The Officer in charge tells me this was not so - therefore the enemy must have been at work. Lights were going up constantly and so they were probably throwing out wire balls. I mentioned a big gap in the evening report and should think they were trying to fill this. I shall make a close telescopic examination of this gap. 2/Lt Holman also reported this and on coming in pointed out the direction to machine gun.

Red flares were sent up but no artillery action followed.

R.B.MELLARD, 2/Lt.

COPY.

28. 6. 16.

Except for one line the enemy wire is still uncut for about 200 X No. of GOMMECOURT RD, it is considerably weaker, but there is still some to cut before the 3 lanes previously reported are through. The entrant lane is now about 20 X wide.

Recnce parties are going out to investigate closer.

H.B.SALTER, 2 Lt.

COPY.

SITUATION REPORT.

27. 6. 16,

At intervals during the day and night we fired on German 2nd & 3rd line wire GOMMECOURT, GOMMECOURT WOOD and communication trenches and tracks leading to it.

<u>Work Done</u>. Assembly trenches etc.

G.W.A.WADE, Lieut.

137th Inf. Bde,
27.6.16.
Machine Gun Co.

COPY.

June 27. 1916.

Patrol.

Patrol consisting of 2 Officers & 2 other Ranks visited gaps in enemy's wire at K.4.a O.S. & K.4.a. $\frac{1}{2}.4\frac{1}{2}$ Patrol started at 12.30 mn. 26th and returned 1.20 a.m. 27th inst. Gaps were found to be in same condition as on previous night – no work had been attempted by enemy and no further cutting had been done by Artillery. Sounds of muffled talking were heard from L.P. between the gaps. Patrol was not fired on and returned safely.

       H.ALLEN, 2/Lt.
        I.O. 5th S.Staffs.
      S.SPEED, 2 Lieut. 5th S.Staffs.

WIRE PATROL.
REPORT.   27. 6. 16.
4th LEIC. REGT.

Patrol went out from No. 1 Sap to entrant about E28D08.
The wire has been cut about 10 yards wide and 15 yards deep
at this point, about another 5 yds has to be cut before lane
is complete. Trip wires still uncut.

A short lane has also been cut at E 28 C 97, another 10 yds
before lane is through.

Two more cuts at about E 28 C 86 and E 28 C 70.55 — these
have demolished the wire to a great extent but they are <u>by no
means through</u> — patrol penetrated about 10 yds in each case.

A complete lane has been cut at E 28 C 65 53 about 12 yds
wide a few trip wires still standing.

<u>The wire is still very strong just N of GOMMECOURT RD for about
150 yds</u>.

H.H.SALTER   2 Lt
4th Leic. Regt.

COPY.

WIRE PATROL REPORT.

5th N.S.Reg.   27. 6. 16.

Patrol went out from No. 2 Sap at 1 a.m. and returned at 3 a.m. and moved from E 28 B 5.5 to E 28 B o.1. At E 28 B 1.1 and E 28 B 5.5 gaps of about 20 yards and 15 yards respectively. In each case a few feet of wire want cutting near parapet before a clearance is effected. About 40 yards from parapet a trip wire was found - there was only a single strand and as we found it by accident on our return it must be fairly well cleared, there is also a partial clearance at E 28 B 2.3 of 15 yds. The enemy appear to have sentries at gaps as we heard 3 men talking at one of them. Map refs are given as accurately as possible, but it is very difficult to locate gaps by night work.

Pte Shenton 5th N.S.Reg. was found about 40 yards in front of our advance trench - we brought his body in - also 2 rifles.

2/Lte L.Holman.

R.B.Mellard, 2nd Lt.

COPY.

To.
    46th Divn., Repeat O. R. A.

Report on enemy wire   aaa   North of sap at about K 4 a.o.5 there is a gap 20 yards wide South of sap a gap 25 yards wide No other gaps in sector South of GOMMECOURT ROAD   aaa   Ar E 28 c.+ 0720 gap 45 yards wide   aaa   At E 28 B 10 gap 30 yards wide except for 6 feet of wire near parapet still standing a   At E 28 b.52 gap 30 yards wide E 28 b.55.45 partly cut   aaa   E 28 b 4.4 partly cut   aaa   From GOMMECOURT ROAD for about 120 yards Northwards wire is untouched – No other gaps reported.

      Inf
From 137/Bde

                        Cyril Ashford.

COPY.

Attached please find patrols reports on wire last night. 4 Patrols went out from trenches 40,41 and worked to the right and from 41 and 43 working to the left.

Except for the Southern party the wire was not found to be smashed though here and there it had been knocked about – still however forming an obstacle. The right patrol which examined wire from K.3.b.9.1 to K.3.d.77 found the wire badly battered and very weak. The Company Commander concerned considers this a good place for a raid.

The 2 gaps at K.4.a.o.5 and K.4.a.0.5.45 appear to be narrow and zig-zag and it appears possible that a certain amount of cutting by hand would be required to make a raid there. These gaps were not guarded.

Signed, Adjt.
4th LINCS.

Time 1.30 a.m.

2/Lieut Quantrelle and 3 men went out at 11 p.m. to inspect enemy wire. They returned at 1.15 a.m. having completed their work satisfactorily. They commenced immediately opposite the left of No. 40 trench. They had no difficulty in keeping close to enemy trench. They report wire all broken up except for loose ends, until the last 10 yards on right which is practically intact. They say that there is no obstacle to keep men from getting into German trench except this last 10 yards.   After arriving at enemy trench they crawled the whole way.   Enemy front line was occupied but probably thinly.   Sentries could be heard talking distinctly.   The trench appears to be very much battered but still a continuous trench.

There is a dyke (not an old C.T.) running from centre of our lines: patrol report this to be quite dry and giving considerable cover all the way.

There was a M.G. active opposite our extreme right not in front line but in supports on edge of trees.

Flares have been going up intermittently, some from front line, but most from supports.

Patrol under 2/Lieut Quantrelle did their work very well and did not return until their task was completed. They followed instructions to the letter.

(Signed) O.C., A.Coy.
4 Lincs.

Patrol Report – 41 trench.

According to instructions I patrolled the German front trench wire in front of 41 trench.   Strength of patrol, 1 Officer, 1 Sergeant, and 2 guides from 5th South Staffs.

Capt Scorer accompanied the party.

Patrol left 41 trench at 11 p.m.

Left Sector.- of space patrolled.   German line opposite No. 4 post 41 trench (Practically the centre of GOMMECOURT

PARK).

Right Sector - about 40 yards beyond GOMMECOURT PARK as corresponding to the right of 41 trench.

Report of German Wire. - On left Sector there is a very narrow opening, which in my opinion has been made by the Germans in order to allow his patrol to get out. This opening is of a zig-zag nature, and would be impossible to get through with a number of men quickly.

About 40 yards to the right of above there is another narrow opening, which again in my opinion has been made to allow patrols to get through. No other openings were seen. The wire being fairly good along the whole of the space patrolled and in places very strong.

The system of wiring is as follows :-

German front line
_____
Trip wire ------------------- Trip wire -------------
_____
.........barbed wire ....
_____
Trip wire ------------------- Trip wire -------------
_____
............Barbed wire ....
_____

Distances between German front line and first wire, ditto second wire, are only approximate.

General remarks - Unless this wire was cut or smashed by Artillery I do not think it would be possible to break through quickly in this sector. Worm standards in places have been bent by shells bursting near them but the wire has not been shattered.

One instance I particularly noticed where a shell had burst within a few feet of the wire making a crater of 12 feet across and about 6 feet deep but had only bent the worm standards and had left the wire intact.

Patrol arrived back in 41 trench at 12-50 a.m.

       (Signed) E. ELLIOTT,
                      Lieut,
                        4 Lincs.

Report on Patrol sent out by B Company on 28/6/16 to examine German wire.

At 11 p.m. 28/6/16 I was in charge of patrol consisting of one Officer and three men. We left our own trench by listening post in 41 trench. A guide was provided. At a distance of 200 yards from our trench the guide went with another patrol to the right, this patrol going to the left. We came to the enemy wire after another 130/160 yards making the distance of the wire from our front line 330/360 yards.

We examined the wire to a distance of 350/400 yards and did not find any gaps. In places it was thinner and had been cut about a good deal but everywhere it provided a big obstacle. The wire is about 8 yards thick where it has not been touched and is very strong.

5 German flares were sent up from the right corner of GOMMECOURT PARK from a position just behind their front

line.   Our own shells were bursting about immediately above our heads the further we got to the left. No German movement of any kind was seen.

        (Signed) G.H.Morris,
             Lieut.
         4 Lincs.

Report on enemy's wire S of FONQUEVILLERS, GOMMECOURT Road as far as E.28.c.40.10.

We went out from the centre of 43 trench at 11 p.m. on the night of 28/29 and on reaching the enemy's wire found it to be very thick and with no gaps cut in the same. The wire is about 3 feet high and mounted on wooden stakes. Depth of wire about 4 yards and very difficult to get through.   We returned at 12.20 a.m.   While on patrol our work was greatly hindered by our own shells either dropping short or coming from a Battery that had not lifted.

        (Signed) W.G.CHAMBERS,
         4 Lincs.

During the night we fired on enemy wire, trenches and communication trenches and GOMMECOURT.

From 1.30 till daylight we fired on enemy wire with 5 guns from our original front line and one gun was flanking their third line wire indirect continuously during the night.

(137 Bde, M.G.Coy).

3.

gap practically untouched.

From E. 28 C. 8.7 to E.28 C.9.7.

German wire which I judged to be near the listening sap K.4.a.0.5. and lay down and listened.

Owing to the noise of the Artillery it was difficult to detect any sound, but during the lull I heard a slight cough and muttered conversation a few yards to the left. A flare light on the left made the wire visible. Around the sap it was very thick but a complete gap of 25 to 30 yards in extent had been made immediately to the right (K.4.a.$\frac{1}{2}$.4)

The patrol then retired 20 yards and watched for a period of 15 minutes.

Only two flares were sent up directly in front and by the light of these the damage done to the wire was clearly discernible.

The destruction appeared to be completed in the gap described - to the right it was partially thinned, but at the point K.4.a.$\frac{1}{4}$.45 little damage had been done.

There was no sound to any enemy transport but ours was quite audible.

The patrol returned at 2.50 a.m.

                L.W.C.CAPSEY,

                  2/Lt.

WIRE REPORT.

I left Barricade on Gommecourt Road at 2 a.m. and proceeded to E.28 C.8.7. There is a gap in the wire about 15 yds wide. This is clear to parapet. The wire from Gommecourt Road to point E.28.C.8.7 is apart from this

To :-

    137th Infantry Bde.

    Herewith original reports on condition of enemy wire.

                       J. LAMOND, Capt & Adjt
                               for Lt/Col.
                 1/5 Bn South Staffs Regt.

To   Adjutant,

    One Sergeant and two men accompanied me on patrol this morning. We left our trenches at No. 4 Post 9 (Ref. K.3.b.23.50) at 1.50 a.m. and proceeded S.E. for about 400 yards where we got to the German wire at about K.4.a.05. The gap made by Artillery runs practically due East and West and is almost free of wire with the exception of loose wire and is roughly 20 yards wide. Ground is churned up also. The grass this side of the gap is well trodden down and has probably been used at this point as a starting point for hostile patrol. Enemy very quiet and no Transport heard.

                         (Signed) H.G.COZENS, 2/Lt.
                             26. 6. 16.

                              June 26. 16.

    The patrol which went out this morning including 1 Cpl, and 2 privates and myself proceeded from the listening sap [~~step~~] of No. 4 Post at 1.45 a.m. After crossing the sunken road the patrol made its way to a point near the

WAR DIARY or INTELLIGENCE SUMMARY

1/6th BATTALION, SOUTH STAFFORDSHIRE REGIMENT

Place	Date	Hour	Summary of Events and Information	Remarks and references to Appendices
SOUASTRE	1-7-16		OPERATION ORDERS by Lt-Col J.H. Thursfield, Comdg. 1/6th Bttn South Staffordshire Regiment, of operations on 1st July 1916. Reference – Map GOMMECOURT Edition II; Fonquevillers, 1/10,000 – Hebuterne, 1/10,000. 1. The Battalion will attack the enemy's position in front and rear of Gommecourt Wood on the 29th instant at an hour to be notified later, in accordance with 137th Infantry Brigade Operation Orders No 63, 137th Infantry Brigade Instructions and Appendices "A" to "O" copies of which have already been issued. 2. The front of the Battalion prior to the attack will be from Gommecourt Road inclusive on the right, to Leicester Street exclusive on the left, at a point in the British front line at E.26.a.5.3 3. The Battalion will be distributed prior to the assault in the advanced trench, present front line, the retrenchment, and Watling Street in the following order :- "C" Coy. From Gommecourt Rd on the right to C.T. "A" inclusive. "A" Coy. From C.T. "A" exclusive to C.T. "A1" inclusive. "B" Coy. From C.T. "A1" exclusive to Sap No 1 inclusive. "D" Coy. From Sap No 1 exclusive to C.T. "B1" inclusive. Company Commanders will dispose their men in the available trenches on their respective fronts in such a manner that the succeeding waves can follow one another at not more than one minutes interval. 4. All ranks will push forward to the final objective without delay, when the assault is commenced, with the exception of one Platoon of "A" Company and one platoon of "D" Coy. who will consolidate Strong Points Nos 2 & 3.	

Army Form C. 2118.

WAR DIARY
or
INTELLIGENCE SUMMARY.
(Erase heading not required.)

1/6th BATTALION
SOUTH STAFFORDSHIRE
REGIMENT

Place	Date	Hour	Summary of Events and Information	Remarks and references to Appendices

			5. The left flank will direct, keeping in touch with the 1/6th North Staffs Regt. throughout the forward movement.
			6. Artillery lifts opposite the front of the 137th Infantry Brigade from zero "hour of attack" will be as follows:-
			    hours minutes.
			Off the enemy's front line ZERO 3
			Off the enemy's second line " 5
			Off the enemy's third line
			    (W. edge of Wood)
			Off the E. edge of the Wood " 15
			Off the Sunken Road " 20
			Off Oxus Trench " 25
			Off Fill Trench " 30
			The time of "zero" (hour of attack) will be issued to all concerned.
			7. The four Lewis Guns detailed to advance with the second and third waves, will protect the advance on the right flank and establish themselves in positions N. of the Gommecourt Road at E.28.c.3.5, 3.5, E.2b.d.0.3, E.2b.d.2.7, 3, and E.28.d.5, 2.5.
			They will remain in such positions until the arrival of the troops specially allotted for the defence of this flank, after which they will rejoin their Companies.
			8. The trained bombers will remain with their Companies and will advance with the assaulting waves, but will be so disposed that they may be readily formed into bombing parties to deal with the enemy C.T's in case the general advance is delayed. They will carry a supply of bombs but will be equipped as other ranks with the exception of the additional S.A.A.
			9. All Company runners will make themselves acquainted with the position of Battalion Headquarters both before and after the advance.	

WAR DIARY
or
INTELLIGENCE SUMMARY.
(Erase heading not required.)

Army Form C. 2118.

Place	Date	Hour	Summary of Events and Information	Remarks and references to Appendices
			10. Four scouts per Company will be detailed to advance at "zero" minus five minutes in order to locate the best routes through the enemy's wire, where they will remain until the arrival of the fourth wave. The scouts will be warned of the action of our artillery, trench mortars, and machine guns.	
			11. The Battalion will parade in Fighting Order at an hour to be notified tomorrow.	
			12. All ranks are reminded that it is of the utmost importance to keep "touch with the troops "whether of their own or other units" on their right and left, and to render mutual support whenever circumstances require it.	
FONQUE-VILLERS	1-7-16		OPERATIONS, 1st July, 1916. The 137th Infantry Brigade having been ordered to attack GOMMECOURT WOOD and VILLAGE, the Battalion took up their position in our old front line trenches between the FONQUEVILLERS - GOMMECOURT ROAD and Leicester Street (E.28. a.5.3) at 1 am. on 1st July. The attack was ordered to commence at 7-30 am in four waves - the Companies advancing by Platoons in depth at a distance of 80 yards - in conjunction with the 1/6th Batcn North Staffordshire Regiment and two Battalions of the 139th Infantry Brigade on our left. The assault was preceded by an intense bombardment of the supporting artillery commencing at 6-25 am. and was also covered by a smoke barrage which opened five minutes before the attack was launched. During the course of this bombardment the enemy replied vigourously with howitzers and field guns upon our front line and communication trenches and at intervals he directed short bursts of machine gun fire on our parapets and exits from the direction of our front and right front.	

Army Form C. 2118.

WAR DIARY
or
INTELLIGENCE SUMMARY.

(Erase heading not required.)

1/6th BATTALION
SOUTH STAFFORDSHIRE
REGIMENT

Place	Date	Hour	Summary of Events and Information	Remarks and references to Appendices
			At 7-30 am the four platoons of the leading wave having moved out to the new front line, under cover of the artillery smoke advanced to the assault of the enemy's position and were followed by the succeeding waves. The fourth wave was delayed for about five minutes by the casualties which blocked the communication trenches leading to the front line and by the heavy load which they were carrying. The disposition of the Companies from right to left was "C" "A" "B" "D" and of these the only Company which was able to penetrate the enemy's line in any strength was "D" Company on the left, who found that the wire was well cut on their frontage: three platoons of this Company obtained a footing in the front line and some men are reported to have gone further but they were outnumbered and accounted for by the enemy. The remaining three Companies on the right, "B" "A" & "C", were held up by the enemy's wire which had been so well cut, and although small parties were able to enter the enemy's line they could not obtain a permanent footing there. Eighty men returned within an hour to our front line where they remained until noon, when they were ordered to occupy our supports, and they were subsequently withdrawn from the trenches. Casualties were 239, out of a fighting strength of 523. The Battalion was then relieved by 1/5th Leicester Regt., and marched to ST. AMAND.	
ST. AMAND	2-7-16		The Battalion rested at ST. AMAND.	
ST. AMAND	3-7-16		The Battalion marched to BERLES-AU-BOIS.	
BERLES.	4-7-16		The Battalion in Brigade Reserve.	
BERLES.	5-7-16		ditto.	
BERLES.	6-7-16		ditto.	

Army Form C. 2118.

WAR DIARY
or
INTELLIGENCE SUMMARY.
(Erase heading not required.)

Instructions regarding War Diaries and Intelligence Summaries are contained in F. S. Regs., Part II. and the Staff Manual respectively. Title pages will be prepared in manuscript.

1/5th BATTALION.
SOUTH STAFFORDSHIRE
REGIMENT

Place	Date	Hour	Summary of Events and Information	Remarks and references to Appendices
BERLES.	7-7-16		The Battalion relieved the 1/5th South Staffs Regt. in the trenches - Right Sector.	
BERLES.	8-7-16		Quiet day.	
BERLES.	9-7-16		ditto.	
BERLES.	10-7-16		ditto.	
BERLES.	11-7-16		ditto.	
BERLES.	12-7-16		ditto.	
BERLES.	13-7-16		ditto.	
BERLES.	14-7-16		The Battalion was relieved in the trenches by the 1/5th South Staffs Regt. and proceeded into Brigade Reserve at BERLES-AU-BOIS.	
BERLES.	15-7-16		In Brigade Reserve.	
BERLES.	16-7-16		ditto. Inspection of Battn by G.O.C. 46th Division.	
BERLES.	17-7-16		ditto. The Strong Points, Fort Gastineau and Point 147, were taken over by two Platoons.	
BERLES.	18-7-16		In Brigade Reserve. Operation of connecting Trenches Nos 104 & 105 carried out.	
BERLES.	19-7-16		In Brigade Reserve.	
BERLES.	20-7-16		In Brigade Reserve.	
BERLES.	21-7-16		The Battalion relieved the 1/5th South Staffs Regt. in the trenches - "C" Sector, "H" Sub-sector.	
BERLES.	22-7-16		Quiet day.	
BERLES.	23-7-16		Quiet day.	
BERLES.	24-7-16		Quiet day.	
BERLES.	25-7-16		Quiet day.	
BERLES.	26-7-16		Quiet day.	
BERLES.	27-7-16		The Battalion was relieved in the trenches by the 1/5th South Staffs. Regt. and proceeded into Divisional Reserve at BAILLEULMONT.	
BAILLEULMONT.	28-7-16		In Divisional Reserve.	
BAILLEULMONT	29-7-16		In Divisional Reserve.	

Army Form C. 2118.

WAR DIARY
or
INTELLIGENCE SUMMARY.
(Erase heading not required.)

Instructions regarding War Diaries and Intelligence Summaries are contained in F. S. Regs., Part II. and the Staff Manual respectively. Title pages will be prepared in manuscript.

Place	Date	Hour	Summary of Events and Information	Remarks and references to Appendices
BAILLEULMONT	30-7-16		In Divisional Reserve.	
BAILLEULMONT	31-7-16		In Divisional Reserve.	

Wilkinson Lieut: Colonel.
Commanding 1/6th Bn. South Staffs Regiment

Army Form C. 2118.

WAR DIARY (79)
or
INTELLIGENCE SUMMARY.

(*Erase heading not required.*)

Instructions regarding War Diaries and Intelligence Summaries are contained in F. S. Regs., Part II. and the Staff Manual respectively. Title pages will be prepared in manuscript.

Place	Date	Hour	Summary of Events and Information	Remarks and references to Appendices
			CASUALTIES FOR MONTH OF JULY 1916.	
			OTHER RANKS.	
			Killed 20	
			Wounded 145	
			" (Accidentally) 1	
			" (At Duty) 13	
			Missing 54	
			Wounded & Missing 14	
			Died of Wounds 7	
			OFFICERS.	
			Killed.	
			2/Lieut R. Page.	
			WOUNDED.	
			Captain A.R.A. Dickens.	
			" J.P. Magrane.	
			Lieut: S.H. Evans.	
			" G.N. Adams.	
			2/Lieut W.G. Davies.	
			" D.H. Robinson.	
			" J.E.T. Sutcliffe.	
			" H.J. Lewis.	
			Wounded (At Duty).	
			Capt & Adjt: R.C. Piper.	
			2/Lieutenant J.G. Gribben.	
			Missing.	
			Lieut R.S. Jeffcock.	
			2/Lieut W.R. Johnson.	
			" T.A. Dickinson.	
			Wounded & Missing.	
			Captain C.W. Evans.	
			Lieut: A.D. Harley.	
			2/Lieut A.E. Flaxman.	

Confidential
War Diary
1st South Staff Regt Y.L.
for the month of
August 1916.

46

1/6 S Stafford Rup

Feb

Vol XIII

Army Form C. 2118.

WAR DIARY
or
INTELLIGENCE SUMMARY.

(80)

(Erase heading not required.)

Instructions regarding War Diaries and Intelligence Summaries are contained in F.S. Regs., Part II. and the Staff Manual respectively. Title pages will be prepared in manuscript.

Place	Date	Hour	Summary of Events and Information	Remarks and references to Appendices
BAILLEUL-MONT.	1.8.16.		In Divisional Reserve.	
"	2.8.16.		The Battalion relieved the 1/5th Battn South Staffs Regiment in the Trenches - "C" Section, "N" Sub-sector.	
BERLES-AU-BOIS.	3.8.16.		Quiet Day.	
"	4.8.16.		Quiet Day.	
"	5.8.16.		Operation Orders No 6 by Lieut-Colonel J.H.Thursfield for raid on enemy's trenches 5.8.16. Reference. Map RANSART 1/10,000, and SECRET SUNPRINT No 6. 1. On the night of 5/6th August 1916 a raiding party of one officer (2/Lieut J.L.C.Swallace) and 30 other ranks of the 1/6th Btn South Staffs Regt, and one office (2Lieut Mansell) and 30 other ranks of the 1/5th Btn South Staffs Regiment, the whole under command of 2/Lieut Wallace will enter the enemy's trenches in his salient, due East of trenches Nos 106, 107, & 108. 2. OBJECT. (i) To destroy enemy's personnel. (ii) To secure identification. (iii) To destroy enemy trenches. (iv) To assist raiding party of 138th Bde on our right. 3. COMPOSITION OF PARTIES. Each of the two detachment will be divided into three parties; those of the 1/6th Btn South Staffs Regt being numbered 1, 2, & 3, and those of the 1/5th Battn South Staffs Regt being numbered Nos 4, 5, & 6. Parties Nos 1, 2 & 3 will be on the Right, and parties Nos 4, 5 & 6 on the Left, and will enter the enemy's trenches through gaps in his wire which are being cut at or about points W23d.85.85 for Nos 1,2 & 3, and W23d.85.95 for Nos34.W5W7&8-'6.	

WAR DIARY or INTELLIGENCE SUMMARY

Army Form C. 2118.

Place	Date	Hour	Summary of Events and Information	Remarks and references to Appendices
BERLES-AU-BOIS.	5.8.16. (contd)		4. COMPOSITION OF PARTIES. No 1 Blocking Party under Corpl Camp to enter at Right Entrace and turning North block enemy's trench. No 2 Bombing Party under L/cpl Morris to enter at same point and work down the trench SOUTHWARDS. No 3 Parapet Party under Sergt Windridge to deal with any enemy appearing above ground and to cover the blocking party and secure the withdrawal of parties Nos 1 & 2. No 4 Blocking Party under Cpl Hutley to enter at Left Entrance and turning South block enemy's trench. No 5 Bombing Party under Corpl Jones to enter at same point and work up trenches Northwards. No 6 Parapet Party under Cpl Bash to deal with any enemy appearing above grounds and to cover the Blocking Party and secure withdrawal of parties Nos 4 & 5. 5. R.E. PARTY. Two parties each of 1 N.C.O and 2 sappers will accompany Parties Nos 2 & 5 and carry out demolition. The greatest care must be taken that none of our men are cut off or endangered. 6. STRETCHER BEARERS. Two Stretcher Bearers with Trench Stretchers will accompany parties Nos 3 & 6. 7. ARTILLERY. Two Batteries of Field Artillery, one section of Howitzers, two guns of Y46 Trench Mortar Battery, and the Stokes Guns of the 137th Trench Mortar Battery will form a barrage on the flanks and on the enemy's support lines at "ZERO" hour, and will continue until the raiding party has withdrawn to our trenches. The Lewis Gun Officer, 1/6th Btn South Staffs Regt, will detail 1 N.C.O and 2 gunners to take out a Lewis Gun in front of our wire to cover return of the parties and protect the right flank. 8. ASSEMBLY. Parties Nos 1, 2 & 3 will assemble in trench No 108, and Parties Nos 4, 5 & 6 in trench No 109.	

WAR DIARY or INTELLIGENCE SUMMARY.

Army Form C. 2118.

1/6th BATTALION, SOUTH STAFFORDSHIRE REGIMENT.

Place	Date	Hour	Summary of Events and Information	Remarks and references to Appendices
BERLES-AU-BOIS.	5.8.16. (contd).		8. ASSEMBLY. (continued). The head of No 1 Party being at L.P.Bay 4, T 108, and head of No 4 Party being at L.P.Bay 1. T109, and will be in position at 10.45 p.m. These parties will leave our front line at "ZERO" minus 15 minutes and will cross in time to enter the gaps in enemy's wire at "ZERO". 9. SIGNALS FOR WITHDRAWAL. 15 minutes after "ZERO" bouquets of 5 white rockets will be fired from W.22b.9.6. near North Street at intervals of three minutes until "ZERO" plus 24. Rockets will give the approximate line back to our own trenches. Parties Nos 3 & 6 will arrange to lay White tape across the open in order to indicate the way back. 10. WITHDRAWAL. Parties will adopt the following method of withdrawal:- The Bombing Parties Nos 2 & 5 will withdraw from the flanks and clear the trench, but will first make certain that the retirement of the Blocking Parties Nos 1 & 4 is protected by the Parapet Parties. The Blocking Parties will then withdraw to the place of entry and leave the trench, and not until then will the Parapet Party be ordered to withdraw. All parties will return to our lines by the outward routes and will occupy their former places of assembly in trenches Nos 108 & 109 and report their arrival immediately to Battn Headquarters. 11. TIME TABLE. "ZERO" will be at 11.25 p.m. Watches will be synchronised by the Btn Signalling Officer who will obtain the correct time from Brigade at 10.0 p.m. 12. BATTALION HEADQUARTERS. Battalion Headquarters will be at the Right Company Headquarters in Nuts Walk. 13. IDENTIFICATION MARKS. All marks of identification must be removed from the men of the raiding party.	

Army Form C. 2118.

1/6th BATTALION,
SOUTH STAFFORDSHIRE
REGIMENT.

No. ....
Date ....

WAR DIARY
or
INTELLIGENCE SUMMARY.
(Erase heading not required.)

(83)

Instructions regarding War Diaries and Intelligence Summaries are contained in F. S. Regs., Part II. and the Staff Manual respectively. Title pages will be prepared in manuscript.

Place	Date	Hour	Summary of Events and Information	Remarks and references to Appendices
BERLES-AU-BOIS.	5.8.16. (contd).		REPORT RE OPERATIONS. The programme as laid down in Battalion Operation Orders was carried out, with the exception that it appeared at 11.10 p.m. that some of our guns were firing upon the sector to be dealt with by this Battalion, whereas at this time no barrage should have been placed on the enemy's lines opposite our front. It appeared that this caused the enemy to send up large numbers of Very Lights and so made it impossible for our men to move without being seen. There is no doubt that the wire had not been completely cut in the gaps, or what is more likely that it had been filled in by the enemy in the evening. He had done some work in the gaps on the previous evening. It would seem to be difficult to keep open such gaps by Machine Gun and Lewis Gun fire.	
"	6.8.16.		Quiet Day.	
"	7.8.16.		Quiet Day.	
"	8.8.16.		Quiet Day. The Battalion was relieved in the Trenches by the 1/5th Btn South Staffs Regt and proceeded into Brigade Reserve at BERLES-SU-BOIS.	
"	9.8.16.		In Brigade Reserve.	
"	10.8.16.		-do-	
"	11.8.16.		-do-	
"	12.8.16.		-do-	
"	13.8.16.		-do-	
"	14.8.16.		-do-	

TJ134. Wt. W708-776. 50000. 4/15. Sir J. C. & S.

WAR DIARY
or
INTELLIGENCE SUMMARY.

(Erase heading not required.)

Army Form C. 2118.

1/5th BATTALION,
SOUTH STAFFORDSHIRE
REGIMENT.

Instructions regarding War Diaries and Intelligence Summaries are contained in F. S. Regs., Part II. and the Staff Manual respectively. Title pages will be prepared in manuscript.

Place	Date	Hour	Summary of Events and Information	Remarks and references to Appendices
BERLES-AU-BOIS.	15.8.16.		The Battalion relieved the 1/5th Battalion South Staffordshire Regiment in the trenches.	
"	16.8.16.		Quiet Day.	
"	17.8.16.		Enemy bombarded the front and support line of Left Centre Coy with Heavy Trench Mortars from 4.20 p.m. to 7.15 p.m. A certain amount of damage was done to our trenches. The enemy eventually quietened down under the fire of our Field Guns and Mortars. Quiet Day on remainder of Battalion Front. At 10.25 p.m. and 11.55 p.m. our artillery bombarded the roads and tracks used by enemy transport.	
"	18.8.16.		Enemy again bombarded from 4.45 p.m. to 5.30 p.m. the trenches of our Left Centre Company, chiefly Trench 114 which was damaged, with his Heavy Trench Mortars. A dug-out containing Grenades and Smoke Bombs was knocked in and a number of the latter detonated which caused a regular cloud of smoke to issue from the Store for about two hours. The enemy desisted under fire from our guns and mortars. Quiet day on remainder of Battalion Front.	
"	19.8.16.		From 6.5 p.m. to 8 p.m. our artillery and trench mortars carried out a combined bombardment of the enemy trenches about his salient at W.23.b. and W.24.a. Enemy replied with a few shells in the Ravine. Otherwise Quiet Day.	
"	20.8.16.		Quiet Day.	
"	21.8.16.		Quiet Day.	
"	22.8.16.		Quiet Day. The Battalion was relieved in the trenches by the 1/5th Btn South Staffs Regt and proceeded into Divisional Reserve at BAILLEULMONT.	

WAR DIARY
or
INTELLIGENCE SUMMARY.

(Erase heading not required.)

Army Form C. 2118.

Place	Date	Hour	Summary of Events and Information	Remarks and references to Appendices
BAILLEUL-MONT.	23.8.16.		Battalion in Divisional Reserve.	
"	24.8.16.		—do—	
"	25.8.16.		—do— Inspection by G.O.C. 46th Division.	
"	26.8.16.		—do—	
"	27.8.16.		—do—	
"	28.8.16.		—do—	
"	29.8.16.		The Battalion relieved the 1/5th Battalion South Staffordshire Regiment.	
BERTES-AU-BOIS.	30.8.16.		Quiet Day.	
"	31.8.16.		Quiet Day.	

Army Form C. 2118.

WAR DIARY
or
INTELLIGENCE SUMMARY.
(Erase heading not required.)

(86)

Instructions regarding War Diaries and Intelligence Summaries are contained in F. S. Regs., Part II. and the Staff Manual respectively. Title pages will be prepared in manuscript.

Place	Date	Hour	Summary of Events and Information	Remarks and references to Appendices
			TOTAL CASUALTIES FOR MONTH OF AUGUST 1916.	
			OFFICERS.	
			Wounded:- 2/Lieut H.R.Paton.	
			2/Lieut J.G.Gribben.	
			2/Lieut A.F.Tait.	
			OTHER RANKS	
			Killed:- 1.	
			Wounded:- 10.	
			Missing:- 1.	
			Died of Wounds:- 2.	
			Wounded At Duty:- 2.	
			[signature] Major,	
			Commanding 1/6th Battalion South Staffordshire Regiment.	

Army Form C. 2118.

1/6th Battalion South Staffordshire Regiment.   WAR DIARY or INTELLIGENCE SUMMARY.

Instructions regarding War Diaries and Intelligence Summaries are contained in F. S. Regs., Part II. and the Staff Manual respectively. Title pages will be prepared in manuscript.

(Erase heading not required.)

Vol. 20

Q 21

Place	Date	Hour	Summary of Events and Information	Remarks and references to Appendices
BERLES-AU-BOIS.	1.9.16.		Battalion in the Trenches. Quiet Day.	
"	2.9.16.		OPERATIONS ORDERS BY MAJOR F.J.TRUMP. (No 8). Map Reference:- TRENCH MAP, RANSART 1/10,000. 1. RAIDING PARTY. On the night of the 2.9.16 the 1/6th Btn South Staffordshire Regiment will carry out a raid on the enemy's trenches between points W23.d.81.74 and W23b. 2. OBJECT. To secure identification of enemy troops holding MONCHY-RANSART Line, by securing prisoners. Killing Germans. 3. COMPOSITION OF PARTIES. The Party will consist of 8 Officers and 100 other ranks under the Command of Captain H.V.MANDER and divided as under:- "A" Party. 2 Officers, 20 O.R. and 3 R.E's. "B" " 2 " 25 " and 3 " "C" " 2 " 24 " and 2 " "D" " 1 " 5 " 22 " Reserve Party 2 N.C.O's and 10 men. 4. OBJECTIVES. "A" Party. To enter by "B" Gap in enemy's wire and seize and block the enemy's front line - Sap and C.T. at W23.d.90.73. "B" Party. Will be subdivided into clearing party 15 men and Parapet Party 10 men. The whole will enter by a Central Gap in wire when the clearing party will endeavour to seize and clear enemy trench by working outwards towards blocking Parties "A" & "C". The Parapet party remaining outside the trench to support the clearing party to take charge of prisoners and assist wounded. "C" Party. To enter by Left Gap proceed to block and hold front line trench and C.T. and suspected sap at W23.b.86.00.	

Place	Date	Hour	Summary of Events and Information	Remarks and references to Appendices
BERLES-AU-BOIS. (continued)	2.9.16. (continued)		4. OBJECTIVES. (continued) "D" Party. To act as Covering Party – to remain outside the enemy wire well on the outer flanks of "R" & "L" gaps – to fire on enemy either side – and to cover withdrawal of "A" "B" & "C" Parties. This party will consist of two Lewis Guns with teams and 10 other ranks. NOTE. In the event of the patrols reporting that there are not three practicable gaps in enemy wire to enable this scheme to be carried out and that only two gaps are cut, O/C. Raid must decide to attack front line in vicinity if gaps, blocking outwards and clearing inwards. Similarly in case of only one gap being found to attack front trench in front of gap and clear outwards. 5. ASSEMBLY. The Raiding Party will assemble as under:- "A" Party. Trench 107. Right Portion. Point of Exit at Lewis Gun Post. "B" Party. Trench 107. Left Portion. Point of Exit Bay 3. "C" Party. Trench 108. Bays 6,7,8,& 9.Point of Exit Bay 7. "D" Party. Right Flank as "A". Left Flank as "C". This Party will commence to move out 15 minutes in advance of "A", "B", & "C" Parties. FINAL ASSEMBLY. In "No Man's Land" about 40 yards away from various gaps. 6. BATTALION HEADQUARTERS. Trench Battalion Headquarters will be established at Top End of NUTS LANE near Trench 107. 7. COMMUNICATION. Communication will be maintained by telephone and runners. O/C. Raid will arrange to maintain communication with O/C. Battalion by a telephone run out into "No Man's Land" – one spare instrument and wire will be taken out. Battalion French Headquarters will be connected by telephone to Battalion and Brigade Headquarters. The Brigade Signalling Officer will arrange signalling communication	

1/6th Btn South Staffordshire Regiment.

WAR DIARY or INTELLIGENCE SUMMARY.

Army Form C. 2118.

Place	Date	Hour	Summary of Events and Information	Remarks and references to Appendices
BERLES-AU-BOIS	2.9.16. (Continued)		**7. COMMUNICATION.** (continued) required by O/C 1/6th South Staffs Regt and will be at Advanced Btn H.Q. at the disposal of the Battalion Commander during operations.	
			8. ARTILLERY. The Centre Group, 46th Divisional Artillery and the two inch Trench Mortar Battery will co-operate in accordance with Artillery Programme which will be submitted.	
			9. EQUIPMENT. All ranks will remove all identification marks, papers etc and will be inspected by their respective party officers before leaving for the trenches.	
			RIFLE MEN. Rifle, Bayonet (darkened) 50 rounds S.A.A. and four bombs in pockets.	
			BOMBERS. No rifle, 12 bombs oh bomb carrying waistcoats. GAS-HELMETS. Gas-Helmets one per man will be taken and carried in the inner coat pocket.	
			Faces to be darkened. White Luminous paint or white cloth to be sewn on under side of collar. Flash Lamps will be carried. Mats for crossing enemy wire will be provided by R.E, also 15 ladders (stretcher pattern). "P" Bombs will be carried by each Party for clearing dug-outs. Each man must be provided with some means of cutting wire.	
			10. SEQUENCE OF OPERATIONS.	
			(1) 6" Howitzers will fire on selected points during the day.	
			(2) At 6 p.m. (or earlier) till 9.15 p.m. general bombardment and wire cutting will take place.	
			(3) At 9 p.m. three patrols, under the three second officers of "A", "B", & "C" will move out for the purpose of locating the three best gaps in enemy wire and taping the routes to same. The patrols will be accompanied by the R.E. Details who will take out the Bangalore Torpedoes. These patrols should return not later that 9.45 p.m. the Artillery will not fire on the objectives but will keep up the bombardment elsewhere.	
			(4) 9.45 p.m. to 10.35 p.m. artillery will maintain sufficient fire to prevent enemy coming out and discovering and mending gaps in wire.	

Army Form C. 2118.

1/6th Btn South Staffordshire Regiment.

WAR DIARY (90)
or
INTELLIGENCE SUMMARY.
(Erase heading not required.)

Instructions regarding War Diaries and Intelligence Summaries are contained in F. S. Regs., Part II. and the Staff Manual respectively. Title pages will be prepared in manuscript.

Place	Date	Hour	Summary of Events and Information	Remarks and references to Appendices
BERLES-au-BOIS	2.9.16. (Continued)		10. SEQUENCE OF OPERATIONS. (continued)	

(5) At 10.35 p.m. to 10.55 p.m. Heavy bombardment by Artillery.
(6) At 10.55 p.m. the Raiding Party will attack as arranged.
(7) At 11.20 p.m. unless object is previously attained the Raiding Party will proceed to withdraw.
(8) At 10.55 p.m. the Artillery will lift off the objective but will continue elsewhere and will not resume firing on objective until O/C Battalion advises Artillery that they may do so.
(9) Machine Guns and Lewis Guns of the 138th Bde will bring fire to bear on enemy's front line trench and saps between W29.b.15.30 and W24.c.01.27 between 9 p.m. and 9.45 p.m. and between 10 p.m. and 10.55 p.m. and from 10.55 p.m. until "Cease Fire".
(10) The 137th Machine Gun Co and the 137th Trench Mortar Bty will co-operate under orders from O/C, 1/6th South Staffs Regiment. They will not bring fire to bear on enemy's lines "S" of W23.b.90.00.
(11) The "Cease Fire" will be ordered by O/C, Battalion through the F.O.O. who will inform Brigade. The Heavy and Divisional F.O.O's will be with O/C, Battalion.
NOTE. The Artillery will lay the necessary wires and test same. Spare Instrument and alternative routes will be arranged for.

11. COUNTERSIGN. O/C, Raid will arrange Countersign on the day of the operations.
12. WITHDRAWAL. The signal to withdraw will only be given by O/C, Raid. This will be done by Klaxon Horns.
NOTE. O/C, Raid will detail exact method of withdrawal.
13. The second officers of "A", "B", & "C" will not enter the enemys trenches, but will remain outside in gaps and ascertain that their parties have entered the enemy's trenches, when they will report to O/C, Raid for instructions at Central Gap. In the event of the O/C, Raid becoming a casualty the senior of these officers will take Command. These three officers will further accompany the patrols who are to do the taping.

1/6th Btn South Staffordshire Regiment.

WAR DIARY or INTELLIGENCE SUMMARY.

Army Form C. 2118.

Place	Date	Hour	Summary of Events and Information	Remarks and references to Appendices
BEUGNES- AU-BOIS	2.9.16. (continued)		14. MEDICAL ARRANGEMENTS. (1) The Medical Officer will establish an Advanced Regimental Aid Post in the dugout in trench 108. (2) "A", "B" & "C" Parties will be accompanied by two stretcher bearers to each party using ladder stretchers - four stretcher bearers with stretchers will accompany O/C. Reid and will be under his direction. Spare bearers will be available at Advanced Trench R.A.P. Five Stretchers with bearers from the 3rd N.M.Field Ambulance will be at Right Company Headquarters. The R.A.M.C. situated in the RAVINE will be in readiness if called upon. 15. R. E. The O/C.1/2nd Field Company R.E. will arrange to provide the necessary Bangalore Torpedoes and the necessary personnel to operate same. The R.E. men will accompany the patrols and on return to own trenches they will attach themselves to the head of "A", "B" & "C" Parties. The O/C.1/2nd F. Co. R.E. will be at Advanced Btn Headquarters during operations to advise the Battalion Commander on technical matters. 16. SILENCE. The importance of absolute silence throughout the operation must be maintained. This must be impressed on all ranks.

(Signed) H.HANFORD. Captain,
Adjutant 1/6th Btn South Staffordshire Regiment.

REPORT RE OPERATIONS.

The Raiding Party assembled in the trenches allotted at 8.0 p.m. At 8.50 p.m. patrols went out and got clear of our own wire. At 9.0 p.m they went forward to investigate the German wire. At about 9.43 p.m. patrol from the right reported that a gap was cut through the two belts of wire, and that the patrol was in with 2/Lt Johnston slightly wounded.

At 9.36 p.m. left party patrol reported that there was an excellent gap in the wire cut oj the left of the position. Centre party patrol reported that they had got up to the German wire, but had been unable to fully investigate owing to our own shrapnel. It was decided that it was unnecessary to use the Bangalore Torpedoes. Captain Mander then ordered the parties to proceed - | |

WAR DIARY or INTELLIGENCE SUMMARY.

Army Form C. 2118.

1/6th Btn South Staffordshire Regiment. (92)

Place	Date	Hour	Summary of Events and Information	Remarks and references to Appendices
BERLES-AU-BOIS	2.9.16. (continued)		REPORT RE OPERATIONS. (continued).	

"A" Party taking the right gap as arranged and "C" Party the left gap as arranged. "B" Party (Centre Party) he then took towards the right gap under his own Command.
Shortly after 10 p.m. all the parties had left our own parapet and successfully negotiated our wire. There was only a very small amount of machine gun fire (from the right) and very little shrapnel. There was not on the points selected for exit.
At 10.21 p.m. a telephone message was received at Battalion H.Q saying them "A" & "B" Parties were in position in front of gaps.
Another message received at 11.3 p.m. stated "Assault has started"
"A" Party has gone through the wire, no more new yet". At 11.6 p.m. bombs were heard thrown at the German front line but no news was to hand.
At 11.12 p.m. two of our wounded men reported that our men were in the German trenches and that Captain Mander had sent forward one Officer and four men to obtain further information.
At 11.16 p.m. Captain Mander reported that "C" Party had gone through the gap and were in the German Trenches. He had seen 2/Lieut McGowan and obtained from him the information.
At 11.18 p.m. Bugle sounded "FALL IN".
At 11.20 p.m. four prisoners were brought in to our trenches.
At 11.30 P.M. Captain Mander came in, and "A", "B" & "C" Parties were also reported in. Bugle then blew "COOK HOUSE DOOR" from our own trenches to withdraw the Covering Party.
The left Covering Party returned at 11.55 p.m. and the right covering Party at 12.20 a.m.
The four prisoners were then sent down under escort to Brigade Headquarters.
Our casualties during the raid were as follows:- 1 Officer (2/Lt Johnston) slightly wounded, 1 other rank missing, and 2 other ranks slightly wounded.

1/5th Btn South Staffordshire Regiment.

Army Form C. 2118.

(93)

WAR DIARY
or
INTELLIGENCE SUMMARY.
(Erase heading not required.)

Instructions regarding War Diaries and Intelligence Summaries are contained in F.S. Regs., Part II. and the Staff Manual respectively. Title pages will be prepared in manuscript.

Place	Date	Hour	Summary of Events and Information	Remarks and references to Appendices
BERLES-AU-BOIS.	3.9.16.		Quiet Day. The was relieved in the Trenches by the 1/5th South Stafford shire Regiment.	
-do-	4.9.16.		In Brigade Reserve.	
-do-	5.9.16.		-do-	
-do-	6.9.16.		-do-	
-do-	7.9.16.		-do-	
-do-	8.9.16.		-do-	
-do-	9.9.16.		The Battalion relieved the 1/5th South Staffordshire Regiment in the Trenches.	
BERLES-AU-BOIS.	10.9.16.		Quiet Day.	
-do-	11.9.16.		Quiet Day.	
-do-	12.9.16.		Two prisoners were captured at about 11.30 p.m. by "B" Coy in front of our wire near No 13a Listening Post in front of Trench 113 (W.23.b.9.8.) Bombs were thrown into our wire at about 11p.m. and rifle fire was opened by our men in the direction of where the bombs exploded. Later, while 2/Lt Harris was in 13A Listening Post, he saw two men crawling on their hands and knees just in front of our wire. After challenging them 2/Lt Harris ordered rifle fire to be opened on them, which evidently wounded one of them. They commenced to creep away but 2/Lt Harris immediately went after them accompanied by Sgt Aston & Pte Clarke. One man was discovered lying in a bed of thistles and was captured without difficulty, and sent back to our lines. 2/Lt Harris and Pte Clarke then went on after the other man. He was eventually discovered hiding in a shell hole, having crawled back some distance from our wire.	

Army Form C. 2118.

WAR DIARY
or
INTELLIGENCE SUMMARY.
(Erase heading not required.)

1/6th Btn South Staffs Regt. (94)

Instructions regarding War Diaries and Intelligence Summaries are contained in F. S. Regs., Part II. and the Staff Manual respectively. Title pages will be prepared in manuscript.

Place	Date	Hour	Summary of Events and Information	Remarks and references to Appendices
BERLES AU-BOIS.	12-9-16. (Contd).		He offered considerable resistance before he could be brought back into our trenches. The enemy, by this time, had become alarmed and was sending up Very Lights and firing, but we suffered no casualties. The prisoners were both VICE FELDWEBELS(Acting Senior N.C.O's) of the 23rd Regiment 12th Division. Their story was that they started out to investigate our Listening Posts,by themselves,but were fired on and could not get away. When captured they had only Very Pistols and Bayonets on them.	
-do-	13-9-16.		Quiet day.	
-do-	14-9-16.		Quiet day.	
-do-	15-9-16.		At about 12-45a.m. a Standing Patrol of "D" Coy engaged an enemy patrol with Rifle fire and bombs at about W23.b.9.9.(N of MONCHY) An Officer, Lt Monk, and four men at once started out to investigate. They found two seriously wounded men(One an officer)about 15 yards in front of enemy wire and proceeded to bring them back to our lines. About half way back a third man was seen moving towards our party. Fire was opened and the man was called upon to surrender,which he did. All three were brought back to our lines. The two seriously wounded prisoners died immediately after being brought in. The third was also wounded in the arm. On examination he proved to belong to the 11th Coy 63rd Regt 12th Division. At about 10 a.m. a fourth man, also wounded, was seen trying to crawl through our wire. Owing to enemy sniping he was unable to reach our trenches. Artillery fire was opened on the enemy trenches which put a stop to the sniping and the man came in. The Battalion was relieved in the trenches by the 1/5th Btn South Staffordshire Regiment.	
BAILLEULMONT.	16-9-16.		In Divisional Reserve.	

1/6th Btn South Staffordshire Regiment.

Army Form C. 2118.

WAR DIARY
or
INTELLIGENCE SUMMARY.
(Erase heading not required.)

Instructions regarding War Diaries and Intelligence Summaries are contained in F. S. Regs., Part II. and the Staff Manual respectively. Title pages will be prepared in manuscript.

Place	Date	Hour	Summary of Events and Information	Remarks and references to Appendices
BAILLEUL-MONT.	17-9-16.		In Divisionel Reserve.	
-do-	18-9-16.		do	
-do-	19-9-16.		do	
-do-	20-9-16.		do	
-do-	21-9-16.		The Battalion relieved the 1/5th Btn South Staffordshire Regiment in the trenches.	
BERLES-AU-BOIS.	22-9-16.		Quiet day.	
-do-	23-9-16.		do	
-do-	24-9-16.		do	
-do-	25-9-16.		do	
-do-	26-9-16.		do	
-do-	27-9-16.		The Battalion was relieved in the trenches by the 1/5th Btn South Staffordshire Regiment.	
-do-	28-9-16.		In Brigade Reserve.	
-do-	29-9-16.		do	
-do-	30-9-16.		do	

LIST OF CASUALTIES FOR MONTH GIVEN ON ATTACHED SHEET.

T.2134. Wt. W708-776. 500090. 4/15. Sir J. C. & S.

Army Form C. 2118.

WAR DIARY (96)
or
INTELLIGENCE SUMMARY.

(Erase heading not required.)

1/6th Btn South Staffordshire Regt.

Instructions regarding War Diaries and Intelligence Summaries are contained in F. S. Regs., Part II. and the Staff Manual respectively. Title pages will be prepared in manuscript.

Place	Date	Hour	Summary of Events and Information	Remarks and references to Appendices
			TOTAL CASUALTIES FOR MONTH OF SEPTEMBER 1916.	
			OFFICERS. Wounded. 2/Lt A.Johnston. 7th Btn The Cameronians(Scottish Rifles) attd 1/6th S.Staffs Rgt. 1	
			OTHER RANKS. Killed. 9	
			Wounded. 9	
			Wounded & at duty. 3	
			Accidentally wounded. 1	
			Missing. 1	
			Stanford Cyrady	
			for Lieut: Colonel.	
			Commanding 1/6th Battn South Staffordshire Regiment.	
			2nd October 1916.	

Army Form C. 2118.

WAR DIARY
or
INTELLIGENCE SUMMARY.
(Erase heading not required.)

1/6th Bn South Staffs Regiment.

Instructions regarding War Diaries and Intelligence Summaries are contained in F. S. Regs., Part II. and the Staff Manual respectively. Title pages will be prepared in manuscript.

6th S. Staffs
Vol 21

Q22

Place	Date	Hour	Summary of Events and Information	Remarks and references to Appendices
BERLES-AU-BOIS.	1.10.16.		In Brigade Reserve.	
"	2.10.16.		-do-	
"	3.10.16.		Battalion relieved the 1/5th South Staffs Regiment in the Trenches.	
"	4.10.16.		Quiet Day.	
"	5.10.16.		-do-	
"	6.10.16.		-do-	
"	7.10.16.		-do-	
"	8.10.16.		-do-	
"	9.10.16.		Battalion relieved in the Trenches by 1/5th South Staffs Regt and proceeded to Divisional Reserve.	
BAILLEUL-MONT.	10.10.16.		In Divisionala Reserve.	
"	11.10.16.		-do-	
"	12.10.16.		-do-	
"	13.10.16.		-do-	
"	14.10.16.		Inspection by G.O.C. 137th Inf: Brigade.	
"	15.10.16.		Battalion relieved the 1/5th South Staffs Regt in the Trenches.	

T2131. Wt. W708-776. 50000. 4/15. Sir J. C. & S.

Army Form C. 2118.

WAR DIARY (98)
or
INTELLIGENCE SUMMARY.
(Erase heading not required.)

1/6th Btn South Staffs Regt.

Instructions regarding War Diaries and Intelligence Summaries are contained in F. S. Regs., Part II. and the Staff Manual respectively. Title pages will be prepared in manuscript.

G. S. Staff.

Place	Date	Hour	Summary of Events and Information	Remarks and references to Appendices
BERLES-AU-BOIS.	16.10.16.		Quiet Day.	
"	17.10.16.		-do-	
"	18.10.16.		-do-	
"	19.10.16.		-do-	
"	20.10.16.		-do-	
"	21.10.16.		Battalion relieved in the Trenches by 1/5th South Staffs Regt and proceeded in-to Brigade Reserve.	
"	22.10.16.		In Brigade Reserve.	
"	23.10.16.		-do-	
"	24.10.16.		-do-	
"	25.10.16.		A raid was carried out on enemy trenches between points W24.a.15.45 and W24.a.40.40. by a party consisting of 8 Officers and 100 other ranks. See Operation Orders No 11 Copy No 1 and report re same attached.	
"	26.10.16.		Battalion relieved the 1/5th South Staffs Regiment in the Trenches.	
"	27.10.16.		Quiet Day.	
"	28.10.16.		Battalion was relieved in the Trenches by the 2nd Yorkshire Regiment, 21st Infantry Brigade, 30th Division, and proceeded into Divisional Reserve at BAILLEULMONT. At 7.0 p.m. the Battalion was relieved in Divisional Res: by the 18th Kings Own Liverpool Regt, 21st I Brigade, 30th [illegible] to COULLEMONT.	

Army Form C. 2118.

C. S. Staff.

WAR DIARY (99)
or
INTELLIGENCE SUMMARY.

(Erase heading not required.)

1/6th Btn South Staffordshire Regiment.

Instructions regarding War Diaries and Intelligence Summaries are contained in F.S. Regs., Part II. and the Staff Manual respectively. Title pages will be prepared in manuscript.

Place	Date	Hour	Summary of Events and Information	Remarks and references to Appendices
GOULLEMONT.	29.10.16.		Battalion marched from GOULLEMONT to LUCHEUX.	
LUCHEUX.	30.10.16.		Resting at LUCHEUX.	
-do-	31.10.16.		Battalion marched from LUCHEUX to BONNIERES.	
			TOTAL CASUALTIES FOR THE MONTH.	
			OFFICERS. Captain F.T.Monk, 7th Btn Cameronians (Scottish Rifles) Wounded 25.10.16.	
			OTHER RANKS. Killed 1.	
			Wounded 8.	
			" (accidentally) 2.	
			" (At Duty) 4.	
			H. Newfoothralty	
			Major.	
			Commanding 1/6th Btn South Staffordshire Regiment.	

T/131. Wt. W708-776. 50C000. 4/15. Sir J. C. & S.

COPIES ISSUED TO:-

1.   War Diary.
2. O.C.   1/5th Btn South Staffs Rgt.
3. O.C.   1/6th Btn South Staffs Rgt.
4. O.C.   1/5th Btn North Staffs Rgt.
5. O.C.   1/6th Btn North Staffs Rgt.
6.   Headquarters.138th Infantry Brigade.
7.   Raiding Party.
8.   Headquarters.137th Infantry Brigade.
9. O.C.   1/6th Btn South Staffs Rgt.
10. O.C. 137th Bde M.G. Company.
11. O.C. Y46.T.M.Bty.
12. O.C. 137th Bde T.M.Bty. Stokes.
13. O.C. 1/2nd Field Coy R.E.
14. O.C. 4th Lincoln Rgt.
15.   C.R.A. 46th Division.
16. O.C. Centre Group. R.F.A.

OPERATION ORDERS NO 11 by LIEUT: COLONEL F.J.TRUMP.
Commanding 1/6th Btn South Staffordshire Regiment.
Dated 18th October 1916.

MAP REFERENCE:- RANSART. 51C.S.E. 3 & 4 (parts of)
Edition 3C. 1/10,000.

1. **RAID.** On the night of the 25th October 1916 the 1/6th Btn South Staffordshire Regt will carry out a raid on enemy trenches between points W24.a.15.45. and W24.a.40.40.

2. **OBJECT.**
   (a) To secure identification by obtaining prisoners.
   (b) To kill Germans.
   (c) To inflict damage.

3. **COMPOSITION OF PARTIES.**
   The Raiding Party will consist of eight Officers & 100 Other ranks under Command of Captain H.V.Mender and detailed as under.
   ("A" Party. 2 Officers & 25 Other Ranks. and 3 R.E's.
     "B" Party. 2   "   " 20   "   "
     "C" Party. 1   "   " 10   "   "
     "D" Party. 1   "   " 15   "   "
     "E" Party. 1   "   " 2 Lewis Gun Teams & 10 Other ranks.

4. **OBJECTIVES.**
   "A" Party to enter by first gap in enemy wire Seize and block enemy front line and Communication Trenches at W24.a.18.43.
   "C" Party to follow seize and block enemy front line at W24.a.40.40.
   "B" Party to enter block Communication Trench at W24.a.32.35. and clear enemy trench and dugouts between the two flank parties.
   "D" Party to act as Parapet party to "B" & "C" Parties. They will take charge of prisoners and assist wounded.
   "E" Party to act as Covering party and to remain outside enemy wire well on the flanks of gap, to fire on enemy on either side and cover withdrawal of Raiding Parties.

5. **ASSEMBLY. PRELIMINARY.**
   "A" Party in front line at foot of Sap 13A in trench 113.
   "C" "B" & "D" Parties in front line at foot of Sap 13C. Trench 113.
   "E" Party right half as for "A" Party. Left half as for "C" "D" & "B" Parties.
   FINAL.
   In "No Man's Land" about 40 yards in front of Gap.

6. **BATTALION HEADQUARTERS.**
   Trench Battalion Headquarters will be established in No 5 Lewis Gun Dugout. Trench 113.

7. **COMMUNICATION.**
   Communication will be maintained by telephone and runners. O/C RAID will arrange to maintain communication with O.C.Battalion by telephone run out in to "No Man's Land". One spare instrument and wire will be taken out. Battalion Trench Headquarters will be connected by telephone to Battalion & Brigade Headquarters.
   The Brigade Signalling Officer will arrange signalling communication required by O.C. 1/6th Btn South Staffordshire Regiment, and will be at Battalion Advanced Headquarters at the disposal of the Battn Commander during operations.

8. **ARTILLERY.**
   Artillery programme (to be issued later) will be arranged by the C.R.A. and 137th Infantry Brigade.

9. **EQUIPMENT.**
   All ranks will remove identification marks, papers etc and will be inspected by their respective party officers before leaving for the trenches.
   RIFLEMEN. Rifle, bayonet (darkened) 50 rounds S.A.A, and four bombs in pockets.
   BOMBERS. No rifle. 12 bombs in bomb carrying waistcoat.
   GAS HELMETS.(One per man) will be carried in the inner coat pocket.
   Flash Lamps will be carried.
   LADDERS. 12 Ladders, stretcher pattern, will be carried.
   P & M.S.K.GRENADES will be carried by each party for clearing dugouts.
   EACH MAN MUST BE PROVIDED WITH SOME MEANS OF CUTTING WIRE.

2.

10. SEQUENCE OF OPERATIONS.

1p.m. to 5p.m.	Artillery cuts a gap at W18.b.60.65. and one 2" Trench Mortar cuts a gap near ALOUETTE-RANSART ROAD. Y46 T.M.Bty aided by 18 pounders cuts gap at W24.a.33.57. (wire reference) W3 u a 15.47. Also a gap at W23.d.90.80.
6-30p.m.	At 6-30p.m. Wire patrols go out to ascertain if Raid can take place. Patrols must return with reports by 8-30p.m. They will leave Standing Patrols to watch gaps. A Lewis Gun will be trained on gap at W23.d.90.80.
9-30p.m.	At 9-30p.m. Ammonal Party and Raiding Parties go out towards objective.
10-15p.m.	Ammonal tubes exploded if necessary, and bombardment as detailed in Artillery Programme commences.
10-18p.m. _artillery_	~~Stokes Mortars~~ firing on objective lifts to other targets gradually.
10-20p.m. ZERO.	Raid goes in, and Stokes Mortars ~~some~~ in RAVINE are withdrawn.
10-50p.m.	Unless the O.C.RAID considers at an earlier time that he has done all that is necessary the main Raiding parties will withdraw on the signal of the O.C.RAID.

From "Zero" until "Cease fire" is ordered by O.C.1/6th Btn South Staffs Rgt the Artillery will continue to fire as ~~at zero~~ _per Artillery Programme_
The 137th M.G.Coy & 137th T.M.Bty will co-operate under orders from O.C.1/6th Btn South Staffs Rgt.
"CEASE FIRE" will be ordered by O.C.Btn through F.O.O's, who will inform Bde.
The Heavy & Divisional F.O.O's will be with the O.C.Btn at Advanced Trench Headquarters ~~from 9-45p.m.~~ _latter at 6.15 P.M._ _former at_

NOTE:- The Artillery will lay the necessary wires and test same. Spare instruments and alternative routes will be arranged for.

11. COUNTERSIGN.
O.C.RAID will arrange countersign on the day of operations.

12. WATCHES.
Watches will be synchronised at 4p.m. through Brigade.

13. WITHDRAWAL.
Signal for withdrawal will be given by O.C.RAID who will detail the exact method of withdrawal in his orders.

14. The second senior officers of "A" & "B" Parties will not enter the enemy trenches but report to O.C.RAID when their parties have entered the trenches. In the event of O.C.RAID becoming a casualty the senior of these officers will take Command.

15. MEDICAL ARRANGEMENTS will be communicated later. _to raiding party_

16. R.E.
The O.C.1/2nd Coy R.E. will arrange to find the necessary Ammonal tubes, and personnel to operate same, providing reserves of tubes & men. The O.C.1/2nd Coy R.E. will be at Advanced Btn Headquarters during the operations to advise the Battalion Commander on technical matters.

17. SILENCE.
The importance of absolute silence throughout the operation must be impressed on all ranks.

(Signed) H.HANFORD. Captain.
Adjutant 1/6th Btn South Staffordshire Regiment.

SEQUENCE OF EVENTS.
---oOo---

On arrival at Battalion Advanced Headquarters at 6p.m. I was informed by Lieut:Wilson 1/5th Btn South Staffs Regt that the enemy was already at work on his wire, and that he had given orders to turn a Lewis Gun on them. This was done and noise of work ceased. The advanced party arrived in good time and after arranging a code by which the Artillery could be put on to enemy working parties 2/Lieut:Shedden and 2/Lieut: Wallace with their Scouts went out at 6-30p.m. accompanied by 2/Lieut: Adams, two Lewis Guns with escort and a telephone.

At 7-10p.m. Lieut Adams reported O.K. and repeated the message at intervals up to 7-25p.m. when he asked for artillery on the gap. The F.O.O. got on to one of the Batteries and the first three rounds came over at 7-29p.m. During the last five minutes three calls came in from the front for artillery. In all some 15 rounds were fired by 7-35p.m. when 2/Lieut: Adams reported two or three German patrols out and asked for instructions. I ordered him to fire on patrols if 2/Lieuts Shedden and Wallace were clear.

At 7-40p.m. 2/Lieut: Adams reported "All quiet".

At 7-41p.m. he reported that 2/Lts Shedden & Wallace had gone forward.

At frequent intervals he reported "O.K." until 8-45p.m.

At 8-50p.m. 2/Lts Shedden and Wallace returned to Advanced Headquarters the former reporting that there was a narrow winding gap extending for some distance into the wire, and that in his opinion one long Amonal tube would complete the passage.

At 8-52 or 8-53p.m. I reported by code to Brigade that the operation would proceed.

At 8-58p.m. 2/Lt Adams again called for Artillery and 6 rounds were fired by 9.6. When he reported "All quiet".

In view of the activity of the enemy working parties and their alertness, it was agreed that the main parties should not go out until 9-45p.m. instead of 9-30p.m. as per programme. The tapes had been properly laid from our two points of exit and there was no object in having the men lying out too long.

2/Lieut: Adams regularly sent in "O.K." reports up to 10p.m.

At 10-4p.m. Captain Mander who had gone out with the main-parties with an independent telephone reported "All parties in position at junction of tapes".

Several "O.K." reports were received up to 10-14p.m. when a report came that Amonal Party had gone forward.

At 10-15p.m. the bombardment started, the Stokes Mortars getting in slightly in advance of time.

At 10-17p.m. "O.K." report received.

At 10-19p.m. a German Machine Gun swept our parapet. Enemy retaliation appeared to consist largely of trench mortar bombs.

10-20p.m. and 10-22p.m. "O.K."

At 10-23p.m. report came in "A" party gone forward.

At 10-24p.m. report "Machine Gun in big gap is firing". I informed Artillery and Stokes Mortars.

10-26p.m. "B" & "C" Parties gone forward.

10-27p.m. All "O.K." 10-29p.m. "O.K." 10-32p.m. "Men in trench, four fishes coming back towards us".

10-33p.m. "Two more coming".

At 10-35p.m. the first prisoner came into my dugout. In all 6 prisoners were brought in. Our casualties being 6 men wounded, one somewhat seriously.

The parties withdrew in good order on Captain Mander's signal, the covering parties remaining out until 11-15p.m.

Lieut: Colonel.

Commanding 1/6th Battn South Staffordshire Regiment.

27th October 1916.

To:- G.O.C.
137th Infantry Brigade.

I have the honour to report that the raid ordered by you for the night of October 25/26th 1916 was successfully carried out by the Raiding Party under Captain H.V.Mander, 6 German prisoners being captured, many casualties inflicted on the enemy, and much damage done to his dugouts and trenches.

The programme was adhered to as far as possible, the activity of the enemy wiring parties and patrols however interfering with the works of the scouting patrols and necessitating the Artillery being turned on the enemy wire on several occasions. In this connection the use of a forward telephone with the covering parties to scouting patrols proved invaluable, and in my opinion is much preferable to any other method of signalling back to Advanced Btn Headquarters.

The wire-cutting of the 2" Trench Mortars was disappointing owing to gun troubles and the sodden nature of the ground which made the mortar foundations unstable.

The work of the Artillery throughout was admirable and the failure to cut a complete gap was due to poor visibility during the period when wire cutting was in progress, also to the difficulty in observing the result of fire owing to the lie of the ground.

The firing of an amsonal tube to complete the gap was conducted at considerable risk by 2/Lieut: Thedden and an efficient squad of R.E's.

During the actual bombardment valuable work was done by the 137th T.M.Bty(Stokes), the 137th Machine Gun Coy, the 139th Machine Gun Coy, and the Lewis Guns of the 5th Btn South Staffordshire Regiment.

The success of the enterprise is largely due to the excellent reconnaissance work of 2/Lieut: Thedden and his patrol under very trying circumstances.

The behaviour of Officers and men was exemplary and in recommending certain officers and men for immediate recognition I again feel the difficulty in discriminating.

Attached to my report are my own notes on the sequence of events and the reports of Captain Mander, and his subordinate Commanders.

After careful consideration of the reports received I beg to recommend the following Officers, N.C.O's and men for immediate recognition.

2/LIEUT: J.A.THEDDEN. Who when in charge of one of the reconnoitring patrols which was twice checked by hostile patrols and wiring parties, succeeded in locating a gap which he successfully explored to within ten yards of the enemy parapet under the very nose of a sentry group whose presence he had detected. After reporting the presence of the gap to the O.C.Raid he again accompanied the advance party, took forward the R.E's with an Amsonal torpedo which was exploded whilst our bombardment was at its height only a few yards away. The success of the operation depended upon his being able to complete the partial gap

CAPTAIN H.V.MANDER. Who earned a Military Cross at NEUVILLE, has twice commanded successful raids by this Regiment, on September 2nd & October 25th. His careful training and management of officers and men resulted on each occasion in complete success. His attitude on both occasions inspired officers and men with confidence of success.

2/LIEUT: T.WALKER. When in the German trench he found that an artificial obstacle prevented the progress of his party. The parapet being blocked with Chevaux-de-frise, he took a party on the parados beyond the block, killed seven and captured two Germans. He then attempted to lead on his party to capture a Machine Gun, but was prevented by our barrage. This is the second occasion in which he has commanded a party in a successful raid.

No 2129 SGT WASHINGTON T.J. Who during the reconnaissance of the gap and the attack on the German trenches behaved with conspicuous gallantry, fearlessly entered dugouts and when his party was being hard pressed formed up a blocking party which effectually kept back a hostile bombing attack.

1.

2.

No 3184 CPL HALE E. Who was recommended by me for his conduct during the raid on 2nd September, showed utter fearlessness in entering dugouts and clearing them out. He also volunteered to go for a Machine Gun on the other side of our barrage.

No 5568 PTE(L'CPL)PALMER C. With his knowledge of German he was able to warn his party officer of an impending bombing attack by a party beyond an artificial block. He took part in the defeat of this party and protected with his bayonet his officer who had dropped his revolver in the struggle.

No 2619 SGT CRAMERIX R.C. Against considerable opposition he handled his party admirably. It was largely due to his courage and energy that the hostile bombing attack was effectively countered.

No 2079 L'CPL HIPKINS W. Personally accounted for two Germans. Behaved admirably throughout the operation.

No 5601 PTE LAMB E. Showed great coolness during the time the right block was hard pressed and helped greatly to hold the trench whilst the dugouts were being cleared.

                                                        Lieut: Colonel.

Commanding 1/6th Btn South Staffordshire Regiment.

27th October 1916.

Army Form C. 2118.

1/6th Battn South Staffs Regt.

WAR DIARY
or
INTELLIGENCE SUMMARY.
(Erase heading not required.)

Instructions regarding War Diaries and Intelligence Summaries are contained in F. S. Regs., Part II. and the Staff Manual respectively. Title pages will be prepared in manuscript.

6th S. Staffs.
Vol 22

Q 23

Place	Date	Hour	Summary of Events and Information	Remarks and references to Appendices
BONNIERES.	1-11-16.		Resting.	
-do-	2-11-16.	do	-do-	
BONNIERES.	3-11-16.		The Battalion marched to new billets at YVRENCHEUX.	
YVRENCHEUX.	4-11-16.		Cleaning of clothing & equipment. Bathing. Boot inspections.	
-do-	5-11-16.		Sunday.	
-do-	6-11-16.		Battalion Training.	
-do-	7-11-16.		ditto	
-do-	8-11-16.		ditto	
-do-	9-11-16.		Inspection by G.O.C. 137th Infantry Brigade.	
-do-	10-11-16.		Battalion Training. Night Operations.	
-do-	11-11-16.		The Battalion marched to ARGENVILLIERS after completing Battalion Training during the morning.	
ARGENVILLIERS.	12-11-16.		Sunday.	
-do-	13-11-16.		Battalion Training.	
-do-	14-11-16.		Battalion Training.	
-do-	15-11-16.		ditto	
-do-	16-11-16.		ditto	
-do-	17-11-16.		ditto Night Operations.	

1/6th Btn South Staffs Rgt. (101).

Army Form C. 2118.

WAR DIARY
or
INTELLIGENCE SUMMARY.
(Erase heading not required.)

G.S. Staff

Place	Date	Hour	Summary of Events and Information	Remarks and references to Appendices
ARGENVILLIERS.	18-11-16.		Battalion Training.	
-do-	19-11-16.		Battalion Parade for Medal Distribution by G.O.C. 46th Division.	
-do-	20-11-16.		Battalion Training.	
-do-	21-11-16.		ditto	
-do-	22-11-16.		The Battalion marched to new billets at CRAMONT-les-MASURES.	
CRAMONT-les-MASURES.	23-11-16.		The Battalion marched to new billets at MOEUX.	
MOEUX.	24-11-16.		Bathing. Cleaning of clothing & equipment.	
-do-	25-11-16.		The Battalion marched to new billets at LE SOUICH.	
LE SOUICH.	26-11-16.		Sunday.	
-do-	27-11-16.		Battalion Training.	
-do-	28-11-16.		Hurdle making at LUCHEUX.	
-do-	29-11-16.		Inspection by G.O.C. 137th Infantry Brigade.	
-do-	30-11-16.		Battalion Training.	
			CASUALTIES FOR MONTH :- Two men accidentally wounded.	
2-12-1916.				

Cecil Coprice
Major.
Commanding 1/6th Btn South Staffordshire Regiment.

Army Form C. 2118.

WAR DIARY
or
INTELLIGENCE SUMMARY.
(Erase heading not required.)

1/6th Bn South Staffordshire Regiment. (102)

Instructions regarding War Diaries and Intelligence Summaries are contained in F. S. Regs., Part II. and the Staff Manual respectively. Title pages will be prepared in manuscript.

6th S. Staffs Regt 46th Div Vol 23

Q24

Place	Date	Hour	Summary of Events and Information	Remarks and references to Appendices
LA SOUICH	1.12.16.		Inspection by the G.O.C.	
—do—	2.12.16.		Battalion Training.	
—do—	3.12.16.		SUNDAY.	
—do—	4.12.16.		Battalion Training.	
—do—	5.12.16.		—do—	
—do—	6.12.16.		The Battalion marched to POMMIER and went in to Brigade Reserve.	
POMMIER	7.12.16.		In Brigade Reserve. Battalion Training.	
—do—	8.12.16.		—do—	
—do—	9.12.16.		—do—	
—do—	10.12.16.		The Battalion relieved the 1/5th South Staffordshire Regiment in the Trenches, two Companies being in the front line system and two Companies in BIENVILLERS.	
BIEN-VILLERS	11-12-16.		Quiet Day.	
—do—	12.12.16.		Quiet Day.	
—do—	13.12.16.		Corps Heavy and Divisional Artillery, and Trench Mortar Batteries bombarded the enemy trenches and positions at MONCHY-AU-BOIS.	
—do—	14.12.16.		Quiet Day.	
—do—	15.12.16.		Battalion relieved in the Trenches by 1/5th South Staff's Regiment and proceeded into Divisional Reserve at ST AMAND.	

T./134. Wt. W708—776. 500000. 4/15. Sir J. C. & S.

Army Form C. 2118.

WAR DIARY
or
INTELLIGENCE SUMMARY. (103)

(Erase heading not required.)

1/6th.Btn South Staffordshire Regiment.

Instructions regarding War Diaries and Intelligence Summaries are contained in F.S. Regs., Part II. and the Staff Manual respectively. Title pages will be prepared in manuscript.

1/6 South Staff

Place	Date	Hour	Summary of Events and Information	Remarks and references to Appendices
ST AMAND.	16.12.16.		In Divisional Reserve.	
-do-	17.12.16.		-do-	
-do-	18.12.16.		-do-	
-do-	19.12.16.		Battalion relieved the 1/5th South Staffordshire Regiment in the Trenches.	
BIEN-VILLERS	20.12.16.		Quiet Day.	
-do-	21.12.16.		Quiet Day.	
-do-	22.12.16.		Quiet Day.	
-do-	23.12.16.		Battalion relieved in the Trenches by the 1/5th Battalion South Staffordshire Regiment, and proceeded into Brigade Reserve at POMMIER.	
POMMIER.	24.12.16.		In Brigade Reserve.	
-do-	25.12.16.		-do-	
-do-	26.12.16.		-do-	
-do-	27.12.16.		The Battalion relieved the 1/5th South Staffordshire Regiment in the Trenches.	
-do-	28.12.16.		Quiet Day.	
-do-	29.12.16.		Quiet Day.	
-do-	30.12.16.		Battalion relieved in the Trenches by 1/5th Battalion South Staffordshire Regiment and proceeded to Brigade Reserve at POMMIER.	
POMMIER.	31.12.16.		Battalion marched to ST AMAND and took up billets in Divisional Reserve.	

T.134. Wt. W708—776. 50C000. 4/15. Sir J. C. & S.

Army Form C. 2118.

WAR DIARY
or
INTELLIGENCE SUMMARY.

(Erase heading not required.)

1/6th Btn South Staffordshire Regiment.

Instructions regarding War Diaries and Intelligence Summaries are contained in F.S. Regs., Part II. and the Staff Manual respectively. Title pages will be prepared in manuscript.

Place	Date	Hour	Summary of Events and Information	Remarks and references to Appendices

TOTAL CASUALTIES FOR MONTH OF DECEMBER 1916.

Officers.

    Killed — 2/Lieut: W.LOGAN.(5h Btn Cameronians$ S.Rifles.)

    Wounded — 2/Lieut: S.W.EDWARDS. (5th South Staffs Regt.)
                2/Lieut: J.L.C.S.WALLACE. (5th Btn K.O.S.B.)

Other Ranks.

    Killed — 2.

    Wounded — 15.

    Died of Wounds — 2.

Lieut-Colonel,

Commanding 1/6th Battalion South Staffordshire Regiment.

Army Form C. 2118.

WAR DIARY (105)
or
INTELLIGENCE SUMMARY.
(Erase heading not required.)

1/6th Btn South Staffordshire Regiment.

Instructions regarding War Diaries and Intelligence Summaries are contained in F.S. Regs., Part II. and the Staff Manual respectively. Title pages will be prepared in manuscript.

Vol 24

Q25

Place	Date	Hour	Summary of Events and Information	Remarks and references to Appendices
ST AMAND	1.1.17.		In Divisional Reserve.	Mis In pt
—do—	2.1.17.		—do—	
BIEN-VILLERS	3.1.17.		Battalion proceeded to the Trenches and relieved the 1/5th Battalion South Staffordshire Regiment.	
—do—	4.1.17.		Quiet Day.	
—do—	5.1.17.		Quiet Day.	
—do—	6.1.17.		Quiet Day.	
—do—	7.1.17.		Battalion relieved in the Trenches by the 1/5th South Staffordshire Regiment, and proceeded to Brigade Reserve at POMMIER.	
POMMIER	8.1.17.		In Brigade Reserve.	
—do—	9.1.17.		—do—	
—do—	10.1.17.		—do—	
—do—	11.1.17.		Battalion relieved the 1/5th Battalion South Staffordshire Regiment in Local Reserve in BIENVILLERS-AU-BOIS.	
BIEN-VILLERS	12.1.17		In Local Reserve.	
—do—	13.1.17.		Battalion relieved the 1/6th Battalion North Staffordshire Regiment in the Trenches.	
—do—	14.1.17.		Quiet Day.	
—do—	15.1.17.		Quiet Day.	
—do—	16.1.17.		Battalion relieved in the trenches by the 1/5th Battalion North Staffordshire Regiment, and proceeded to Divisional Reserve at ST AMAND.	

Army Form C. 2118.

WAR DIARY
or
INTELLIGENCE SUMMARY.
(Erase heading not required.)

1/6th Battalion South Staffordshire Regiment.

*Instructions regarding War Diaries and Intelligence Summaries are contained in F. S. Regs., Part II. and the Staff Manual respectively. Title pages will be prepared in manuscript.

Place	Date	Hour	Summary of Events and Information	Remarks and references to Appendices
ST AMAND.	17.1.17.		In Divisional Reserve.	
-do-	18.1.17.		-do-	
-do-	19.1.17.		-do-	
-do-	20.1.17.		Battalion relieved the 1/5th Battalion South Staffordshire Regt in the trenches at BIENVILLERS-AU-BOIS.	
BIENVILLERS AU-BOIS.	21.1.17.		Quiet Day.	
-do-	22.1.17.		Battalion relieved Bn in the trenches by 1/5th Battalion North Staffordshire Regiment and proceeded to Local Reserve at BIENVILLERS-AU-BOIS.	
-do-	23.1.17.		In Local Reserve.	
-do-	24.1.17.		Battalion relieved by the 1/5th Battalion North Staffordshire Regiment and proceeded to Brigade Reserve at POMMIER.	
POMMIER.	25.1.17.		In Brigade Reserve.	
-do-	26.1.17.		-do-	
-do-	27.1.17.		-do-	
-do-	28.1.17.		Battalion relieved the 1/5th Battalion South Staffordshire Regt in Local Reserve at BIENVILLERS-AU-BOIS.	
BIENVILLERS AU-BOIS.	29.1.17.		In Local Reserve.	
-do-	30.1.17.		Battalion relieved the 1/6th Battalion North Staffordshire Regt in the trenches.	
-do-	31.1.17.		Quiet Day.	

T2134. Wt. W708-776. 500000. 4/15. Sir J. C. & S.

Army Form C. 2118.

1/6th Battalion South Staffordshire Regiment.

WAR DIARY (107)

or

INTELLIGENCE SUMMARY.

(Erase heading not required.)

Instructions regarding War Diaries and Intelligence Summaries are contained in F. S. Regs., Part II. and the Staff Manual respectively. Title pages will be prepared in manuscript.

Place	Date	Hour	Summary of Events and Information	Remarks and references to Appendices
			Total Casualties for Month of January 1917.	
			Other Ranks.	
			Killed 1.	
			Wounded 8.	
			Wounded (At Duty) 1.	
			J. J. _____	
			Lieut-Colonel.	
			Commanding 1/6th Battalion South Staffordshire Regiment.	

Army Form C. 2118.

(108)
WAR DIARY
or
INTELLIGENCE SUMMARY
(Erase heading not required.)

1/6th Btn South Staffordshire Regiment.

16th South Staff Regt 46 Div.

Vol 25

46. Div.

Q26

Instructions regarding War Diaries and Intelligence Summaries are contained in F.S. Regs., Part II and the Staff Manual respectively. Title Pages will be prepared in manuscript.

Place	Date	Hour	Summary of Events and Information	Remarks and references to Appendices
ST AMAND.	1-2-17		In Divisional Reserve.	
"	2-2-17		--do--	
POMMIER.	3-2-17.		The Battalion moved from Divisional Reserve at ST AMAND to Divisional Reserve at POMMIER.	
"	4-2-17.		Battalion Training. (Attack practices).	
"	5-2-17.		--ditto--	
"	6-2-17.		The Battalion relieved the 1/5th Btn South Staffs Regt in the trenches.	
BERLES-AU-BOIS.	7-2-17.		Quiet day.	
"	8-2-17.		Trench Mortar activity by enemy.	
"	9-2-17.		Battalion relieved in the trenches by the 1/5th Btn South Staffordshire Regt, and proceeded into Brigade Reserve, having two Companies in Berles-Au-Bois, and two Companies in Bienvillers, with Btn Headquarters at Berles-Au-Bois.	
BERLES-AU-BOIS.	10-2-17.		In Brigade Reserve.	
"	11-2-17.		--ditto--	
"	12-2-17.		--ditto-- until after dinners, when the Battalion relieved the 1/5th Btn South Staffs Regt in the trenches, with 2 Coys 2/7th London Regt attached for instruction.	
"	13-2-17.		2 Coys of 2/7th London Regt relieved in the trenches and went to BERLES-AU-BOIS. Quiet day except for trench mortaring by enemy.	

2449 Wt. W14957/M90 750,000 1/16 J.B.C. & A. Forms/C.2118/12.

1/6th Btn South Staffs Regt.

Army Form C. 2118.

WAR DIARY
INTELLIGENCE SUMMARY

(Erase heading not required.)

16th South Staffs Regt
46 Div

Place	Date	Hour	Summary of Events and Information	Remarks and references to Appendices
BERLES-AU-BOIS.	13-2-17. (Contd).		Headquarters and two Companies of the 2/9th London Regt attached to the Battalion for training in the line.	
"	14-2-17.		Quiet day.	
"	15-2-17.		The Battalion relieved in the trenches by the 1/5th Btn South Staffordshire Regt and proceeded into Div: Reserve at POMMIER.	
POMMIER.	16-2-17.		In Divisional Reserve. Battalion Training "The Attack".	
"	17-2-17.		" " " " " "	
"	18-2-17.		The Battalion relieved the 1/5th Btn South Staffs Regt. in the trenches.	
BERLES-AU-BOIS.	19-2-17.		Heavy T.M.Bombardment by enemy at 5-30p.m.and again at 7-30p.m. Our 18pdrs and 4.5 Hows retaliated.	
"	20-2-17.		Quiet day.	
"	21-2-17.		Battalion relieved in the trenches by the 1/6th Btn South Staffordshire Regiment,and proceeded into Brigade Reserve, having Headquarters and two Coys at BERLES and two Coys at Bienvillers.	
"	22-2-17.		In Brigade Reserve.	
"	23-2-17.		--ditto--	
"	24-2-17.		The Battalion relieved the 1/5th Btn South Staffordshire Rgt in the Trenches.	
"	25-2-17.		Quiet day.	

Army Form C. 2118.

6th South Staff Rgt
46 Division

WAR DIARY
or
INTELLIGENCE SUMMARY
(Erase heading not required.)

1/6 Btn South Staffs Regt.

Instructions regarding War Diaries and Intelligence Summaries are contained in F.S. Regs., Part II. and the Staff Manual respectively. Title Pages will be prepared in manuscript.

Place	Date	Hour	Summary of Events and Information	Remarks and references to Appendices
BERLES-AU-BOIS.	26-2-17.		The enemy appeared to suspect a relief in our Sector, and Bombarded NEWARK ST: FISH STREET: NUTTS LANE & NOODLES AVENUE from noon to 4p.m.	
"	27-2-17.		The Battalion was relieved in the trenches by the 1/5th Btn South Staffs Regiment, and proceeded into Divisional Reserve at POMMIER.	
"	28-2-17.		In Divisional Reserve. Battalion Training.	

—oOo—

CASUALTIES FOR MONTH of FEBRUARY 1917.

Officers.   2/Lieut: D.N.GORDON.   Killed.
            Captain E.W.PAGE.   Wounded.

O'Ranks.   Killed   3
            Wounded.   8
            Died of wounds.   1

—oOo—

D.J. Downing Lieut:Colonel.
Commanding 1/6th Btn South Staffordshire Regiment.
3-3-1917.

Army Form C. 2118.

WAR DIARY
or
INTELLIGENCE SUMMARY.
(Erase heading not required.)

1/6th Btn South Staffordshire Regiment. (111).

Vol 26
Q 27

Place	Date	Hour	Summary of Events and Information	Remarks and references to Appendices
POMMIER	1.3.17.		In Divisional Reserve. Battalion Training.	
"	2.3.17.		Battalion relieved the 1/5th Battalion South Staffordshire Regiment in the Trenches. Enemy shelled transport route at night.	
BERLES-AU-BOIS.	3.3.17.		Quiet Day. Enemy bombarded the Ravine with lachrymatory shells during the evening.	
"	4.3.17		Quiet Day.	
"	5.3.17		Battalion relieved in the trenches during the afternoon by the 2/7th Battalion London Regiment, and proceeded into Divisional Reserve at POMMIER. Enemy shelled NOBS WALK and BERLES-AU-BOIS during relief.	
POMMIER	6.3.17		In Divisional Reserve.	
"	7.3.17		Battalion moved into Rest Billets at POMMERA.	
POMMERA	8.3.17		Battalion Training.	
"	9.3.17		-do-	
"	10.3.17		-do-	
"	11.3.17		Battalion moved to new billets at BAYENCOURT.	
BAYENCOURT	12.3.17		Battalion Training.	
"	13.3.17		Battalion moved to BIEZ WOOD in reserve to 1/5th Battalion South Staffordshire Regiment for attack on BUCQUOY.	
BIEZ WOOD	14.3.17		Battalion relieved and returned to Rest Billets at BAYENCOURT.	
BAYENCOURT	15.3.17		Battalion resting.	

Army Form C. 2118

1/6th Btn South Staffordshire Regiment.

(112) **WAR DIARY** or **INTELLIGENCE SUMMARY**.

(Erase heading not required.)

Instructions regarding War Diaries and Intelligence Summaries are contained in F. S. Regs., Part II. and the Staff Manual respectively. Title pages will be prepared in manuscript.

Place	Date	Hour	Summary of Events and Information	Remarks and references to Appendices
BAYENCOURT	16.3.17.		Battalion Training.	
"	17.3.17		-do-	
"	18.3.17		The Battalion relieved the 5th Corps Mounted Troops in the HANNESCAMP SECTOR during the afternoon, and found them in the act of pursuing the Germans who had evacuated their positions. Two companies were pushed forward and formed an Outpost Line, 1½ miles in rear of the original German front line. Patrols pushed forward but were unable to get in touch with the enemy. At 10 pm instructions were received for the Battalion to stand fast as it was being squeezed out by two converging Divisions.	
HANNESCAMPS	19.3.17.		Battalion withdrawn to HANNESCAMPS and carried out salvage work in our own trenches, and clearing of barricades on roads	
"	20.3.17.		Battalion continued salving operations, and cleaning roads.	
"	21.3.17.		-ditto-	
"	22.3.17.		-ditto-	
"	23.3.17		Battalion marched to BUS-EN-ARTOIS, & took up billets there.	
BUS-EN-ARTOIS	24.3.17		Battalion marched to CONTAY and took up billets there.	
CONTAY	25.3.17.		Battalion marched to BERTANGLES and took up billets there.	
BERTANGLES	26.3.17.		The Battalion embussed on the AMIENS Road and was conveyed to SALEUX, to take up billets at BOVELLES. Instructions were received en route that billets at latter place were not available and that the Battalion would be billeted at SALEUX. Billets at SALEUX not being obtainable the Battalion march/to DURY and took up billets there arriving at 11 pm.	

Army Form C. 2118.

1/6th Btn South Staffordshire Regiment. (213) WAR DIARY or INTELLIGENCE SUMMARY.

Instructions regarding War Diaries and Intelligence Summaries are contained in F. S. Regs., Part II. and the Staff Manual respectively. Title pages will be prepared in manuscript.

(Erase heading not required.)

Place	Date	Hour	Summary of Events and Information	Remarks and references to Appendices
DURY.	27.3.17.		Battalion resting.	
"	28.3.17.		Battalion entrained at SALEUX Station at 11.30 pm.	
"	29.3.17.		Battalion de-trained at LILLERS and marched to LESPRESSES and billeted there.	
LESPRESSES	30.3.17.		Battalion Training.	
"	31.3.17.		Battalion marched to AUCHY-AU-BOIS and took up billets there.	

TOTAL CASUALTIES FOR MONTH OF MARCH 1917.

Officers   nil.

Other Ranks. Wounded   4.
" (Gassed) 1.
" (Gassed - At duty) 1.
Died of Wounds 1.

A. Raymond Capel(?)
Lieut-Colonel,
Commanding, 1/6th Battalion South Staffordshire Regiment.

(114).
WAR DIARY
or
INTELLIGENCE SUMMARY.
(Erase heading not required.)

Army Form C. 2118.

1/6th Bn. South Staffs Regt.

Instructions regarding War Diaries and Intelligence Summaries are contained in F. S. Regs., Part II. and the Staff Manual respectively. Title pages will be prepared in manuscript.

1/6 S Staffs Rgt
QP 27
Q 28

Place	Date	Hour	Summary of Events and Information	Remarks and references to Appendices
AUCHY- AU-BOIS	1-4-17.		Battalion Training.	
"	2-4-17.		—ditto—	
"	3-4-17.		—ditto—	Inspection of "A" & "D" Companies by the Commanding Officer.
"	4-4-17.		—ditto—	Inspection of the Battalion by the Commanding Officer.
"	5-4-17.		Brigade Route March.	
"	6-4-17.		Battalion Training.	
"	7-4-17.		—ditto—	
"	8-4-17.		EASTER-DAY. Divisional	
"	9-4-17.		Brigade Route March (See O.O. No 1 attached).	
"	10-4-17.		Battalion Training.	
"	11-4-17.		—ditto—	
"	12-4-17.		The Battalion marched to new billets at BARHUN. (see O.O. No 2 attached).	
BARHUN	13-4-17.		Battalion at disposal of Company Commanders.	
"	14-4-17.		Battalion Training.	
"	15-4-17.		Battalion Kit Inspection by the Commanding Officer.	
"	16-4-17.		Battalion Training.	

Army Form C. 2118.

No. 10 Bn South Staff Regt

115.

WAR DIARY or INTELLIGENCE SUMMARY.

Place	Date	Hour	Summary of Events and Information	Remarks and references to Appendices
Bethune	17.4.17		Battalion Training.	
"	18.4.17		Battalion Route March. Repeated but cancelled owing to Operations. (See Operation Orders. No. 4 attached).	
Lewis	18.4.17		Operations: The Battalion relieved the 3rd Battn the Rifle Brigade (24th Division) in support in "ZIE" Line	
	19.4.17		Relief of 1st Royal Fusiliers by the Bn. 1st S. Staff Regt. (in the line) (See Operation Orders. No 5. attached).	
"	20.4.17		Battalion holding the "line". This consisted of 2 OP Coys in Outposts among the houses, with two Coys back in a well defined line with two strong posts in it. This latter position well known to the enemy who shelled it very accurately, frequently. The posts were not quite so well spotted but were nevertheless possible heavily though somewhat indiscriminately.	
	21.4.17		As above; patrols sent out but no special incidents occurred.	
	22.4.17		During the afternoon orders were received that the position vacated by our right would be attacked by the NOTTS & DERBIES operating at 9.0 till (6.5) communic during the period in our front, well wired + entrenched. It was assumed that if their attack succeeded, the enemy would abandon his position in our front, in front of LENS, + we were ordered out from patrols to ascertain this, occupy his trenches if possible. During the night, 5 ops reported to have been out, were examined by small patrols + only one gap found.	

Place	Date	Hour	Summary of Events and Information	Remarks and references to Appendices
LIEVIN	23.4.17	4.45AM	This fring ZERO hour, fighting patrols of two sections each under an officer supported by the remainder of the platoon. Unfortunately the attack on the ght strong points CENOTTS & BOOIES were preceded in getting in, was not successful & our patrols, were heavily fired on by the enemy & had to withdraw. 2'Lieut Jopham was killed & 2 other Ranks, whilst 4 O.R. were wounded. The Patrols were withdrawn very skilfully under difficult conditions. 2' Lieut Bullock, Sergt Cox, Pte LITTLE, JONES, & Pte Holmes were recommended for gallantry.	

Army Form C. 2118.

WAR DIARY
or
INTELLIGENCE SUMMARY.
(Erase heading not required.)

Instructions regarding War Diaries and Intelligence Summaries are contained in F. S. Regs., Part II and the Staff Manual respectively. Title pages will be prepared in manuscript.

Place	Date	Hour	Summary of Events and Information	Remarks and references to Appendices
Fenin	23.4.17		The Battalion was relieved in the trenches by the 7th Bn Israel Staff. Regt. (See Operation Orders).	
Fenin	24.4.17		The Bn marched to Rest Billets at Saine-en-Gohelle.	
Saine-en-Gohelle	25.4.17		Inspections at disposal of Company Commanders.	
do.	26.4.17		— ditto —	
do.	27.4.17		Battalion Training	
do.	28.4.17		— ditto — Lt Colonel F.J. Young DSO returned from 3 weeks sick leave at GT MARTIN	
do.	29.4.17		Sunday. Service by Major HALES. Sermon by the Bishop of KHARTOUM.	
do.	30.4.17		Battalion relieved the 6th Bn North Stanley Regt. in Brigade Reserve. (See Operation Orders No. 9 attached).	

WAR DIARY or INTELLIGENCE SUMMARY

Army Form C. 2118.

1/4th Bn North Staff Regt. (17)

Summary of Events and Information

Total casualties for month of April 1917:-

Officers: 2/Lieut: H.J. Stephens — Killed.

Other ranks —
- Killed. 1
- Wounded. 29.
- Wounded at duty. 3.
- Missing. 1.

H. Stratford Ansley
Major for Lt Colonel.
Comdg 1/4th Bn North Staff Regt.

3/5/17

OPERATION ORDERS No. 1.   Copy No. 7
                           by
                      MAJOR R. EVANS,
           Commanding, 1/6th Battalion South Staffordshire Regiment.

                        Sunday, 8.4.1917.

Reference:- HAZEBROUCK Map, 1/100,000.

1. The Battalion will take part in a Brigade Route March on Monday, 9th April 1917.

2. ORDER OF MARCH. Order of March will be:- Brigade H.Q. & Signal Section, 1/6th South Staffs Regt - 230th Field Artillery Brigade - 137th Machine Gun Coy - 137th Trench Mortar Battery - 1/5th North Staffs - etc.

3. STARTING POINT. The Starting Point for the Battalion will be CROSS ROADS, Northern Exit of AUCHY.

4. TIME. Pass Starting Point at 10.8 a.m. There will be a half hours halt from 11.50 a.m. to 12.20 p.m.

5. ASSEMBLY POINT. The Battalion will assemble South of Starting Point and of the WESTRHEM - AUCHY Road.

6. BATTALION ORDER OF MARCH. Signallers - "D" Co. - "A" Co. - Drums - "B" Co. - "C" Co. - Transport Echelon "A".
Transport Echelon "B", less 2 limbers, will be Brigaded under the Brigade Transport Officer

7. ROUTE. On arrival at ESTRIE BLANCHE the 230th Field Artillery Brigade will march back to billets via Road on North side of River. Remainder of 137th Brigade Group will march back to billets via LOMGREM - LINGHEM - ST HILAIRE.

8. REPORTS to head of column.

9. RATIONS. Haversack rations will be carried.

10. The Battalion and Transport will assemble at 9.50 a.m. Transport of Echelon "A" will assemble on the Orderly Room Road with the head up to the AUCHY - RELY Road at 9.50 a.m.
Transport Echelon "B" will assemble on the AUCHY - RELY Road with head at Cross Roads Northern exit of AUCHY at 10.45 a.m. and will join in with the column under Brigade Transport Officer in same order as their Battalion.

11. DRESS. Marching Order - Steel Helmets will be worn. Transport will be packed.

12. Acknowledge.

                              (Signed) H. BARFORD. Captain,
              Adjutant, 1/6th Battalion South Staffordshire Regiment.

    Issued to Commanding Officer   No 1. Copy.
       "   " Adjutant   " 2.   "
       "   " O/C, "A" Company   " 3.   "
       "   " O/C, "B"   "   " 4.   "
       "   " O/C, "C"   "   " 5.   "
       "   " O/C, "D"   "   " 6.   "
       "   " Transport Officer   " 7.   "
       "   " Quartermaster   " 8.   "
       "   " War Diary   " 9.   "

BATTALION

Copy No. 8

OPERATION ORDERS NO. 2
BY
MAJOR R. EVANS
Commanding 1/6th Battalion South Staffordshire Regiment.

Reference:- HAZEBROUCK 5A 1/100,000

1. **MOVE** — The Battalion will move to new billets in BETHUNE tomorrow.

2. STARTING POINT — Cross Roads — Northern Exit of AUCHY.

3. TIME — Battalion will pass the Starting Point at 9.15 a.m.

4. INTERVAL — An interval of 500 yards to be maintained between Battalions.

5. TRANSPORT — The transport will accompany the Column. Lewis Gun Hand-Carts will march in the rear of the Battalion.

6. ORDER OF MARCH — "C", "D", DRUMS, "B", "A".

7. BLANKETS — Blankets will be stacked at the Quartermaster's Stores by 7.45 a.m.

8. OFFICERS' VALISES — Officers' Valises will be stacked at the Quartermaster's Stores by 8 a.m.

9. MESS BASKETS — Officers' mess baskets will be loaded at the following times and places:-
   Headquarters, "B" & "C" Companies at Headquarter Mess at 8 a.m.
   "A" & "D" Companies at the Quartermaster's Stores at 8.30 am

10. PARADE — The Battalion will parade at 9.10 a.m. HEAD OF COLUMN — Cross Roads — N exit of AUCHY.

11. DRESS — Full Marching Order — Steel Helmets will be worn — Box Respirators and Smoke Helmets will be carried on the person.

12. BILLETING PARTY. — All Company Q. M. Sergeants and Corporal Bradley will report to 2/Lieut: WOOD at Orderly Room at 8.30 a.m. This Party will report to the Staff Captain at 10.30 a.m at point where Railway crosses the main CHOQUES-BETHUNE ROAD just South of HU in VENDIN-LEZ-BETHUNE. Bicycles will be provided at Orderly Room.

13. CERTIFICATES — Certificates re Cleanliness of Billets and Damage to Billets to be handed to the Adjutant on parade.

14. DINNERS — Dinners will be served en route.

15. LOADING OF LEWIS GUN LIMBERS — Three limbers will report to "A", "B" & "D" Companies respectively at 7 a.m — Lewis Gunners will have all their Guns and Stores in the street ready to load at this hour. One L. G.N.C.O will accompany each limber and will not leave it until it is unloaded in the new billets.
   Three horses report to "C" Company at 8.15 a.m to draw the hand-carts. These hand-carts will be ready loaded in the street at this hour.

16. ACKNOWLEDGE.

(Signed) H. HANFORD, Captain,
Adjutant, 1/6th Battalion, South Staffordshire Regiment.

11th April, 1917.

Copy 1 — A Co   Copy No 2 — B Co   Copy No 5 — Q.M.   Copy 4 — H.Q.
" 3 — C "   " 4 — D   " 6 — T.O.   " 8 "

OPERATION ORDERS No 4,
by
MAJOR R. EVANS,
Commanding, 1/6th Battalion South Staffordshire Regt.

Copy No 8

Wednesday, 18th April 1917.

1. MOVE. The Battalion will move to-day to LIEVIN.

2. PARADE. The Battalion will Parade in the Road outside the Tobacco Factory, head of Column facing S.E., at E.18.a.5.5. at 4.15 p.m.
Order of March:- Signallers, "D" - "A" - "B" - "C".

3. ROUTE. Via BEUVRY - SAILLY LA BOURSE to G.20.a.3.2. thence South to GRENAY, where Guides will meet the Battalion at 7.30 pm. From SAILLY LA BOURSE movement will be by Companies and from G.20.a.3.2. by Platoons.

4. WATCHES. Watches will be synchronised at Orderly Room at 3.0 p.m. and halts observed independently. After dark connecting files will be maintained between units, and care must be taken not to loose touch at the halts.

5. VALISES & BLANKETS, MESS KITS. Officers valises will be delivered to the Q.M.Stores by 2.0 p.m.
Officers Mess Kits will be at the Q.M.Stores at 3.15 p.m. Blankets will/neatly rolled in bundles of tens and taken to the Cooks Shed, in Barrack Yard, at 12.30 p.m.

6. TEA. Tea will be served at 3.0 p.m.

7. TRANSPORT. Transport will accompany the Battalion.

8. CERTIFICATES & CLEANING OF BILLETS. Officers Commanding Companies will render to Orderly Room at 3.0 p.m. certificates re Damage to Billets. They will see that billets etc are left clean.
O/C, "D" Company will detail a party to pay special attention to the cleanliness of the Barrack Yard.

9. STORES. Care must be exercised in taking over all stores, specially regarding Pack Saddlery and Gum-boots. Transport Officer will see that all Pack Saddlery is complete.

10. ACKNOWLEDGE, at once.

(Signed) H. HANFORD. Captain,
Adjutant, 1/6th Battalion South Staffordshire Regiment.

Issued at 11.5 a.m.

```
Copy No  1 issued to Commanding Officer.
  "    2    "     "  O/C, "A" Company.
  "    3    "     "   "    "B"    "
  "    4    "     "   "    "C"    "
  "    5    "     "   "    "D"    "
  "    6    "     "  Transport Officer.
  "    7    "     "  Quartermaster.
  "    8    "     "  Orderly Room.
  "    9    "     "  War Diary.
```

OPERATION ORDERS NO 5.   Copy.
by   No 6.
MAJOR R.EVANS.
Commanding 1/6th Btn South Staffordshire Regiment.
Dated 19-4-1917.

1. The Battalion will relieve the 1st Royal Fusiliers in the trenches tonight.

2. "A" Company will relieve their "A" Company in the Right forward trenches.
"B" Company will relieve their "C" Company in the Left forward trenches.
"C" Company will relieve their "D" Company in the Right Support Trench.
"D" Company will relieve their "B" Company in the Left Support Trench.

3. One guide per Platoon will be at the 1st R.Fusiliers Btn H.Q. at 8p.m.

4. Lewis Gunners will carry 6 panniers per Gun.

5. Packs will be stored under Company arrangements. Great-coats may be taken.

6. Rations will be issued if received in time. If not the Support Coys ("C" & "D") will leave 25 men per Company to carry rations from ROLLINCOURT to BTN HEADQUARTERS, and thence to the Line. Support Companies are responsible for the rations of Companies in the Line.

7. Water-Bottles will be filled.

8. Acknowledge.

(Signed) H.HANFORD. Captain.
Adjutant 1/6th Btn South Staffordshire Regiment.

Copies issued to:-
No 1.   "A" Company.
No 2.   "B"   "
No 3.   "C"   "
No 4.   "D"   "
No 5.   Commanding Officer.1/6th S.Staffs Rgt.
No 6.   War Diary.
No 7.   O/C. 1st Btn Royal Fusiliers.

OPERATION ORDERS NO 8.   Copy No 7.
by
MAJOR R.EVANS.
Commanding 1/6th Btn South Staffs Regiment.

Dated 23-4-1917.

1. RELIEF.   The 1/5th Btn South Staffs Regt will relieve the 1/6th
Btn South Staffs Regt in the trenches tonight.
"A" & "D" Coys will send one guide for each Platoon, to
be at Battalion Headquarters at 7p.m.
"B" Coy will send 2 guides to Btn H.Q. at 7p.m. and two
guides to the 2 Platoons of "B" Coy of 1/5th Btn South
Staffs Regt, at present in Reserve to "B" Coy.

"B" Company 1/5th South Staffs will relieve "B" Coy.) 1/6th
"D"   "   "   "   "   "   "   "D" ") South
) Staffs.

All water tins will be handed over on relief and a
separate receipt taken, this receipt to be handed to the
Adjutant tonight. A list of Stores handed over to be
sent to Orderly Room tonight.
"C" Coy will return to Orderly Room all long-handled wire
cutters sent to them yesterday.

Lewis Gunners will bring their Lewis Gun magazines back
with them

Bombs and rifle grenades at present on the men will be
handed over on relief.

O/C Companies will report personally to Headquarters that
relief is complete.

The Battalion will return to same billets in LIEVIN as
occupied before going into the trenches.

The Battalion will move to SAINS-EN-GOHELLE tomorrow
night. Orders will be issued regarding the move later.

2. ACKNOWLEDGE.

(Signed) H.HANFORD.Captain.
Adjutant 1/6th Btn South Staffs Regiment.

Copies issued to:-
No 1.   Commanding Officer.1/6th Btn S.Staffs Rgt.
No 2.   O/C. "A" Coy.
 " 3.   "   "B" "
 " 4.   "   "C" "
 " 5.   "   "D" "
 " 6.   "   1/5th Btn South Staffs Regt.
 " 7.   War Diary.

OPERATION ORDERS No 9.   Copy No...... 6
by
LIEUT:COLONEL F.J.TRUMP. D.S.O.
Commanding 1/6th Btn South Staffordshire Regt.

SUNDAY. 29th April 1917.

1. **ROUTINE.**
Reveille	6-30a.m.
Breakfast	7-0 a.m.
Sick Parade	8-0 a.m.
Orderly Room	12 noon.

   GUARD. "A" Company will detail 1 N.C.O.(full rank) 3 men and 1 Drummer for Battalion Guard to mount on arrival at Trench H.Q.

   ORDERLY OFFICER FOR TOMORROW:- 2/Lieut:L.J.SHELTON.
   ORDERLY SERGEANT FOR TOMORROW:- C.S.M.Dangerfield J.

2. **MOVE.** Reference Map Sheet 36B & 36C. 1/40,000.

   The Battalion will relieve the 6th Btn Notts & Derby Regt in BRIGADE RESERVE tomorrow afternoon.

3. **PARADE AND STARTING POINT.** The Battalion will move by Platoons at 5 minutes intervals, commencing at 4p.m.
   Starting Point:- R3.c.20.60.

4. **ORDER OF MARCH.**   "H.Q" "A" "D" "C" "B".

5. **ROUTE.** R3.c.20.60. via AIX-NOULETTE to Road Junction R29.d.60.50. to M26.d.8.2.
   Guides will be at Road Junction M26.d.8.2. at 5-30p.m. (Entrance to ANGRES).

6. **DRESS.** Full Marching Order.

7. **BLANKETS** to be at the Quartermaster's Stores by 10a.m.
   OFFICERS VALISES " " " " " " 12 noon.
   MESS BASKETS required for the Trenches to be at the Q.M.Stores at 1-45pm
   The remainder of the MESS STUFF to be at the Q.M.Stores at 3p.m.

8. **LEWIS GUNS.** will be loaded at the Q.M.Stores at 1p.m. Two Lewis Gunners to accompany each Limber. Remainder of Lewis Gunners will march with their Companies.

9. **BTN H.Q.** Will close here at 4p.m. and re-open at RED MILL on arrival.

10. **TRANSPORT.** Transport and Rations will leave here at 2p.m. C.Q.M.Sgts and Cooks will accompany it.

11. **COOKING UTENSILS.** Cooking Utensils will not be taken to the trenches.

12. **DAILY SICK PARADE.** Sick Parade whilst in the Trenches will be at 11a.m. daily.

13. **TRAINING FOR TOMORROW MORNING.** Companies are at the disposal of Company Commanders during the morning.

14. **ACKNOWLEDGE.**

(Signed)   H.HANFORD. Captain.
Adjutant 1/6th Btn South Staffordshire Regiment.

Copies issued to:-
No 1. O/C. "A" Company.
No 2. "   "B"   "
No 3. "   "C"   "
No 4. "   "D"   "
No 5. "   1/6th Btn South Staffs Rgt.
No 6 War Diary.
No 7 Transport Officer.
No 8 Quartermaster.

Army Form C. 2118.

WAR DIARY
or
INTELLIGENCE SUMMARY.
(Erase heading not required.)

1/6th Btn South Staffordshire Regt. (118)

Instructions regarding War Diaries and Intelligence Summaries are contained in F.S. Regs., Part II. and the Staff Manual respectively. Title pages will be prepared in manuscript.

Sheet 1   Vol 28   Q29

Place	Date	Hour	Summary of Events and Information	Remarks and references to Appendices
RED MILL. ANGRES.	1-5-17.		In Brigade Reserve.	
	2-5-17.		-do-	
	3-5-17.		-do-	
	4-5-17.		The Battalion relieved the 1/6th Btn North Staffs Regt in the Trenches.(See Operation Orders No 10 dated 3-5-17.attached).	
	5-5-17.		Quiet day.	
	6-5-17.		Quiet day.	
	7-5-17.		Quiet during day. Enemy bombarded Battalion Headquarters and areas in rear with Gas Shells during the evening	
	8-5-17.		The 1/6th Btn North Staffs Regt relieved the Battalion in the Trenches (See Operation Orders No 11.dated 7-5-17.attached), the latter Btn going into Brigade Reserve, with Headquarters in the RED MILL, ANGRES.	
ANGRES.	9-5-17.		In Brigade Reserve.	
	10-5-17.		-do-	
	11-5-17.		-do-	
	12-5-17.		The Battalion being relieved by the 5th Btn Leicester Rgt, proceeded to SAINS-EN-GOHELLE (Divisional Reserve). See Operation Orders No 12.dated 11-5-17.attached).	
SAINS-EN-GOHELLE.	13-5-17.		Bathing and cleaning of clothing and equipment.	

WAR DIARY or INTELLIGENCE SUMMARY

Army Form C. 2118.

1/6th Btn South Staffs Regt. (119).

Place	Date	Hour	Summary of Events and Information	Remarks and references to Appendices
SAINS-EN-GOHELLE.	14-5-17.		Rifle & Kit Inspections. Specialists training under Specialist Officers.	
"	15-5-17.		"B" & "D" COMPANIES INOCULATED. "A" & "C" Box Respirator Drill.Rapid Loading.Platoon Drill and rapid marching. The Brigade Signal Officer lectured all Officers of the Btn at 5-15p.m.on the use of the Pigeon,and how to send Messagesby same.	
"	16-5-17.		"B" & "D" COYS resting after Inoculation. "C" & "C" Battalion Training.	
"	17-5-17.		Battalion Training.	
"	18-5-17.		The Battalion was ordered to relieve the 7thBtn Sherwood Foresters in the Left Sub-Sector(See Operation Orders No 13.dated 18-5-17 attached)but this was cancelled by a subsequent order which stated that the 1/6th Btn South Staffs Regt would relieve the 8th Btn Sherwood Foresters in the LEFT SUPPORT LINE(See Operation Orders No 14.dated 18-5-17.attached). The two Orders were then cancelled and the Battalion ordered to "STAND FAST".	
"	19-5-17.		The Battalion relieved the 7th Btn Sherwood Foresters in the LEFT SUB-SECTOR(See Operation Orders No 13.dated 18-5-17) as mentioned for the 18-5-1917.	
PETIT LOOS.	20-5-17.		Quiet day.	
"	21-5-17.		Quiet day.	
"	22-5-17.		The Battalion wasrelieved in the trenches by the 1/6th Btn North Staffordshire Regiment(See Operation Orders No 15.dated 22-5-17. attached).	

Army Form C. 2118.

WAR DIARY
or
INTELLIGENCE SUMMARY.

(Erase heading not required.)

1/6th Btn South Staffs Rgt.

Instructions regarding War Diaries and Intelligence Summaries are contained in F.S. Regs., Part II. and the Staff Manual respectively. Title pages will be prepared in manuscript.

(120)

Sheet 3

Place	Date	Hour	Summary of Events and Information	Remarks and references to Appendices
IN FRONT OF LENS.	23-5-17. 24-5-17.		In Brigade Reserve. The Battalion in support to the 1/6th Btn North Staffs Regt, who were due to make an attack on the Front Line German Trench about 350 yards long. This attack took place at 7p.m. and was very successful though the whole of the objective was not taken. The 1/6th Btn South Staffs Regt suffered very little from the ENEMY BARRAGE. (See Operation Orders No 16 dated 23-5-17.attached)	
"	25-5-17. 4a.m.		The enemy laid a very heavy barrage for an hour on the areas behind the FrontLine in which the Battalion was lying. Again we suffered little from the shelling. During the morning two Platoons of "C" COY(2/Lieut:BULLOCK R.N.Commanding) were sent forward to stiffen the captured line,the other two Platoons being in immediate Support.	
		11a.m.	The enemy laid an unusually heavy barrage of 77c.m. 10.5c.m. 5.9 and 8" Shells and at about 11-30a.m. they Counter-attacked up the trenches and over the open. The attack was made in considerable force and our men were obliged to withdraw from the trench. The casualties of the 1/6th Btn South Staffs Regt in the 24 hours amounted to 38,amongst which were five killed, and seven missing. A report by 2/Lieut:TEETON P.R. is appended. The Battalion relieved the 1/6th Btn North Staffs Regt on the night of the 25/26th May 1917.	
PETIT LOOS.	26-5-17.			
	27-5-17.		The 1/5th Btn South Staffs Regt relieved the Battalion in the Trenches,which Battn went into Brigade Reserve,with Btn H.Q. at ELVASTON CASTLE.(See Operation Orders No 18.dated 27-5-17.attached)	
ELVASTON CASTLE.	28-5-17.		In Brigade Reserve.	
"	29-5-17.		-do-	
"	30-5-17.		The Battalion relieved the 1/5th Btn North Staffs Rgt in Pl.Sub-Sector.(See Operation Orders No 19.dated 30-5-17.attached).	

A5834 Wt.W4973/M687 750,000 8/16 D.D.&L.Ltd. Forms/C.2118/13

Army Form C. 2118.

WAR DIARY
or
INTELLIGENCE SUMMARY.

1/6th Btn South Staffs Rgt.   (121).

(Erase heading not required.)

Instructions regarding War Diaries and Intelligence Summaries are contained in F. S. Regs., Part II. and the Staff Manual respectively. Title pages will be prepared in manuscript.

Sheet 4

Place	Date	Hour	Summary of Events and Information	Remarks and references to Appendices
	31-5-1917.		TOTAL CASUALTIES FOR MONTH OF MAY 1917.	
			Major R.Evans. 4th Btn Leicestershire Rgt(attached) Wounded and at Duty.	
			Captain W.A.Adam. Wounded.	
			2/Lieut:M.L.G.C.Sullivan.1/5th S.Staffs Rgt(attached) Wounded(Gassed)	
			OTHER RANKS.	
			Killed. 17	
			Missing. 7	
			Died of Wounds. 2	
			Wounded Accidentally. 6	
			Wounded,Self-Inflicted. 1	
			Wounded. 52(51)	
			Wounded & At Duty. 8	
			_____	
			92	
			R.J.Drury Lieut:Colonel.	
			Commanding 1/6th Btn South Staffordshire Regiment.	
			3rd June 1917.	

APPENDIX TO DAR DIARY. MAY 1917.   1/6th Btn S.Staffs Rgt.

COPY OF REPORT BY 2/Lieut:P.R.TEETON, Commanding "C" Coy. on Operations of 24/25th May 1917.

I received orders from Lieut:Colonel Trump, Commanding 1/6th Btn South Staffs Regt, that my Company was to support the 1/6th Btn North Staffs Regt, and that I was under the direct orders of Lt Col:Stoney, Commanding 1/6th Btn North Staffs Regt.

I received orders to take two Platoons to Saps in BUGS WALK and two Platoons to dig in at M.6.c.65.80 in existing trench, with my Coy Headquarters at N.1.c.15.90.

My Company was in position at 4-45p.m. on the 24th inst.

At 12-10a.m. Captain Shedden, 1/6th Btn North Staffs Regt, asked me to send him a Platoon to support him in NETLEY TRENCH in case of a counter attack, as he was unable to collect sufficient men of his own Company.
This Platoon returned at 4a.m.

At 7-30a.m. on the 25th I received orders to send two Platoons to report to Major Macnamara at M.6.a.90.45 and to move my other two Platoons up to BUGS WALK.
I sent 2/Lt R.N.BULLOCK with Nos 11 & 12 Platoons to Major Macnamara, who, later ordered him to take one Platoon up into NASH ALLEY to 2/Lieut: EDGE.
2/Lieut:Bullock posted the Lewis Gun Team in a good position midway between the two flank bombing posts, the remainder of the Platoons were divided and posted to the two flank Bombing Posts. The Left Bombing Post was ordered to push their post up O.G.1 trench and two of my Sergeants were included in this party; a shell burst and wounded both Sergeants.

Shortly after the enemy was seen massing troops on the Right and 2/Lieut:Edge sent word by one of my Cpls to Major Macnamara.

2/Lieut:Bullock returned to Major Macnamara after posting the platoon as per instructions and was ordered to stand by with the other platoon in the dugout at N.1.a.20.65.

My Lewis Gun Team saw the enemy advancing and fired twenty-two Magazines, causing heavy casualties to the enemy; then the gun was thrown out of action. The Team were then ordered by Major Macnamara to take up bombs and slowly withdraw over the top to O.G.1 trench at N.1.a.5.8.
The Bombing Section posted to the right bombing post was heavily pressed from NETLEY TRENCH on both sides of NASH ALLEY, and were told to withdraw, and as they withdrew they took up firing positions in a Sap running West from NASH ALLEY. At least ten of the enemy were killed by rifle fire before the party withdrew over the top to O.G.1.
The party on the Left bombing post withdrew with the 1/6th North Staffs Regt down O.G.1.trench.

Four of my men were wounded and seven are missing.

During the heavy bombardment from 11-30a.m. to 1-15p.m. I had the remainder of my Company all ready to move, and also I had previously arranged firing positions in BUGS WALK in case the enemy should attempt to break through.
               (Signed)   P.R.TEETON. 2/Lieutenant.
28-5-1917.   O/C. "C" Company 1/6th Btn S.Staffs Rgt.

Operation Orders No 10   Copy No. 1
Lieutenant Colonel C/ T. J. Trump. D.S.O.   War Diary
Commanding 6th Battalion South Staffordshire Regiment
3rd May 1917.

Reference Map Loos Sheet S.W. 1/10,000.

1. **Move.** The 6th South Staffs Regt will relieve the 6th N Staff Regt in the line tomorrow night. Relief to be complete by 2 a.m. 4th inst.

2. **Scouts.** Each Company will detail two smart intelligent men to act as runners. These men will proceed to the trenches with their Companies and when relief is complete will report to Battn HQ for duty.

3. **Dispositions.** Right Company — "D"
   Centre   " — "A".   Reserve Company "B".
   Left   " — "C"

4. **Relief.** Companies of 6th South will relieve Companies of 6th North as under:—
                  6th South   6th North.
                  "D"   relieves   "A"
                  "A"   "   "B"
                  "C"   "   "C"
                  "B"   "   "D"

5. **Guides.** Guides for Left Company will be at Loos N.25.d.50.85 at 10 p.m.
Guides for remainder at Red Mill at 9 p.m.
Lewis Gun Officer will arrange relief of Teams.

6. **Advance Party.** Company Commanders plus one Officer per Company & 1 N.C.O. per Platoon will report to present Company H.Q., 6 N. North, Road J.5.a.4. at 9 p.m. tonight (May 3rd). Company Commanders only return at dawn, remainder must be prepared to stay until end of tour.

7. **Rations.** Rations will be delivered to Reserve Coy H.Q. during daylight. All C.Q.M.Sgts will remain with the Reserve Company & will lay off the rations. These will then be carried up to the firing line at night by fatigue parties found by the Reserve Company. Rations for tomorrow will be issued before leaving for the trenches. Water bottles to be filled.

8. **Flanks.** 5th South Staffs on left flank - Canadian Infantry Brigade on right.

9. **Dress.** Fighting Order. All packs to be dumped at Battn HQ by 1pm tomorrow. Small parties only to be used carrying packs to avoid congestion on the route.

10. **Mills Cups.** The Mills Cups issued to Companies on April 29th will be taken into the firing line. These Cups are on Company charge and must not be handed over on relief.

11. **Trench Stores.** All Trench Stores taken over will be carefully checked before giving receipt.

12. **Reports.** Number of daily reports required from Companies will be issued & the time stated hereon must be strictly complied with.

13. **Petrol Tins.** Ten filled tins per Company will be taken over on relief.

14. Relief complete will be sent to Battn HQ by code message.

(Signed) H. Hanford, Captain
Adjutant 6th Battalion South Staffs Regiment.

Operation Orders No 13
by
Lieut-Colonel F. W. Trott. D.S.O.
Commanding, 1/6th Battalion South Staffordshire Regiment.

Friday, 18th May 1917.

Copy No 9.

1. **RELIEF.** The 1/6th Btn South Staffs Regt will relieve the 7th Bttn Sherwood Foresters Regt in the Left Sub-sector (N.2.sector) from RAILWAY - ST MARTIN'S Railway (inclusive) to Brigade northern Boundary, "D" in SEC SLAGHT at N.2.a.6.5.

2. **MOVE.** The Battalion will leave ORMS AS MAIDAN in following order:-
   Headquarters - "B" - "C" - "A" - "D".
   Platoons at 200yards interval at 6.30 p.m.

3. **GUIDES.** One guide per platoon and one for Headquarters will be at Cross Roads N.34.d.5.4. at 5.0 p.m.

4. **DETAILS & SPECIAL- -ISTS.** Details and specialists will march as follows:-
   B.T.Signallers under 2/Lieut ____ parade at Orderly Room at 4.30 p.m.
   R.S.M. & Pioneer Sgt   -ditto-
   4 R.E.Sappers   -ditto-

   NOTE:- The Headquarter Runners will reconnoitre the route to all Company Headquarters immediately on ___ arrival. The Company runners attached to Headquarters will proceed to the Trenches with their Companies and then return to Headquarters when the relief is complete. "A" Company.
   All Snipers will parade with ____ ____ and will be met by a separate Guide. Snipers will be rationed by Headquarters.

5. **MESS ORDERLY.** Sergeant Salter and one Cook per Company will remain at the Transport Lines. Two Pioneers(Carpenters) will report to the Transport Officer to complete repairs to Limbers.

6. **LEWIS GUNS & SIGNALLERS EQUIPMENT.** All Lewis Guns and S.A.A. as detailed by the L.G.Officer will be at the Quartermasters Stores at 5p.m. Transport Officer to arrange for two Limbers to be ready at that hour.
   The L.G.Officer will detail suitable party to march with these Limbers. Guns etc will then be dumped at the British Cemetery ____ and picked up by Companies as they march by. Signallers equipment and rest of Lewis Gun S.A.A. to be loaded at Q.M.Stores at 6p.m. and will be sent to Trench Headquarters.

7. **DUMPS.** ____ ____ WAY DEPOT 15, and SECOND ____.

8. **BLANKETS, PACKS.** All Blankets to be at the Q.M.Stores by 12-30p.m. All Packs to be at the Q.M.Stores by 2-30p.m. All Officers Valises to be at the Q.M.Stores by 3p.m. All Mess Baskets not for the trenches to be at the Q.M.Stores by 5-30p.m. All Mess Baskets for the trenches to be at the Q.M.Stores by 6p.m. Officers Servants will go with the Mess Cart and carry their stuff from the Dump to Company Headquarters.

9. **WATER AND RATION PARTIES.** The Reserve Company carries all rations and water to the other Companies. SPECIAL NOTE:- As all water is sent up in petrol Tins the next day's supply entirely depends on the number of empty Tins returned to Headquarters by Ration Parties.

10. **DISPOSITIONS IN THE LINE.** Companies will relieve 7th Sherwoods in the Line and be distributed as follows:-

	LEFT Coy.	RIGHT Coy.	SUPPORT Coy.	RESERVE Coy.
6th S.Staffs.Regt.				
7th S.Foresters.	"B"			

11. **RELIEF COMPLETE.** To be wired to Headquarters by O.A.D. ____.

12. **H.Q.** Will be at N.3.d.7.1. near SHELL DUMP.

13. **TRENCH MAPS.** All copies Sheet ____. 36c.N.W. 3.1/10,000 issued today are to be treated as Trench Stores and handed over at the end of the tour. Copies of Trench Stores taken over are to be sent to Orderly Room as soon as possible.

14. **DOC AID POST.** Is at Battalion Headquarters.

15. **INTELLIGENCE.**

(Signed) F.W.Trott. Capt Lt.
Adjubant 1/6th Btn South Staffordshire Regiment.

Copies Issued to:- No 1. Commdg Officer. No 2,3,4,5. O/C "A","B","C","D" Companies.
No 6. O/C 7th Btn S.Foresters. No 7. Transport Officer. ____

Copy No. 10

OPERATION ORDERS No 14.
by
LIEUTENANT COLONEL F.J.TRUMP. D.S.O.
Commanding 1/6th Btn South Staffordshire Regiment.
Dated 18th May 1917.

1. **RELIEF.** The 1/6th Btn South Staffs Regt will relieve the 8th Btn Sherwood Foresters in the LEFT SUPPORT LINE tonight.

2. **GUIDES.** Guides of the 8th Btn Sherwood Foresters will meet Companies at G.34.d.3.4. at 9-30p.m.

3. **MOVE AND ORDER OF MARCH.** The Battalion will move by Platoons at 200 yards intervals at 7-0p.m.
Order of March:- "C" "A" "B" "D".

4. **DISTRIBUTION.**
On arrival Companies will be distributed as under:-
"A" COY. MUSIC TRENCH. H.Q. M.5.d.60.30.
"B" " OLD GERMAN FRONT LINE.M.5.c.71.41.
"C" " MARTYRS ALLEY.H.Q. M.6.d.15.45.
"D" " KING STREET. H.Q. M.5.a.49.21.

5. **L.GUNS AND S.A.A.** To be at Q.M.Stores at 5p.m. The Lewis Gun Officer will detail suitable party to accompany the limbers.
These will be dumped at exit of MAROC, to be picked up by Companies as they pass.
Remainder of Lewis Gun S.A.A. to be sent to Btn Headquarters from the Transport Lines.

6. **SIGNALLERS EQUIPMENT** to be loaded at the Quartermaster's Stores at 7p.m.
MESS BASKETS FOR TRENCHES " " " " " " " " " " " "
TRENCH STORES " " " " " " " " " " " "

7. **BLANKETS, VALISES & MENS PACKS.** To be sent to the Quartermaster's Stores at once.

8. **MESS BASKETS NOT FOR TRENCHES.** To be sent to the Quartermaster's Stores at 6-30p.m.

9. **RUNNERS.** Company runners attached to Btn Headquarters will accompany their Companies to the trenches, and return to Btn H.Q. when RELIEF is complete.

10. **BTN H.Q.** Will be at G.34.d.9.3.

11. **RELIEF COMPLETE.** to be notified to Btn Headquarters as soon as possible.

12. **ACKNOWLEDGE.**

(Signed) H.HANFORD. Captain.
Adjutant 1/6th Btn South Staffordshire Regiment.

Copies issued to:-
No 1. Commanding Officer.
No 2. O/C. "A" Company.
No 3. " "B" "
No 4. " "C" "
No 5. " "D" "
No 6. Transport Officer.
No 7. Quartermaster.
No 8. O/C. 8th Btn Sherwood Foresters.
No 9. Orderly Room.
No 10 War Diary

Operation Orders No. 16
by
Lieut. Colonel L. J. Trump D.S.O.
Commanding 1/6th Bttn South Staffordshire Regiment

20th May 1916

1. The 1/6th Bttn North Staffordshire Regt will relieve the 1/6th Bttn South Staffordshire Regiment in trenches tonight as follows:—

	Left Coy	Right Coy	Support Coy	Reserve Coy
1/6th S.S.R.	C	D	B	A
1/6th N.S.R.	C	D	A	B

2. One guide per platoon will be at H.Q. at 8.15 p.m. These guides are reconnoitering the way this afternoon. The Companies will take over the trench ordnance of the Companies of 1/6 N.S.R. that relieve them.

3. Times of Coys leaving HARTS CRATER are 1/6 N.S.R. "B" Coy 9.30 p.m. "C" Coy 9.50 p.m. "D" Coy 10.10 p.m.

4. "D" Coy 1st S Staffs will exchange places with "A" Coy 1/6 North Staffs at 10.30 p.m. O.C. "D" Coy will reconnoitre the place at once.

5. Rations and water will be dumped at about M52.b5 $?$ on LENS—BETHUNE Road and Companies will send fatigue parties to fetch water when they are relieved. All water tins in the line are to be brought down and dumped at Battle Trench H.Q. A list of trench stores handed over to be sent to H.Q. as soon as possible.

6. Companies will carry their own mess stuff out of trenches.

7. Relief complete to be phoned by B.A.B. without delay to Trench H.Q.

8. Lewis gun magazines and panniers and all special equipment must be brought out of trenches by Companies.

9. Gas mask recently issued (P. Helmet) to be handed over and receipt obtained for same. Receipt to be forwarded to Orderly Room without [delay?].

Signed
Adjutant 1/6th South Staffordshire Regiment

Copy No. 9

Operation Order No. 6
by
Lieut. Colonel T. J. Trench. D.S.O.
Commanding 1/6th South Staffordshire Regiment

May 23rd 1917

Reference Maps LENS & LOOS 1/5000

1. The 1/6th North Staffs Regt. will attack and capture NASH ALLEY from N12 98.40 to N18 92.98 and NETLEY TRENCH between NASH and NOYEL ALLEYS on Thursday 24th May 1917. Zero hour to be notified later.

2. Two Companies of 1/6th Bn. South Staff Regt. (C & D) will be in immediate support to and under the orders of O.C. 1/6th North Staffs Regt.

3. "D" Coy. will move from MARTYRS ALLEY and relieve "D" Coy. 1/6th North Staffs Re in NOYEL TRENCH, between NETLEY TRENCH and NEW TRENCH. Two platoons near Coy. H.Q. (N1C 45.45) and two platoons in the line. This relief to be carried out tonight under orders from O.C. 1/6th North Staffs Regt.

4. "C" Coy. will move as follows:-
   Coy. H.Q. in TRIANGLE at N1C 15.90
   2 Platoons in BUGS WALK.
   2   "   in CRASSIER TRENCH or any dugouts in the immediate neighborhood. First platoon to reach new Coy. H.Q. at 3 p.m. Company relief to be complete by 4 p.m. tomorrow.

5. "B" Coy. will occupy:-
   Coy. H.Q. and dugouts about M6d 35.45
   First party to reach new Coy. H.Q. at 4 p.m. Relief to be complete by 5 p.m. tomorrow.

6. "A" Coy. will occupy:-
   Coy. H.Q. in MARTYRS ALLEY
   Coy. distributed in M6d 15.45 and dugouts near.
   Relief to commence at 5 p.m. and to be complete by 6 p.m. tomorrow.

7. Companies will reconnoitre covered daylight routes to their new positions at dawn. During the relief Companies will move by small parties preferably sections and the greatest care will be taken to avoid observation from FOSSE III and neighbouring houses. The success of these operations largely depends upon the secrecy with which these movements of troops are made.

Operation Orders No 18
by
Lieut: Colonel F. J. Trump D.S.O.
Commanding 16th Bn South Staffordshire Regiment

Copy No 9

27th May

1. The 16th South Staffs Regt will relieve the 16th South Staffs on 27/28 May.
2. Companies will send one guide per platoon to Battn H.Q. at 12 noon. "A" & "D" Coys will also send a guide from their attached platoon.
3. Companies will be relieved as follows:—

	Left Coy B	Right Coy B	Support Coy	Reserve Coy
16th	"A" + 1 Pln "B" Coy	"D" + 1 Pln "C" Coy	"B"	"C"
16th South	"B" + 1 Pln "C" Coy	"A" + 1 Pln "C" Coy	"C"	"D"

4. On completion of relief the Battn will be in Brigade Reserve distributed as under:
   Two Coys in support to 1/S South in R2 Subsector Btn H.Q. M6a 7.1
      i.e. "B" Coy in MARTYRS TRENCH.
           "C" Coy in MUSIC TRENCH.
   Two Coys in support to 1/S North Staffs in R1 Subsector Btn H.Q. N11 b 66.15
      i.e. "D" Coy in near PUITS 11 bis.   CITÉ ST PIERRE
           "A" Coy in - - - - - - - -
   Battn H.Q. will be at Elraston Castle G 34 d 90 30
   The platoons attached to "A" & "D" Coys will rejoin their Coys as soon as relieved.
5. Guides referred to in Para 2. will reconnoitre routes to new position and return to Btn H.Q. They will meet the Battn at night at Btn H.Q 9 p.m. to guide them into trenches. These men will, on completion of relief lead their own platoons out to the new positions that they reconnoitred this morning.
6. On the day after relief Coy Commanders will send small parties to collect their greatcoats and issue them.
7. "B" & "C" Coys will be directly under the orders of O.C. 1/S South Staffs.
   "A" & "D"   "   "   "   "   "   "   " O.C. 1/S North Staffs.
   and will notify the respective Commanding Officers and also my Orderly Room of the location of their Coy H.Q. when in position.
8. Rations.   Ammunition. Water will be dumped at —
   "B" & "C" Coys at M6a 85.75 LENS & BETHUNE ROAD.
   "A" & "D" Coys at M10a 90.00.
   C.Q.M. Sgts will accompany rations.

— 2 —

6. All petrol tins will be handed over to 5th South Staffs.

7. Lewis Gun S.A.A. and specialist equipment in charge of Coy. Snipers to be brought out of trenches on relief. List of trench stores handed over to be sent to Supply Coy by 6 p.m.

8. Relief [?] fulls to be sent by B.A.B. Code as usual.

(Signed) H. HANFORD Captain

Adjutant 5th South Staffs Regiment

Copies to:
1. "C.O." 5th South Staff Regt
2. Staff
3. C.O. 1/5th South Staffs Regt
4. C.O. 5th North Staffs Regt
5-8. Companies
9. War Diary

Army Form C. 2118.

1/6th Bn. South Staffordshire Regiment. (122) WAR DIARY or INTELLIGENCE SUMMARY.

Instructions regarding War Diaries and Intelligence Summaries are contained in F.S. Regs., Part II. and the Staff Manual respectively. Title pages will be prepared in manuscript.

(Erase heading not required.)

Vol 29

137/46

Q 30

Place	Date	Hour	Summary of Events and Information	Remarks and references to Appendices
CITE ST PIERRE	1.6.17		Battalion in Trenches CITE ST PIERRE. Quiet day.	
"	2.6.17		Quiet Day.	
"	3.6.17.		Quiet Day. Battalion relieved in the line by 1/5th Btn North Staff's Regiment and proceeded to Brigade Reserve in CITE ST PIERRE. See Operation Orders No 20 attached.	
"	4.6.17		In Brigade Reserve.	
"	5.6.17		—do—	
"	6.6.17		—do—	
"	7.6.17		The Battalion relieved the 1/5th Btn North Staffs Regiment in the line. See Operations Orders No 21 attached.	
"	8.6.17		Quiet day. Operations carried out by 138th and 139th Infantry Brigades on our Right and by the 1/5th Bn South Staffs Regiment on our Left. See Operation Orders No 22 attached.	
"	9.6.17		Quiet Day.	
"	10.6.17		Quiet Day	
"	11.6.17		Quiet Day. "A" & "D" Companies relieved in the line by 1/5th Btn North Staffs Regiment and proceeded on to Brigade Reserve at CITE ST PIERRE. "B" & "C" Companies remained in Support under direct orders of O/C. 1/5th Btn North Staffs Regiment. See Operation Orders No 24 attached.	
"	12.6.17		In Brigade Reserve.	

Army Form C. 2118.

1/6th Btn South Staffordshire Regiment. (123) WAR DIARY or INTELLIGENCE SUMMARY.

Instructions regarding War Diaries and Intelligence Summaries are contained in F. S. Regs., Part II. and the Staff Manual respectively. Title pages will be prepared in manuscript.

(Erase heading not required.)

Place	Date	Hour	Summary of Events and Information	Remarks and references to Appendices
CITE ST PIERRE	13.6.17		"B" & "C" Companies joined remainder of Battalion in Brigade Reserve in ST PIERRE.	
"	14.6.17		In Brigade Reserve.	
"	15.6.17		Battalion relieved in Brigade Reserve by 6th Battalion Sherwood Foresters and proceeded into Divisional Reserve at BOUVIGNY - BOYEFFLES. See Operation Orders No 25 attached.	
BOUVIGNY BOYEFFLES	16.6.17		In Divisional Reserve. Battalion Resting.	
"	17.6.17		—do— Sunday - Church Parade.	
"	18.6.17		—do— Battalion Training at MARQUEFFLES FARM.	
"	19.6.17		—do—	
"	20.6.17		—do—	
"	21.6.17		—do—	
"	22.6.17		Battalion moved to CALONNE and relieved the 8th Battalion Sherwood Foresters in Reserve. Relief complete by 11.30 p.m.	
CALONNE	23.6.17		The Battalion relieved the 1/5th Btn South Staffs Regiment in Support billets in LIEVIN. Relief complete by 11 pm. See Operation Orders No 27 attached.	
LIEVIN	24.6.17		In accordance with Operations Orders No 28 (see copy attached) "A" & "D" Companies assembled in their assembly positions in the slag heap at 7.30 p.m. At 9.26 p.m. the 2 companies advanced in single file in parallel lines over the slag heap over the ground in between FOSSE 3 and the "L" shaped building	

Army Form C. 2118.

1/6th Btn South Staffordshire Regiment. (124) WAR DIARY or INTELLIGENCE SUMMARY.

Instructions regarding War Diaries and Intelligence Summaries are contained in F. S. Regs., Part II. and the Staff Manual respectively. Title pages will be prepared in manuscript.

(Erase heading not required.)

Place	Date	Hour	Summary of Events and Information	Remarks and references to Appendices
LIEVIN	24.6.17		(Continued from sheet 123) When within 200 yards of their objective they halted taking as much cover from buildings as was possible and at 9.30 pm "ZERO HOUR" the two lines advanced simultaneously to the fringe of our barrage where they again halted. at "ZERO" plus 6 the lines again moved forward. "A" Company on the Left in the direction of AHEAD TRENCH with "D" Company on the Right in the direction of ADMIRAL TRENCH. Some difficulty was found on the right in locating the trench owing to the bombardment in the afternoon having practically obliterated it. The Artillery Barrage which should have lifted from the first 50 yards, on both trenches mentioned, had not however done so, and it was found necessary to take cover which held the advance up for a few seconds, when it was resumed, in spite of the fact that our own Artillery intermittently shelled. No opposition was encountered when the advance on the main trenches continued steadily and it was found that the rate of the barrage lifts was not quick enough for the rate of the advance. It was necessary therefore to keep a tight hold on the men to prevent them from running into our own barrage. The objective was gained by 9.55 p.m. and posts were immediately pushed forward up AHEAD TRENCH as far as the third house and up ADMIRAL TRENCH as far as the fourth house. No opposition was encountered whatsoever from Machine-gun or Rifle fire or bombs. It is more than probably that the enemy had evacuated the trench on account of the heavy bombardment directed against it during the course of the afternoon and evening. One prisoner was taken unwounded, who was found hiding in a shell hole, and only one other enemy dead body was seen. The bombardment by our heavies in the course of the day had done great destruction to the enemy trenches and in places it was very difficult to follow the front line of AHEAD TRENCH at all; in the case of ADMIRAL TRENCH this was practically blotted out of existence, and the communication trenches in bwteen AHEAD & ADMIRAL were equally difficult to follow. With the exception of three, the dugouts were completely destroyed.	

Army Form C. 2118.

WAR DIARY
or
INTELLIGENCE SUMMARY.

1/6th Btn South Staffordshire Regiment. (125)

Instructions regarding War Diaries and Intelligence Summaries are contained in F. S. Regs., Part II. and the Staff Manual respectively. Title pages will be prepared in manuscript.

(Erase heading not required).

Place	Date	Hour	Summary of Events and Information	Remarks and references to Appendices
LIEVIN	24.6.17		(continued from Sheet 124) When the objective was gained and the Forward Posts pushed out up AHEAD & ADMIRAL TRENCHES and also in front of ADMIRAL TRENCH, consolidation was begun immediately, aided by "C" Company who followed up very quickly upon the Assaulting Companies. This work was carried on with through the night. There was no retaliation from the enemy artillery, and quickly fire positions were made and Lewis guns mounted covering our immediate front and our Left front. On the Right connection was quickly gained with the Canadian Division who had also gone forward.	
"	25.6.17		On the morning of the 25th a Reconnaissance Party (under 2/Lieut: Walker) reconnoitred the RESERVOIRS on the Crest of Hill 65 which were found to be unoccupied by the enemy, a Lewis Gun Post was thereupon established. After further reconnaissance it was decided to push forward Outpost Groups into shell-holes on the inner-brow of Hill 65 on a line from the RESERVOIRS on our Right to the end house of the row of houses running parallel with AHEAD TRENCH. When placing these Outpost Groups and enemy Balloon was seen to ascend and shortly afterwards Hill 65 was swept with 5.9's and 4.2's, a Machine Gun also opened fire from CITE ST THEODORE. The ground gained up to the crest of HILL 65 gives a commanding view of the Country round LENS and South East of it The Battalion was relieved in the trenches by 5th Battalion Lincolnshire Regiment and proceeded to Divisional Reserve in BULLY GRENAY. Relief was not completed until 4.30 am (26th) owing to one Company of the relieving Battalion going astray. See Operation Orders No 29 attached.	
"	26.6.17			
BULLY GRENAY	26.6.17.		Bathing, cleaning-up etc.	
"	27.6.17		The Battalion relieved the 1st Monmouthshire Regiment in Support billets in LIEVIN. Relief complete 11 pm. See Operation Orders No 30 attached.	

A5834 Wt.W4973/M687 750,000 8/16 D. D. & L. Ltd. Forms/C.2118/13

Army Form C. 2118.

1/6th Btn South Staffordshire Regiment. (126) WAR DIARY or INTELLIGENCE SUMMARY.

Instructions regarding War Diaries and Intelligence Summaries are contained in F. S. Regs. Part II and the Staff Manual respectively. Title pages will be prepared in manuscript.

(Erase heading not required.)

Place	Date	Hour	Summary of Events and Information	Remarks and references to Appendices
LIEVIN.	28.6.17.		The Battalion took part in a successful attack on the enemies defences West of LENS, assisting in the capture of ADJACENT and ADJUNCT trenches. They also dug a support trench from M24.d.50.37 to M24.b.01.29. The attack took place at 7.10 p.m. in a thunder-storm which afforded excellent cover to view. Activity was marked throughout the day increasing to intense barrage at intervals. (See Operation Orders No 31 attached.)	
"	29.6.17.		The Battalion was withdrawn to Support Billets in LIEVIN.	
"	30.6.17.		Preparations completed for an attack on Cite de Moulin which it was decided to launch in the early hours of July 1st, and the Battalion took up its position in the assembly trenches.	

TOTAL CASUALTIES FOR MONTH OF JUNE 1917.

OFFICERS:- 2/Lieut: J.G.GRIBBEN. Killed 11.6.17.
" A.R.HARTLEY. Wounded 24.6.17.
Captain E.W.PAGE. " 24.6.17.

OTHER RANKS:- Killed   10.
Wounded   104.
" (At Duty) 3.
Missing   nil.
Died of Wounds 4.
N.Y.D.N.   3.

F. S. Dumm,
Lieut-Colonel,
Commanding 1/6th Battalion South Staffordshire Regiment.

No 9.

                                                                    Btn

         D   B
      anies   materials R
      tomorrow   dump as soon as
complete
Gun S A A &c   1/5   16
list of Stores, S A A
by 12 noon
pecialist Officers
to at 4 pm.
Relief complete to be sent to HQ by code word
Battalion password for night 7/8 June

SECRET.   OPERATION ORDERS. No 22.   Copy No 2
                                  by
                  LIEUTENANT-COLONEL F.J.TRUMP. D.S.O.
                  Commanding 1/6th Btn South Staffordshire Regt.

                                              Dated 7th June 1917.

1. Operations will be carried out on June 8th 1917 by the 138th and
   137th Infantry Brigades at 8-30p.m.

2. The 138th Infantry Brigade will raid the ENEMY LINE from SOUCHEZ
   RIVER at M.30.d.3.3. to M.24.d.6.4. All troops will return to
   our trenches by dawn on the 9th inst,except for that portion
   from M.30.d.3.3. to M.30.b.½.2.which will be held and consolidated.

3. Operations by the 137th Infantry Brigade will be carried out at the
   same date and time as under:-
        The 1/5th Btn South Staffs Regt will carry out a RAID.
        Two Companies will remain in NASH ALLEY until dark.
        The 5th Company R.E. will construct BOOBY TRAPS before
        leaving.

4. A feint attack with dummy targets representing a Battalion of
   Infantry advancing from COWDEN TRENCH will be carried out.

   AT ZERO PLUS 2½ minutes the rear wave will appear followed by
   third,second and first waves at ½ minute intervals.
   A feint attack will also be carried out in continuation of right
   of attack by the 1/5th Btn South Staffs Regt from NETLEY TRENCH
   about N.1.a.7.2. to RAILWAY N.1.c.85.55.

   O/C.1/6th Btn North Staffs Regt will arrange to Support this
   Attack with Lewis Gun & Rifle Fire.

5. SMOKE. At Zero minus 2. No 4.Special Coy R.E.will(wind permitting)
   put up a smoke screen between CITE ST EDOUARD & CITE ST ELIZABETH,
   also a thin screen across open ground North of CITE ST THEODORE.

6. GAS.   At 2a.m. on the 9th inst."B" Special Coy R.E. will
   (wind permitting) project Gas into area:-
                (1) CITE ST LAURENT.
                (2) CORNWALL & CUTEY TRENCHES.
                (3) N.13.c.

7. From Zero plus 3 to ZERO plus 30,the 139th Infantry Brigade will
   make a demonstration with Lewis Guns and Rifle Fire from its
   present line of Posts.

8. The 6th Division are co-operating to assist the Operations with
   a Smoke Barrage all along their Front and Raids on ENEMY'S
   TRENCHES.

9. All Watches to be synchronised at 1-15p.m. and 5-15p.m. on the
   8th inst.

10. All Box Respirators must be worn in the ALERT POSITION.

11. As retaliation must be expected for the Gas projected on our
    Front and the smoke and dummy Battalion Attack on the right
    and left of the Battalion Front,the following precautions will
    be taken:-
         The Coys in the Front Line will keep their men under
    cover as much as possible,the minimum number of men to be on
    the posts. The remainder being under cover as near at hand as
    possible. Companies in Support to keep in dugouts and be
    ready to move to Support at a moments notice.
    All ranks to be warned in case Gas blows back.

                    (Signed)   H.HANFORD. Captain.
ACKNOWLEDGE.   Adjutant 1/6th Btn South Staffordshire Regiment.
    Copies issued to:- No 1. Commanding Officer.
                        " 2. Adjutant.
                        " 3/6. O/C Companies.
                        " 7   War Diary.
                        " 8   File.

SECRET.   OPERATION ORDERS No 24   Copy No 1
                              by
              LIEUTENANT-COLONEL F.J.TRUMP, D.S.O.
              Commanding 1/6th Btn South Staffs Regiment.
                                        Dated 11-6-1917.

1.   Operation Orders No 23 are cancelled.
     Two Companies of the 1/5th Btn North Staffs Regt will relieve
     "A" & "D" Coys in the trenches tonight, relief commencing
     at 10-30p.m.

     "B" & "C" Companies will remain in Support as at present, and
     come under the direct orders of the O/C.1/5th Btn North
     Staffs Regt.

     "A" & "D" Companies will take up the same billets as
     occupied last time in the ST PIERRE AREA.

     1 N.C.O. from "A" & "D" Coys to be sent to take over from
     the 1/5th Btn North Staffs Regt at 7p.m.

     Rations for these two Companies will be at Support Btn H.Q.
     Dump.

     Rations for "B" & "C" COYS will be at present Btn Dump at
     10-30p.m.

     RELIEF COMPLETE to be wired to Btn Headquarters by word
     "ELEPHANT".

     Pass-word   "THUNDER-STORM".

                    (Signed)   H.HANFORD, Captain.
              Adjutant 1/6th Btn South Staffordshire Regiment.

     Copies issued to:-

              No.1 Commanding Officer.
              No 2. O/C 1/5th Btn North Staffs Regt.
              No 3. "   "A" Company.
              No 4. "   "B"   "
              No 5. "   "C"   "
              No 6. "   "D"   "
              No 7. War Diary.
              No 8. File.

Reference map

1. ...

2. ...

3. BOUVIGNY — FOSSE ?? — GRENAY BRIDGE — ?? GRENAY — FOSSE 10 — BOYEFFLES — BOUVIGNY

4. ...will meet their companies at ?????? O.24.b.80.40.

5. Each company will send an N.C.O. to meet 2/Lt ?? Noel at Q.M. Stores

6. ...BOUVIGNY...

Operation Orders No 24
by
Lieutenant-Colonel L. J. Trumps D.S.O.
Commanding 16th Batt. South Staffordshire Regiment.

Copy No. 1.

23rd June 1917.

1. The 16th Btn South Staffordshire Regiment will relieve 15th Btn South Staffordshire Regiment in LIEVIN tonight and will be in support.

2. One Sergeant per Company will report to Orderly Room at 5.30 p.m. and will proceed to LIEVIN with the billeting Officer.

3. Companies will move in the following order :- "B" "C" "D" "A" by platoons at 200 yards interval. first platoon to leave at 10 p.m.

4. Route - Australian Road

5. Billeting N.C.Os will meet their companies at FOSSE 3.1 (M 28 a 40 45)

6. Mess Baskets, Lewis Guns and Panniers to be at Batt. H.Q at 10 p.m.

7. Water-Bottles will be filled before leaving.

(Signed) J.M. FREW 2Lt.
A/Adjutant 16th Btn. South Staffordshire Regiment.

Copies issued to :-
  No 1. Commanding Officer
  - 2-5 Companies
  - 6. Regt Sergt Major.
  - 7. War Diary
  - 8. File

Operation Orders No 28.   Copy No 11

Lieutenant-Colonel H. J Trump D.S.O
Commanding 16th Battn. South Staffordshire Regiment

24th June 1917.

1. The 16th South Staffs Regt will, on June 24th, capture and consolidate the German First and Second Lines, AHEAD and ADMIRAL TRENCHES. The line to be consolidated will run along BOOT TRENCH, thence to M.30.b.5.4, thence along ADMIRAL to M.30.b.35.98, thence to M.24.d.22.20. The attack will be carried out from South to North, by two Companies with one Company in Support and one Coy in Reserve. Two Companies 1/5th Btn South Staffordshire Regiment are placed at the disposal of the O.C 16th South Staffs Regt to be used if necessary.

2. ZERO hour will be at 9.30 p.m.

3. ASSEMBLY. The attacking Companies will assemble about M.30 central, Support Company in trenches M.30 a.+c. Reserve Company will "Stand to" in Chocolate Factory. M.28 d.   Completion of Assembly will be notified by sending word ARAB.

4. ARTILLERY. The Corps Heavy artillery will bombard objective from 11.45 am until ZERO.
At ZERO an 18-pdr barrage will be put down on German front and second line for 6 minutes, and will then lift Northwards at the rate of 50 yards every 3 minutes. On reaching the junction of AHEAD and ADMIRAL TRENCHES the Artillery will lift and form a standing barrage about 200 yards east of, and parallel to ADMIRAL TRENCH. This will become the S.O.S. line.

5. TRENCH MORTARS. Trench Mortars will co-operate as follows:-
2" Mortars will cut wire in front of AHEAD TRENCH from ALICE TRENCH to M.24 d 22.20.
9.45" Trench Mortars will bombard AGNES TRENCH east of M.24.d.40.30.
Stokes' Mortars will support the attack. Instructions have been issued separately.

6. MACHINE GUNS. 12 Guns from CITE JEANNE de ARC will barrage HILL 65 east of the road running from M.24.d.40.30 to M.24.d.53.00. 2 Guns from about M.30.a.80.50 will barrage HILL 65 and Southern Slope.

7. The 10th Canadian Infantry Brigade at ZERO will advance their posts to the embankment at M.30.d.9-4 to the pit at M.25.c.1-9.

— 2 —

8. The Headquarters of 6th Bn South Staffordshire Regiment will be established in the CITE des GARENNES about M.29.a.70.50. An advanced report centre will be established at M.30.c.40.95.

9. The Dressing Station will be in the vicinity of Battn Headquarters at M.29.d.40.50.

10. Watches will be synchronised at 4 p.m.

11. PRISONERS. O.C. 5th Bn South Staff. Regt will arrange to escort prisoners from Battn H.Q.

12. A Straggler Post will be formed at junction of ASSERT and CAVALRY TRENCHES M.29.c.

13. COMMUNICATION. A Power Buzzer has been established at advanced Report Centre with amplifier at Battn H.Q. There is also a buried route from advanced Report Centre to Battn H.Q.

14. SIGNALS. Attainment of objective will be signalled by two White Very Lights. The S.O.S. signal will remain unaltered — a succession of REDS.

15. DUMPS. A forward dump has been established at M.30 central, a Bomb store at M.30.a.60.30, R.E. store at Quarry Dump M.29.c.

16. ACKNOWLEDGE.

(Signed) J.M. FREW. 2nd Lieut
& Adjutant 6th Bn South Staffordshire Regiment.

Copies issued to:-
1. Commanding Officer
2. Adjutant
3-6. Companies
7. O.C. 3rd Infantry Brigade.
8. O.C. 5th Bn South Staff Regt.
9. O.C. 6th Bn North Staff Regt.
10. War Diary.
11. File.

Warning Orders to:
Lieut Colonel F. J. Trump DSO.
Commanding 6th Battn South Staffordshire Regiment

23rd June 1917

1. The 6th Battn South Staffordshire Regiment will attack and consolidate AHEAD, ADMIRAL, ALCOVE and BOOT Trenches on 24th June.

2. "A" & "D" Companies will carry out the assault.
"C" Company will be in close support and will assist in consolidation of BOOT Trench.

3. The assaulting Companies will be in position in cellars around M30a 60.10 at dawn on ZERO day.

4. ZERO hour will be notified later.
Operation Orders to follow.

5. Acknowledge.

A.W. Trew A/Lt
A/Adjutant 6th Battn South Staffordshire Regt.

Copies issued to:-
No 1   Commanding Officer
 - 2.   Adjutant
 - 3   H.Q. 34th Infantry Brigade
 - 4-7   Companies
 - 8   War Diary.
 - 9   File.

Operation Orders No 29   Copy No 7
by
Lieutenant Colonel J H Lomax DSO
Commanding 16th Btn South Staffordshire Regiment

June 25th 1917

1. The 5th Lincolnshire Regiment will relieve the 16th Btn South Staffordshire Regiment in the right sub-sector.
   The 16th Btn South Staffordshire Regiment will be withdrawn to Reserve in BULLY GRENAY.
   Relief to be complete by 4 a.m.

2. Lewis Gun material, thoss baskets, empty water tins, and salvage will be dumped at Quarry Dump.

3. Company Commanders will prepare a list of Trench Stores to be handed over and will render same to Orderly Room as soon as possible.

4. Relief complete to be notified by telephone to Battn HQ by word ALSO.

                                                    [signature]
                                                    2 Lieut.
A/Adjutant 16th Btn South Staffordshire Regiment.

Copies issued to:-
   No 1. Commanding Officer
   - 2-5. Companies
   - 6.   War Diary
   - 7.   File.

Copy No 11

OPERATION ORDERS No 30
by
LIEUT:COLONEL F.J.TRUMP. D.S.O.
Commanding 1/6th Btn South Staffordshire Regiment.
Dated 27th June 1917.

1. **MOVE.** The Battalion will move into Support Billets at LIEVIN tonight.
Movement will be by Platoons at 200 yards Interval, first Platoon to pass GREEN BRIDGE at 10p.m.

Order of march:- "C" "D" "A" "B".

2. **BILLETING PARTY**
2/Lieut J.S.Harris and one Sergeant per Company will report to Orderly Room at 2-30p.m. for the purpose of billeting the Battalion.

3. **PACKS. VALISES etc.**
Men's Packs to be at Q.M.Stores at 5p.m.
Officers Valises -do-   at 6p.m.
Lewis Guns and Signallers Equipment also Headquarter Details Equipment to be at Q.M.Stores at 8-45p.m.
Officers Mess B Sheets, for the trenches, and not for the trenches, to be ready for loading at 9-45p.m.

4. **ACKNOWLEDGE.**

(Signed)   J.A.FREW. 2/Lieutenant.
Acting/Adjutant 1/6th Btn South Staffordshire Regiment.

COPIES ISSUED TO:-

No 1. Commanding Officer.
No 2. Adjutant.
No 3. O/C "A" Company.
No 4. "   "B"   "
No 5. "   "C"   "
No 6. "   "D"   "
No 7. Quartermaster.
No 8. Transport Officer.
No 9. Regt Sergeant-Major.
No 10. War Diary.
No 11. "   "   (Duplicate).
No 12. File.
No 13. "

OPERATION ORDERS No 31.
by
LIEUT:COLONEL F.J.TRUMP. D.S.O.
Commanding 1/6th Btn South Staffordshire Regiment.
Dated 27th June 1917.

1. The Battalion will form part of an attack on the enemies defences West of LENS on the 28th June.

2. ZERO hour will be notified later.

3. "A" Company will dig a trench from M.24.d.50.37 to M.24.b.01.29 40 picks and 80 shovels will be drawn from R.E. Store at RIVER Dump. Tape for marking out the trench may be drawn from Battalion Headquarters LIEVIN.

"B" Company will act as "moppers-up" to 1/6th Btn North Staffs Regt. They will be under orders of O/C 1/6th Btn North Staffs Regt from noon to-morrow (28th).

"C" Company will act as carrying party to the 1/5th Btn South Staffs Regt for carrying purposes.

"D" Company will supply carrying parties for the 1/6th Btn North Staffs Regt.

4. Watches will be synchronised at 1.0 p.m.

5. "A" & "B" Companies will return all Yellow arm bands in possession to Orderly Room by 5.0 p.m. to-night.

6. Straggler Posts will be found at M.23.c.10.90 by the Regtl Police. They will be in position at 5.0 p.m. to-morrow (28th) and will remain there until relieved.

Acknowledge.

2/Lieut:

Actg/Adjutant, 1/6th Btn South Staffordshire Regiment.

Copies issued to:-

No 1. Commanding Officer.
   2. Adjutant.
   3. 137th Infantry Brigade.
   4. O/C, 1/5th Btn South Staffs Regt.
   5. "   1/6th Btn North Staffs Regt.
   6. Quartermaster.
   7. Transport Officer.
   8. O/C, "A" Company.
   9. "   "B"   "
  10. "   "C"   "
  11. "   "D"   "
  12. Regtl Sgt-Major.
  13. War Diary.
  14.   "
  15. File.
  16.   "

WAR DIARY or INTELLIGENCE SUMMARY

Army Form C. 2118.

Place: LEVIN
Date: 1/7/17

Q31

The Battalion took part in the attack on the Western defences of LENS on the early morning of July 1st 1917. A Coy. met with no real opposition for the 1/5 North Staffords Regt. B Coy. met with slight, Major W. C. B. D Coy. were confronted to the ambush Regt. A Coy. performed its task successfully & offered heavy opposition, beaming all to others. C & D Coys attacked thus, and had instructions but not a little support to active operators during the fight. B Coy was organised into four parties of 20 men, each party being attached to the leading Platoon of the four companies of the 5th North Stafford Regt who performed the assaulting troops. (commander of party was recalled but two of the ACONITE trench at the foot of LENS but were unable to remove the flank brigade toward that objective. Genmace were holding & lieut H. P. Jones, B Coy found himself in charge of the remnants of two companies of N. Staffs. as well as his own men in the trench at Cimetiere Square CITE DUNDOLIN. He consolidated the ground & disposed of his men in support of the unsuccessful companies incidentally capturing & burning 3 machine guns. In the early part of the afternoon the enemy largely outnumbering our & the 5th N. Staffords were forced to retire to AVFS Trench thus leaving the ACONITE/N. hostile in enemy's hand. The men in ACONITE were either killed or taken prisoner. At 6 PM orders were received from the C.O. 1/5 South Staffords who had taken over command of the Brigade forces to withdraw & 1/5 N.M. as a great amount was being harrassed at midnight. The Battalion reached LEVIN at 3 am 2nd July.

Army Form C. 2118.

1/6th Btn South Staffs Regiment.

WAR DIARY
or
INTELLIGENCE SUMMARY.

(127)

(Erase heading not required.)

Instructions regarding War Diaries and Intelligence Summaries are contained in F.S. Regs., Part II. and the Staff Manual respectively. Title pages will be prepared in manuscript.

Place	Date	Hour	Summary of Events and Information	Remarks and references to Appendices
LIEVIN.	2-7-17.		Battalion relieved in Support by 24th French-Canadian Regt. and embussed at LES BREBIS for BURBURE.	
BURBURE.	3-7-17.		Resting.	
"	4-7-17.		Battalion Training.	
"	5-7-17.		—do—	
"	6-7-17.		—do— and Inspection of Companies by the Commanding Officer.	
"	7-7-17.		—do—	
"	8-7-17.		S U N D A Y.	
"	9-7-17.		Battalion Training.	
"	10-7-17.		—do—	
"	11-7-17.		—do— and Inspection of Battalion by the Commanding Officer.	
"	12-7-17.		—do—	
"	13-7-17.		—do—	
"	14-7-17.		—do— and Inspection of Transport Section by Cmdg Officer.	
"	15-7-17.		S U N D A Y.	
"	16-7-17.		Battalion Training. Competitors left for Divisional Rifle Meeting.	
"	17-7-17.		—do—	
"	18-7-17.		Battalion inspected by G.O.C.46th (N.M).Division.	

A5834 Wt.W4973/M687 750,000 8/16 D.D. & L. Ltd. Forms/C.2118/13

Army Form C. 2118.

WAR DIARY (128)
or
INTELLIGENCE SUMMARY.
(Erase heading not required.)

1/6th Btn South Staffs Regt.

Instructions regarding War Diaries and Intelligence Summaries are contained in F.S. Regs., Part II. and the Staff Manual respectively. Title pages will be prepared in manuscript.

Place	Date	Hour	Summary of Events and Information	Remarks and references to Appendices
BURBURE.	19-7-17.		Battalion Training.	
"	20-7-17.		—do—	
"	21-7-17.		—do—	Party returned from Div:Rifle Meeting.
"	22-7-17.		S U N D A Y.	
"	23-7-17.		Battalion Training.	
"	24-7-17.		—do—	
"	25-7-17.		Battalion marched to FOUQUIRES.See O.O.No 32.	
FOUQUIERES.	26-7-17.		Battalion Training.	
LABOURSE.	27-7-17.		Battalion marched to LABOURSE.	
"	28-7-17.		Battalion Training.	
"	29-7-17.		S U N D A Y. Battalion Training.	
"	30-7-17.		Battalion Training.	
"	31-7-17.		—do—	

A5834 Wt.W4973/M687 750,000 8/16 D.D. & L. Ltd. Forms/C.2118/13

Army Form C. 2118.

WAR DIARY
or
INTELLIGENCE SUMMARY.

(Erase heading not required.)

1/6th Bsn South Staffs Regt.

Place	Date	Hour	Summary of Events and Information	Remarks and references to Appendices
			LIST OF PRIZES WON AT DIVISIONAL RIFLE MEETING.	
			G.O.C's Cup. 3rd Prize.	
			Inter-Company Competition. 2nd Prize.	
			Knock-Out Competition. 3rd Prize. "D" Coy.	
			Snapshooting Competition. 1st Prize. L'Cpl Turner J.	
			LIST OF OFFICERS & O'RANKS AWARDED DECORATIONS DURING MONTH OF JULY 1917.	
			Captain E.W.Pege. Military Cross.	
			Lieut:P.H.Highfield-Jones. Military Cross.	
			240197 L'Sgt Morris J. Military Medal.	
			241967 L'Cpl Welmsley W. -do-	
			240976 Pte Whitehouse F. -do-	
			241938 " Oldfield J. -do-	
			242613 " Potter W.E. -do-	
			240408 Cpl Leason W.E. -do-	
			242582 " Sheldon R. -do-	
			242591 L'C Jones H. -do-	
			CASUALTIES FOR MONTH OF JULY 1917.	
			2/Lieut: Hon:W.B.Wrottesley. Wounded.	
			" S.Summers. -do-	
			" W.H.Newborough. -do- Shell Shock.	
			14 O'Ranks. Killed.	
			54 Wounded.	
			3 Died of Wounds.	
			3 Shell-Shock. Wounded.	
			17 Missing.	
			Commdg 1/6th Bsn South Staffordshire Rgt. Lieut:Colonel.	

Copy No 1

OPERATION ORDERS No 32
by
LIEUTENANT-COLONEL F.J.TRUMP. D.S.O.
Commanding 1/6th Btn South Staffordshire Regt.
Dated Tuesday 24th July 1917.

1. **MOVE.** The 1/6th Btn South Staffs Regt,less Transport,will march to FOUQUIERES tomorrow the 25th inst.

2. **ROUTE.** LOZINGHEM - MARKES-les-MINES - LA PUGNOY - LABEUVRIERE - FOUQEREUIL.

3. **STARTING POINT.** Road Junction C.4.c.9.9. Head of column to pass starting point at 9-30a.m.

4. **INTERVALS.** of 500 Yards will be maintained between Battalions.

5. **TRANSPORT.** will march independantly under Lieut:G.F.Smith.

6. **TRANSPORT ROUTE & TIME.** BURBURE - ALLOUAGNE -main CHOCQUES -BETHUNE ROAD to Cross Roads E.3.a.7.6. - E.10.d.3.2, and will start at 10a.m.

7. **PARADE & ORDER OF MARCH.** The Battalion will parade on the Sports Ground at 9-10a.m.
DRUMS."B"."C"."D"."A".

8. **BILLETING PARTY.** 2/Lieut:P.G.Hickman,Cpl Bradley & 4 cyclists will parade at Orderly Room at 4p.m. and will report to the Town Major,HESDIGNEUL at 6p.m. today.

9. **DRESS.** Full Marching-order. Water-bottles to be full.

10. **MESS BASKETS.** to be ready at Company Headquarters at 8-15a.m. All surplus mess stuff to be at the Q.M.Stores by 10p.m. tonight.

11. **OFFICERS VALISES** to be ready at Company Headquarters at 8-15a.m.

12. **BAGGAGE WAGONS.** will report at the Q.M.Stores this evening,and will be returned to H.Q.453rd Coy A.S.C. NOEUX-les-MINES not later than 10a.m. 26th inst.

13. **DINNERS** etc will be served on arrival. Cooks will accompany the Cookers. Officers servants will march with their Companies.

14. **BILLETS.** to be cleaned and ready for inspection by 8-30a.m.

15. **RETURNS.** Marching Out States etc and Billeting Certificates to be at Orderly Room by 8a.m.

16. **ACKNOWLEDGE.**

(Signed) H.HANFORD. Captain.
Adjutant 1/6th Btn South Staffordshire Regiment.

Copies issued to:-
No 1. Commanding Officer.
No 2. O/C "A" Company.
No 3. "   "B"   "
No 4. "   "C"   "
No 5. "   "D"   "
No 6. Quartermaster.
No 7. Transport Officer.
No 8. War Diary.
No 9. File.

Copy No_____

OPERATION ORDERS NO 33,
by
LIEUTENANT-COLONEL F. J. TRUMP. D.S.O.,
Commanding 1/6th Battalion South Staffordshire Regiment.

Thursday, 26th July 1917.

Reference Map 36B 1/40,000.

1. MOVE. The 1/6th Battalion South Staffordshire Regiment will march to LABOURSE to-morrow the 27th instant.

2. DRESS. Full Marching Order, Steel Helmets to be worn.

3. ROUTE. VERQUIN - VERQUIGNEUL - LABOURSE.

4. BILLETING. 2/Lieut: Hickman and 5 cyclists will Parade at Orderly Room at 7.30 a.m. The C.Q.M.Sgts will proceed to LABOURSE at 9 a.m.

5. PARADE & ORDER OF MARCH. Head of Column at B.15.d.50.40. Order of March:- Drums "C" - "D" - "A" - "B" - Transport. Parade at 10.30 a.m.

6. MESS BASKETS. Mess Baskets to be ready at 8.30 a.m. Surplus stores to be at Q.M.Stores at 8.0 a.m.

7. OFFICERS VALISES to be at Company Headquarters at 8.30 a.m.

8. LEWIS GUNS to be loaded at Transport Lines at 8.0 a.m.

9. RETURNS. Marching Out States etc and Billet Certificates to be at Orderly Room at 8.0 a.m.

10. BILLETS. Billets are to be ready for Inspection at 9.30 a.m.

11. BAGGAGE WAGONS will report to the Q.M.Stores this evening.

ACKNOWLEDGE.

(Signed) H. HANFORD. Captain,

Adjutant, 1/6th Battalion South Staffordshire Regiment

Copies Issued to:-

No 1. Commanding Officer.
   2. O/C, "A" Company.
   3. "   "B"   "
   4. "   "C"   "
   5. "   "D"   "
   6. Quartermaster.
   7. Transport Officer.
   8. War Diary.

46/37

Army Form C. 2118.

1/6th Btn South Staffordshire Regiment.

WAR DIARY (128)
or
INTELLIGENCE SUMMARY.
(Erase heading not required.)

Instructions regarding War Diaries and Intelligence Summaries are contained in F. S. Regs., Part II. and the Staff Manual respectively. Title pages will be prepared in manuscript.

Q31

Place	Date	Hour	Summary of Events and Information	Remarks and references to Appendices
1-8-17/31-8-1917.				
LABOURSE	1-8-1917.		In Reserve.	
"	2-8-1917.		-do-	
"	3-8-17.		The Battalion relieved the 4th Btn Lincoln Regt in the Right Section.(See Operation Orders No 33.attached).	
TRENCHES S.W. of Hulluch	4.8.17.		Quiet Day.	
"	5.8.17.		-do-	
"	6.8.17.		-do-	
"	7.8.17.		-do-	
"	8.8.17.		The Battalion was relieved in the Trenches by 1/5th Battalion South Staffordshire Regiment and proceed to Support in MAZINGARBE.(See Operation Orders No 34 attached).	
MAZINGARBE.	8.8.17.			
"	9.8.17.		Battalion employed in Bathing and Cleaning up.	
"	10.8.17.		Battalion Training.	
"	11.8.17.		-do-	
"			The Battalion relieved the 1/5th Battalion in the Trenches during the evening. (See Operation Orders No 35 attached).	
TRENCHES S.W. of HULLUCH	12.8.17.		Quiet Day.	
"	13.8.17.		-do-	
"	14.8.17.		The Battalion was relieved in the Trenches during the evening by 1/5th Battalion South Staffordshire Regiment and proceeded to Brigade Reserve in NOEUX-LES-MINES. (See Operation Orders No 36 attached).	
NOEUX-LES-MINES.	15.8.17.		Battalion employed in Bathing and Cleaning up.	
"	16.8.17.		Battalion Training.	
"	17.8.17.		The Battalion relieved the 1/5th Battalion South Staffordshire Regiment in the Trenches. (See Operation Orders No 37 attached).	
TRENCHES S.W. of HULLUCH	18.8.17.		Quiet Day.	
"	19.8.17.		-do-	
"	20.8.17.		-do-	
"	21.8.17.		The Battalion was relieved in the evening by 1/5th Btn South Staffs Regt and proceed to Brigade Support in MAZINGARBE.(See Operation Orders No 38 attached).	

Army Form C. 2118.

1/6th Btn South Staffordshire Regiment.   WAR DIARY (129)
                                            or
Instructions regarding War Diaries and Intelligence   INTELLIGENCE SUMMARY.
Summaries are contained in F.S. Regs., Part II.
and the Staff Manual respectively. Title pages
will be prepared in manuscript.
                                          (Erase heading not required.)

Place	Date	Hour	Summary of Events and Information	Remarks and references to Appendices
MAZINGARBE	22.8.17.		Battalion Training.	
"	23.8.17.		Battalion Training.	
"	24.8.17.		Battalion Training. Operation Orders No 39 (see attached) issued with regard to proposed discharge of Gas installed on Brigade Front.	
"	25.8.17.		The Battalion relieved the 1/5th Battalion South Staffordshire Regiment in the Trenches. (See Operation Orders No 40 attached.)	
TRENCHES S.W. of HULLUCH	26.8.17.		Quiet Day.	
"	27.8.17.		Proposed Raid on enemy Trenches postponed.	
"	28.8.17.		In accordance with instructions contained in 137th Infantry Brigade Order No 162 the raid was successfully performed by Captain E.W.Page M.C., 4 Officers, and 100 other ranks, assisted by 6 Sappers of the 466th Field Company R.E. The Raiders were assembled in the front line trench at 7.30 p.m. and at 8.3 p.m., the ZERO hour, went over the top with the first shots of the barrage. All parties carried out their instructions to the letter, except that the forward parties failed to enter the German Second Line on the Right and Left flanks owing to the proximity of our barrage. In the centre of the second line this trench was found to be unoccupied and practically obliterated. The allotted task having been completed the raiders were withdrawn at ZERO plus 30 minutes. Total casualties 2 killed, and 17 wounded. Estimated enemy casualties 30 to 40. Prisoners taken 5. Unit 3rd Battalion, 393rd Regiment, VII Division. (See Operation Orders No 41, Appendix "A" and Appendix "B" attached). On completion of Raid "C" and "D" Companies occupied Front Line as per Operations Orders No 42 attached.	
"	29.8.17.		The Battalion was relieved in the Trenches, The Right Front and Support Companies by 1st Kings Shropshire Light Infantry, and the Left Front and Support Companies at 1/6th Battalion North Staffordshire Regiment. (See Operation Orders No 43 attached.)	

Army Form C. 2118.

WAR DIARY (130)
or
INTELLIGENCE SUMMARY.
(Erase heading not required.)

1/6th Battalion South Staffordshire Regiment.

Instructions regarding War Diaries and Intelligence Summaries are contained in F.S. Regs., Part II. and the Staff Manual respectively. Title pages will be prepared in manuscript.

Place	Date	Hour	Summary of Events and Information	Remarks and references to Appendices
MAZINGARBE	29.8.17.		The Battalion employed on Pioneer work. "A" & "B" Companies being billeted in MAZINGARBE and "C" & "D" Companies in TENTH AVENUE.	
"	30.8.17.		- ditto -	
"	31.8.17.		- ditto -	
			TOTAL CASUALTIES FOR MONTH OF AUGUST 1917.	
			OFFICERS. 2/Lieut: H.W. Wootton. Wounded 5.8.17.
			" D. Martin. " 19.8.17.
			Lieut: G.F. Smith. (At Duty) " 20.8.17.
			OTHER RANKS. Killed 6.
			Wounded 34.
			Died of Wounds 1.

Commanding 1/6th Battalion South Staffordshire Regiment. Lieut-Colonel.

Operation Orders No 33   Copy No 8
by
Lieutenant-Colonel F.J.Trump. D.S.O.,
Commanding 1/6th Battalion South Staffordshire Regiment.

Wednesday, 1st August 1917.

1. The 1/6th Btn South Staffs Regt will relieve the 4th Lincoln Regiment in the Right Section to-morrow night 2/3rd August.

2. Movement to be by Companies at 200 yards intervals beyond Sailly Labourse and by Platoons at 200 yards intervals from Cross Roads Philosophe.

3. All Trench Stores, Maps & Aeroplane Photos will be taken over. Serial numbers of all Secret Maps taken over to be forwarded to Orderly Room with copy of Trench Stores by 9 am 3rd instant.

4. Transport Lines, Q.M.Stores, & Canteen will remain at Sailly Labourse.

5. Coy Q.M.Sgts and Company Cooks, except one Cook of "A" & "C" Coys, will remain at the Q.M.Stores.

6. Guides will meet Platoons near Fosse 3 Philosophe, where the track commences, at 9.30 p.m.

7. Order of March - H.Q'rs, "B" - "D" - "A" - "C". "B" Company to move off at 8.15 p.m.

8. Packs to be stored at Q.M.Stores under Company arrangments not later than 4 p.m. Officers valises to be at Company Headquarters at 6.0 p.m. Mess baskets for the trenches to be at Coy H.Q'rs at 7.0 p.m. Boxes etc not for the trenches to be ready at same time.

9. Lewis Guns to be loaded at Transport Lines at 10.15 a.m. These Guns and 6 panniers per team will be dumped at Philosophe, where track commences near Fosse 3, and picked up by Companies as they pass. Remainder of panniers will be sent to Battalion H.Q. by rail. Signal Officer will arrange for 'phones etc.

10. Regtl Sgt-Major and Pioneer Sergt will take over from 4th Lincs at 8 p.m. Runners will accompany the R.S.M. and will reconnoitre all routes to Coy H.Q. and Brigade etc immediately on arrival.

11. No cooking or fires will be allowed in front or support lines. Cooking and carrying to be done by the two Companies in reserve. Rations etc arrive at Battalion H.Q. dump by rail about 11 pm.

12. "B" & "D" Companies will be in the line, "A" & "C" Coys in Support. "B" & "A" on the right of front and support line respectively.

13. Relief complete to be notified to Btn H.Q. by word "Bird".

14. On account of the wet state of the trenches whale oil is to be used regularly.

15. Certificates etc to be rendered to Orderly Room by 7 pm, and billets ready for inspection by the Medical Officer at 7.30 pm.

16. Dress - No 2 Fighting Order, filled water bottles. Rations for 3rd August to be carried on the man. Great coats will not be taken to the trenches.

17. Acknowledge.

(Signed) H.Hanford. Captain,
Adjutant, 1/6th Battalion South Staffordshire Regiment.

Operation Orders No 314.   Copy No. 11.
by
Lieutenant Colonel F. J. Trump. D.S.O.
Commanding 16th Bn. South Staffordshire Regiment.

                                                Monday 6th August 1917.

1. The 15th Bn. South Staffordshire Regiment will relieve the 16th Bn. South Staffordshire Regiment in Right subsector tomorrow night 7/8 August.

2. Companies will be placed as follows:—

	Right Coy.	Left Coy.	Right Support	Left Support
16th South Staffs	B	D	A	C
15th South Staffs	A	B	C	D

3. One guide per platoon will report to Battn. H.Q. at 6 p.m. to proceed to FOSSE 3 to meet 15th South Staffs.

4. Lewis gun S.A.A. panniers will be handed over on relief. All other Specialist equipment and box periscopes will be brought out of trenches. Lewis Guns will be carried out.

5. Officers Mess baskets and cooks utensils to be at H.Q. at 9.30 p.m. to go down by rail. Servants may accompany them.

6. On completion of relief the Battn. less "A" Coy will be in Brigade Reserve at MAZINGARBE.
   "A" Coy will be in immediate support in dugouts near 15th North Staffs H.Q.

7. O.C. A Coy will send 3 men to report to 2/Lieut. S. Wood at Btn. H.Q. at 9 a.m. to reconnoitre position of dugouts. Rations for A Coy will be delivered at 15th North Staffs Dump. One of the 3 men will remain in charge of the dugouts and will also receive the rations on arrival. O.C. A Coy will take what cooking utensils he requires with him and return the rest if any to Battn. H.Q. to be sent down by rail as per para 5.
   This Company will be under the orders of 137th Brigade.

8. Coy. Q.M.S.'s less A Coy will take over billets in MAZINGARBE and will meet Companies on arrival.

9. Relief complete to be notified to H.Q. by code word LEAVE.

                              (Signed). H. HANFORD Captain.
                    Adjutant 16th Bn. South Staffordshire Regiment.

Copies issued:- No.1. Commanding Officer. No 2/5. Companies. No.6. R.S.M. No.7 War Diary.
No.8 File. No.9 T.O. No.10 Q.M.

Operation Orders No 35,   Copy No 11
by
Lieutenant-Colonel F.J.Trump. D.S.O.,
Commanding 1/6th Battalion South Staffordshire Regiment.

Friday, 10th August 1917.

1. <u>Relief</u>.   The 1/6th Battalion South Staffordshire Regiment will relieve the 1/5th Battalion South Staffordshire Regiment in the Right Subsector to-morrow the 11th instant.

2. <u>Distribution</u>.   Right Coy. Left Coy. Right Support Coy. Left Support Coy.
                        "A" Co.   "C" Co.   "B" Co.   "D" Co.

3. <u>Parade</u>.   8 p.m. at Company Headquarters.

4. <u>Dress</u>.   Fighting Order No 2 and filled water bottles.

5. <u>Order of March</u>. Headquarters, "B" Coy, "C" Coy, "D" Coy. Companies will march by Platoons with 200 yards intervals. "A" Company will move from Tenth Avenue as soon as light permits.

6. <u>Rations</u>.   Rations for the 12th will be carried on the men.

7. <u>Stores</u>.   Lists of Trench Stores taken over to be carefully checked and forwarded to Battalion Headquarters by 9 a.m. on the 12th.

8. <u>Advance Party</u>. Specialist Officers, R.S.M., and Pioneer Sergeant will report to 1/5th Battalion South Staffordshire Regiment at 8 p.m. to-morrow.

9. <u>Relief Complete</u>. Relief to be complete by 2 a.m. the 12th instant. Relief complete to be notified to Battalion Headquarters by sending code word "Bay".

10. <u>Battn H.Q</u>.   Battalion Headquarters will close at Mazingarbe at 8.0 p.m.

11. <u>Acknowledge</u>.

                         (Signed) H.Hanford. Captain,
Adjutant, 1/6th Battalion South Staffordshire Regiment.

Copies Issued to:-

        No 1. Commanding Officer.
           2. G.O.C., 137th Infantry Brigade.
           3. O/C, 1/5th Btn South Staffs Regt.
           4.   "   "A" Company.
           5.   "   "B"   "
           6.   "   "C"   "
           7.   "   "D"   "
           8. Transport Officer.
           9. Quartermaster.
          10. R.S.M.
          11. War Diary.
          12.   "   "   (Duplicate)
          13. File.
          14. O/C, Left Battalion.

SECRET.   Operation Orders No. 36.   Copy No. 10

Lieutenant Colonel H. Vivian S.O.
Commanding 16th Bn. South Staffordshire Regiment.

Monday Aug 3rd 1914.

1. **RELIEF.** The 15th Bn. South Staffordshire Regiment will relieve the 16th Bn. South Staffordshire Regiment in trenches tomorrow night 4/5 Aug.

2. **MOVE.** On completion of relief, the Battalion will march to NOEUX-LES-MINES to Brigade Reserve.

3. **ROUTES.** H. Qrs. "A" Coy & "B" Coy via POSEN ALLEY — RATION DUMP — RAILWAY TRACK — VICTORIA STN — track to MAZINGARBE — NOEUX-LES-MINES.
"C" Coy & "D" Coy via VENDIN ALLEY — QUARRY DUMP — LAMBERT TRACK — VICTORIA STN — track to MAZINGARBE — NOEUX-LES-MINES.

4. **MOVEMENT** By platoons at 200 yards intervals.

5. **LEWIS GUNS &c.** Lewis Guns and S.A.A. will be brought out of the line on relief and carried to Church at MAZINGARBE where they will be loaded into limbers. All Specialist equipment on charge of Companies will also be brought out. List of Trench Stores to be handed over, to reach Battn. H.Q. not later than 3.30 p.m.

6. **MESS BASKETS &c.** Mess Baskets and cooks utensils to be at Posen Dump at 9.30 a.m.

7. **BILLETING.** Lieut. J. Wood and Coy. Q.M. Sgts. will report to Town Major NOEUX-LES-MINES at 3 p.m.

8. **DISTRIBUTION**

	Right Coy.	Left Coy.	Right Support	Left Support
16th South Staffs.	A	C	B	D
15th South Staffs.	C	D	A	B

9. Relief to be complete by 2 a.m. 5th instant and notified to Battn. H.Q. by code word "BALL".

10. **ACKNOWLEDGE.**

(Signed) H. HANFORD Captain
Adjutant 16th Bn. South Staffordshire Regiment.

Copies issued to:-
1. Commanding Officer.   4/7. Companies   10. O/C War Diary
2. 13th Infantry Brigade.   8. T.O.   12/13 File
3. O.C. 15th South Staffs.   9. Q.M.   14. R.S.M.

Operation Orders No 37.   Copy No 11
1/6th Battalion South Staffordshire Regiment.

1. **Relief.** The Battalion will relieve the 1/5th Battalion South Staffordshire Regiment in the right subsector to-morrow night, 17/18th instant.

2. **Distribution.** Right Coy. Left Coy. Right Support. Left Support.
                  "B"   "D"   "A"   "C"

3. **Move.** Companies will move by Platoons at 200 yards interval to Mazingarbe. Starting Point L.19.a.35.75. Tea will be had in the Brigade Headquarter Grounds. March to the trenches will be continued at 8 p.m.

4. **Order of March.** Headquarters - "B" - "D" - "A" - "C".

5. **Parade.** 5.0 p.m. at Company Headquarters.

6. **Dress.** No 2 Fighting Order.

7. **Rations.** Rations for the 17th instant will carried on the man. Water bottles to be filled.

8. **Stores.** List of trench stores taken over to be checked and forwarded to Battalion Headquarters by first runner 18th instant.

9. **Advance Party.** Specialist Officers, R.S.M. and Pioneer Sergeant will proceed to the trenches at 6.0 p.m.

10. **Relief Complete.** Relief to be complete by 2.0 a.m. 18th instant, and notified to Battalion Headquarters by code word "Beer".

11. **Battalion Headquarters** will close at Noeux Les Mines at 5.0 p.m. and re-open at Curzon Street on arrival.

12. **Acknowledge.**

(Signed) H.Hanford. Captain,
Adjutant, 1/6th Battalion South Staffordshire Regt.

Copies Issued to:-
1. Commanding Officer.
2. G.O.C., 137th Infantry Brigade.
3. O/C, 1/5th Btn South Staffs Regt.
4. " "A" Company.
5. " "B" "
6. " "C" "
7. " "D" "
8. Transport Officer.
9. Quartermaster.
10. R.S.M.
11. War Diary.
12. " " (Duplicate).
13. File.
14. O/C, Left Battalion.

Operation Orders No 38.
"6th Batt: South Staffordshire Regiment"

Copy No 10

20th August 1917.

1. **RELIEF.** 15th Btn South Staffordshire Regiment will relieve the 6th Btn South Staffordshire Regiment in Right Sub-sector on night of 21/22 August. Relief to be complete by 2 a.m.

2. **MOVE.** The Battalion less "C" Coy will move into Brigade Support at Mazingarbe. "C" Coy will be in immediate support in Tenth Avenue. This Company will be under orders of 137th Infantry Brigade.

3. **L.G. S.A.A.** Lewis Gun S.A.A. will be handed over on relief. "C" Coy will take over Lewis Guns S.A.A. in Tenth Avenue. Lewis Gun Officer will send a N.C.O. to Mazingarbe to take over L.G. S.A.A. from 15th Btn South Staffs Regt at 4 p.m.

4. **MESS BASKETS & ETC.** Mess Baskets and cooks Utensils to be at Battalion Dump at 1.30 p.m. All specialist equipment on charge of Companies to be brought out of trenches.

5. **BILLETS.** 2/Lieut J. Peacock and Coy Q.M. Sergts will report to Town Major's Office Mazingarbe at 4 p.m.

6. **MOVEMENT.** All movement will be by properly formed bodies and strict march discipline is to be maintained. No individuals or parties will move over the open till after dark.

7. **STORE LISTS.** List of Trench Stores to be handed over to be at Orderly Room by 3.30 p.m.

8. **RATIONS.** Q.M. will send rations for "C" Coy up with 6th North Staffs trucks. Coy Q.M. Sergt. will see them delivered.

9. **RELIEF COMPLETE.** To be notified to Batta H.Q. by code word FOAM.

10. **ACKNOWLEDGE.**

(Signed) H. HANFORD Captain,
Adjutant 6th Btn South Staffordshire Regiment.

Copies issued to:-
No 1. Commanding Officer.   No 4/7. Companies.   No 11. War Diary.
" 2. 137th Infantry Brigade.   " 8. Transport Officer.   12/13. File.
" 3. O.C. 6th Btn South Staffs.   " 9. Quarter Master.   14. R.S.M.

SECRET

No 10

Operation Orders No 39,
1/6th Battalion South Staffordshire Regiment.

24th August 1917.

. The Gas installed on Brigade Front between trenches 66 and 72 a will be discharged by "C" Special Company R.E., as soon as wind is favourable.

. "Zero" hour for discharge will be communicated later as per code attached. This will not be before 1 a.m. to-night.

. Artillery and Machine Guns will co-operate from "Zero" plus 4 minutes to "Zero" plus 30 minutes. "P" Section No 4 Special Company R.E. will co-operate against enemy trench junction - firing to commence at "Zero" plus 3 minutes.

. The following precautions will be taken:-
(a) Front and Support Lines from Trench 63 to Trench 73 will be cleared except for a post about junction of Vendin Alley and Support Line.
(b) Respirators will be worn by all troops forward of Battalion Headquarters. These will be adjusted at "Zero" minus 5 minutes and will not be removed until the Gas Officer reports "All Clear".
(c) A Section Officer of "C" Special Company R.E. will be at Company Headquarters H.19.a.1.7. and H.19.a.3.2.

. All messages regarding these operations will be by runner.

. Watches will be synchronised at 7.15 p.m.

. About 2 hours notice will be given of the "Zero" hour.

. Trenches as per para 4a will be cleared by "Zero" minus 15 minutes.

. When gas has been discharged it is not safe to send out patrols until four hours afterwards.

. Acknowledge.

H. Hanford
Captain,

Adjutant, 1/6th Battalion South Staffordshire Regiment.

Copies Issued to:-

       No 1. Commanding Officer.
          2. 137th Infantry Brigade.
          3. O/C, "A" Company.
          4. "   "B"   "
          5. "   "C"   "
          6. "   "D"   "
          7. Transport Officer.
          8. Quartermaster.
          9. R.S.M.
         10. War Diary.
         11. "   "   (Duplicate)
         12. File.

1/6th Battalion South Staffordshire Regt.
-:-:-:-:-:-:-:-:-:-:-:-:-:-:-:-:-:-:-:- :-:-:-:-:-:-

C O D E

Issued in conjunction with Operation Orders No 39.

Gas will be discharged to-night   - Balloon.
Gas will not be discharged to-night - Slumber.

"Zero" hour will be -

       Periwinkle - 1 = Q.
                 2 = H.
                 3 = S.
                 4 = B.
                 5 = K.
                 6 = R.
                 7 = F.
                 8 = Z.
                 9 = A.
                 0 = W.

            A.M. = Sun.
            P.M. = Moon.

Example -

    "Zero hour will be 2.37 a.m."

        will read - "Periwinkle H.SF Sun."

24th August 1917.

SECRET   No 11

Operation Orders No 40.
1/6th Battalion South Staffordshire Regiment.

24th August 1917.

1. Relief.   The 1/6th Btn South Staffs Regt will relieve
                    the 1/5th Btn South Staffs Regt in the Right
                    sub-sector to-morrow night 25/26th August.
                    Relief to be complete by 2 a.m. 26th August.

2. Distribution.   Right Company -- "A" Company.
                    Left   "   -- "C"   "
                    Right Support -- "B"   "
                    Left Support   -- "D"   "

3. Move.   Starting Point - road junction B.23.b.20.80.
                    Order of March - "A" - "C" - "H.Q." - "B".
                    First Platoon of "A" Company to pass starting
                    point at 7.50 p.m., remaining Platoons at
                    200 yards distance. "D" Company will move
                    from Tenth Avenue at dusk.

4. Dress.   Fighting Order.

5. Rations.   Rations for the 26th instant will be carried
                    on the men. Water bottles to be filled.

6. Stores.   Lists of Trench Stores taken over to be sent to
                    Orderly Room first runner on the 26th instant.

7. Advance   Specialist Officers and the Regimental Sergeant-
   Party.   Major will proceed to the trenches at 6.0 p.m.

8. Relief complete to be notified by code word "Bread".

9. Battalion Headquarters will close at Mazingarbe at 7.30 p.m.
   and re-open at Curzon Street on arrival.

10. Movement.   No movement over the open will be allowed until
                    after dusk.

11.   Acknowledge.

                                                H. Hanford
                                                Captain,

Adjutant, 1/6th Battalion South Staffordshire Regiment.

Copies Issued to:-

                    No 1. Commanding Officer.
                        2. 137th Infantry Brigade.
                        3. 1/5th Btn South Staffs Regt.
                        4. O/C, "A" Company.
                        5. "   "B"   "
                        6. "   "C"   "
                        7. "   "D"   "
                        8. Transport Officer.
                        9. Quartermaster.
                       10. R.S.M.
                       11. War Diary.
                       12. "   "   (Duplicate.
                       13. File.
                       14. Left Battalion.

Secret.   Operation Orders No 41,   Copy No 21
1/6th Battalion South Staffordshire Regiment.

25th August 1917.

Reference:- LOOS, 36c N.W.3. Edition 8b, 1/10,000.

1. **Raid.** On 27th August 1917 the 1/6th Btn South Staffs Regt will carry out a daylight raid on the enemy Front and Support Trenches between points Posen Crater (H.19.d.35.10) and H.25.b.45.55. "Zero" hour to be notified later.

2. **Object.**
   (a) To secure identification by obtaining prisoners.
   (b) To kill Germans.
   (c) To inflict damage.

3. **Strength.** The Raiding Party will consist of 5 Officers and 100 other ranks under the Command of Captain L.W. Page.

4. **Composition of Raiding Party.**
   "A" Company - 3 parties of 10 O.R. and 2 Lewis Gun Teams.
   "B" Company - 3 parties of 10 O.R. and 2 Lewis Gun Teams.
   Six Sappers of No 466th Company R.E. will be under orders of O/C Raid for dug-out destruction.

5. **Assembly.** At "Zero" minus 30 minutes the Raiding Party will form up in front line between trenches 63 and 64 opposite the gaps cut in our wire. "B" Company having moved up to shafts in front line under cover of darkness on night of 26/27th August.

6. **Objectives.** The three parties of "A" Company will proceed direct to enemy second line as soon as barrage lifts allows and clean up the trench, establishing blocks on the outer flanks.
   The three parties of "B" Company as under:-
   The two outer parties will attack Posen Crater and the long sap at H.25.b.45.55, and having cleared same will leave two Lewis Guns in Posen Crater and one Lewis Gun in the long sap and will with the third party and one Lewis Gun enter enemy front line which they will thoroughly mop up by working outwards and establishing blocks on the outer flanks.

7. **Advanced Headquarters.** Advanced Battalion Headquarters will be established in Right Company Headquarters, Posen Alley.

8. **Raid C.O's Headquarters.** Will be in a central position in German front line trench.

9. **Communication.** A forward telephone will be established in Medical Officers dug-out in Support Line near Dalkey Trench.

10. **Artillery.** Artillery programme to be issued later will be arranged by the C.R.A. and 137th Infantry Brigade.

11. **Equipment.** All ranks will remove identification marks, papers etc, and will be inspected by their respective party Officers before leaving front line trench. Each Officer and man will be provided with a label bearing his name, Regtl Number, and special Raid Number. On the return of the raid these labels will be handed in to the Assistant Adjutant who will be on duty in the trench.

- 2 -

11. **Equipment.** (continued)	Each man will carry a Rifle with fixed bayonet and one bandolier S.A.A. (50 rounds) and a slit sandbag containing six bombs. Lewis Gunners to be equipped as detailed by O/C, Raid. Two men in each party will carry Rifle Grenades. O/C, Raid will ensure that ample means for wire cutting are carried.
12. **Sequence of Operations.**	(a) At "Zero" intense barrage opens on enemy front line trenches and Raiding Party leaves British front line trench. (b) At "Zero" plus two minutes barrage lifts to enemy second line followed by Raiding Party into German front line trench. (c) At "Zero" plus four minutes barrage lifts from enemy second to enemy third line and remains there during the operations. "A" Companies parties enter German second line and clean up same. (d) The 137th Machine Gun Company will co-operate in the barrage and will obtain all assistance possible from neighbouring Machine Gun Units. (e) 137th Trench Mortar Battery will assist in the barrage under orders of O/C, 1/6th Battalion South Staffordshire Regiment. 2" Trench Mortars will fire under orders of C.R.A. (f) A F.O.O. detailed by the O/C, Hulluch Group will be with Battalion Commander at Advanced Battalion Headquarters. The Artillery will lay the necessary wires and test the same, spare instruments and alternative routes will be arranged for. (g) The order to cease fire will be given by O/C, 1/6th Battalion South Staffs Regiment to the F.O.O. who will communicate same to the Artillery.
13. **Watches.**	Watches will be synchronised daily under Brigade arrangements until the Raid takes place.
14. **Withdrawal.**	There will no light or sound signal for withdrawal. Orders for withdrawal will be given by O/C, Raid when the task is completed, but all Raiders must be clear of enemy trenches by "Zero" plus 30 minutes.
15. **Command.**	In the event of O/C Raid becoming a casualty Captain P.H.Highfield Jones M.C. will assume Command.
16. **Identification.**	Each Officer and N.C.O. is responsible for securing identification by means of shoulder straps, papers, etc, from the bodies of dead or badly wounded Germans. Slightly wounded Germans will be brought back with other prisoners.
17. **Medical arrangments.**	The Medical Officer, 1/6th Bn South Staffs Regt, will establish a Regimental Aid Post in dug-out in support line off Dakkey Trench and will arrange for the necessary R.A.M.C. personnel required.
18. **Movement & Silence.**	Movement in "Posen" and neighbouring trenches will be reduced to the absolute minimum on the 27th August 1917, and on no account are conversations relating to this operation to take place over the telephone.

- 3 -

19. **Prisoners.** Prisoners will be sent by O/C, Raid to a selected shaft entrance in British Front Line where they will be taken over by the Regimental Police who will take charge of them until they can be sent to rear Battalion Headquarters. The prisoners will be searched by the Assistant Adjutant.

20. **Orders.** O/C, Raid will issue detailed orders to the Raiding Party and communicate the Raid password on the night of the operations.

21. **Acknowledge.**

H. Hanford
Captain,

Adjutant 1/6th Battalion South Staffordshire Regt.

25th August 1917.

Copies Issued to:-

No 1. Commanding Officer.
2. Second in Command.
3. Adjutant.
4. 137th Infantry Brigade.
5. O/C, "A" Company.
6. O/C, "B" Company.
7. O/C, "C" Company.
8. O/C, "D" Company.
9 to 13. O/C, Raid.
14. C.R.E.
15. O/C, Hulluch Group, R.A.
16. O/C, Left Battalion.
17. O/C, Right Battalion.
18. R.S.M.
19. Quartermaster.
20. Transport Officer.
21. War Diary.
22. War Diary. (Duplicate).
23. File.
24. File. (Duplicate).
25. O/C, 137th Machine Gun Coy.
26. O/C, 137th Trench Mortar Bty.

APPENDIX "A".

Medical Arrangements.

1. The Medical Officer will establish an Advanced Dressing Station in the dugout in the Support Line near DALKEY TRENCH.

2. Stretcher Bearers of "A" "B" & "C" Companies will report to O/C Raid at a time to be notified later and will be attached two to each party of Raiders.

3. They will use the "Trench-ladder-stretcher" in place of the ordinary stretchers.

4. Two Stretcher Bearers of "D" Company will report to O/C. "C" Company to be attached for duty for period of the Raid.

5. Four R.A.M.C. Bearers from Field Ambulance will be accomodated, in the dugout near the LOOS-HULLUCH ROAD where it crosses POSEN ALLEY, for the purpose of evacuation.

6. Eight R.A.M.C. Bearers from Field Ambulance will be accomodated in the Machine Gun dugout 40 yards "E" of the junction of RESERVE TRENCH and POSEN ALLEY. These men will hold themselves in readiness to assist in the evacuation of wounded when called upon.

7. An M.O. from the Field Ambulance will report to Battalion Headquarters at 6.0 p.m. on "Z" day and will take up his position in the "R.A.P." in PONT STREET.

8. Eight R.A.M.C. bearers will be accomodated in the Bearer Post in PONT STREET and will be under the direct orders of the M.O. at the R.A.P. in PONT STREET.

                        (Signed) H.D.LANE. Captain, R.A.M.C.

                        M.O. 1/6th Btn South Staffs Regt.

26th September 1917.

Orders by O/c Raid
16th Battn South Staffs Regiment.

26th August 1917

Reference LOOS 36c. N.W. 10,000 & Battn Operation Orders No 41.

1. A & B Coys will carry out a daylight raid on the enemy's front and support lines between "POSEN CRATER" H19d 35.10 and H25b 15.55. Zero hour to be notified later.

2. OBJECT (a) To secure identification by obtaining prisoners.
   (b) To kill Germans.
   (c) To inflict damage.

3. COMPOSITION OF PARTIES.
   (1) /Lieut N.L. Dickson and 11 O.R.
   (2) Sergt Sheldon   "   11 "
   (3) /Lieut C.W. Wickers "   12 "
   (4) /Lieut J.G. Brady   "   12 ", 1 Lewis Gun Team, and 3 R.E's.
   (5) Sergt G.W. Burton   "   11 ", and 1 Lewis Gun Team.
   (6) Capt. T.A.H. Jones   "   12 ", 2 Lewis Gun Teams, and 3 R.E's.

4. Assembly will be as per Battalion Operation Orders No 41, parties in the following order:-
   "No 6" - "No 3" - "H.Qrs" - "No 5" - "No 2" - "No 1" - "No 4".

5. OBJECTIVES.
   No 1 Party, will proceed to enemy support line at H25b 75.81 and will there form a block and clear the trench to H25b 18.84 (trench junction)
   No 2 Party will proceed direct to enemy support line at H25b 68.84 and will clear the trench to H19d 60.00.
   No 3 Party will proceed direct to enemy support line to trench junction at H19d 56.10 - form a block there and clear the trench to H19d 60.00.
   No 4 Party will seize the long sap at H25b 15.55 and having cleared same will establish a Lewis Gun to cover the right flank. They will then proceed to block front line trench at H25b 55.60 and mop up the trench in the immediate neighbourhood

— 1 —

2.

5. OBJECTIVES (continued)

No. 5 Party will enter the enemy front line at H25b 50.80 and will mop up the trench outwards to the flank parties. The Lewis Gun Team of this party will act as reserve for Oc. Raid.

No. 6 Party will seize POZEN CRATER and having cleared same will establish its two Lewis Guns to cover the left flank. They will then proceed to block the enemy's front line at H19d 35.13 and mop up the trench in the immediate neighbourhood.

NOTE. The R.E's detailed for parties Nos 4 & 6 will carry explosives for the demolition of dugout, etc. Party leaders must warn all ranks that they must keep clear of enemy dugout entrances at the time of demolition which should take place just previous to the withdrawal.

6. RAID HEADQUARTERS will be formed in German front line about H25b 50.80.

7. EQUIPMENT as per Battalion Operation Orders No 41, and Lewis Gunners will be equipped as follows:-
No 1. Revolver, Lewis Gun and Spare Parts.
" 2. Revolver and two Panniers.
Nos 3,4,5 & 6. Rifle and Bayonet, 2 Magazines, and 6 Rifle Grenades each.

8. SEQUENCE OF EVENTS as per Battalion Operation Orders No 41. After getting clear of our own wire parties will deploy and cross "NO MAN'S LAND" in two waves at ten paces distance, and will proceed to their various objectives in that formation as far as possible.

9. WATCHES will be synchronised daily

— 3 —

10. <u>WITHDRAWAL</u>. At "ZERO" + 20 Parties 1, 2, + 3 on completion of their tasks will withdraw to enemy front line where they will remain until "ZERO" + 30. They will then continue their withdrawal followed by parties No 4, 5 + 6. The Lewis Gun teams of Parties Nos. 4 + 6 will remain in position until all parties are well clear of enemy wire when they will themselves withdraw.

11. In the event of O/C. Raid becoming a casualty Captain S. H. Highfeld Jones M.C. will take over command.

12. <u>IDENTIFICATION</u>. Each Officer and N.C.O. is responsible for securing some identification. This is of the utmost importance.

13. <u>MEDICAL ARRANGEMENTS</u>, as per Battalion Operation Orders No. 11. Two Stretcher Bearers will accompany each of Parties Nos 1, 3, 4 + 6 and 4 S.B's with O/C. Raid.
<u>NOTE</u>. It is of the greatest encouragement to others if slightly wounded men continue to carry out their duties.

14. <u>PRISONERS</u> will be immediately sent to O/C. Raid at Raid Hd. to await removal to collecting stations in our front line.

15. <u>COUNTER-SIGN</u> will be arranged and notified to all concerned before "ZERO" hour.

16. <u>PARTY LEADERS</u> will be held responsible for the reading of Operation Orders to their parties.

17. <u>MOVEMENT</u>. Party Leaders must warn their parties that there must be the least possible movement in POGEN and neighbouring trenches immediately preceding the hour of "ZERO".

18. Party Leaders will inspect all ranks by 7.0 p.m and must be absolutely certain that all badges, papers, identity discs, etc, and any marks by which the Regt. can be identified, in case a man is made prisoner, are removed.

26.8.17.   O/C. 1/6th Btn. South Staffs Regiment, Captain Raiding Party

SECRET   Operation Orders No. 4a   Copy No. 9

1/6th Bn. South Staffordshire Regiment

27th August 1917

1. **MOVES**   On completion of Hill 60 fight the Right Company front will be taken over as under and the Raiding party withdrawn via POSEN ALLEY to Reserve Line.
   At 10 p.m. or earlier if situation allows 4 Lewis Gun teams of "C" Coy will move from Left front company along firing line and take over the Right front company. 4 Lewis Guns of "D" Coy will occupy posts vacated by "C" Coy Lewis Gunners. Relief to be complete by 11 p.m.

2. **TRAFFIC.**   From 11 p.m. onwards POSEN ALLEY will be used by 1/5th South Staffs Regt. and will be kept clear of all other troops.

3. **SECOND RAID.**   The 1/5th South Staffs Regt. will carry out a raid from trenches Nos 63 & 64 between 1 a.m. and dawn. They will be in position by 1 a.m.

4. **ROUTES**   The 1/5th South Staffs Regt. routes to position of assembly are: TENTH AVENUE — CURZON STREET — POSEN ALLEY.

5. **RELIEF AND FINAL DISPOSITION.**   At 3.15 a.m. or earlier if situation allows, "C" Company will move from Left front company along firing line and take over the Right front company. "D" Company from Left Support will take over Left Front company. The Battalion will then be distributed:—
   C Company – Right Front   D Company – Left Front
   B   "   – Right Support   A   "   – Left Support.
   Relief to be complete by 3.35 a.m. and notified to Battalion Headquarters by code word "GOOD".

6.   O/c 1/5th South Staffs Regt. particularly requests that all ranks of 1/6th South Staffs Regt. refrain from entering into conversation or communicating with any of 1/5th South Staffs Regt. until all operations are completed.

7. **HEAD-QUARTERS**   Advanced Battalion Headquarters will close at Right Company Headquarters at 10 p.m.

—1—

~ 2 ~

8. During the said periods the first line trenches will be considerably thinned, especially in the sectors containing gas.

9. ACKNOWLEDGE.

H Hanford
Captain,
Adjutant, 1/5th Batt. South Staffs. Regiment.

27th August 1917.

Copies Issued to :-
No 1. Commanding Officer
 2. O/C "A" Company.
 3. " "B" "
 4. " "C" "
 5. " "D" "
 6. 137th Inf. Brigade.
 7. 1/5th South Staff. Regt.
 8 & 9. War Diary.
 10. File
 11. R.S.M.

Secret.   Operation Orders No 43   Copy No
             7th Bn South Staffordshire Regiment
                                              29th August 1917

1. RELIEF. (a) A.Os, A & B Companies on completion of relief
            tonight will move to MAZINGARBE.
            (b) "C" & "D" Coys will move into dug-outs in 10th Avenue.
            (c) The 1st K.S.L.I. will relieve "C" Company as far as
            Trench 67 exclusive, & B Coy in Reserve Line. The 7th Bn North
            Staffs Regt will relieve "D" Company and take over
            the line from Trench 67 exclusive to ESSEX LANE, and
            A Coy in Reserve Line

2. LEWIS   All Lewis Gun panniers etc and specialist equipment
   GUN   in charge of Companies will be brought out of the
   SAK etc Trenches.   A & B Coys will carry their Lewis Guns
            and Magazines to MAZINGARBE, and "C" & "D" Coys to
            their new quarters in 10th AVENUE.

3. TRENCH   A list of Trench Stores to be handed over to be sent
   STORES. to Headquarters by 5pm, and also a list signed by the
            O/C relieving Company to be sent to H.Qrs by first
            orderly on 30th August, together with a list of Secret
            Maps handed over, showing serial numbers.

4. WORK ETC. C & D Companies will be under orders of the O/C,
            Battalion holding the line for tactical purposes.
            Orders regarding the scheme of work will be issued
            later.

5. MESS   H.Q, A & B. Coys mess baskets to be at POZEN DUMP by
   BASKETS 9.30 pm.   A & B. Coys will hand over their
   AND COOKS duties to C & D Coys respectively as soon as possible.
   UTENSILS

6. RELIEF   To be notified to Headquarters by code word
   COMPLETE. "RUM".

7.   ACKNOWLEDGE.
                                            H Hanford
                                                Captain,
            Adjutant 7th Battn South Staffs Regt

WAR DIARY or INTELLIGENCE SUMMARY

Army Form C. 2118.

6th SOUTH STAFFS REGT.

Vol 32

(131)

Q32

Place	Date	Hour	Summary of Events and Information	Remarks and references to Appendices
MAZINGARBE	11.9.17 to 14.9.17		The Battalion employed on Pioneer work. "A" & "B" Companies in MAZINGARBE attached to 3rd Australian Tunnelling Company. "C" & "D" Companies in TENTH AVENUE attached to 466th Field Company R.E.	
do.	15.9.17		"A" & "B" Companies relieved in MAZINGARBE by 1/6th Bn. North Staffordshire Regiment. "C" & "D" Companies relieved in TENTH AVENUE by 1/5th Bn. South Staffordshire Regiment. On completion of relief the Battalion moved to billets in VERQUIN. (See Operation Orders 160 Attached)	
VERQUIN	19.9.17		Battalion Training and Bathing.	
do	20.9.17		Battalion Training	
do	21.9.17		Battalion Training. "A" & "B" Companies inspected by Commanding Officer.	
do	22.9.17		do. "C" & "D" do.	
do	23.9.17		do. up to 12.30 p.m. At 6 p.m. the Battalion marched to Fosse Billets in NOYELLES.	
NOYELLES	24.9.17		The Battalion relieved the 1/6th Bn. North Staffordshire Regiment in the HULLUCH RIGHT SUB-SECTOR (See Operation Orders 160 H.S. attached)	
TRENCHES S.W. of HULLUCH	25.9.17		Quiet Day	
do.	26.9.17		do	
do	27.9.17		do	
do	28.9.17		The Battalion was relieved in the evening by the 1/6th Battalion North Staffordshire Regiment (See Operation Orders 160 H.B. attached) and moved as follows:- Battn. H.Q. & MAZINGARBE, "B" Coy to dugouts in RESERVE LINE. "A", "C" & "D" Companies to dugouts in TENTH AVENUE.	

WAR DIARY or INTELLIGENCE SUMMARY

Army Form C. 2118.

6th SOUTH STAFFS REGT.

Place	Date	Hour	Summary of Events and Information	Remarks and references to Appendices
MAZINGARBE	29.9.17		In Brigade Reserve	
	30.9.17		"B" Company relieved in RESERVE LINE by 10th Bn North Staffordshire Regt. and proceeded to huts in MAZINGARBE.	
			Total casualties for Month of September 1917	
			Officers.	
			1 Lieut (A/Capt) L.S.Shears. Wounded (At Duty) 26.9.17.	
			" Q.G.Hickman " 28.9.17	
			Other Ranks.	
			Killed. 1	
			Wounded 7	
			Died of Wounds. 1	

J.S. [Innes?]
Lieut. Colonel
Commanding 6th Bn South Staffs Regt.

2.10.17

SECRET.   Operation Orders No 44,   Copy No 11.
             1/6th Battalion South Staffordshire Regiment.

1. Relief.   The 1/6th Btn North Staffs Regt will relieve "A"
                  and "B" Companies 1/6th Btn South Staffs Regt in
                  Mazingarbe to-morrow afternoon 18th September.
                  The 1/5th Btn South Staffs Regt will relieve "C"
                  and "D" Companies in Tenth Avenue to-morrow night
                  18/19th September.

2. Move.   On completion of relief the Battalion will move to
                  Verquin.

3. Order of   H.Q., "A" & "B" Coys. Parade 3.0 p.m. on Sailly-
   March and   Labourse Road by Huts. Dress - Full Marching Order.
   Dress.   "C" & "D" Companies will march from the trenches
                  via Philosophe-Sailly Road. Dress - No 2 Fighting
                  Order.

4. Routes.   Track to Sailly Labourse - Labourse - Verquineuil -
                  Verquin.

5. Movement.   By Platoons at 200 Yards interval.

6. Billeting.   2/Lieut: Ames and 1 N.C.O. per Company will Parade
                  at Orderly Room at 9 a.m. This party will report
                  to the Billet Warden at Orderly Room, 1/6th Btn
                  North Staffs Regt, Verquin at 10 a.m. C.Q.M.Sgts
                  will join billeting party after dinner.

7. Working   The parties of "B" Company attached to the 3rd
   Parties.   Australian Tunnelling Company will cease work at
                  2.0 p.m. and return to Camp. These parties will
                  collect their equipment at the Camp and March to
                  Verquin under 2/Lieut N.R.Dickson M.C. No
                  parties will proceed to the Tunnell to-morrow.

8. Packs.   Packs of "C" & "D" Companies, and the Tunnelling
                  Party of "B" Company at present in the line, will
                  be loaded at 12 noon.
                  Lewis Guns & S.A.A. to be loaded at 11 a.m.
                  Officers Valises will be collected at 12 noon.
                  Mess baskets of H.Q. "A" & "B" Coys will be
                  collected at 2.0 p.m.
                  All spare mess stuff will be sent with the Officers
                  Valises at 12 noon.
                  Lewis Guns, Mess baskets, and Cooks utensils of
                  "C" & "D" Coys will be met at Kingsbridge Station
                  to-morrow night. The Transport Officer will
                  detail the necessary limbers.

9. Inspection.   Company Orderly Officers will meet the Second-in-
                  Command at Orderly Room at 2.30 p.m. Billets will
                  be clean and ready for inspection at that time.

10. Trench   Lists of Trench Stores handed over by "C" & "D"
    Stores.   Companies to be rendered to Orderly Room on
                  return to Verquin.

11. Certificates. Certificates re Cleanliness of and Damage to Billets,
                  and marching out states will be rendered to Orderly
                  Room by 2.0 p.m. Return re number of Men who fell
                  out on the march will be rendered to Orderly Room on
                  arrival.

12. Relief Com-   "C" & "D" Companies will notify Battalion Headquarters
    plete.   when the men arrive in billets.

                                 - 1 -

13. <u>Headquarters</u>. Battalion Headquarters will close at
    Mazingarbe at 3.0 p.m. and re-open at
    Verquin on arrival.

14. <u>Acknowledge</u>.

H Hanford

Captain,

Adjutant, 1/6th Battalion South Staffordshire Regiment.

<u>17th September 1917.</u>

<u>Copies Issued to:-</u>

No 1. Commanding Officer.
   2. 137th Infantry Brigade.
   3. O/C, "A" Company.
   4. "   "B"   "
   5. "   "C"   "
   6. "   "D"   "
   7. Quartermaster.
   8. Transport Officer.
   9. 1/6th Btn North Staffs Regt.
 10. 1/5th Btn South Staffs Regt.
 11. War Diary.
 12. War Diary. (Duplicate).
 13. File.

SECRET.   Operation Orders No 45.   Copy No 11
                 1/6th Btn South Staffordshire Regiment.

1. **Relief.**   The Battalion will relieve the 1/6th Btn North
                     Staffs Regt in the Right-Subsector on the night of
                     the 24/25th inst.

2. **Boundaries.**   N - Broadway. S - Chalk Pit Alley to H.26.c.17.68.

3. **Distribution.** Companies will relieve corresponding Companies of
                     the 1/6th N.Staffs Regt, and on completion of relief
                     will be distributed as follows.

                     Right Line Coy. Centre Line Coy. Left Line Coy.
                         "B"   "C"   "D"
                     with "A" Company in Support.

4. **Move.**   Companies will move by Platoons in the following order:-
                     "D" "B" "C" "A" "H.Q". First Company to move off
                     at 7p.m., the others following at five minute
                     intervals.
                     Starting point:- Junction of <u>Cambrin Rd</u> with <u>Lens-
                     Bethune Road</u> in <u>Noyelles</u>.

5. **Guides.**   Two guides per Company will meet each "B" "C" & "A"
                     Companies at G.20.d.60.20.(Victoria Station) at
                     7-30p.m.
                     Two guides will meet "D" Company at Junction of
                     Posen Alley and Tenth Avenue at 6p.m.
                     The left Company will use Posen Alley, and the
                     remaining Companies Chalk Pit Alley.

6. **Rations.**   Rations for the 25th inst will be carried on the
                     men. Water Bottles to be filled.
                     The Ration Dump for all Companies will be Chalk
                     Pit Dump, and for Headquarters - Posen Dump.

7. **Dress.**   No 2 Fighting Order.

8. **Stores.**   Lists of Trench Stores taken over will be checked
                     and forwarded to Btn Headquarters by first runner
                     on the 25th inst.

9. **Advance Pty.** The Regt Sgt Major, Pioneer Sgt, and Sniping N.C.O.
                     will proceed to the trenches at 2p.m.

10. **Headquarters.** Btn Headquarters will close at <u>Noyelles</u> at 7-45p.m.
                     and open at <u>Curzon Street</u> on arrival.

11. **Relief complete** will be notified to Btn H.Q. by code word <u>Dundee.</u>

12. **Acknowledge.**

                                                               2/Lieutenant.
                     A/Adjutant 1/6th Btn South Staffordshire Regiment.

          Copies issued to:-

     No 1. Commanding Officer.   No 8. Transport Officer.
     No 2. G.O.C.137th I.Brigade.   No 9. Quartermaster.
     No 3. O/C.1/6th Btn N.Staffs Regt.   No 10. Regt Sgt Major.
     No 4. O/C "A" Company.   No 11. War Diary.
     No 5. " "B"   "   No 12. "   "   (Duplicate).
     No 6. " "C"   "   No 13. File.
     No 7. " "D"   "

SECRET   Operation Orders No.   Copy No. 11
                       1st/6th Bn. North Staffordshire Regiment
                                                                   28th October 1916.

Reference Map Sheet No. 3
   RELIEF   The 6th Bn. North Staffordshire Regiment will be relieved by the 6th Bn. North
                   Staffordshire Regiment in the HULLUCH RIGHT subsector on the night of 28/29 inst.
                   A Coy. will take over the line at ... to be relieved by B Coy. on the North Staffs
                   B   "
                   C   "
                   D   "

2. LEWIS GUN   Each Company will hand over 20 Magazines per Gun on being relieved,
   AMMUNITION   and will take over a corresponding quantity.

3. RELIEF COMPLETE will be notified to Battalion H.Q. by the code word EDINBURGH.

4. MOVES   On completion of relief the following moves will take place:-
                   A Company to TENTH AVENUE near HAY ALLEY.
                   B   "   RESERVE LINE   about G.24.d.8.
                   C   "   TENTH AVENUE near VENDIN ALLEY
                   D   "   POSEN ALLEY
                   Battalion H.Q. to MAZINGARBE.
                   One Officer and one N.C.O. per company will proceed to their locations
                   on the afternoon of the 28th inst. to take over from the Companies of the
                   6th Bn. North Staffordshire Regiment.

5. RATIONS   On the night of the 28/29 inst. rations will be supplied as follows:-
                   Rations for A Company on HAY DUMP
                           "   B   "   POSEN DUMP
                           "   C   "   QUARRY DUMP
                           "   D   "   POSEN DUMP
                   Companies will arrange to draw their own rations from these dumps
                   about 2.30 a.m. on the 29th inst.
                   The Transport Officer will arrange to collect H.Q. baggage from POSEN DUMP
                   at 6.00 p.m. for transport to MAZINGARBE.

6. STORES   Lists of all stores to be handed over will be sent to Battalion H.Q. by
                   2nd runner on the 28th inst.

7. ACKNOWLEDGE

                                                              W. H. Ames   2/Lt.
                                                     Adjutant 1st/6th Bn. North Staffordshire Regiment.

— 2 —

Copies issued to :—

    No. 1   Commanding Officer.
    " 2   G.O.C. 13th Infantry Brigade.
    " 3-6   Companies
    " 7   O.C. 9th Bn. North Staff Regt.
    " 8   Transport Officer
    " 9   Quartermaster
    " 10   Regt. Sergt. Major.
    " 11 & 12   War Diary
    " 13   File

Army Form C. 2118.

1/6th Bn South Staffs Regiment.

WAR DIARY
or
INTELLIGENCE SUMMARY.
(Erase heading not required.)

Instructions regarding War Diaries and Intelligence Summaries are contained in F. S. Regs. Part II. and the Staff Manual respectively. Title pages will be prepared in manuscript.

Vol 33

Q33

Place	Date	Hour	Summary of Events and Information	Remarks and references to Appendices
Mazingarbe	1-10-1917.		In Brigade Reserve.	
Hulluch.	2-10-1917.		The Btn relieved the 1/6th Btn North Staffs Regt in the HULLUCH Right Subsector.(See O.O.No 47 attached).	
"	3-10-1917.		Quiet day.	
"	4-10-1917.		-do-	
"	5-10-1917.		-do-	
"	6-10-1917.		The Battalion was relieved in the trenches by the 1/5th Btn North Staffordshire Regt, and proceeded to billets in VERQUIN(Divisional Reserve). (See O.O.No 48 attached).	
VERQUIN.	7-10-1917.		Bathing,Cleaning up and Church Services.	
"	8-10-1917.		Battalion Training.	
"	9-10-1917.		-do-	
HULLUCH.	10-10-1917.		The Battalion relieved the 1/6th Btn North Staffs Regt in the HULLUCH Left Sub-sector.(See O.O.No 49 attached).	
"	11-10-1917.		Quiet Day.	
"	12-10-1917.		-do-	
"	13-10-1917.		"B" Company carried out a silent Raid on enemy post at H.13.c.50.65 LOOS.36C.NW.3.Edition 8a.1/10,000.(See O.O.No 50 attached). COPY OF 40th DIV:MEMO No G727/206.15-10-17. " Corps " " 283/GB1. 14-10-1917. "The Corps Commander wishes to draw attention to an excellent piece of work done by the 1/6thsStaffordshire Rgt last night. By careful patrolling a post had been accurately located in the enemy's front line. At 9p.m.on the 13th a party of (Contd).	

Army Form C. 2118.

1/6th Bn South Staffordshire Regt.

(134)
WAR DIARY
or
INTELLIGENCE SUMMARY.
(Erase heading not required.)

Instructions regarding War Diaries and Intelligence Summaries are contained in F. S. Regs., Part II. and the Staff Manual respectively. Title pages will be prepared in manuscript.

Place	Date	Hour	Summary of Events and Information	Remarks and references to Appendices
HULLUCH	13-10-1917 (Continued)		One Officer(2/Lt P.W.Burgess) 1 N.C.O.(Sgt A.Cox) and 8 O.R. attacked this post, killed three Germans and captured one without a single casualty. It is enterprises of this nature which the Corps Commander is particularly anxious to encourage - they are the fruits of good patrol work, and the initiative and dash which are essential to make them a success not only raise the moral of our men but lowers that of the enemy". 2/Lieut:P.W.BURGESS and No 240087 SERGEANT A.COX have been subsequently awarded the MILITARY CROSS and DISTINGUISHED CONDUCT MEDAL respectively.	
"	14-10-1917		Quiet Day. The Battalion was relieved in the Trenches by the 1/5th Btn North Staffs Regt. "A" & "C" Companies proceeded to MAZINGARBE and "B" COMPANY to TENTH AVENUE with "D" COMPANY at JUNCTION of LONE TRENCH and TENTH AVENUE.	
"	15			
MAZING- ARBE.	15-10-1917		In Brigade Reserve.	
"	16-10-1917		"A" COMPANY relieved "B" Company in TENTH AVENUE. "C" " "D" " " " " " "	
"	17-10-1917		In Brigade Reserve.	
HULLUCH	18-10-1917		The Battalion relieved the 1/6th Bn North Staffs Regt in the HULLUCH Right Subsector.(See O.O.No 52 attached).	
"	19-10-1917		Quiet Day.	
"	20-10-1917		-do-	
"	21-10-1917		-do-	
"	22-10-1917		The Battalion was relieved in the trenches by the 1/6th Btn North Staffordshire Regt, and proceeded to VERQUIN(Divisional Reserve).	We O.O. No 53 attached
VERQUIN	23-10-1917		Bathing, Cleaning up etc.	
"	24-10-1917		Battalion Training.	

1/6th Btn South Staffordshire Regt.   (135).

Army Form C. 2118.

WAR DIARY
or
INTELLIGENCE SUMMARY.
(Erase heading not required.)

Instructions regarding War Diaries and Intelligence Summaries are contained in F.S. Regs., Part II and the Staff Manual respectively. Title pages will be prepared in manuscript.

Place	Date	Hour	Summary of Events and Information	Remarks and references to Appendices
VERQUIN	25-10-1917		Battalion Training.	
"	26-10-1917		The Battalion relieved the 1/5th Btn North Staffs Regt in the HULLUCH Left Subsector.(See O.O.No 54 attached).	
HULLUCH	27-10-1917		Quiet Day.	
"	28-10-1917		-do-	
"	29-10-1917		-do- A deserter(probable)of the German Artillery was brought into our Lines.	
"	30-10-1917		The Battalion was relieved in the trenches by the 1/5th Btn North Staffs Regt.(See O.O.No 55)"B" & "D" COMPANIES proceeded to MAZINGARBE, "A" COMPANY proceeded to NINTH AVENUE and "C" COMPANY to JUNCTION of LONE TRENCH and TENTH AVENUE.	
MAZING-ARBE.	31-10-1917		In Brigade Reserve.	

TOTAL CASUALTIES FOR MONTH:-

  1 O'Rank.Killed.in.Action.
  3 O'Ranks Wounded.
  2 " " & at duty.

FOR OFFICER COMMANDING.1/6th BTN SOUTH STAFFORDSHIRE RGT.

         MAJOR.

3-11-1917.

SECRET.   Operation Orders No 47.   Copy No 12

1/6th Btn South Staffordshire Regiment.

1. **Relief.** The 1/6th Btn South Staffs Regt will relieve the 1/6th Btn North Staffs Regt in the Hulluch Right Subsector on the night of the 2/3rd inst.

2. **Distribution.** "A" Company S.Staffs Regt relieve "D" Coy 1/6th N.S.Rgt.
   "B"   "   "   "   "   "A"   "   "
   "C"   "   "   "   "   "C"   "   "
   "D"   "   "   "   "   "B"   "   "

   On completion of relief Companies will be distributed as follows:-

   <u>Left Line. Right Line. Left Support. Right Support.</u>
      "A"   "C"   "B"   "D"

3. **Move.** Companies will move by Platoons at the following times:- "C" Coy 7p.m. "A" Coy. 7-15p.m. "D" Cy 7-30p.m.
   "B" Company will move from Mazingarbe at 6-45p.m.
   Headquarters   "   "   "   "   " 7-15p.m.
   Care will be taken to avoid congestion in Posen Alley.

4. **Rations.** In the case of "B" Coy and Headquarter details Rations for the 3rd inst will be carried on the men. Water-bottles to be filled.
   Ration Dump for all Companies will be 'Chalk Pit Alley Dump' and for Headquarters 'Posen Dump'.
   During this tour "B" Coy will carry for "A" Coy, and "D" Coy for "C" Coy.

5. **Lewis Gun S.A.A.** Each Company will leave behind in its present location eighty magazines in panniers to be taken over by the incoming Unit, and will take over a corresponding quantity in the line.

6. **Dress.** No 2 Fighting Order.

7. **Advance Party.** The Regt Sgt Major, Pioneer Sgt, and senior Snipers will report at 6p.m. at Curzon Street to take over.
   One officer per Company will proceed to the Line in advance, not later than 6p.m.

8. **Stores.** A list of Trench Stores taken over will be checked and forwarded to Btn H.Q. at Curzon Street, by first runner on the 3rd inst.

9. **Headquarters.** will close at Mazingarbe at 7-15p.m. and open at Curzon Street on arrival.

10. Relief complete will be notified to Btn H.Q. by code word "Dunbar".

11. **Acknowledge.**

                                    A Williams
                                    2/Lieutenant.
               A/Adjutant 1/6th Btn South Staffordshire Regt.

Copies issued to:-
No 1. Commanding Officer.   No 7. O/C 1/5th Btn N.Staffs Rgt.
No 2. G.O.C.137th I.Brigade.   No 8. "   1/6th "   "   "
No 3. O/C "A" Company.   No 9. Transport Officer.
No 4. " "B"   "   No10. Quartermaster.
No 5. " "C"   "   No 11.Regt Sgt Major.
No 6. " "D"   "   No12. War Diary.
                                    No 13. "   "   (Duplicate).
                                    No 14. File

SECRET

Operation Orders No 48.   Copy No 10
6th Bn South Staffordshire Regiment

5th October 1917.

1. RELIEF. The 6th Bn South Staffordshire Regiment will be relieved by the 16th Bn North Staffordshire Regiment in the Bulluch Right Subsector tomorrow night 6/7th October. The 6th Bn South Staffordshire Regt. will proceed to billets in Verquin (6 miles) and will be in Divisional Reserve.

2. ROUTE. Bone Track – Philosophe – Sailly Labourse.

3. GUIDES. 2 Guides per Company will report to O's C Companies 16th Bn North Staffs Regt at 6.15 a.m.
  A Coy guides will report to OC C Coy 16th North Staffs Regt at Coy HQ junction of Bone Trench and Tenth Avenue.
  B Coy will be relieved by A Coy 16th N.S.R. No guides will be required.
  C "   "   "   "   "   B "   "   "   "   – Coy HQ junction of Posen & Tenth Avenue
  D "   "   "   "   "   D "   "   "   "   – Coy HQ old Bn HQ Tenth Avenue.

4. LEWIS GUNS & S.A.A. 20 Magazines per Gun in panniers will be handed over at the gun positions. All other Lewis Gun S.A.A. will be taken out of the trenches. Lewis Guns and surplus S.A.A. to be loaded on Lorries at Chalk Pit Dump immediately on relief. All Specialist equipment to be taken out of trenches.

5. MESS BASKETS &c. Mess Baskets, cooking utensils etc to be at Chalk Pit Dump at 9.20 p.m.

6. HORSES. Coy Commanders will notify Orderly Room the time and place they wish their horses.

7. BILLETING. The Quartermaster and Coy Quartermasters will proceed to Verquin to billet the Battalion. The Batn will occupy as far as possible billets previously occupied.

8. STORES. A list of Trench Stores to be handed over will be rendered to Orderly Room by 2nd dinner tomorrow.

9. COMPLETION OF RELIEF. To be notified to Orderly Room by B.A.B code.

10. ACKNOWLEDGE.

J M Frew
Captain
Adjutant 6th Bn South Staffordshire Regiment.

Copies send to:

1. Commanding Officer
2. GOC 8/Z Infantry Brigade
3. 15th Btn. North Staff Regt.
4, 5, 6, 7. Companies
8. Transport Officer

9. Quartermaster
10, 11. War Diary
12, 13. File
14. Regt. Sergt. Major

5-10-1917

Secret

Operation Orders No 49,   Copy No 11.
1/6th Battalion South Staffordshire Regiment.
           Tuesday, 9th October 1917.

1. **Relief.**   The Battalion will relieve the 1/6th Btn North
                     Staffs Regt in the Hulluch left sub-sector
                     to-morrow night.

2. **Distribution.** The line at present is held:-
                     Right Company "C"   Right Centre Coy "B".
                     Forward Company "D"   Left Company "A",
                     and on completion of relief will be held:-
                     Right Company "D"   Right Centre Coy "C"
                     Forward Company "B"   Left Company "A".

3. **Move, etc.**   The Battalion will Parade in Full Marching
                     Order at 2.0 p.m. in the following order:-
                     Headquarters, "D" Coy,"B" Coy,"A" Coy,"C" Coy.
                     Head of Column:- Orderly Room.
                     Tea will be served en route.

4. **Guides.**   Guides for "A", "B" & "C" Coys will be at the
                     junction of Hay Track and Tenth Avenue by 7 pm,
                     and for "D" Company at Quarry Dump at 7 pm.

5. **Lewis Guns.**   Lewis Guns and 12 Magazines per Gun in pouches
                     will be at Orderly Room at 10 am ready to be
                     transported to cross-roads Philosophe, where
                     they will be picked up by Lewis Gun Teams.
                     The Lewis Gun Officer will detail 4 Lewis
                     Gunners to proceed with the Guns & Ammunition.

6. **Advance Party.** One Officer per Company and one N.C.O. per
                     platoon will report to the 1/6th N.Staffs Regt
                     Companies at 2.0 p.m.

7. **Blankets etc.** Blankets, Officers valises, and Mess Stores not
                     for the trenches to be stacked outside Company
                     Headquarters at 1.30 p.m.   Mess Stores for the
                     trenches to be stacked at 2.0 p.m.

8. **Acknowledge.**

                                                 Captain,
              A/Adjutant, 1/6th Battalion South Staffs Regiment.

    Copies Issued To:-

    No 1. Commanding Officer.   No 8. Transport Officer.
       2. 137th Infantry Bde.   9. Quartermaster.
       3. O/C,1/6th N.Staffs Rgt.   10. Regtl Sgt-Major.
       4. "   "A" Company.   11. War Diary.
       5. "   "B"   "   12. "   "   (Duplicate).
       6. "   "C"   "   13. File.
       7. "   "D"   "

SECRET.   Operation Orders No 50   Copy No 11
16th Btn South Staffordshire Regiment

13th October 1917.

1. "B" Company will carry out a Silent Raid on enemy post at H.13.c.50.65
2. The Raiding party will consist of 2 Officers and 16 O.R.
3. Equipment – as detailed by Raid Commander. All identification will be removed and all O.R will be inspected by Raid Commander.
4. Stokes Mortars – The 137th Stokes Mortar Battery will arrange to barrage enemy trenches at points previously arranged.
5. Communication – The signal for barrage will be a GREEN VERY LIGHT fired due North. The Battalion Signal Officer will arrange a chain of communication through our forward post to the Stokes Mortar.
6. ZERO hour will be 9 p.m.
7. O.C. "A" Company will detail 8 Men to form part of Garrison in No 1 Post. O.C. "C" Company will detail 8 Men to form part of Garrison in No 4 Post. These Men should report as soon as possible.
8. PASSWORD for to-night will be TABLE-SPOON
9. Patrols will be furnished after midnight by "A" & "D" Companies.

Andrew
Captain

13-10-17.   A/Adjutant 16th Btn South Staffordshire Regiment.

Copies to:-
No.1 Commanding Officer.   No.9 Quartermaster
  2 GOC 13th Infantry Brigade.   10 Regtl Serg Major
  3 O.o.[?] both Rifle Regt.   11 O/C b Bn North [?] Lgt
                                      12 War Diary
  8 Transport Officer.   13 File.

SECRET

Operation Orders No. 51.

No. 12

1/6th Battn. South Staffordshire Regiment.

13th October 1915.

1. RELIEF
The Battalion will be relieved in the HULLUCH LEFT SUBSECTOR by the 1/5th Bttn. Prince of Wales's (North Staffs) Regiment tomorrow night 14/15th inst.

2. DISPOSITION
On completion of relief the Battalion will be disposed as follows:—
"A" & "C" Companies in MAZINGARBE
"B" Company — Old Battn. H.Q. in TENTH AVENUE
"D" Company — Junction of LONE TRENCH and TENTH AVENUE.
Companies in reserve will be under the tactical command of the Left Battalion Commander.

On the night of the 16th "A" Company will relieve "B" Company and "C" Company will relieve "D" Company, "B" & "D" Companies moving into huts in Northern Camp, Mazingarbe.

3. GUM BOOTS
All Gumboots, except those actually in use, will be collected at "Gum Boot Store", Lone Trench tomorrow morning. Those in use will be handed in as soon as possible after relief.

4. TRENCH STORES
A list of Trench Stores to be handed over to reach Battn. H.Q. by 2nd Runner.

5. CANTEEN
The Canteen will occupy dugout opposite "D" Company H.Q. and will be established by 5 p.m.

7. ADVANCE PARTY
One Officer each of "B" & "D" Companies will recconoitre positions in advance.

8. MESS STORES etc.
"B" & "D" Coys Mess Stores and cooking utensils to be at HAY DUMP at 6.30 p.m. All wet socks to be delivered at HAY DUMP by 6 p.m. All Specialist equipment will be taken out of the trenches.

9. BILLETING
The Quartermaster will arrange billets for H.Q., "A" & "C" Companies. All men of the Battn. Football Team will be billeted in Mazingarbe.

10. ACKNOWLEDGE

Capt.
1/6 Bttn. South Staffordshire Regiment.

Secret.　　　　　　Operation Orders No 52,　　　　　Copy No
　　　　　　　　1/6th Battalion South Staffordshire Regiment.
　　　　　　　　　　　　　Wednesday, 17th October 1917.

1. **Relief.**　　　The Battalion will relieve the 1/6th Btn North
　　　　　　　　Staffs Regiment in the Hulluch Right Subsector
　　　　　　　　to-morrow night.

2. **Distribution.** On completion of relief Companies will be
　　　　　　　　distributed as follows:-
　　　　　　　　Right Subsector　"C" Coy.　　Left Subsector　"A" Coy.
　　　　　　　　Right Support　　"D"　"　　　Left Support　　"B"　"

3. **Move.**　　　"A" & "C" Companies will move at 5.30 p.m.
　　　　　　　　"B" & "D" Companies will move by Platoons at 200
　　　　　　　　yards interval, in the order "B" → "D", first
　　　　　　　　Platoon to pass Brigade Headquarters at 5 p.m.
　　　　　　　　Headquarters will move at 5.30 p.m.
　　　　　　　　Dress:- Fighting Order No 2 (greatcoat additional).

4. **Blankets,**　Officers Valises, Mess Stores not for the trenches,
   Packs etc.　blankets and Mens packs will be stacked outside
　　　　　　　　billets at 3.0 p.m.
　　　　　　　　Mess Stores and Cooking Utensils for the trenches
　　　　　　　　will be ready for loading at Company Headquarters
　　　　　　　　at 5.0 p.m.

5. **Lewis Guns.**　80 Lewis Gun Magazines per Company will be taken
　　　　　　　　over from 1/6th Btn N.Staffs Regt, and 80 magazines
　　　　　　　　per Company will be handed over to the 1/5th Btn
　　　　　　　　N.Staffs Regt.
　　　　　　　　"B" & "D" Companies will send up one man per Lewis
　　　　　　　　Gun Team in advance to take over Lewis Guns and
　　　　　　　　Ammunition at present in reserve in Tenth Avenue.

6. **Whale Oil.**　All men will rub their feet and legs with whale oil,
　　　　　　　　under Company arrangments, before proceeding to the
　　　　　　　　trenches.

7. **Administrative** Gum-boots.　"A" & "C" Companies will draw all
   Arrangments.　available gumboots from Brigade Gumboot Store, Lone
　　　　　　　　Trench, to-morrow afternoon.　A further supply will
　　　　　　　　arrive with the rations.
　　　　　　　　Dumps.　H.Q. "A" & "B" Coys will use Posen Dump. "C"
　　　　　　　　& "D" Coys will use Chalk Pit Dump.　The rations will
　　　　　　　　be delivered in bulk to these Dumps to-morrow and
　　　　　　　　succeeding nights.　The Companies in Support will
　　　　　　　　carry rations for support and front line Companies.
　　　　　　　　Socks. One clean pair of socks per man will be
　　　　　　　　delivered with the rations on the nights of 19th,
　　　　　　　　20th, and 21st.　One dirty pair per man will be
　　　　　　　　returned on these nights.

8. **Acknowledge.**

　　　　　　　　　　　　　　　　　　　　　　　Captain,
　　　　　　　A/Adjutant, 1/6th Bth South Staffordshire Regiment.

Copies Issued To:-

　　No 1. Commanding Officer.　　　　　No 9. Transport Officer.
　　　2. 137th Infantry Brigade.　　　　10. Quartermaster.
　　　3. O/C, 1/6th N.Staffs Regt.　　　11. Regtl Sgt-Major.
　　　4. " 　1/5th N.Staffs Regt.　　　12. War Diary.
　　　5. " 　"A" Company.　　　　　　　13. " 　" (Duplicate).
　　　6. " 　"B"　 "　　　　　　　　　 14. File.
　　　7. " 　"C"　 "
　　　8. " 　"D"　 "

SECRET   Operation Orders No 53   Copy No 11.
                    16th Bn. South Staffordshire Regiment.
                                                Sunday 21st October 1917.

1. RELIEF.   The 16th Bn. South Staffordshire Regiment will be relieved in the
                  HULLUCH RIGHT Sector by the 16th Bn. Prince of Wales's (North Staff.) Regt.
                  on the night of 22/23rd October 1917.

2. MOVE.   On completion of relief, Battalion will move to VERQUIN (5 miles)
                  and will be in Divisional Reserve.

3. ROUTE.   MAZINGARBE — NOEUX-LES-MINES — CITE-DE-VERQUIN.

4. TEA.   Tea will be served in CHATEAU GROUNDS MAZINGARBE.

5. COOKING UTENSILS. Cooking Utensils etc. will be at Dumps at 6pm

6. MESS STORES   Officers Mess Stores, Lewis Guns and Lewis Gun Ammunition
 & LEWIS GUNS etc. (except with the Teams) will be at Dumps as soon as possible
                  after Relief.

7. GUM BOOTS.   Gum Boots will be tied in pairs and delivered at LONE TRENCH
                  Stores at 10 A.M.

8. GUARD.   "A" Company will detail a Guard of 1 N.C.O. & 3 Men to mount over the
                  R.E. Yard, MINE, VERQUIN at 12-noon.

9. TRENCH STORES List of Trench Stores to be handed over will reach Orderly Room
                  by 12 noon.

10. COMPLETION OF RELIEF to be notified to Bath. H.Q. by B.A.B. Code.

11. ACKNOWLEDGE.
                                                        J.W. Frew
                                                        Captain
                                            Adjutant 16th Bn. South Staffordshire Regiment

Copies issued to:-
    1. Commanding Officer.   9. Quartermaster
    2. G.O.C. 10th Inf. Bde.   10. Regt. Sergt. Major
    3. O.C. 16th Bn. N. Staff. Regt. 11. War Diary
    4-7. Companies.   12. File
    8. Transport Officer.

Secret.   Operation Orders No 54.   Copy No 11.
1/6th Battalion South Staffordshire Regiment.
Thursday, 25th October 1917.

1. **Relief.** The 1/6th Btn South Staffs Regt will relieve the 1/5th Btn Prince of Wales (North Staffs) Regt in the Hulluch Left Sub-sector to-morrow night 26/27th instant.

2. **Distribution.** On completion of relief the Battalion will be distributed as follows:-
   Right Company   "C".   Right Centre Company   "D".
   Outpost Company   "A".   Left Company   "B".

3. **Move.** The Battalion will parade in Fighting Order No 2 plus greatcoat, at 1.30 p.m. in the following order:-
   Headquarters, "A" - "B" - "C" - "D".
   Head of Column:- Regtl Aid Post.
   Tea will be served at Mazingarbe.

4. **Advance Party.** One Officer per Company and one N.C.O. per platoon will proceed to the trenches in advance.

5. **Rear Party.** A Rear Party of 3 men per Company and one junior N.C.O. from "A" Company will parade ~~under the Orderly Officer at Orderly Room at 1.30 p.m.~~ in their billets.

6. **Lewis Guns.** Lewis Guns will be loaded at Orderly Room at 11 a.m. and will be conveyed to the cross-roads Philosophe where they will be picked up by Lewis Gun Teams. One man per Gun will proceed with the limber.

7. **Blankets etc.** Officers Valises, Mens packs and blankets to be stacked outside Company Headquarters at 11 a.m. Mess stores for trenches and not for trenches to be stacked outside Company Headquarters at 1.15 p.m. Tea urns will be sent up to the trenches with the rations.

8. **Gum Boots.** O/C "C" Company will draw 15 pairs of gum-boots at Lone Trench Gum-boot store.

9. **Acknowledge.**

                                          [signature]
                                          Captain,
A/Adjutant 1/6th Battalion South Staffs Regiment.

Copies Issued To:-

   No 1. Commanding Officer.   No 8. Transport Officer.
      2. 137th Infantry Brigade.   9. Quartermaster.
      3. O/C, 1/5th N.Staffs Regt.   10. Regtl Sgt-Major.
      4. "   "A" Company.   11. War Diary.
      5. "   "B"   "   12. "   "   (Duplicate)
      6. "   "C"   "   13. File.
      7. "   "D"   "

SECRET
Operation Orders No. 15
1st Bn. South Staffordshire Regiment
29th October 1917

1. RELIEF   The 1st Bn. South Staffordshire Regiment will be relieved by the
             10th Bn. Prince of Wales's (North Staffs) Regiment in the
             HULLUCH LEFT SUBSECTOR on the night of October/October.

2. MOVES   On completion of relief the Battalion will proceed to Bde. Reserve
             at MAZINGARBE less 2 Companies. "A" Company will relieve 10th
             Batt. H.Q. NINTH AVENUE and "C" Company at junction of LONE
             TRENCH and TENTH AVENUE. One Officer per Company and N.COs
             per platoon will proceed to new area in advance.

             A Company will be under the orders of the Left Battn. Commander
             for tactical purposes and under the Australians Commanding R.E.
             for work.

             C Company will be under the orders of the Right Bn. Commander
             for tactical purposes and under the R.E. for work.

             Coy. Comdr. will send a representative to the Commanding Coy. and
             R.E. before relief for orders.

3. CANTEEN   Canteen will move to Junction of LONE TRENCH and TENTH AVENUE at 4 p.m.
             O.C. "A" Coy will supply the necessary carrying party.

4. GUM BOOTS All Gum Boots issued or taken will be returned to the Gum Boot
             Drying Room LONE TRENCH immediately on relief.

5. LEWIS GUNS
   & S.A.A. Lewis Guns of "A" & "B" Coys. will be taken to "A" Coy
             H.Q., Lewis Guns of "C" & "D" Coys will be taken to "C" Coy H.Q.
             Companies will hand out and take over 20 rounds per Lewis Gun.

6. TRENCH STORES Lewis of Trench Stores to be handed over to each Batt. H.Q. after
                  Relief.

7. MESS STORES Officers Mess Stores, cooking utensils etc. of B & D Companies
                to be at dumps by 6.30 p.m.

8. CHARGERS Company Commanders will notify Orderly Room time and time
             they require their horses.

9. ACKNOWLEDGE

                                                    D. West
                                                    Captain
                              Adjutant 1st Bn. South Staffordshire Regiment

Copies issued to:-

No. 1. Commanding Officer.
" 2. G.O.C. 137th Bde.
" 3. O.C. 1/5th Bn N. Staffs Regt
" 4.
" 5.
" 6.
" 7.

            do   Duplicate
B. Lie.

CONFIDENTIAL.

WAR DIARY

of

1/6th BTN SOUTH STAFFORDSHIRE REGIMENT.

From 1st November 1917 to 30th November 1917.

1/6th Bn South Staffs Regt.   (156) WAR DIARY or INTELLIGENCE SUMMARY.   Army Form C. 2118.

Instructions regarding War Diaries and Intelligence Summaries are contained in F.S. Regs., Part II. and the Staff Manual respectively. Title pages will be prepared in manuscript.

(Erase heading not required.)

Place	Date	Hour	Summary of Events and Information	Remarks and references to Appendices
MAZINGARBE	1-11-1917		The Battalion in Brigade Reserve less two Companies in Support in Tenth Avenue. The Btn Football Eleven defeated the 230th RFA Eleven by two goals to NIL.	
"	2-11-1917		Battalion Training. The two Companies in Mazingarbe relieved the two Companies in Tenth Avenue.	
"	3-11-1917		The Battalion relieved the 1/6th Btn North Staffs Regt in the HULLUCH Right Subsector.(See O.O.No 57. Our patrols were out in 'No Man's Land' and wiring took place on the whole Battalion Front.	
HULLUCH.	4-11-1917		The day was very quiet, but at night an enemy wiring party was scattered with bombs.	
"	5-11-1917		An internal relief took place at night. During the night the enemies Machine Guns were specially active.	
"	6-11-1917		The day was very quiet. At night we patrolled "No Man's Land" and located some enemy posts.	
"	7-11-1917		The Battalion was relieved in the trenches by the 1/6th Btn North Staffordshire Regiment.(See O.O.No 58), and proceeded into Divisional Reserve Billets at VERQUIN.	
VERQUIN.	8-11-1917		Bathing and cleaning up.	
"	9-11-1917		Specialist Training carried out in the morning. Inter-Company Football Matches played in the afternoon, between "D" & "B" Coys, the former coming out victorious by 3 goals to 1.	
"	10-11-1917		Battalion carried out a Route March to HESDIGNEUL, and carried on with Battalion training there prior to returning at 4p.m. to billets. In the evening a very successful Concert was held.	
"	11-11-1917		In the forenoon the Btn attended Church Parade. The Btn marched to NOYELLES immediately after dinner, had tea there, and then proceeded to the Trenches to relieve the 1/5th Btn North Staffordshire Regt in the HULLUCH Left Sub-Sector.(See O.O.No 59).	
HULLUCH.	12-11-1917		The day was very quiet. Six patrols out during the night, locating enemy posts with a view to attacking them the following night.	

Army Form C. 2118.

1/6th Btn South Staffs Regt.

(137) WAR DIARY
or
INTELLIGENCE SUMMARY.

(Erase heading not required.)

Instructions regarding War Diaries and Intelligence
Summaries are contained in F. S. Regs., Part II.
and the Staff Manual respectively. Title pages
will be prepared in manuscript.

Place	Date	Hour	Summary of Events and Information	Remarks and references to Appendices
HULLUCH.	13-11-1917 14-11-1917		Day very quiet. Our patrols were active at night. Very quiet day. At 10-30p.m. 700 Gas Projectors were discharged from our sector into HULLUCH. The enemy put up an intense barrage about 11p.m. which lasted for 10 minutes.	
"	15-11-1917		The Battalion was relieved by the 1/6th Btn North Staffs Rgt and moved into Brigade Reserve as follows:- HQ and two Companies to MAZINGARBE and two Companies to TENTH AVENUE. (See O.O.No 60)	
MAZINGARBE.	16-11-1917		Bathing and cleaning up. In the afternoon the Btn Football Team played the 1/5th Btn South Staffs Eleven in the Div:League. A very exciting and keenly contested game ended in a draw of 2 goals each. In the evening the "Whizzbangs" gave a performance.	
"	17-11-1917		The two Companies in Mazingarbe relieved the two Companies in Tenth Avenue in the evening.	
"	18-11-1917 19-11-1917		Bathing, cleaning up, and Btn Training. The Btn Football Eleven played the 139th Bde H.Q.Eleven and won the match by 2 goals to nil. Late in the afternoon the Btn moved into the Line and relieved the 1/5th Btn North Staffordshire Regt in the HULLUCH Right Sub-Sector.(See OO 61)	
HULLUCH.	20-11-1917		Very quiet day until late in the afternoon when the enemy put down a barrage all along the Btn Front in retaliation to a bombardment of ours on his trenches. At night our patrols were active on the Battalion Front.	
"	21-11-1917		In the early morning(at dawn)our Divisional Artillery bombarded the enemy trenches while the Division on our RIGHT raided the enemy lines. The enemy then put down a slight barrage on our front. Patrols were again aggressive at night.	
"	22-11-1917		The enemy bombarded our trenches at dawn, most of his barrage was on our Right Company. At the same time he raided the Btn on our immediate right.i.e. the 4th Leicesters. The remainder of the day was quiet. At night patrols were out and our men were employed clearing the trenches as the result of the morning's "STRAFFE".	

Army Form C. 2118.

1/6th Bn South Staffordshire Regt.   (138) WAR DIARY or INTELLIGENCE SUMMARY.

Instructions regarding War Diaries and Intelligence Summaries are contained in F. S. Regs., Part II and the Staff Manual respectively. Title pages will be prepared in manuscript.

(Erase heading not required.)

Place	Date	Hour	Summary of Events and Information	Remarks and references to Appendices
HULLUCH.	23-11-1917		The day was quiet, and late in the afternoon the Battalion was relieved by the 1/6th Btn North Staffs Regt, and moved into Divisional Reserve Billets at VERQUIN. (See O.O.No 62)	
VERQUIN.	24-11-1917		Bathing and cleaning up.	
"	25-11-1917		Battalion Training and Church Parade. The Btn Eleven played the 466th Field Company R.E. and defeated them by 10 goals to nil.	
"	26-11-1917		A route march was carried out to HESDIGNEUL and carried on with Battalion training there prior to returning to Billets at 4p.m. In the evening the "WHIZZBANGS" (Div; Concert Pty) gave a performance.	
"	27-11-1917		The morning was spent in packing up etc. At 1p.m. the Btn marched off to the trenches to relieve the 1/5th Btn North Staffs Regt. The journey was broken at NOYELLES where tea was served and the Btn then proceeded to the HULLUCH Left Sub-Sector. (See O.O.No 63).	
HULLUCH.	28-11-1917		Gas was discharged into HULLUCH and CITE ST ELIE, causing the enemy to shell our lines, otherwise the day was quiet.	
" b	29-11-1917		Divisional Artillery bombarded the enemy lines and he retaliated on the whole of the Btn Front. Our patrols were active at night.	
"	30-11-1917		The day was very lively, the enemy shelling and Trench Mortaring our Lines the greater part of the forenoon. In the afternoon he raided the Brigade on our left without success. Our patrols again active.	

CASUALTIES FOR MONTH OF NOVEMBER 1917.
O'Ranks.   Wounded.   7
            " At duty.   2
            " Accidentally 2.

3-12-1917.   Commanding 1/6th Btn South Staffordshire Regiment.
                                                        Major:-

SECRET. Operation Orders No 57.   Copy No 12
1/6th Btn South Staffordshire Regiment.
Dated 2nd November 1917.

1. **Relief.** The 1/6th Btn South Staffordshire Regiment will relieve the 1/6th Btn Prince of Wales's (North Staffordshire) Regt, in the HULLUCH Right Sub-Sector, tomorrow night 3/4th November 1917.

2. **Distribution.** On completion of relief Companies will be distributed as follows:-
   Right Company. "D"   Left Company. "B"
   Right Support. "C"   Left Support "A"

3. **Move.** "B" & "D" Companies will move at 5-15p.m.
   "A" & "C" Companies will march to the trenches by platoons, in the order:- "A" "C".
   First Platoon to pass Brigade Headquarters at 4-30p.m.
   Route for "A" & "C" Companies:- Philosophe - Lamberts Track.

4. **Gum Boots.** O/C "D" Company will draw Gum Boots for his Company from the Gum Boot Store in Lone Trench. He will also draw 25 pairs for "C" Company and hand them over at Right Support Company H.Q. A further 35 pairs for Right Support Company will arrive with the Rations at Chalk Pit Dump. Gumboots are not required in the Left Company Sector.

5. **Whale Oil.** All O.R. will rub their feet with Whale Oil before proceeding to Right Sub-Sector.

6. **Blankets. Packs, etc.** Officers Valises, Mens Packs and Blankets will be stacked ready for loading at 12 noon. Mess Stores for the trenches and not for the trenches will be stacked outside Company H.Q. at 3-30p.m.

7. **Socks.** Socks will be changed under same arrangements as made for the last tour.

8. **Rations.** Rations will be delivered in Bulk at the usual Dumps. Tea Urns will be taken to the trenches.

9. **Working Party.** The Right Support Company will detail a party of one Officer and twenty-five Other-Ranks to be at Chalk Pit Dump at 2p.m. daily, where a guide from the X/46th T.M.Bty will meet them.

10. **Headquarters** will close at Mazingarbe at 5-30p.m. and will open at Curzon Street on arrival.

11. **Relief complete** to be notified to Orderly Room by 'BAB' Code.

12. **ACKNOWLEDGE.**

                                            Captain.

A/Adjutant. 1/6th Btn South Staffordshire Rgt.

Copies issued to:-
   No 1. Commanding Officer.   No 9. Transport Officer.
   No 2. G.O.C.137th I.Brigade.   No 10. Quartermaster.
   No 3. O/C.1/6th N.Staffs Rgt. No 11. Regt Sgt Major.
   No 4. " "A" Company.   No 12. War Diary.
   No 5. " "B"   "   No 13. "   "   (Duplicate).
   No 6. " "C"   "   No 14. File.
   No 7. " "D"   "
   No 8. " 1/5th N.Staffs Rgt.

SECRET   Operation Order No 58   Copy No. 11
                  1/6th Bn. South Staffordshire Regiment
                                        Tuesday, November 6th 1917

1. Relief.   The 1/6th Bn. South Staffordshire Regiment will be relieved in the
                  HULLUCH RIGHT Subsector by the 1/6th Bn. Prince of Wales's (North Staff) Regt.
                  tomorrow night 7/8th November 1917.

2. Move.   On completion of relief the Battalion will move (march) in companies
                  (8 mins) and will form Divisional Reserve.

3. Route.   Mazingarbe – Noeux-les-Mines – Verquin.

4. Tea.   Hot tea rations will be issued at Mazingarbe. One N.C.O. per
                  Coy will proceed in advance to supervise the issue of it.

5. Supper.   Supper will be ready on arrival at Verquin.

6. Coats.   Mens coats will be carried from Brigade H.Q. to Verquin. Coy Commdrs
                  will ensure that no congestion occurs.

7. Cookers.   All Cookers, tied in pairs, will be drawn at its Loco. Water Line at
                  7.30 pm. The Pioneer Sergt. will check returns.

8. Box Respirators. Off'rs Mess Cook, Cooking Utensils & Coy. Lists will be loaded on
                  Trucks at Dumps at 6.45 pm.

9. S.A.A.   10 Magazines and 20 rounds per Gun with the
                  1/6th Bn. North Staff Regt. and taken over from 1/6th South Staff Regt.
                  One relief to new lines and S.A.A. as previous will be loaded on trucks at
                  Dumps under Coy party ....

10. Trench Stores. Ammunition etc will be taken Bomb M.O. and Rocket.

11. Bombs.   [illegible] .... 4 C.T. Hullech [illegible] on N.H.E Dump
                  .... Nov 8th 1917. These .... be checked .... of stores
12. Rocket Gunners. .... verified by T.B.R. ......
13. Ammunition.
                                                           [signature]

                  Alapura Dobalis   [illegible] Staffordshire Regiment
Distribution:
No.1 Commanding Officer   6. Coy Capt....   No.10 Regt Sergt......
  " 2 ....   Adj Adn   " 7. Transport Officer   " 11 Coy Digr
  " 3 ....   Staff Dy   " 9. Quartermaster   "13 Lds

Secret.   Operation Orders No 59.   Copy No 11
                 1/6th Battalion South Staffordshire Regiment.
                                Saturday, 10th November 1917.

1. **Relief.**   The 1/6th Btn South Staffs Regiment will relieve
                    the 1/5th Btn Prince of Wales's (North Staffs) Regt
                    in the Hulluch Left Sub-sector to-morrow night
                    11/12th instant.

2. **Distribution.** On completion of relief the Battalion will be
                    distributed as follows:-
                    Right Company   "D".   Right Centre Coy   "C".
                    Outpost Company   "B"   Left Company   "A"

3. **Move.**   The Battalion will parade at 1.0 p.m.
                    Order of March:-   H.Q. "D" "A" "B" "C".
                    Dress:-   Fighting Order No 2, plus greatcoats.
                    Head of Column:-   Regtl Aid Post.
                    Tea will be served at Noyelles.

4. **Advance Party.** One Officer per Company and one N.C.O. per Platoon
                    will proceed to the trenches in advance.

5. **Rear Party.** A Rear Party of 3 men per Company, and 1 Junior
                    N.C.O. from "B" Coy, will parade in their billets
                    at 1.0 p.m., and will be marched to the trenches
                    by the Orderly Officer.

6. **Lewis Guns.** Lewis Guns will be loaded at Orderly Room at 11 a.m.
                    and will be conveyed to the Cross-roads Philosophe
                    where they will be picked up by the Lewis Gun Teams.
                    One man per gun will proceed with the limber.

7. **Blankets,**   Officers' Valises, mens packs and blankets to be
   Stores etc. stacked outside Company Headquarters at 11 a.m.
                    Mess Stores for the trenches and not for the trenches
                    to be stacked outside Company Headquarters at 12.45 pm.

8. **Gum-boots.**   O/C, "D" Company will draw 15 pairs of Gum-boots
                    at Lone Trench Gum-boot Store.

9. **Tea-urns.**   Tea-urns will not be taken to the trenches.

10. **Acknowledge.**

                                              [signature]
                                              Captain,

                    A/Adjutant, 1/6th Btn South Staffordshire Regiment.

Copies Issued to:-

   No 1. Commanding Officer.   No 8. Transport Officer.
      2. 137th Infantry Brigade.   9. Quartermaster.
      3. 1/5th Btn N.Staffs Rgt.   10. Regtl Sgt-Major.
      4. O/C, "A" Company.   11. War Diary.
      5. "   "B"   "   12. "   "   (Duplicate)
      6. "   "C"   "   13. File.
      7. "   "D"   "   14. "   (Duplicate)

SECRET   Operation Orders No. 60.   Copy No. 12

1/6th Bn. South Staffordshire Regiment

14th October 1917

1. RELIEF   The Battalion will be relieved in the Kultschof Loop Sub-sector by the
                   1/6th Bn. Prince of Wales's (North Staff.) Regt tomorrow night 15/16th inst.

2. DISPOSITION   On completion of relief the Battalion will move into support
                   and will be disposed as follows :—
                   A & C Companies in Marguingarbe.
                   B Coy — Old Battery S. in Tenth Avenue.
                   D Coy — Junction of Loone Trench and Tenth Avenue.

3. LEWIS GUNS   20 Panniers and 80 Magazines per Company will be handed over on
   & S.A.A   relief. Usual number of unused amount taken over in new positions.
                   A Company will dump the remainder of S.A.A. and the Lewis Guns
                   at Tenth Avenue Coy H.Q. and C Company at Company H.Q. near
                   Loone Trench, on relief.

4. GUM BOOTS   All Gum Boots, except those actually in use will be handed in at
                   Gum Boot store Loone Trench tomorrow morning. The remainder will be
                   handed in as soon as possible after relief.

5. CANTEEN   The Canteen will move to Tenth Avenue. Move to be complete by 5 p.m.
                   15th. B Company will provide a pte-10 carrying party.

6. MESS STORES   Mess Stores of A & C Companies to leave Ray Dump at 6.30 p.m.

7. S.E.   All Specialist equipment will be taken out of trenches. Each Company
                   will hand over to the relieving Battn 2 Mops. The remaining Mops and Hoppers
                   will be collected at Coy H.Q. Loone Trench and Tenth Avenue and divided
                   equally between the 2 Companies in Tenth Avenue. This should be done
                   before relief.

7. ADVANCE PARTY   1 Officer and 1 N.C.O. per Company will proceed to new positions in advance.
8. TRENCH STORES   A list of Trench Stores to be handed over will be rendered to O.R. by 2nd Runner
9. RELIEF COMPLETE Relief complete to be notified to Battn. Group H.Q. by the 3rd code.
10. ACKNOWLEDGE

                                                                    W H Ames
                                                                    Lieutenant.
                                                Adjutant 1/6th Bn. South Staffordshire Regiment.

Secret.   Operation Orders No 61,   Copy No 14
                      1/6th Battalion South Staffordshire Regiment.
                                Sunday, 18th November 1917.

1. **Relief.**   The 1/6th Battalion South Staffordshire Regiment
                     will relieve the 1/5th Battalion Prince of Wales's
                     (North Staffs) Regiment in the Hulluch Right Sub-
                     sector on the night of the 19/20th instant.

2. **Distribution.** On completion of relief Companies will be
                     disposed as follows:-
                     Right Company   "C".   Left Company   "A".
                     Right Support Coy   "D".   Left Support Coy   "B".

3. **Move.**   "A" and "C" Companies will move from Tenth Avenue
                     at 3.30 p.m.
                     "D" Coy, "B" Coy, and Headquarters will march from
                     Mazingarbe by Platoons at 200 yards interval.
                     First Platoon to pass Brigade H.Q. at 3.30 p.m.
                     Route:- Lambert's Track.
                     Dress:- Fighting Order No 2, plus greatcoat.

4. **Advance   One Officer per Company and one N.C.O. per Platoon
   Party.**   will proceed to the trenches in advance and take
                     over in daylight.
                     3 Lewis Gunners per Team will parade under the Lewis
                     Gun Sergeant at 3.0 p.m. and proceed to the trenches
                     in advance.

5. **Gum-boots.**   "C" Company will draw 70 pairs of Gum-boots from Lone
                     Trench Store.
                     "D" Company will draw 30 pairs as detailed below.

6. **Working   "D" Company will detail 1 N.C.O. and 15 men to be at
   Parties.**   Quarry Dump at 3.0 p.m. to-morrow (19th instant) where
                     they will be met by a guide from X/46th T.M.B.
                     They will carry trench mortars to Vendin Post and
                     complete two journeys. These men on completion of
                     their task will draw 2 pairs of gum-boots per man from
                     Lone Trench Store and convey same to trenches.
                     The Right Support Company will detail a party of one
                     Officer and 25 O.R. to be at Chalk Pit Dump at 2 p.m.
                     daily, where a guide from X/46th T.M.B. will meet them.

7. **Whale Oil.**   Whale oil will be used by all ranks before proceeding
                     to the trenches.

8. **Blankets   Officers Valises, mens packs, and blankets will be
   Packs etc.**   collected at 1.30 p.m. to-morrow.
                     Mess Stores for the trenches and not for the trenches
                     will be stacked outside Company Headquarters at 3.30 pm.

9. **Canteen.**   O/C. "C" Company will move the Canteen to Curzon Street
                     H.Q. before 3.30 p.m.

10. **Pass-word.**   The Pass-word for the night will be "Leave-train".

11. **Books.**   Books will be changed under same arrangements as made
                     for last tour.

12. **Relief   Relief Complete will be notified to Headquarters by
    Complete.**   Fullerphone in "B.A.B." Code.

13. **Acknowledge.**

                                                               Captain,
                     A/Adjutant, 1/6th Battalion South Staffordshire Regt.

Copies issued to:-
No 1. Commanding Officer.   No 6. "B" Company.   No 11. Regtl Sgt-Major.
   2. 137th Inf: Brigade.   7. "C"   "   12. War Diary.
   3. 1/5th N.Staffs Rgt.   8. "D"   "   13. "   "   (Duplicate)
   4. 1/6th N.Staffs Rgt.   9. Transport Officer.   14. File.
   5. "A" Company.   10. Quartermaster.   15. "   "   (Duplicate)

SECRET.   OPERATION ORDERS NO 62.   Copy No 11
            1/6th Battalion South Staffordshire Regiment.
                        Thursday, 22nd November 1917.

1. RELIEF.   The 1/6th Battalion South Staffordshire Regiment will
                be relieved by the 1/5th Battalion Prince of Wales's
                (North Staffs) Regiment in the HULLUCH Right Sub-sector
                on the night of the 23/24th instant.

2. MOVE.   On completion of relief the Battalion will move to
                VERQUIN (8 miles) and form Divisional Reserve.

3. ROUTE.   CHATEAU SIDINGS - SAILLY LABOURSE - VERQUIGNEUL.

4. TRANSPORT.   "A" and "C" Companies and H.Q. details will entrain at
                CHATEAU SIDINGS at 6.30 p.m. Tea will be served in
                Q.M. Stores on arrival. The Transport Officer will
                arrange transport of greatcoats to VERQUIN.
                "B" and "D" Companies will march to Brigade Headquarters
                MAZINGARBE. Tea will be served in Brigade Grounds.
                Transport Officer will arrange transport of greatcoats
                to VERQUIN. They will entrain at CHATEAU SIDINGS at
                8.0 p.m. and march from SAILLY LABOURSE.

5. SUPPER.   Supper will be served on arrival in billets.

6. GUMBOOTS.   All Gum-boots, tied in pairs, will be returned to Gum
                Boot Store at 12 noon.

7. MESS   Officers Mess Stores, cooking utensils etc, will be
   TINS.   loaded on trucks at DUMP at 5.0 p.m.

8. LEWIS GUNS   Lewis Guns and S.A.A. will be loaded under Company
   & S.A.A.   arrangements after completion of relief.

9. TRENCH   Accurate lists of Trench Stores will reach Battalion
   STORES.   Headquarters by 2nd runner to-morrow.

10. COOKING   Two boilers and one fryer per company will be handed
    UTENSILS.   over on relief.

11. RELIEF   Relief complete will be notified to Battalion Headquarters
    COMPLETE.   by code word "OLD MORTALITY".

12. ACKNOWLEDGE.

                                                    Drew
                                                    Captain,

                A/Adjutant, 1/6th Battalion South Staffordshire Regiment.

Copies Issued to:-

        No 1. Commanding Officer.
           2. 137th Infantry Brigade.
           3. 1/5th Btn North Staffs Rgt.
           4. O/C, "A" Company.
           5. "   "B"   "
           6. "   "C"   "
           7. "   "D"   "
           8. Transport Officer.
           9. Quartermaster.
          10. Regtl Sgt Major.
          11. War Diary.
          12. "   "   (Duplicate)
          13. File.
          14. "   (Duplicate)

Secret. Operation Orders No 63, Copy No IV
1/6th Battalion South Staffordshire Regiment.
Monday, 26th November 1917.

1. **Relief.** The 1/6th Btn South Staffs Regt will relieve the 1/5th Btn Prince of Wales's (North Staffs) Regt in the Hulluch Left Sub-sector to-morrow night 27/28th instant.

2. **Distribution.** On completion of relief the Battalion will be distributed as follows:-
    Right Company   "D".   Right Centre Company   "C".
    Outpost Company   "B".   Left Company   "A".

3. **Move.** The Battalion will parade at 1.0 p.m.
    Order of March:- "H.Q." - "D" - "A" - "B" - "C".
    Dress:-   Fighting Order No 2.
    Head of Column:- Regimental Aid Post.
    Tea will be served at Loyelles.

4. **Advance Party.** One Officer per Company and one N.C.O. per Platoon will proceed to the trenches in advance.

5. **Rear Party.** A Rear Party of 3 men per Company and 1 junior N.C.O. from "B" Coy, will Parade in their billets at 1.0 p.m., and will be marched to the Trenches by the Orderly Officer.

6. **Lewis Guns.** Lewis Guns will be loaded at Orderly Room at 11 a.m. and will be conveyed to the cross-roads Philosophe, where they will be picked up by the Lewis Gun Teams.
    One man per gun will proceed with the limber.

7. **Blankets, Stores, etc.** Officers Valises, mens packs, blankets, and rolled greatcoats to be stacked outside Coy H.Q's at 11.0 a.m.
    Mess stores for the trenches and not for the trenches to be stacked at same place at 12.45 p.m.

8. **Gum-Boots.** O/C, "D" Company will draw 25 pairs of Gum-boots from Lone Trench Gum-boot Store.

9. **Tea-Urns.** Tea-urns will be taken to the trenches.

10. **Whale Oil.** Whale oil will be used by all ranks before proceeding to the trenches.

11. **Socks.** Socks will be changed under the same arrangements as made for last tour.

12. **Canteen.** The Battalion Canteen will be established in Hulluch Tunnel.

13. **Relief Complete.** Relief complete will be notified to Headquarters by Fullerphone in "B.A.B" Code.

14. **Acknowledge.**

15. **Pass-word** - "Pickwick Papers".

Captain,
A/Adjutant 1/6th Battalion South Staffordshire Regiment.

Copies Issued to:-

    No 1. Commanding Officer.   No 9. Transport Officer.
       2. 137th Inf: Brigade.   10. Quartermaster.
       3. 1/5th N.Staffs Regt.   11. Regtl Sgt Major.
       4. 1/6th N.Staffs Regt.   12. War Diary.
       5. O/C, "A" Company.   13. "   "   (Duplicate).
       6. "   "B"   "   14. File.
       7. "   "C"   "   15. "   (Duplicate).
       8. "   "D"   "

SECRET.

OPERATION ORDERS No 64.
1/6th Battalion South Staffordshire Regt.

Copy No 12

FRIDAY, 30th NOVEMBER 1917.

1. The Battalion will be relieved in the HULLUCH Left Sub-sector on the night of the 1/2nd December by the 1/5th Prince of Wales's (North Staffs) Regiment.

2. On completion of relief the Battalion will be in Close Support and will be distributed as follows:-
   "H.Q.", "C" and "D" Coys   ---   NOYELLES.
   "A" and "B" Companies   ---   TENTH AVENUE.

3. "A" Company will move into dugouts in NINTH AVENUE. The Company will be under O/C, 1/6th Btn North Staffs Regiment tactically and O/C, 3rd Australian Tunnelling Company for work. "B" Company will move into dugouts in TENTH AVENUE. The Company will be under O/C, 1/5th Btn North Staffs Regiment tactically and O/C, 466th Field Coy, R.E., for work.

4. One Officer per Company and one N.C.O. per Platoon will proceed in advance and take over.

5. CANTEEN. The Canteen will move to junction of LONE TRENCH and TENTH AVENUE at 5.0 p.m. O/C, "B" Company will detail the necessary carrying party.

6. TEA URNS will be taken out of the trenches.

7. MESS STORES of "C" and "D" Companies will be at DUMPs at 5 p.m.

8. LISTS OF TRENCH STORES to be handed over will be rendered to Orderly Room by second runner to-morrow.

9. RELIEF COMPLETE. Relief Complete will be notified by Fullerphone to Battalion Headquarters by code word:-
   "DAVID COPPERFIELD".

                                           Captain,
   A/Adjutant 1/6th Battalion South Staffordshire Regiment.

Copies Issued to:-

No 1. Commanding Officer.
   2. 1/5th N. Staffs Regt.
   3. 1/5th N. Staffs Regt.
   4. 137th Infantry Bde.
   5. O/C, "A" Company.
   6. "   "B"   "
   7. "   "C"   "
   8. "   "D"   "

No 9. Transport Officer.
  10. Quartermaster.
  11. Regtl Sgt-Major.
  12. War Diary.
  13. "   (Duplicate)
  14. File.
  15. "   (Duplicate)

CONFIDENTIAL

WAR DIARY.

1/6th Bttn South Staffordshire Regiment.

FROM:- 1st December 1917 TO 31st December 1917.

1/6th Bn South Staffs Regt.

Army Form C. 2118.

(159)

WAR DIARY
or
INTELLIGENCE SUMMARY.

(Erase heading not required.)

Instructions regarding War Diaries and Intelligence Summaries are contained in F.S. Regs., Part II. and the Staff Manual respectively. Title pages will be prepared in manuscript.

Place	Date	Hour	Summary of Events and Information	Remarks and references to Appendices
HULLUCH	1.12.17.		At 12.30 am we called for artillery retaliation as the enemy was pounding our lines. He tried a raid on our left again. The day was very lively. In the afternoon Corps and Divisional Heavy Artillery bombarded the enemy lines at HULLUCH. The Battalion was relieved in the evening by the 1/6th Bn North Staffs Regt and moved into Brigade Reserve at NOYELLES. (Two Companies and H.Q., leaving 2 Coys in Close Support).	See O.O. No 64.
NOYELLES	2.12.17.		At 8.15 am a shell fell on the Battalion Officers Mess, killing the Commanding Officer (Lieut-Colonel F.J. Trump D.S.O.), also the H.Q. Company Cook, and wounding two other ranks. The Camp was vacated. Officers were billeted in other billets whilst the men occupied the School House and Chateau loft. Training and cleaning up etc.	
"	3.12.17.		On the night of the 3rd the two Companies from Brigade Reserve relieved the two Companies in Support in Tenth Avenue. The late Commanding Officer was buried in the British Cemetery at SAILLY LABOURSE.	
"	4.12.17.		Bathing and cleaning up. The Bn Football Eleven played the 1/1st Field Ambulance and lost two goals to one.	
HULLUCH	5.12.17.		MAJOR C. LISTER M.C. Northamptonshire Regt assumed Command of the Battalion. The Battalion relieved the 1/5th Bn North Staffs Regt in the HULLUCH Right Subsector. All was very quiet on the Battalion front. Patrols and wiring parties were out.	See O.O. No 65.
"	6.12.17.		Enemy planes were active during the day. Our patrols were out at night examining the enemy wire. Machine gun fire was normal throughout the night.	
"	7.12.17.		Enemy 'plane brought down by our Machine Gun Company and fell near PHILOSOPHE. Enemy 'planes were active. Enemy put a barrage down on HILL 70, and our artillery and trench mortars retaliated.	
"	8.12.17.		Patrols were out during the night. Two O.R's killed in NEW CUT by a 77 mm. Machine Gun fire normal. Artillery fairly active.	

Army Form C. 2118.

1/6th Btn South Staffordshire Regt.

(140).

WAR DIARY
or
INTELLIGENCE SUMMARY.
(Erase heading not required.)

Instructions regarding War Diaries and Intelligence Summaries are contained in F. S. Regs., Part II. and the Staff Manual respectively. Title pages will be prepared in manuscript.

Place	Date	Hour	Summary of Events and Information	Remarks and references to Appendices
NOEUX-LES-MINES.	9-12-1917		Quiet throughout the day. The Battalion was relieved by the 1/6th Btn North Staffs Regt and moved into Divisional Reserve at Noeux-les-Mines. A Battalion Officers Mess came into force.	See O.O. No. 66.
"	10-12-1917		Bathing and cleaning up.	
"	11-12-1917		The Commanding Officer inspected "A" & "B" Companies. "C" & "D" Coys carried out Musketry during the morning. "A" & "B" Coys played "C" & "D" Coys in a Football Match in the afternoon, the former winning by six goals to NIL. Colonel T.F.Waterhouse(a former Commanding Officer of this Battalion)came to Dinner.	
"	12-12-1917		The Commanding Officer inspected "C" & "D" Companies. "A" & "B" Companies fired on the Rifle Range during the morning. Lecture to all officers on Trench Discipline. The Commanding Officer & Lieut;Dickson attended a meeting at Army Headquarters on 'Adjutant's General's work and staff'.	See O.O. No 67
"	13-12-1917		Battalion Training during the morning. Battalion left Noeux-Les-Mines at 2p.m. to take over in the HULLUCH left Sub-Sector from the 1/5th Btn North Staffs Rgt. All was quiet during the night. Our patrols went out.	
HULLUCH.	14-12-1917		Minenwerfers active on VENDIN POST and Tunnel Posts. Artillery normal. Our patrols and wiring parties were out during the night.	
"	15-12-1917		Patrols and working parties out during the night. Our snipers were active,firing from craters. Enemy very quiet.	
"	16-12-1917		Enemy active with Machine Guns. Hostile Aircraft (8)over our lines.Driven off by our Lewis Guns. Enemy hit M.G.position and put Gun out of action covering VENDIN POST. Enemy manned front line during the night. A new Battle position was built in HAY ALLEY. Our patrol struck a Wiring party. Leader turned on Trench Mortars and 18 Pounders.	
"	17-12-1917		A very quiet day. At 6-30p.m.the Battalion was relieved in the line by the 1/6th Btn North Staffs Regt. H.Q., "B" & "D"COYS going into Brigade Reserve at 16 N.Y.L.I. leaving "A" & "C" Coys in Support at G.35.d.44.G.29.b.13.N.28.d.73.N.35.b.70.N.35.b.79.c.c. in Tenth Avenue.	See O.O.No 68.

Army Form C. 2118.

1/6th Btn. South Staffs Regt.

WAR DIARY or INTELLIGENCE SUMMARY.

(140)

(Erase heading not required.)

Instructions regarding War Diaries and Intelligence Summaries are contained in F. S. Regs. Part II. and the Staff Manual respectively. Title pages will be prepared in manuscript.

Place	Date	Hour	Summary of Events and Information	Remarks and references to Appendices
NOYELLES.	18-12-1917		Bathing, cleaning up., and Battalion Training.	
"	19-12-1917		Battalion Training carried out during the morning. The Bt In the afternoon "B" & "D" Companies relieved "A" & "C" Coys in Support in Tenth Avenue.	
"	20-12-1917		Bathing, cleaning up. Kit Inspection.	
"	21-12-1917		Battalion Training and 'routine' prior to the trenches. At 3p.m. "A" & "C" Companies left NOYELLES. The Battalion relieved the 1/5th Btn North Staffs Regt in the HULLUCH Right Sub-Sector. The Canadians relieved the 11th Division on HILL 70. Our patrols and Working Parties were out during the night.	See O.O. No. 69.
HULLUCH.	22-12-1917		Throughout the night of 21/22nd December 1917, enemy Machine Guns were very active. Enemy Balloons up at 8a.m. and remained up during the morning. Enemy Artillery and Trench Mortars active on Left-Sub-Sector.	
"	23-12-1917		Enemy quiet during the morning. In the afternoon enemy H.T.M's active. A bombing raid by our aeroplanes took place during the morning. Machine Guns active during the night. Gas reported in enemy front lines by the Canadians.	
"	24-12-1917		During 'Stand to' enemy Machine Guns swept our parapets. Our front during the remainder of the day was quiet. Our patrols were out throughout the night. Heavy Artillery activity on our Northern Flank.	
"	25-12-1917		At 'Stand to' the Bosche called across "A HAPPY XMAS STAFFS". Very quiet throughout the day. Enemy hardly seen. At 6-30p.m. the Battalion was relieved by the 1/6th Btn North Staffs Regt and moved into Divisional Reserve at NOEUX-LES-MINES.	See O.O. No. 70.
NOEUX-LES-MINES.	26-12-1917		Bathing, cleaning up etc. OFFICERS XMAS DINNER.---'SOME NIGHT'.	
"	27-12-1917		A little training was done during the morning, and inspection of clothing etc by the Commanding Officer. MENS XMAS DINNER TOOK PLACE, and FOOTBALL GAMES (Inter-Platoons) during the afternoon.	
"	28-12-1917		All Companies proceeded to the Rifle Range and fired five rounds RAPID (per man). In the afternoon the Btn Football Eleven played Divisional H.Q. Eleven and won 5 goals to one goal.	

1/6th Btn South Staffordshire Regt.

Army Form C. 2118.

(141).

WAR DIARY
or
INTELLIGENCE SUMMARY.

(Erase heading not required.)

Instructions regarding War Diaries and Intelligence Summaries are contained in F. S. Regs., Part II. and the Staff Manual respectively. Title pages will be prepared in manuscript.

Place	Date	Hour	Summary of Events and Information	Remarks and references to Appendices
NOEUX-LES-MINES.	29-12-1917.		Trench Routine prior to proceeding to the trenches. The Battalion relieved the 1/5th Bn North Staffs Regt in the HULLUCH Left Sub-Sector.	See OO.No.71.
HULLUCH.	30-12-1917.		Our patrols and working parties were out throughout the night. The day was fairly quiet. Sergeant KELLY J. DCM.was killed and two men wounded by a Priester bomb. During the early part of the night the enemy was active with machine Guns. Three of our patrol were wounded by a Hostile Patrol of greater strength.	
"	31-12-1917.		Fairly quiet during the day. Very little movement of the enemy seen. No aerial activity. At night our patrols were active.	

TOTAL CASUALTIES FOR MONTH OF DECEMBER 1917.

Lieut:Colonel F.J. TRUMP. DSO.(1st Monmouthshire Rgt attd) Killed in Action 2-12-1917.

4 O"Ranks Killed in Action.
1 " Died of Wounds.
11 " Wounded.
4 " Wounded and "At Duty".

---oOo---

3-1-1918.

[signature] MAJOR.
Commanding 1/6th Btn South Staffordshire Rgt.

Secret.   Operation Orders No 65.   Copy No 12
                    1/6th Battalion South Staffordshire Regiment.
                              Tuesday, 4th December 1917.

1. **Relief.**   The 1/6th Btn South Staffs Rgt will relieve the 1/5th
                  Btn Prince of Wales's (North Staffs) Rgt in the Hulluch
                  Right Sub-sector on the night of the 5/6th instant.

2. **Distribution.** On completion of relief Companies will be distributed
                  as follows:-
                  Right Company   "C".   Left Company.   "A".
                  Right Support Company "D"   Left Support Company "B".

3. **Move.**   "C" and "D" Companies will move from Tenth Avenue at
                  3.30 p.m.
                  "A" and "B" Companies will march from Lovelles by
                  Platoons at 200 yards interval, followed by Btn H.Q.Coy.
                  First Platoon to pass N.11.c.99.20 at 3.30 p.m.
                  Route:-   Lamberts Track.
                  Dress:-   Fighting Order No 2, plus greatcoat.

4. **Advance   1 Officer per Company and 1 N.C.O. per Platoon will
   Party.**   proceed to the trenches and take over in daylight.
                  3 Lewis Gunners per Team will parade under Cpl Everitt
                  at 3.0 pm and proceed to the trenches in advance.

5. **Gum-Boots.** O/C, "C" and "D" Companies will draw required number of
                  pairs from Long Trench Store.

6. **Whale-oil.** Whale Oil will be used by all ranks before proceeding
                  to the trenches.

7. **Blankets,   Officers valises, mens packs, and blankets will be
   Packs etc.**   collected at 1.30 p.m. to-morrow.
                  Mess stores for the trenches and not for the trenches
                  will be stacked outside Company H.Q'rs at 3.0 p.m.

8. **Canteen.**   O/C, "D" Company will move the Canteen to Curzon Street
                  Headquarters before 3.30 p.m.

9. **Password.** The Pass-word for the night will be "Aston Villa".

10. **Socks.**   Socks will be changed under the same arrangements as
                  were made for last tour.

11. **Relief   Relief Complete will be notified to Btn H.Q. by
    Complete.**   Fullerphone in "B.A.B" Code.

12. **Acknowledge.**

                                                              Captain,
                        A/Adjutant, 1/6th Battalion South Staffs Regiment.

    Copies Issued to:-

    No 1. Commanding Officer.   No 9 Transport Officer.
       2. 137th Infantry Brigade.   10. Quartermaster.
       3. 1/5th Btn North Staffs Rgt.   11 Regtl Sgt-Major.
       4. 1/6th Btn North Staffs Rgt.   12. War Diary.
       5. O/C, "A" Company.   13. "   "   (Duplicate).
       6. "   "B"   "   14 File.
       7. "   "C"   "   15. "   (Duplicate).
       8. "   "D"   "

SECRET.   Copy No

OPERATION ORDERS NO 66,
1/6th Battalion South Staffordshire Regiment.

8th December 1917.

1. The 1/6th Battalion South Staffordshire Regiment will be relieved in the HULLUCH Right Subsector by the 1/6th Battalion Prince of Wales's (North Staffs) Regiment on the night of the 9/10th December 1917.

2. On completion of relief the Battalion will move by Companies to NOEUX-LES-MINES and form Divisional Reserve.
Company Q.M. Sergeants will meet their Companies at Railway Crossings on the MAZINGARBE - NOEUX-LES-MINES Road.

3. Tea will be served at Brigade Headquarters MAZINGARBE, supper on arrival in billets.
Two boilers and one fryer per Company will be handed over on relief.

4. Officers Mess Baskets etc to be at Dumps at 5.0 p.m.

5. One truck will remain at GUN and CHALK PIT DUMPS for Lewis Guns and ammunition.

6. Relief complete will be notified to Battalion Headquarters by code word:-
        "DUCK".

7. Acknowledge.

Captain,
A/Adjutant 1/6th Battalion South Staffordshire Regiment.

Copies issued to:-

    No 1. Commanding Officer.
    2. 137th Infantry Brigade.
    3. 1/6th Btn North Staffs Regiment.
    4. 1/5th Btn South Staffs Regiment.
    5. O/C. Right Battalion.
    6.   "   "A" Company.
    7.   "   "B"   "
    8.   "   "C"   "
    9.   "   "D"   "
    10. Transport Officer.
    11. Quartermaster.
    12. Regtl Sgt-Major.
    13. War Diary.
    14.   "   "   (Duplicate)
    15. File.
    16.   "   (Duplicate)

SECRET.

Secret.　　　　　　　Operation Orders No 67,　　　　　　Copy No 14.
　　　　　　　1/6th Battalion South Staffordshire Regiment.

　　　　　　　　　　　　　　　　Wednesday, 12th December 1917.

1. The 1/6th Battalion South Staffordshire Regiment will relieve
   the 1/5th Battalion Prince of Wales's (North Staffordshire)
   Regiment in the Hulluch Left Subsector on the night of the
   13/14th December.

2. Dispositions.　On completion of relief the Battalion will be
   distributed as follows:-
   Right Company　　　　　　"C".　　Right Centre Coy　　　　"D".
   Outpost Company　　　　　"A"　　 Left Company　　　　　　"B"

3. The Battalion will parade in Fighting Order No 2, plus greatcoat,
   at 2.0 p.m. outside the Huts and march to Mazingarbe, by
   Companies at 200 yards interval, in the following order:-
   　　"Headquarters" - "C" - "A" - "D" - "B".
   Companies will march to the trenches by Platoons at 200 yards
   interval from Mazingarbe, first Platoon to leave Brigade
   Headquarters at 3.30 p.m.

4. Packs and Blankets will be collected at 10.30 a.m.

5. Advance Party.　An Advance Party consisting of 1 Officer per
   Company, 1 N.C.O. per Platoon, Regtl Sgt-Major, H.Q. and Company
   Gas N.C.O's and Company Cooks will parade at noon and proceed
   to the trenches and take over in advance.

6. Officers Mess Stores, Lewis Guns and Lewis Gun S.A.A. will be
   collected at 12 noon.

7. O/C, "C" Company will draw 20 pairs of Gum-boots from Lone
   Trench Gum-boot Store.

8. Whale Oil will be used by all ranks before proceeding to the
   Trenches.

9. Socks will be changed under the same arrangements as were made
   for last tour.

10. Relief Complete will be notified to Battalion Headquarters in
    "B.A.B". Code.

11. Acknowledge.

　　　　　　　　　　　　　　　　　　　　　　J M Trew
　　　　　　　　　　　　　　　　　　　　　　Captain,
　　A/Adjutant, 1/6th Battalion South Staffordshire Regiment.

　　Copies issued to:-

　　　　　　　No 1. Commanding Officer.
　　　　　　　　 2. 137th Infantry Brigade.
　　　　　　　　 3. 1/5th Btn North Staffs Regt.
　　　　　　　　 4. 1/6th Btn North Staffs Regt.
　　　　　　　　 5. 1/5th Btn South Staffs Regt.
　　　　　　　　 6. O/C, "A" Company.
　　　　　　　　 7. "   "B"   "
　　　　　　　　 8. "   "C"   "
　　　　　　　　 9. "   "D"   "
　　　　　　　　10. Transport Officer.
　　　　　　　　11. Quartermaster.
　　　　　　　　12. O/C, Left Battalion.
　　　　　　　　13. Regtl Sgt-Major.
　　　　　　　　14. War Diary.
　　　　　　　　15. "   " (Duplicate).
　　　　　　　　16. File.
　　　　　　　　17. "   (Duplicate).

BATTALION ORDERS No 66.   Copy No 13.
1/6th Bn North Staffordshire Regiment
                                    Sunday 16th December 1917.

Reference 36 B 1/40,000.

1. The Battalion will be relieved in the HULLUCH LEFT Sub-sector
   on the night of the 17/18th December by the 1/6th Bn Prince
   of Wales's (North Staffs) Regiment.

2. On completion of relief Headquarters, "B" & "D" Companies will
   march by platoons to billets in NOYELLES. Guides will meet
   Companies at L 17 b 40.

3. "A" Company will be billeted in HULLUCH TOWER, will work under
   orders of O.C.170th(?) Tunnelling Co. but will be tactically
   under the orders of the O.C. Left Battalion.

   "C" Company will be billeted at junction of LONE TRENCH and
   TENTH AVENUE, will work under orders of O.C. 466th Field Coy R.E.

4. Officers Mess Stores, Cooking Utensils etc., will be on Dumps at
   4.30 p.m.

5. Two cooking boilers and one fryer per Company will be handed over
   on relief.

6. Tea will be served on completion of relief.

7. Lists of Trench Stores to be handed over will reach Orderly Room
   by first runner tomorrow.

8. Relief complete will be notified to Battalion Headquarters by
   code word 'OXFORD'.

9. ACKNOWLEDGE.

                                                          Captain.
              A/Adjutant.1/6th Bn North Staffordshire Regiment.

Copies issued to :-

No 1. Commanding Officer.   No 9. Transport Officer.
   2. 1/6th North Staffs Regt.   10. Quartermaster.
   3. 1/5th North Staffs Regt.   11. Regt Sgt Major.
   4. 137th Infantry Brigade.   12. War Diary.
   5. O.C. "A" Company.   13.   do   (Duplicate)
   6. "   "B"   "   14. File.
   7. "   "C"   "   15.   do   (Duplicate).
   8. "   "D"   "

Operation Orders No 70.   Copy No 13.
1/6th Btn South Staffordshire Regiment.
                                   Monday 24th December 1917.

1. **RELIEF.**   The 1/6th Btn South Staffordshire Regiment will be
                    relieved in the HULLUCH RIGHT subsector by the 1/5th
                    Btn Prince of Wales's (North Staffs) Regiment on the
                    night of the 25/26th December 1917.

2. **MOVE.**   On completion of relief the Battalion will move by
                    Companies to NOEUX-LES-MINES and form Divisional Reserve.
                    Company .M. Sergeants will meet their Companies at
                    Railway Crossing on the MAZINGARBE – NOEUX-LES-MINES Road.

3. **TEA.**   Tea will be served at Brigade Headquarters MAZINGARBE
                    Supper will be served on arrival in billets.

4. **MESS STORES** Officers' Mess Baskets etc will be at Dump at 4.45 p.m.

5. **LEWIS GUNS
   A.A.A.**   One truck will remain at GUN and CHALK PIT DUMPs for
                    Lewis Guns and Ammunition.
                    Cpl Everitt will be responsible for the loading and
                    unloading of the Battalion Lewis Guns.

6. **TRENCH STORES.** A list of Trench Stores to be handed over will be
                    rendered to Orderly Room by 2nd Runner tomorrow.

7. **RELIEF
   REPORT.**   Relief Complete will be notified to Battalion H.Q. by
                    code word 'PORK'.

8. **ACKNOWLEDGE.**

                                                J W Drew
                                                    Captain.
                Adjutant 1/6th Btn South Staffordshire Regiment.

   Copies issued to :-

        No 1. Commanding Officer.
           2. 137th Infantry Brigade.
           3. 1/5th Btn North Staffordshire Regiment.
           4. 1/5th Btn South Staffordshire Regiment.
           5. O.C. Right Battalion.
           6. O.C. "A" Company.
           7. "   "B"   "
           8. "   "C"   "
           9. "   "D"   "
          10. Transport Officer.
          11. Quartermaster.
          12. Regt Sgt-Major.
          13. War Diary.
          14.   do.   (Duplicate).
          15. File.
          16.   do.   (Duplicate).

Operation Orders No 71. Copy No 13.
1/6th Btn South Staffordshire Regiment.
Friday, 28th December 1917.

1. The 1/6th Btn South Staffordshire Regiment will relieve the 1/5th Battalion Prince of Wales's (North Staffs) Regiment in the HULLUCH Left sub-sector on the night of the 29/30th December 1917.

2. **Dispositions.** On completion of relief the Battalion will be distributed as follows:-
   Right Company   "C"   Right Centre Company   "D"
   Outpost Company   "A"   Left Company   "B"

3. The Battalion will parade in fighting order No 2, plus greatcoat, at 2 p.m. outside the Huts and march to Mazingarbe, by Companies at 100 yards interval, in the following order:-
   Headquarters - "C" - "A" - "D" - "B".
   Companies will march to the trenches by platoons at 100 yards interval from Mazingarbe, First Platoon to leave Brigade Headquarters at 3.30 p.m.

4. **Packs and Blankets and Officers' Valises** will be collected at 10.0 a.m.

5. **Advance Party.** An Advance Party consisting of 1 Officer per Company, 1 N.C.O. per Platoon, Regt Sgt-Major, Headquarters and Company Gas N.C.O's and Company Cooks will parade at noon and proceed to the Trenches and take over in advance.

6. Officers' Mess Stores, Lewis Guns and Lewis Gun S.A.A. will be collected at 12 noon.

7. O.C. "C" Company will draw 20 pairs of Gum-Boots from Lone Trench Gum-Boot Store.

8. Two Tea-urns and one Fryer per Company will be taken over on relief.

9. **Whale Oil** will be used by all ranks before proceeding to the Trenches.

10. **Socks** will be changed under the same arrangements as were made for last tour.

11. **Relief Complete** will be notified to Battalion Headquarters in "B.A.B" Code.

12. Acknowledge.

TM Frew
Captain.
Adjutant, 1/6th Btn South Staffordshire Regiment.

Copies issued to:-

No 1. Commanding Officer.   No 9. Transport Officer.
   2. 137th Infantry Brigade.   10. Quartermaster.
   3. 1/5th Btn North Staffs Regt.   11. O.C. Left Battalion.
   4. 1/5th Btn South Staffs Regt.   12. Regt Sergt-Major.
   5. O.C. "A" Company.   13. War Diary.
   6. O.C. "B"   "   14.   "   "   (Duplicate).
   7. O.C. "C"   "   15. File.
   8. O.C. "D"   "   16.   "   (Duplicate).

CONFIDENTIAL.

WAR DIARY.

1/6th Btn South Staffordshire Regiment.

From 1st January to 31st January 1918.

1/6th Btn South Staffordshire Regiment.   WAR DIARY or INTELLIGENCE SUMMARY.   Army Form C. 2118.

Place	Date	Hour	Summary of Events and Information	Remarks and references to Appendices
HULLUCH	1-1-18		At 5.15 a.m. enemy endeavoured to raid our No 1 Tunnel Post but was unsuccessful in obtaining identification. The Raiding Party left behind 2 Ammonal Tubes. The enemy was very quiet throughout the remainder of the day. The Battalion was relieved by the 1/6th Btn North Staffordshire Regiment and went into Brigade Reserve at MAZINGARBE 2 Companies in close support in TENTH AVENUE & TUNNELS and 2 Companies in Huts.	See 80. No 14.
MAZIN-GARBE.	2-1-18.		Two Companies and Headquarters bathed and had M.O's inspection and cleaning up generally. In the evening a heavy bombardment was put on Right Brigade and Left Brigade.	
"	3-1-18.		Two Companies went up to pass through Gas Test. Physical Drill and Company Drill afterwards. "A" & "C" Companies relieved "B" & "D" Companies during the afternoon.	
"	4-1-18.		"B" & "D" Companies - Bathing, M.O.'s inspection and cleaning up generally. In the afternoon Major Hutchence and Lieut W.R. Dickson inspected Tracks and Village Line of Centre Brigade.	
"	5-1-18.		Commanding Officer inspected "B" & "D" Companies. Routine prior to Trenches was carried out. Games in the afternoon.	
"	6-1-18		Church Parade in the morning. Lt.Colonel C.Lister M.C. returned from Leave. The Battalion relieved the 1/5th Btn North Staffs Regiment in the HULLUCH Right Subsector. During the night our Patrols were active	See 80. No 15.
HULLUCH	7-1-18.		Enemy active with Light T.M's on No 65 Trench which was being re-opened. Wiring done of South of Battalion front North of CANADIAN CUT. Our Patrols were active.	
"	8-1-18.		Very quiet during the day. Enemy busy during the night wiring his front line in. Machine Guns active forming covering party for enemy wiring party which was being French Mortared. Our Patrols were out later but none of the enemy were found.	

Army Form C. 2118.

(145)
WAR DIARY
or
INTELLIGENCE SUMMARY.
(Erase heading not required.)

1/6th Btn South Staffordshire Regiment.

Instructions regarding War Diaries and Intelligence Summaries are contained in F. S. Regs., Part II and the Staff Manual respectively. Title pages will be prepared in manuscript.

Place	Date	Hour	Summary of Events and Information	Remarks and references to Appendices
HULLUCH	9-1-1918.	8.0 a.m.	Enemy aeroplanes up over our Lines but too high for our Lewis Guns. None of our 'planes were up. Our Snipers were very active, 4 hits were claimed. Parties of mensseen in enemy front line carrying timber. Our Patrols were out during the night.	See O.O. No 14.
"	10-1-1918.		Some Trench Mortaring on front line. POSEN, CHALK PIT and GUN DUMPS shelled with 4.2s. The Battalion was relieved by the 1/6th Btn North Staffordshire Regiment and moved into Divisional Reserve at NOEUX LES MINES.	
NOEUX LES MINES.	11-1-1918.		The Battalion cleaning up and bathing during the morning. Football and games played during the afternoon.	
"	12-1-1918.		Physical Drill and Bayonet Fighting. Inspection by Company Commanders. Football in the afternoon No 16 Platoon won the Inter Platoon 6 a side competition. The Battalion played the "WYVERNS" and won by 9 goals to 2.	
"	13-1-1918.		Companies inspected by Commanding officer. Physical Training and Bayonet Fighting. Church Parade at 11 a.m.	
"	14-1-1918.		Routine prior to Trenches. The Battalion moved off at 2.0 p.m and relieved the 5th Btn Prince of Wales's (North Staffs) Regiment in the HULLUCH LEFT Subsector. Our Patrols were out during the night. The situation was quiet on the Battalion front. Canadians made a raid on HILL 70. American officer attached for instruction.	See O.O. No 15.
HULLUCH	15-1-1918.		During the morning the enemy did a destruction shoot round WING'S WAY with 77 mm. and 4.2s. At 3.0 p.m. the enemy again started on WING'S WAY but stopped on our Guns opening out. Our Patrols were out during the night. Divisional Relief posponed owing to thaw precautions.	
"	16-1-1918.		The morning was quiet. In the afternoon enemy shelled and Trench Mortared "A" and "B" Companies. One of our 'planes brought down by M.G. fire from hostile 'plane at 10.0 a.m.	

Army Form C. 2118.

WAR DIARY
1/6th Btn South Staffordshire Regiment. (144)
or
INTELLIGENCE SUMMARY.

Instructions regarding War Diaries and Intelligence Summaries are contained in F. S. Regs., Part II. and the Staff Manual respectively. Title pages will be prepared in manuscript.

(Erase heading not required.)

Place	Date	Hour	Summary of Events and Information	Remarks and references to Appendices
HULLUCH	17-1-1918.		During the morning the Trenches continued to fall in. The intelligence officer of 9th Btn Notts & Derby Regiment came up with 15 snipers to take stock of Line. Our snipers had four hits during the afternoon. Our Patrols were active at night.	See O.O. No %.
"	18-1-1918.		The morning was quiet without any event other than the continuance of the line falling in. The Battalion relieved by the 1/6th Btn Prince of Wales' (North Staffs) Regiment. and moved into Close Support "A", "B" & "C" Companies in TENTH AVENUE & TUNNELS, "D" Company and Headquarters at MAZINGARBE. Captain E.A. Wilson (1/5th North Staffs Regt) acting 2nd in Command during absence of Major Hutchence.	
MAZINGARBE	19-1-18.		"D" Company and Headquarters bathed during the morning and Scabies inspection by M.O. Cleaning up generally in the afternoon.	
"	20-1-1918.		Church Parade in the morning. In the afternoon "D" Company relieved "A" Company. Rumours of an earlier Divisional Relief.	
"	21-1-1918.		"A" Company bathed and had Scabies inspection in the morning, cleaning up in the afternoon. Still rumours of an early Relief	
"	22-1-1918.		Training and Routine prior to proceeding to the Trenches took place in the morning. The Battalion relieved the 1/6th Btn Prince of Wales' (North Staffs) Regiment in the HULLUCH Left Subsector.	
HULLUCH	23-1-1918. 24-1-1918.		Quiet day. Our Patrols were out during the night. The Battalion was relieved by the 9th Btn Sherwoof Foresters (11th Division) and moved to rest billets at VAUDRICOURT.	See O.O. No 71.
VAUDRI-COURT	25-1-1918.		The Battalion Bathing and cleaning up.	See O.O. No 72.
"	26-1-1918.		Cleaning up and Kit Inspections etc.	
"	27-1-1918.		Church Parade. Demonstration of "Inspection of a Platoon" to Subaltern Officers and Sergeants.	
"	28-1-1918.		Battalion Training.	
"	29-1-1918.		Battalion Training. Officers' Riding School.	
"	30-1-1918.		The Battalion engaged in Wiring.	

Army Form C. 2118.

(C145)

WAR DIARY
or
INTELLIGENCE SUMMARY.

(Erase heading not required.)

1/6th Btn South Staffordshire Regiment.

Instructions regarding War Diaries and Intelligence Summaries are contained in F. S. Regs., Part II. and the Staff Manual respectively. Title pages will be prepared in manuscript.

Place	Date	Hour	Summary of Events and Information	Remarks and references to Appendices
VAUDRICOURT.	31-1-1918.		The Battalion engaged in Wiring. Officers attended a demonstration at Divisional Training Battalion, ALLOUAGNE.	
			CASUALTIES FOR THE MONTH.	
			WOUNDED. 2 O.R.	
			WOUNDED AT DUTY. 1 O.R.	

C'hister Lieut:Colonel.
Commanding 1/6th Btn South Staffordshire Regiment.

2nd February 1918.

Operation Orders No 75.
1/5th Bn South Staffordshire Regiment.
Tuesday, January 1st 1916.

Reference 36.B.1/40,000.

1. The Battalion will be relieved in the RUE DU BOIS LEFT subsector on the night of the 2/3rd January by the 1/5th Bn Prince of Wales's (North Staffs) Regiment.

2. On completion of relief, Headquarters, "A" & "C" Companies will march by platoons to billets in ESTAIRES. Guides will meet Companies at Brigade Headquarters.

   "B" Company will be billeted in ENGLISH TUNNEL, will work under orders of O.C. 170th (N) Tunnelling Company and will be tactically under the orders of the O.C. Left Battalion.

   "D" Company will be billeted at junction of A&Y TRENCH and 7 8TH AVENUE and will work under orders of O.C. 466 Field Company R.E.

3. Officers' Mess Boxes, Cooking Utensils etc will be on dumps at 4.30pm.

4. Two Cooking Boilers and one Fryer per Company will be handed over on relief.

5. Tea will be served on completion of relief.

6. List of Trench Stores to be handed over will reach Orderly Room by first runner tomorrow.

7. Relief complete will be notified to Battalion Headquarters by code word "NYGH".

8. ACKNOWLEDGE.

J M Frew
Captain.
Adjutant 1/5th Bn South Staffordshire Regiment.

Copies issued to:-

No 1. Commanding Officer.
   2. 137th Infantry Brigade.
   3. 1/5th Bn North Staffs Regt.
   4. 1/5th Bn North Staffs Regt.
   5. O.C. "A" Company.
   6. "   "B"   "
   7. "   "C"   "
   8. "   "D"   "
   9. Transport Officer.
   10. Quartermaster.
   11. Regt Sergt-Major.
   12. Diary.
   13. "   " (Duplicate).
   14. File.
   15. "   " (Duplicate).

SECRET.   Operation Orders No 73.   Copy No 13
                  1/6th Btn South Staffordshire Regiment.
                                        Saturday, 5th January 1918.

1. Relief.   The 1/6th Btn South Staffordshire Regiment will relieve
                    the 1/5th Btn Prince of Wales's (North Staffs) Regt. in
                    the HULLUCH RIGHT Sub-sector on the night of the 6/7th
                    instant.

2. Distribution.   On completion of relief Companies will be distributed
                    as follows:-
                    Right Company   "C"   Left Company   "A"
                    Right Support Company   "D"   Left Support Company "B"

3. Move.   "A" and "C" Companies will move from TENTH AVENUE at
                    3.30 p.m.
                    "B" and "D" Companies will march from MAZINGARBE by
                    Platoons at 200 yards interval, followed by H.Q. Compy.
                    First Platoon to pass Brigade Headqurters at 3.30 p.m.
                    Route:- Lamberts Track.
                    Dress:- Fighting Order No 2 plus Greatcoat.

4. Advance   1 Officer per Company and 1 N.C.O. per Platoon will
   Party.   proceed to the trenches and take over in daylight.
                    3 Lewis Gunners per Team will parade under Sergt.
                    Wooldridge at 3.15 p.m. and proceed to the trenches in
                    advance.

5. Gum-boots.   O's C. "A" and "C" Companies will draw required number
                    of pairs from Lone Trench Store.

6. Whale-Oil.   Whale-oil will be used by all ranks before proceeding
                    to the trenches.

7. Blankets,   Officers' Valises, Mens Packs and blankets will be
   Packs etc.   collected at 10.30 A.M. tomorrow. (10 a m)
                    Mess stores for the trenches and not for the trenches
                    will be stacked outside Company H.Q. at 3.0 p.m.

8. Canteen.   O.C. "A" Company will move the Canteen to Curzon Street
                    Headquarters before 3.30 p.m.

9. Password.   The password for the night will be 'NEW-YEAR'.

10. Socks.   Socks will be changed under the same arrangements as
                    made for last tour.

11. Tea-urns.   Two Tea-urns and one Fryer per Company will be taken
                    over on relief.

12. Relief   Relief Complete will be notified to Battalion H.Q. by
    Complete.   Fullerphone in 'B. & B' Code.

13. Acknowledge.

                                                            Captain.
                    Adjutant 1/6th Btn South Staffordshire Regiment.

Copies issued to:-

  No 1. Commanding Officer.   No 9. Transport Officer.
     2. 137th Infantry Brigade.   10. Quartermaster.
     3. 1/5th Btn North Staffs Regt.   11. Right Battalion.
     4. 1/5th Btn South Staffs Regt.   12. Regt Sergt-Major.
     5. O.C. "A" Company.   13. War Diary.
     6. "   "B"   "   14. "   "   (Duplicate).
     7. "   "C"   "   15. File.
     8. "   "D"   "   16. "   (Duplicate).

SECRET.   Operation Orders No 74,   Copy No. 13.
                         1/5th Battalion South Staffordshire Regiment.
                                               Wednesday, 9th January 1918.

1. RELIEF.   The 1/5th Btn South Staffordshire Regiment will be
                  relieved in the MONACUE RIGHT subsector by the 1/6th
                  Btn Prince of Wales's (North Staffs) Regiment on the
                  night of the 10/11th January 1918.

2. MOVE.   On completion of relief the Battalion will move by
                  platoons to MARIMBERT and thence by companies to
                  MORBEQUE and form divisional reserve.
                  Company Q.M.Sergeants will meet their Companies at the
                  entrance to the Camp.

3. TEA.   Tea will be served at Brigade Headquarters MARIMBERT.

4. MESS STORES   Officers Mess baskets etc will be at Dumps at 4.45 p.m.
   ETC.

5. MA VANS &   Two tea urns and one fryer per company will be handed
   FRYERS.   over on relief.

6. LEWIS GUNS   One truck will remain at GUN and CHALK PIT DUMPs for
   & S.A.A.   Lewis Guns and ammunition.
                  Cpl Everitt will be responsible for the loading and
                  unloading of the Battalion Lewis Guns at KING BARLOW
                  station.

7. TRENCH   A list of trench stores to be handed over will be
   STORES.   rendered to Orderly Room by first runner to-morrow.

8. RELIEF   Relief Complete will be notified to Battalion Headquarters
   COMPLETE.   by code word "ROSE".

9. ACKNOWLEDGEMENT.

                                              J.H.Wood
                                              Lieut,
                  A/Adjutant 1/5th Battalion South Staffordshire Regiment.

   Copies issued to:-

            No 1. Commanding Officer.
               2. 137th Infantry Brigade.
               3. 1/6th Btn North Staffs Rgt.
               4. 1/5th Btn South Staffs Rgt.
               5. O/C. Right Battalion.
               6. "A" Company.
               7. "B"   "
               8. "C"   "
               9. "D"   "
              10. Transport Officer.
              11. Quartermaster.
              12. Regtl Sgt-Major.
              13. War Diary.
              14. "   "   (Duplicate).
              15. File.
              16. "   (Duplicate).

Secret.   Operation Orders No /5.   Copy No /3
             1/6th Battalion South Staffordshire Regiment.
                              Sunday, 13th January 1918.

1. The 1/6th Battalion South Staffordshire Regiment will relieve the
   1/5th Battalion Prince of Wales's (North Staffs) Regiment in the
   Hulluch Left Subsector on the night of the 14/15th instant.

2. <u>Dispositions.</u> On completion of relief the Battalion will be
   distributed as follows:-
   Right Company   "C".   Right Centre Company   "D"
   Outpost Company   "A".   Left Company   "B"

3. The Battalion will Parade in fighting order No 2, plus greatcoat,
   at 2.0 p.m. outside the Huts and march to Mazingarbe, by Companies
   at 200 yards interval, in the following order:-
       "C" Coy - "A" Coy - "D" Coy - "B" Coy - "Headquarters".
   Companies will march to the trenches by Platoons from Mazingarbe
   at 200 yards interval. First Platoon to pass Brigade Headquarters
   at 3.30 p.m.

4. <u>Packs, Blankets and Officers valises</u> will be collected at 10 a.m.

5. <u>Advance Party.</u> An Advance Party consisting of 1 Officer per Company
   1 N.C.O. per Platoon, Regtl Sgt-Major, Headquarters and Company
   Gas N.C.O's, and Company Cooks will parade at noon and proceed to
   the trenches and take over in advance.

6. Officers' Mess Stores, Lewis Guns and Lewis Gun S.A.A. will be
   collected at 12 noon.

7. O/C, "C" Company will draw 20 pairs of Gum-boots from Lone Trench
   Gum-boot store.

8. Two tea-urns and one Fryer per Company will be taken over on
   relief.

9. Whale Oil will be used by all ranks before proceeding to the
   trenches.

10. Socks will be changed under the same arrangements as were made for
    last tour.

11. Relief Complete will be notified to Battalion Headquarters in
    "B.a.B." Code.

12. <u>Acknowledge</u>.

                                                      J R Wood
                                                        Lieut:
A/Adjutant 1/6th Battalion South Staffordshire Regiment.

<u>Copies issued to</u>:-

No 1. Commanding Officer.   No 9. Transport Officer.
   2. 137th Infantry Brigade.   10. Quartermaster.
   3. 1/5th Btn North Staffs Rgt.   11. O/C, Left Battalion.
   4. 1/5th Btn South Staffs Rgt.   12. Regtl Sgt-Major.
   5. O/C, "A" Company.   13. War Diary.
   6. "   "B"   "   14. "   "   (Duplicate)
   7. "   "C"   "   15. File.
   8. "   "D"   "   16. "   (Duplicate).

SECRET.   Operation Orders No 76.   Copy No 12
          1/6th Battalion South Staffordshire Regiment.

                              18th January 1916.

1. The Battalion will be relieved in the HULLUCH Left subsector on the night of the 18/19th inst by the 1/6th Battalion Prince of Wales's (North Staffs) Regiment.

2. On completion of relief Headquarters and "D" Company will march by platoons to billets in MAZINGARBE. Guides will meet Coys at Brigade Headquarters.
"B" Company will be billeted in HULLUCH Tunnel and will work under orders of O/C 170th (A) Tunnelling Company and will be tactically under orders of O/C, Left Battalion.
"A" Company will be billeted at the junction of LONE TRENCH and TENTH AVENUE and will work under orders of 466th Field Coy R.E.
"C" Company will be billeted in POSH ALLEY and will work under orders of O/C 466th Field Coy R.E.
"A" and "C" Coys will be tactically under the orders of O/C Right Battalion.
"A" "B" & "C" Coys will send an officer to take over stores & dugouts previously.

3. Headquarters and "D" Coys Officers Mess Stores, Cooking utensils etc will be at Dumps at 4.50 p.m.

4. Two cooking boilers and one fryer per Company will be handed over on relief.

5. Tea will be served on completion of relief.

6. Lists of Trench Stores to be handed over will be rendered to Orderly Room by first runner to-day.

7. Relief complete will be notified to Battalion Headquarters by code word "SHAMROCK".

8. ACKNOWLEDGE.

                              J P Wood
                              Lieut:
   A/Adjutant 1/6th Battalion South Staffordshire Regiment.

Copies issued to:-

       No 1. Commanding Officer.
          2. 137th Infantry Brigade.
          3. O/C. 1/6th Btn North Staffs Rgt.
          4. " 1/5th Btn North Staffs Rgt.
          5. " "A" Company.
          6. " "B"   "
          7. " "C"   "
          8. " "D"   "
          9. Transport Officer.
         10. Quartermaster.
         11. Regtl Sgt-Major.
         12. War Diary.
         13. "   "   (Duplicate).
         14. File.
         15. File (Duplicate).

Secret.   Operation Orders No 7,   Copy No 14
1/6th Battalion South Staffordshire Regiment.

Monday, 21st January 1918.

1. The 1/6th Battalion South Staffordshire Regiment will relieve the 1/6th Battalion Prince of Wales's (North Staffs) Regiment in the Hulluch Left Subsector on the night of the 22/23rd January 1918.

2. On completion of relief the Battalion will be distributed as follows:-
   Right Company   "D".   Right Centre Company   "C"
   Outpost Company   "A"   Left Company   "B"

3. "B" "C" & "D" Companies will move from Close Support to the line at 4.0 p.m.
   "A" Company and H.Q.Details will march from Mazingarbe by Platoons at 200 yards interval, in the order mentioned. First Platoon to pass Brigade Headquarters at 3.45 p.m.
   Dress:- Fighting Order No 2, plus greatcoats.
   Route:- Lone Track.

4. An Advance Party consisting of 1 Officer per Company, 1 N.C.O. per Platoon, Regtl Sgt-Major, Headquarters and Company Gas N.C.O's and Company Cooks will proceed to the trenches in advance and take over in daylight.

5. Whale Oil will be used by all ranks before proceeding to the trenches.

6. Officers Valises, Mens Packs and blankets will be ready for loading at 12 noon.
   Mess stores for the trenches and not for the trenches will be stacked at the Q.M.Stores by 3.0 p.m.

7. O/C "B" Company will detail the necessary party to move the Canteen to Hulluch Tunnel before 3.30 p.m.

8. Sicks will be changed under the same arrangements as were made for last tour.

9. Two tea-urns and one fryer per Company will be taken over on relief.

10. The Battalion pass-word for the night will be "War Bond".

11. Relief complete will be notified to Battalion Headquarters by Fullerphone in "B.A.B." Code.

12. Acknowledge.

J R Wood
Lieut:
A/Adjutant, 1/6th Battalion South Staffordshire Regiment.

Copies issued to:-

No 1. Commanding Officer.   No 9. Transport Officer.
   2. 137th Infantry Brigade.   10. Quartermaster.
   3. 1/6th Btn North Staffs Regt.   11. O/C, Left Battalion.
   4. 1/5th Btn South Staffs Regt.   12. 1/5th Btn N.Staffs Regt.
   5. O/C, "A" Company.   13. Regtl Sgt-Major.
   6. " "B"   "   14. War Diary.
   7. " "C"   "   15. "   "   (Duplicate)
   8. " "D"   "   16. File.
                                        17. "   (Duplicate).

MURRAY.   Operation Orders No 78.   Copy No 13
              1/6th Battalion South Staffordshire Regiment.
                                          Wednesday, 23rd January 1918.

1. The 1/6th Battalion South Staffordshire Regiment will be relieved by the
   9th Btn Sherwood Foresters in the line on the night of January 24/25th.
      "A" Coy 9th Sherwood Foresters will relieve Outpost (A) Coy 1/6th S.S.R.
      "D" "   "   "   "   "   Left   (B) "   "   "
      "B" "   "   "   "   "   Centre (C) "   "   "
      "C" "   "   "   "   "   Right   (D) "   "   "

2. On relief the Battalion will move to Billets in VAULXCOURT.
   Headquarters and the first two Companies relieved will entrain at
   CHATEAU DE HEM and detrain at SAILLY LABOURSE. Tea and rum will be
   provided there.
   The last two Companies will entrain at CHATEAU DE HEM and detrain at
   Ration Dump, LABOURSE. Tea and rum will be provided there. The Q.M.
   will provide guides from detraining point to place where tea is to be
   drawn.
   Companies will proceed independently from detraining point to
   VAULXCOURT, via VERQUIGNEUL and VER NIE.

3. Officers' Mess Stores, Cooking Utensils (including 2 cooking boilers
   and 1 fryer per Company) and all Stores to be taken out of the trenches
   will be on Dumps at 4.30 p.m.

4. Defence Schemes, Aeroplane Photos and all Maps except those of 1/10,000
   1/20,000, 1/40,000, 1/100,000 and 1/250,000 scales will be handed over.

5. All Lewis Gun Panniers and Magazines will be taken out and conveyed to
   KING GEORGE on trucks. Sergt Boalsridge will be responsible for loading
   and unloading of Lewis Guns and Panniers at KING GEORGE.

6. 1 guide per platoon and 2 for Headquarters will report to Captain
   Wilson at Brigade Headquarters at 4.30 p.m. to guide platoons of
   9th Btn Sherwood Foresters to the Trenches.

7. Lists of Trench Stores to be handed over will reach Orderly Room by
   1st runner on 24th instant. Receipted Lists in duplicate will be
   obtained for all Stores handed over.

8. The Q.M. Stores and Transport Lines will be taken over by the 7th Btn
   South Staffordshire Regiment on 24th instant.
   Certificates will be obtained from the Town Major concerned that
   Billets and Horse-lines have been left clean and tidy. These will
   be sent to Orderly Room on relief.

9. Relief Complete will be reported to Headquarters by code word 'MURRAY'.

10. ACKNOWLEDGE.

                                              J.W.Trent
                                              Captain,
    Adjutant, 1/6th Battalion South Staffordshire Regiment.

    Copies issued to:-

    No 1. Commanding Officer.   No 9. Transport Officer.
       2. 137th Infantry Brigade.   10. Regtl Sgt Major.
       3. O/C, 9th Btn Sherwood F.   11. O/C, 1/5th Btn South Staffs Rgt
       4. "   "A" Company.   12. "   Left Battalion.
       5. "   "B"   "   13. War Diary.
       6. "   "C"   "   14. "   " (Duplicate).
       7. "   "D"   "   15. File.
       8. Quartermaster.   16. "   (Duplicate).

Confidential

War Diary.

1/6th North Staffordshire Regt.

From 1st February to 28th February 1918.

Army Form C. 2118.

WAR DIARY
or
INTELLIGENCE SUMMARY.

(Erase heading not required.)

1/6th Btn South Staffs Regt.   (M5)

Instructions regarding War Diaries and Intelligence
Summaries are contained in F.S. Regs., Part II.
and the Staff Manual respectively. Title pages
will be prepared in manuscript.

Place	Date	Hour	Summary of Events and Information	Remarks and references to Appendices
VAULX LOOKRE	1.2.18.		Battalion Training.	
"	2.2.18.		—do—	
"	3.2.18.		The Battalion Paraded for Divine Service in the forenoon, in the afternoon a Boxing Competition was held.	
"	4.2.18.		Battalion Training. In the afternoon a successful Cross-Country Race was held.	
"	5.2.18.		Battalion Training. In the afternoon the Battalion Football Team played the 1/1st North Midland Field Ambulance in the Semi-Final of the Divisional Football Cup and won by 4 goals to 1.	
"	6.2.18.		Battalion Training.	
"	7.2.18.		—do— In the afternoon the Officers played the Officers of the 1/6th Btn North Staffs Regt at Football and won by 5 goals to nil. In the evening a successful concert was held.	
"	8.2.18.		Battalion Training.	
"	9.2.18.		The Battalion formed a Unit in the Brigade Tactical Scheme in a march to the "BOMY" area, marching under sealed orders was arrived and stayed the night at BURBURE.	
BURBURE	10.2.18.		The Battalion left BURBURE in the morning and arrived at FONTAINE-LEZ-BOULANS late in the afternoon.	
FONTAINE-LEZ-BOULANS	11.2.18		The Day was spent in cleaning up, bathing etc.	
"	12.2.18.		Battalion Training.	
"	13.2.18.		—do—	
"	14.2.18.		—do—	
"	15.2.18.		—do—	
"	16.2.18.		—do— The preliminary rounds of the Battalion Tug-of-War Competition were pulled in the afternoon.	
"	17.2.18.		The Battalion Paraded for Divine Service. After the Service the Final of the Battalion Tug-of-War Competition was pulled, ending in a victory for "D" Coys team. In the afternoon the Battalion Football Team played the 1/5th Btn North Staffs Rgt in the Final of the Divisional Football Cup at CREPY and won by 4 goals to nil before 2,000 spectators.	

Army Form C. 2118.

WAR DIARY
or
INTELLIGENCE SUMMARY.

(Erase heading not required.)

1/6th Bn South Staffs Regt.

Instructions regarding War Diaries and Intelligence Summaries are contained in F. S. Regs., Part II and the Staff Manual respectively. Title pages will be prepared in manuscript.

(147)

Place	Date	Hour	Summary of Events and Information	Remarks and references to Appendices
FONTAINE-LES-BOULANS	18.2.18.		Battalion Training, including A.R.A. Competition.	
"	19.2.18.		Battalion Training.	
"	20.2.18.		—do— In the afternoon the Battalion Football Team played and defeated the 1/6th Btn North Staffs Regiment at Football by 7 goals to 3.	
"	21.2.18.		Battalion Training.	
"	22.2.18.		—do—	
"	23.2.18.		—do— In the afternoon a successful Battalion Boxing Competition was held.	
"	24.2.18.		In the morning the Battalion Paraded for Divine Service. In the afternoon the Battalion Football Team played and defeated the 1/5th Btn South Staffs Rgt team by 1 goal to nil.	
"	25.2.18.		Battalion Training. In the afternoon the Battalion Football Team played and defeated the 465th Field Company R.E. by 6 goals to nil.	
"	26.2.18.		Battalion Training.	
"	27.2.18.		—do— In the afternoon the Battalion Football played the 1/3rd (N.M.) Field Ambulance. The game ended in a draw of four goals each. In the evening a Battalion Concert was held.	
"	28.2.18.		Battalion Training and bathing.	

TOTAL CASUALTIES FOR MONTH OF FEBRUARY 1918.

Wounded (Accidentally)   1 O.R.

Chester Lieut-Colonel,
Commanding 1/6th Battalion South Staffordshire Regiment.

Secret. Operation Orders No 80, Copy No. 10
1/6th Battalion South Staffordshire Regiment.
Thursday, 28th February 1918.

Reference:- Map Sheets, Lens 11 and Hazebrouck 5a, 1/100,000.

The Battalion will move to the Auchy-au-Bois area.

1. The Battalion will parade in mass on Area No 5 to-morrow. Signallers and Band will Parade as Units.
Dress:- Full Marching Order.

2. Zero hour will be notified later.

3. <u>Officers Valises & Blankets</u>. Officers Valises will be at the Q.M.Stores at zero minus 2 hours. Blankets tightly rolled in bundles of tens will be stacked at the Q.M.Stores at zero minus 2 hours.

4. <u>Billeting Party</u>. Lieut: J.P.Wood and billeting party consisting of Regtl Q.M.Sgt, 4 Coy Q.M.Sgts, 1 N.C.O. "D" Coy, and 1 N.C.O. H.Q.Details will parade at Orderly Room at zero minus 3 hours.

5. <u>Transport</u>. Transport will parade on the Fontaine - Palfart Road. Head of Column:- South end of Area No 5, facing North, at zero plus 30 minutes.

6. The usual certificates will be rendered to Orderly Room at zero minus 2 hours.

7. <u>Watches</u> will be synchronised at Orderly Room at zero minus 3 hours.

8. <u>Billets</u> will be inspected at zero minus 30 minutes.

9. <u>Acknowledge</u>.

Captain,
Adjutant 1/6th Battalion South Staffordshire Regiment.

<u>Copies issued to</u>:-

No 1. Commanding Officer.
2. 137th Infantry Brigade.
3. O/C, "A" Company.
4. "   "B"   "
5. "   "C"   "
6. "   "D"   "
7. Transport Officer.
8. Quartermaster.
9. File.
10. War Diary.
11. "   "   (Duplicate).

1/6th BATTALION,
SOUTH STAFFORDSHIRE
REGIMENT.
No. ....
Date ....

War Diary,
1st to 31st.
March 1918.

(148 - 150)

WAR DIARY
or
INTELLIGENCE SUMMARY

1/6th Bn South Staffs Regt. (A48)

Army Form C. 2118.

Instructions regarding War Diaries and Intelligence Summaries are contained in F.S. Regs., Part II. and the Staff Manual respectively. Title pages will be prepared in manuscript.

(Erase heading not required.)

Place	Date	Hour	Summary of Events and Information	Remarks and references to Appendices
FONTAINE-les-BOULANS	1.3.18.		The Battalion moved from rest billets at Fontaine-les-Boulans to Auchy-au-Bois. The night was spent there. (See Operation Orders No 80 attached).	
AUCHY-AU-BOIS.	2.3.18.		The Battalion moved to La Miquellerie and remained there until the 5th March.	
LA MIQUELLERIE	5.3.18.		The Battalion moved to Beuvry. (See Operation Orders No 82 attached).	
BEUVRY.	6.3.18.		The Battalion moved into Brigade Reserve with two Coys and Battalion Headquarters in ANNEQUIN and two Companies in LE PREOL remaining there until the 9th March. (See Operation Orders No 83 attached).	
ANNEQUIN	9.3.18.		The Battalion relieved the 1/5th Bn South Staffs Regiment in the CUINCHY Sector during the morning with "A" & "B" Coys in the line and "C" & "D" Coys in Support.(0.0.84 attd)	
CUINCHY	10.3.18.		Quiet Day.	
"	11.3.18.		-do-	
"	12.3.18.		-do-	
"	13.3.18.		The 1/5th Bn South Staffs Regiment relieved Btn H.Q'rs "A" "B" & "C" Coys and the 1/6th Btn North Staffs Regt relieved "D" Company in the line during the morning. the Battalion proceeded to Brigade Reserve with Btn H.Q'rs and "A" & "B" Coys in ANNEQUIN and "C" & "D" Coys in the CAMBRIN LOCALITY. (See Operation Orders No 85 attached).	
ANNEQUIN.	14.3.18.		In Brigade Reserve.	
"	15.3.18.		"A" & "B" Companies relieved "C" & "D" Companies in the CAMBRIN LOCALITY. (See Operation Orders No 66 attached).	
"	16.3.18.		In Brigade Reserve.	
"	17.3.18.		The Battalion relieved the 1/5th Bn South Staffs Regt in the CUINCHY SECTOR during the morning, with "D" "A" & "B" Coys in the Front Line and "C" Company in Support. Relief was complete by 11 a.m. (See Operation Orders No 87 attd). Light and Medium Trench Mortars were active during the greater part of the day. Hostile aeroplanes were particularly active between 11 and 1 p.m. crossing our front line at several places.	

Army Form C. 2118.

WAR DIARY
or
INTELLIGENCE SUMMARY

(Erase heading not required.)

1/6th Btn South Staffs Regt. (149).

Instructions regarding War Diaries and Intelligence
Summaries are contained in F. S. Regs., Part II
and the Staff Manual respectively. Title pages
will be prepared in manuscript.

Place	Date	Hour	Summary of Events and Information	Remarks and references to Appendices
CUINCHY	18.3.18.		Nothing of importance occurred during the day.	
"	19.3.18.		The morning opened wet and rain fell throughout the day. In consequence of the weather there was little activity. Companies carried out an inter-platoon relief.	
"	20.3.18.		A dull morning which greatly improved at mid-day. Enemy artillery was very active between 1 & 1.30 pm and 3 & 3.45 pm in the vicinity of Battalion Headquarters. The observation post at Mountain House received a direct hit. A light trench mortar store was blown up in the afternoon "strafe".	
"	21.3.18.		The Battalion was relieved by the 1/6th Btn Prince of Wales's (North Staffs) Regt in the Cuinchy Sector in the morning, and went into Support in the Cambrin Locality. Three Companies in the Village Line and "D" Coy and Btn H.Q'rs in ANNEQUIN. (See Operation Orders No 88 attached), also O.O No 88a.) All reliefs were successfully completed by 1.0 p.m.	
ANNEQUIN	22.3.18.		On the night of the 21/22nd about mid-night the enemy raided attacked on the Cambrin and Hohenzollern Sectors after a heavy bombardment. We took up our battle positions and "Stand down" was given at 1.50 p.m. The remainder of the night was quiet.	
"	23.3.18.		The day was spent in bathing and drill with box respirators. "D" Company relieved "A" Company in the CAMBRIN Village Line	
"	24.3.18.		The day was very quiet, in the afternoon Battalion Headquarters moved to the Command Post Position (Cambrin) and "A" Company to the Cambrin locality, as an extra precaution the Battalion was held in readiness to man the defences at 5 minutes notice.	
CAMBRIN	25.3.18.		The Battalion was relieved by 1/6th Btn North Staffs Regt and moved to Divisional Reserve at LE PREOL. The Battalion was employed during the afternoon and evening digging a cable trench. (See Operation Orders No 89 attached).	
LE PREOL	26.3.18.		In Divisional Reserve.	
"	27.3.18.		The Battalion moved from LE PREOL to SOUCHEZ taking over Columbia Camp from the 75th Canadians. The move was made by bus from BEUVRY to AIX NOULETTE and thence by march to SOUCHEZ.	
SOUCHEZ	28.3.18.		The Battalion relieved the 87th Canadians in the Right Sub-Sector LENS SECTION during the evening. (See Operation Orders No 90 attached).	

Army Form C. 2118.

WAR DIARY
—of—
INTELLIGENCE SUMMARY.
(Erase heading not required.)

1/6th Btn South Staffs Regt.   (1507)

Instructions regarding War Diaries and Intelligence Summaries are contained in F. S. Regs., Part II. and the Staff Manual respectively. Title pages will be prepared in manuscript.

Place	Date	Hour	Summary of Events and Information	Remarks and references to Appendices
LENS	29.3.18.		Quiet Day.	
"	30.3.18.		-do-	
"	31.3.18.		-do-	
			TOTAL CASUALTIES FOR MONTH OF MARCH 1918.	
			Killed 2 O.R.	
			Wounded 3 "	
			Wounded (at duty) 2 "	
			C. Mister Lieut-Colonel,	
			Commanding 1/6th Btn South Staffordshire Regiment.	
			2nd April 1918.	

Secret.   Operation Orders No 32.   Copy No 10
              1/6th Battalion South Staffordshire Regiment.
                                                        Monday, 4th March 1918.
Reference:- HAZEBROUCK 5a.

1. The 1/6th Battalion South Staffordshire Regiment will march to
    BEUVRY (9 miles) to-morrow and on arrival will form Brigade Reserve.

2. The Battalion will Parade at 10.0 a.m. on the LA MIQUELLERIE - BUSNES
    Road facing EAST.
    Order of March:- Sigs - "D" - "A" - Drums - "B" - "C" - Transport.
    Head of Column:- Orderly Room.
    Dress:-   Full Marching Order.

3. Billeting Party. A billeting party consisting of:-
                     R.Q.M.Sgt,
                     4 Coy Q.M.Sgts,
                     1 N.C.O. Transport and
                     1 N.C.O. Headquarters,
    will Parade at the Q.M.Stores at 8.30 a.m.   They will report to
    Lieut: J.P.Wood at UNION JACK SHOP, BEUVRY, at 10 a.m.

4. Blankets neatly rolled will be delivered to the Q.M.Stores at
    7.30 a.m.   Officers valises will be delivered to the Q.M.Stores
    by 8.0 a.m. and mess boxes by 8.30 a.m.

5. Watches will be synchronised at Orderly Room at 7.30 a.m.

6. Billets will be ready for inspection at 9.0 a.m.

7. Acknowledge.

                                                    Captain,
    Adjutant 1/6th Battalion South Staffordshire Regiment.

                                                       (P.T.O.)

Copies Issued to:-

No 1. Commanding Officer.
   2. 137th Infantry Brigade.
   3. O/C, "A" Company.
   4.   "   "B"   "
   5.   "   "C"   "
   6.   "   "D"   "
   7. Quartermaster.
   8. Transport Officer.
   9. Regtl Sgt-Major.
 10. War Diary.
 11. "   "   (Duplicate).
 12. File.

SECRET.   Operation Order No 5.   Copy No. 10
                    1/6th Bn. South Staffordshire Regt.

Reference:- Ground Map.

1. The Battalion will move to billets at ANEUQIN and LA FLAMENGRIE tomorrow:- Dress:- Full marching order.

2. DISPOSITION.   Headquarters 'A' & 'B' Coys.   — — ANEUQIN.
                  'C' & 'D' Coys. Transport and
                  Q.M. Stores.   — — LA FLAMENGRIE.

3. Companies will proceed by Platoons at 5 minutes interval. 'A' & 'B' Companies will leave at "ZERO".

4. "ZERO" hour will be notified later.

5. A Billeting party of one Officer and two N.C.O's from 'A' & 'B' Coys will report to Lieut: J.R.Wood at Orderly Room at 9a.m.

6. Officers valises will be at the Q.M.Stores at 9-30a.m.

7. Cookers and Blankets will be taken to ANEUQIN & LA FLAMENGRIE.

8. Battalion Headquarters will be at billet '4' ANEUQIN.

9. Report completion of move to Battalion Headquarters.

10. Acknowledge.

                                              T.W.Frew
                                              Captain.
                              Adjutant 1/6th Bn. South Staffordshire Regt.
                                                           (P.T.O).

5/3/18

Copies issued to:-
        No 1.   Commanding Officer.
        No 2.   G.O.C. 15/th I.Brigade.
        No 3.   O/C "A" Coy.
        No 4.   " "B" "
        No 5.   " "C" "
        No 6.   " "D" "
        No 7.   Transport Officer.
        No 8.   Quartermaster.
        No 9.   Regtl Sgt Major.
        No 10. War Diary.
        No 11.   "   "   (Duplicate).
        No 12. File.

SECRET.
Operation Orders No 84.
1/6th Btn South Staffordshire Regt.

Copy No 14

Friday, March 8th 1918.

Reference Map 36CH.W.1. 1/10,000.

1. The 1/6th Btn South Staffordshire Regiment will relieve the 1/5th Btn South Staffordshire Regiment in the Canal Centre Sector tomorrow morning.

2. Dispositions.

Right Coy. "A" Coy 1/6th South Staffs will relieve "C" Coy 1/5th S. Staffs
Left Coy. "B" Coy   "   "   "   "   "   "   "D" Coy   "   "
Support Coy "C" Coy   "   "   "   "   "   "   "A" Coy   "   "
Reserve Coy "D" Coy   "   "   "   "   "   "   "B" Coy   "   "

Routes.
"A" & "B" Coys - CAMBRIN-LA BASSEE ROAD - HARLEY STREET.
"C" & "D" Coys - CANAL BANK - CUINCHY STN - PONT FIXE.

3. Companies will proceed by Platoons at 250 yards interval. First platoon will leave at 9.0 a.m. Dress:- Fighting Order plus Greatcoat.

4. Guides for "A" & "B" Coys will be at Road Junction P 20 b 35.70.
            "   "C" & "D" "   "   " Pont Fixe   P 14 d 20.75.

5. Lewis Guns and 24 Magazines per Gun will be collected and dumped at meeting point for Guides at 9.0 a.m.
All other Lewis Gun Ammunition will be returned to Quartermaster who will hand over 90 Panniers to Quartermaster 'GUY'

6. Mess Stores and Cooking Utensils (2 Tea Urns & 1 Fryer per Company) will be collected and delivered with Lewis Guns.
Officers' Mess Stores not for the Trenches will be collected at 9.0 a.m.

7. Packs, Blankets & Officers' Valises of "C" & "D" Coys will be delivered to Q.M.Stores at 7.15 a.m. "A" & "B" Coys will be stacked outside Guard Room at 7.45 a.m.

8. Rations for the 9th instant will be carried on the Man.

9. Relief complete will be notified to Battalion Headquarters by Fullerphone by Code Word - 'SUN'

10. ACKNOWLEDGE.

Captain.
Adjutant 1/6th Btn South Staffordshire Regiment.

Copies issued to:-

No 1. Commanding Officer.
   2. O.C. Right Battalion.
   3. O.C. Left Battalion.
   4. 137th Infantry Brigade.
   5. O.C. "A" Company.
   6. O.C. "B"   "
   7. O.C. "C"   "
   8. O.C. "D"   "

No 9. Transport Officer.
   10. Quartermaster.
   11. Regtl Sergt Major.
   12. War Diary.
   13. "   "   (Duplicate)
   14. File.
   15. "   (Duplicate)

SECRET.   Operation Orders No 65.   COPY No 13.
                1/6th Btn South Staffordshire Regiment.
                                                  15th March 1916.

1. The 1/6th Btn South Staffordshire Regiment will be relieved in the CURGHY sector to-morrow 13th/16th March by the 1/5th Btn South Staffordshire Regiment.

2. The Battalion will hold the CURGHY locality.

3. Dispositions.
   Btn Headquarters, "A" & "B" Companies - AUBIGNY.
   "C" & "D" Companies - VILLAGE LINE "E" OF CURGHY - At RAILWAY HEAD taking over line as held by two Companies of 1/5th Btn South Staffordshire Regiment.

4. Stores.
   Lewis Gun Ammunition will be taken out.
   "C" & "D" Companies will take Lewis Gun ammunition to VILLAGE LINE.
   Battalion reserve of 90 panniers will be handed over to 1/5th Btn South Staffs Regt.
   Camp Kettles will be taken out.

5. Report relief complete to Btn Headquarters by "W.T.S." code.

6. Acknowledge.

                                             [signature]
                                             Captain,
                Adjutant 1/6th Btn South Staffordshire Regiment.

Copies issued to:-

No 1. Commanding Officer.
2. 137th Infantry Brigade.
3. 1/6th Btn North Staffs Regt.
4. 1/5th Btn South Staffs Regt.
5. 1/8th Btn Kings Liverpool Regt.
6. O/C. "A" Company.
7. "   "B"   "
8. "   "C"   "
9. "   "D"   "
10. Transport Officer.
11. Quartermaster.
12. Regtl Sgt-Major.
13. War Diary.
14. "   "   (Duplicate).
15. File.
16. "   (Duplicate).

SECRET.   Operation Orders No 66.   Copy No 10
            1/6th Btn South Staffordshire Regt.
                      Dated 14th March 1916.

1. The Companies billeted in ANZIN will relieve the Companies
   in the VILLAGE LINE tomorrow morning.
   Dress:- Fighting Order plus greatcoat.
   "A" Company will relieve "C" Company in the Right Sector. They
   will proceed by Platoons at 5 minutes interval. First Pltn will leave at
   Guides will report at Company Headquarters ANZIN at 8-30a.m.(?a.m.

   "B" Company will relieve "D" Company in the Left Sector.
   Guides:- 1 Platoon at Junction CAMBRIN-LA BASSEE Road and HARLEY
            Street at 9-__a.m. Platoon will leave ANZIN 8-45a.m.
            3 Platoons at Junction of DAMON Street and HARLEY Street
            at 9-45a.m. First Platoon will leave ANZIN at 9-20a.m.

   Cooking Utensils and Lewis Gun Ammunition will be handed over.
   A Limber will report to O/C "A" Company at 8-30a.m. to convey
   Mess Stores, ~~cooking utensils~~ and Lewis Guns to Ration Dump, and
   will pick up "C" Companies Lewis Guns, Mess Stores.
   A Limber will report to O/C "B" Company at 8-30a.m. and convey
   Mess Stores etc to PONT FIXE, returning with "D" Companies Stores.

   Blankets will be stacked outside Company Headquarters, neatly
   rolled and tied in bundles of tens, at 7-30a.m.
   Officers Valises to be outside Company Headquarters ready for
   loading at 8-30a.m.
2. ACKNOWLEDGE.
                                        (signed)
                                              Captain.
                Adjutant 1/6th Btn South Staffordshire Regt.

   Copies issued to:-   No 1. O.C. 137th I. Brigade.
                        " 2. Commanding Officer.
                        " 3. O/C "A" Company.
                        " 4.   " "B"   "
                        " 5.   " "C"   "
                        " 6.   " "D"   "
                        " 7. Transport Officer.
                        " 8. Quartermaster.
                        " 9. O/C 1/5th Btn South Staffs Regt.
                        " 10. War Diary.
                        " 11.   "   "   (Duplicate).
                        " 12. File.

SECRET. Operation Orders No 87.   Copy No 13
         1/6th Btn South Staffordshire Regt.
                                              Saturday, 16th March 1918.

1. The 1/6th Btn South Staffordshire Regiment will relieve the 1/5th Btn
   South Staffordshire Regiment in the CUINCHY Sector tomorrow morning
   17th instant.

2. "A" & "B" Companies will take over previous Line dispositions, moving
   at 9.0 a.m.
   "C" Coy 1/6th South Staffs Regt will relieve "D" Coy 1/5th South Staffs
   Regt in Close Support. They will move by Platoons at 200 yds intervals.
   First Platoon will leave at 9.0 a.m. via Route 10.
   "D" Coy 1/6th South Staffs Regt will relieve "C" Coy 1/5th South Staffs
   Regt in Right Front Company. 1 Guide per Platoon will meet Platoons
   at junction CAMBRIN-LA BASSEE ROAD - HARLEY STREET at 9.30 a.m.

3. Movement on top will be reduced to a minimum.

4. Dress:- Fighting Order No 2 plus Groundsheet.

5. 1 Limber will report to O.C. "C" Coy and 1 Limber to O.C. "D" Coy at
   8.30 a.m. to convey stores to Dumps.

6. Cooking Utensils and Lewis Gun Ammunition will be taken into the
   Trenches.

7. Usual Certificates will be rendered to Orderly Room immediately on
   arrival in the Trenches.

8. Relief Complete will be notified to Battalion Headquarters by B.A.B.
   Code.

9. ACKNOWLEDGE.

                                                       Captain.
            Adjutant 1/6th Btn South Staffordshire Regiment.

Copies issued to:-

No 1. Commanding Officer.   No 9. O.C. "D" Company.
   2. G.O.C. 137th Infantry Brigade.   10. Transport Officer.
   3. O.C. 1/5th Btn South Staffs Regt.   11. Quartermaster.
   4. O.C. Right Battalion.   12. Regtl Sergt Major.
   5. O.C. Left Battalion.   13. War Diary.
   6. O.C. "A" Company.   14. "   "   Duplicate
   7. O.C. "B" Company.   15. File.
   8. O.C. "C" Company.   16. "

SECRET.   Operation Orders No 26.   Copy No 13.
                        1/6th Battalion South Staffordshire Regt.
                                                    27th March 1916.

1. Reference Operation Orders No 25.
   Please cancel para 2 and substitute:-
   On completion of relief the Battalion will defend the GASTON
   LOCALITY.   It will be disposed as follows:-

   Headquarters -   AUTH RUE (Headquarters and Billet).

   Right Company (B)   Company Headquarters and two platoons - Cellars
                         in vicinity of GASTON Church.
                         Two Platoons - VILLAGE LINE Lewis Keep (inclusive)
                         to RICHARD WAY (inclusive).

   Centre Company (A)   Company Headquarters and one Platoon - Houses
                         around X.20.a.7½.6½.
                         One Platoon - VILLAGE LINE RICHARD WAY (exclusive)
                         to HARFORD STREET (exclusive).

   Left Company (C)   Company Headquarters and one Platoon - R.WAY
                         STREET and BOND WIRE.
                         Three Platoons - VILLAGE LINE North of HARFORD
                         STREET.

   Support Coy (D)   AUTH RUE.

2. Acknowledge.

                                                    [signed]
                                                    Captain,
                                   Adjutant 1/6th Battalion South Staffordshire Regt.

                                                            (P.T.O).

Copies issued to:-

No 1. Commanding Officer.
   2. 137th Infantry Brigade.
   3. 1/5th Bn North Staffs Regt.
   4. 1/5th Bn South Staffs Regt.
   5. Right Battalion.
   6. O/C. "A" Company.
   7. "   "B"   "
   8. "   "C"   "
   9. "   "D"   "
  10. Transport Officer.
  11. Quartermaster.
  12. Regtl Sgt-Major.
  13. War Diary.
  14. "   "   (Duplicate).
  15. File.
  16. Left Battalion.

SECRET   Operation Orders No.90   Copy No.
16th Bn. South Staffordshire Regt.
27th March 1918

Reference LENS 36c S.W.1 1/10,000

1. The 16th Bn. South Staffordshire Regt will relieve the 87th Canadian Bn. in the Right Subsector, LENS Section tomorrow night 28/29th.

2. The Bn will march by Platoons at 200 yards interval. Order of March :- 16th - A - D - C - B. First platoon will pass starting point at 1.0 pm.
Starting point - SOUCHEZ Cross Roads
Dress :- Fighting Order, plus greatcoat.
Guides from 87th Canadian Bn will report to Coy Commanders at 3.30 pm
Lewis Guns and Panniers will be dumped at M 23 c 40.50 and will be collected by Platoons there.

3. On completion of Relief the Battn will be disposed as follows:-
Right Company "A"   Left Company "D"
Support   "C"   Reserve   "B"

4. Coys will take over Maps, Documents, Trench Stores etc from outgoing Bn. They will give receipts for same and forward to a copy to Orderly Room by first DR

5. Report relief complete by B.A.B code

6. ACKNOWLEDGE.

M.Andrew
Captain
Adjutant 16th Bn. South Staffordshire Regt

SECRET.
Operation Orders No 89,
1/6th Btn South Staffordshire Regiment.
25th March 1918.

Reference --- Map GORRE 1/20,000.

1. The 1/6th Btn North Staffs Regt will relieve the Battalion to-day in the Cambrin Locality.
On completion of relief the Battalion will be billeted at LE PREOL and will form Divisional Reserve.
2. Billeting Party. 1 N.C.O. per Company will report to 2/Lieut: W.S.Brand at F.15.b.25.05 at 10 a.m. to take over billets from the outgoing Battalion.
3. The Battalion will take over 80 panniers of L.G.Ammunition from 1/5th Btn South Staffs Regt and hand over 80 panniers to 1/6th Btn North Staffs Regiment.
4. Cooking utensils etc will be at Company Headquarters at 11.30 a.m.
5. Lists of Trench Stores to be handed over will be forwarded to Orderly Room immediately.
6. Acknowledge.

(Sgd) J.M.Frew Captain,
Adjutant 1/6th Btn South Staffs Regiment.

137th Brigade.
46th Division.

1/6th BATTALION

SOUTH STAFFORDSHIRE REGIMENT

APRIL 1918.

Army Form C. 2118.

WAR DIARY

1/6th Bttn South Staffordshire Regiment. (151).

INTELLIGENCE SUMMARY.

(Erase heading not required.)

Instructions regarding War Diaries and Intelligence Summaries are contained in F. S. Regs., Part II and the Staff Manual respectively. Title pages will be prepared in manuscript.

Place	Date	Hour	Summary of Events and Information	Remarks and references to Appendices
	APRIL 1918.			
LENS.	1-4-18.		The Battalion was relieved by the 1/6th Bttn North Staffordshire Regt in the Right Sub-Section LENS Sector, and moved into Brigade Reserve at LIEVIN. During the day five of our Observation Balloons were fired by an enemy areoplane. Machine Gun and Trench Mortar, and Artillery fire normal during the day. Aerial activity above normal in the evening. We sent over 'GAS' during the night of the 1/2nd April 1918.	
LIEVIN.	2-4-1918.		Bathing and interior economy. Activity normal throughout the day. A dud shell entered one of "C" Coys Billets killing one man and wounding two men.	
"	3-4-1918.		Companies at the disposal of Company Commanders for interior economy. No 32691 Pte Wannop A.(Killed on the 2-4-18) was buried at AIX-NOULETTE British Cemetery. The Bttn relieved the 1/5th Bttn South Staffs Regt in the Left Lens Sector in the evening.	
LENS.	4-4-1918.		The Sector was exceptionally quiet.	
"	5-4-1918.		New dispositions were made in the LEFT LENS SECTOR. Bttn Headquarters being moved back to LIEVIN. General Situation 'Quiet'.	See OO to R.
"	6-4-1918. 7-4-1918.		Nothing of interest occurred during the day. The Bttn was relieved by the 1/6th Bttn North Staffs Regt in the Left Subsector, LENS SECTOR. Between 7p.m. and 11-30p.m. the enemy shelea heavily the railway track and main roads, causing considerable delay to the relief. At about 12 midnight an Enemy Aircraft dropped nine bombs on our Transport Lines killing Hon:Captain & Quartermaster J.WILLNER and wounding No. 240484 Sergeant JONES S.P.	
LIEVIN.	8-4-1918.		A heavy gas bombardment occurred between 3a.m. and 4a.m. Captain J.WILLNER was buried at AIX-NOULETTE British Cemetery.	
"	9-4-1918.		A quiet day. Dull and misty. The Bttn relieved the 1/5th Bttn South Staffs Regt in the LENS RIGHT SUBSECTOR. Very quiet. Our patrols were active but failed to discover any Apos Us.	See OO to R.

W4973/M687 750,000 8/16 D.D.&L. Ltd. Forms/C.2118/13

Army Form C. 2118.

WAR DIARY
INTELLIGENCE SUMMARY.
(Erase heading not required.)

1/5th Btn South Staffordshire Regt. (152).

Instructions regarding War Diaries and Intelligence Summaries are contained in F.S. Regs. Part II. and the Staff Manual respectively. Title pages will be prepared in manuscript.

Place	Date	Summary of Events and Information	Remarks and references to Appendices
LENS.	APRIL 1918. 10-4-1918.	Ineffective Gas shelling of our centres of activity. Division dropped a bombshell and told us to get ready to come out of it.	
"	11-4-1918.	Canadians running about like mice in all directions. Adjutant very surprised at our small staff.	
FOSSE 10.	12-4-1918.	Btn quartered in Fosse 10 for the night -place packed with troops -very little accomodation available. Relief very late owing to a breakdown on the Light Railway. Relief not completed until 4a.m.13-4-1918.	
DIVION.	13-4-1918.	The Battalion marched to DIVION - Corps Reserve.	
"	14-4-1918.	Troops given a complete rest. Sports in the afternoon. The most amusing item being 'Wrestling on Mules'. Jwing to the rope breaking the 'Tug-of-War' broke down hopelessly. Prizes were distributed by the Commanding Officer. The Brigade Band was in attendance,and was greatly appreciated.	
"	15-4-1918.	Bathing in the morning. Lectures by O/C Companies in the afternoon. A Grand Concert was given by the First Army Concert Party in the LA BRA-SAY Theatre in the evening.	
"	16-4-1918.	Full training programme carried out throughout the day including Range Practices. The Btn Football Eleven defeated the Canadian M.G.Corps Depot Team by 3 goals to two. A Concert was arranged in the Y.M.C.A., the Canadian Depot M.G Corps Troupe rendering a fine programme.	
"	17-4-1918.	Full training programme carried out throughout the morning. At 12-15p.m. we received orders to quit, the Btn to be clear of billets by 3p.m. The Btn moved to Concentration Camp at HALLICOURT,but as it was next to No 6 C.C.Station,objection was raised,which was upheld by Divisional General. However we stayed there for the night.	

1/6th Bttn South Staffordshire Regt. (153).

Army Form C. 2118.

WAR DIARY
or
INTELLIGENCE SUMMARY
(Erase heading not required.)

Instructions regarding War Diaries and Intelligence Summaries are contained in F.S. Regs., Part II and the Staff Manual respectively. Title pages will be prepared in manuscript.

Place	Date	Hour	Summary of Events and Information	Remarks and references to Appendices
HALLICOURT.	APRIL 1918. 18-4-1918		In the morning in bitterly cold weather a camp was pitched by the Railway Embankment near the village of HALLICOURT, the 1/5th Bttn South Staffs Regt shared the Field. In the evening the officers played a scratch footer match. The Commanding Officer's Team beating the 2nd in Command's Team by 3 goals to NIL.	
"	19-4-1918.		The weather continued cold. Full training programme of work was carried out throughout the morning. In the afternoon the Brigade Band played selections on the Camp Square. Football. Our officers played the officers of the 1/5th Bttn South Staffs Regt, and after a keen and well fought game we won by 3 goals to two.	
"	20-4-1918.		Training carried out during the morning including Range Practice by "A" and "C"Companies. Football. Our officers Eleven played the officers of the 231 Bde R.F.A. and won by 2 goals to Nil.	
"	21-4-1918.		Heavy rain fell during the evening. SUNDAY. A Joint Bttn Church Parade was held at 11a.m. on our Camp Square. Captain S.G.I.KEANS officiated. Brigadier General J.V.CAMPBELL. VC. DSO.Commanding 137th Infantry Brigade was present. The Brigade Band was in attendance. Private Mountford R.H.was presented with the Military Medal Ribbon in the afternoon by Major-General W.THWAITES.CB Commanding 46th (NM)Division.	
"	22-4-1918. 23-4-1918. 24-4-1918.		Training Programme carried out throughout the day. —ditto— The Battalion marched to FOUQUIERES and was billeted in the Corps Rest Camp.	
LOISNE	25-4-1918.		The Bttn moved into the Line taking over the LOISNE Left Brigade Sector. Prior to moving off the enemy shelled the Rest Camp Area. We had no casualties. The Bttn relieved the King's Own Bttn. 55th Division. Nothing of importance occurred after relief was complete.	

Army Form C. 2118.

1/6th Btn South Staffordshire Regiment. (154). **WAR DIARY**
INTELLIGENCE SUMMARY.
(Erase heading not required.)

Instructions regarding War Diaries and Intelligence
Summaries are contained in F.S. Regs. Part II
and the Staff Manual respectively. Title pages
will be prepared in manuscript.

Place	Date APRIL 1918.	Summary of Events and Information	Remarks and references to Appendices
LOISNE	26-4-1918.	Route "A" Keep fell into the hands of the enemy after a very hard and stubborn fight.	
"	27-4-1918.	A quiet day.	
"	28-4-1918.	The 1/5th Btn South Staffs Regt, at midnight attacked Route "A" Kepp, took same and consolidated. Casualties about 50. 4 Officers being killed, including Captain R.C.PIPER who was in Command. The enemy's Barrage was intense, and in consequence we suffered slight casualties. 3 men killed 6 wounded.	
"	29-4-1918.	Artillery Duels.	
"	30-4-1918.	Quiet day. The Btn was relieved by the 1/5th Btn South Staffs Regt and went into Support in GORRE. Relief complete by 1a.m. No casualties.	

TOTAL CASUALTIES FOR MONTH OF APRIL 1918.
Hon: Captain & Quartermaster J.WILLNER. Killed in Action.
                            4 O'Ranks.   "   "
                            17 "   Wounded.
                            4 "   " (At duty).
                            1 "   Died of wounds.

My Lieut: Colonel.
Commanding 1/6th Btn South Staffordshire Regiment.

SECRET

Operation Orders No 93.
16th Btn South Staffordshire Regiment.

Copy No. 12

Saturday, 6th April 1918.

Reference LENS 36 c S.W.1 1/10.000

1. The 16th Btn South Staffordshire Regt will be relieved by the 16th Btn Prince of Wales's (North Staffs) Regt. in the LEFT Subsector LENS Sector tomorrow night 7/8th April.

2. On completion of relief the Battn will move to LIEVIN and will form Brigade Reserve.

3. Dispositions :—   Left Sector   "D" Company.
                    Centre   -   "B"   -
                    Right   -   "A"   -
                    Right Support Sector "C"   -

4. Guides will report to Coy. H.Q. 16th Btn North Staffs Regt at 7 p.m.

5. Report relief complete by code word "AMEN" and completion of move by Runner to Battalion H.Q. at M 22 b 18.12.

6. ACKNOWLEDGE.

F.W. Trew
Captain.
Adjutant 16th Btn South Staffordshire Regiment.

Copies issued to :—

No 1 Commanding Officer.
2. 137th Infantry Brigade
3. O.C. 16th Btn North Staffs Regt.
4. O.C. 15th Btn South Staffs Regt.
5-8. Companies.
9. Transport Officer.

No 10. Quartermaster
11. War Diary
12.   do   (Duplicate)
13. File.
14.   do   (Duplicate)
15. O.C. 1st Sherwood Foresters.

6th Bn. South Staffs. Regt.
8th April 1918

Operation Order No. 1.

1. The Battalion will relieve the 7/5th Bn South Staff Regt. in the Rear Subsection I & N8 Sector tomorrow night 9/10th April 1918.

2. On completion of relief the Battalion will be disposed as follows:—
   Right Company — "A"
   Left Company — "B"
   Left Support Company — "C"
   Right Support Company — "D"

3. Companies will move by Platoons at 200 yards interval at dusk.

4. Lists of Trench Stores to be handed over will be rendered to Orderly Room by noon tomorrow.

5. Companies will report Relief complete by "A.A.B." Code.

6. Acknowledge D.T.E.

T.W. [signed]
Captain
Adjutant 6th Bn South Staffs Regiment.

Reference Copies to:—
1. Commanding Officer
2. 138th Infantry Brigade
3. 1/5th Bn South Staff Regt.
4. 1/6 Bn North Staff Regt.
5. Transport Officer
6. Quartermaster
7. Regt. Sgt. Major
8. Orderly Battalion
9. "A" Company
10. "B" "
11. "C" "
12. "D" "
13. War Diary
14. " " (Duplicate)
15. File
16. " (Duplicate)

SECRET

Operation Orders No 95.
16th Btn South Staffordshire Regiment

Copy No. 13

Friday, 12th April 1918.

Reference. LENS II 1/100,000. LENS 36c S.W.1.

1. The 16th Btn South Staffordshire Regiment will be relieved by the Royal Canadian Regiment tonight April 12/13th 1918.
2. On completion of relief the Battalion will move to FOSSE 10.
3. 10 Guides per Company will meet incoming Battalion at M 28d 75.65, time will be notified later.
4. Trench Stores and Aeroplane Photos will be handed over on relief.
5. Relief complete will be notified to Battalion H.Q. by code word "FOOTBALL".
6. Acknowledge.

Pm Frew
Captain
Adjutant, 16th Btn South Staffordshire Regiment.

Copies issued to:-

Nos 1. Commanding Officer.
2. 18/th Infantry Brigade
3. 4th Btn North Staffs Regt
4. O.C. "A" Company
5. " "B" "
6. " "C" "
7. " "D" "
8. Transport Officer.

9. Quartermaster.
10. Regtl Sergt Major.
11. Royal Canadian Regiment
12. War Diary
13. do (Duplicate)
14. File.
15. do (Duplicate)

Vol 40

Major Russell

Q 40.

CONFIDENTIAL.

W A R   D I A R Y.

1/6th Btn South Staffordshire Regiment.

From 1st MAY 1918 to 31st MAY 1918.

Pages 155 to 157.

Army Form C. 2118.

WAR DIARY
or
INTELLIGENCE SUMMARY.

(Erase heading not required.)

1/6th Btn South Staffordshire Rgt. (155).

Instructions regarding War Diaries and Intelligence Summaries are contained in F.S. Regs., Part II. and the Staff Manual respectively. Title pages will be prepared in manuscript.

Place	Date	Hour	Summary of Events and Information	Remarks and references to Appendices
GORRE	1-5-18.	4am	The enemy opened out a gas shell bombardment which lasted for four hours, causing casualties. The remainder of the day was quiet.	
	2-5-18.		Headquarter Details suffered heavy casualties from Gas, 90% reporting to the Dressing Station. The Battalion moved into Reserve at VAUDRICOURT WOOD, under canvas.	
VAUDRICOURT WOOD.	3-5-18.		Resting and Bathing.	
	4-5-18.		Range Practice by all Companies.	
	5-5-18.		SUNDAY. A wet day. No Church Parades.	
	6-5-18.		The Battalion relieved the 1/5th Btn Leicestershire Rgt in the Right Subsection, Left Brigade ESSARS Sector. Enemy carried out harrassing fire on main roads giving an anxious time to our Transport.	See O.O. No 96.
ESSARS	7-5-18.		Quiet day and night.	
	8-5-18.		Quiet day and night.	
	9-5-18.		Very quiet day. Enemy was expected to attack at dawn on the 10th, but nothing happened.	
	10-5-18.		The Battalion was relieved by the 1/5th Btn South Staffs Rgt, and went into Brigade RESERVE at ESSARS. In RESERVE.	See O.O. No 98.
	11-5-18.		The Battalion relieved the 1/6th Btn NORTH Staffs Regt in the Left Subsection, ESSARS Sector.	O.O. No 100.
	12-5-18.			
	13-5-18.		Quiet day.	
	14-5-18.		The Battalion was relieved by the 1/5th Btn SHERWOOD FORESTERS in the ESSARS Left Subsection and went into Rest Billets at VERQUIN.	O.O. No 101.
VERQUIN.	15-5-18.		Cleaning up etc and Bathing.	
	16-5-18.		At about 2-30a.m. the enemy shelled the main VERQUIN-BEUVRY Road obtaining direct hits on "D" & "B" Companies billets causing considerable casualties. "B" Coy had 1 man killed and 10 men wounded, whilst 'D' Coy had 4 men killed and 11 men wounded. in addition to the casualties much food was destroyed. The Chaplain of the Cyclist Corps rendered valuable assistance in attending to the wounded. 'B' & 'D' Coys went into VAUDRICOURT WOOD under canvas.	

Army Form C. 2118.

1/6th Btn South Staffs Regt. (156).

WAR DIARY
or
INTELLIGENCE SUMMARY.

(Erase heading not required.)

Instructions regarding War Diaries and Intelligence Summaries are contained in F. S. Regs., Part II and the Staff Manual respectively. Title pages will be prepared in manuscript.

Place	Date	Hour	Summary of Events and Information	Remarks and references to Appendices
VERQUIN.	17-5-18.		The Battalion attended a Ceremonial Decoration Parade by the Divisional General at HESDIGNEUL. Extremely hot day.	O.O.67.A.
GORRE.	18-5-18.		The Battalion relieved the 5th Btn Leicestershire Regt in the Right Subsection Right Brigade.	O.O.67.B
"	19-5-18.		At 2-0a.m. Btn Headquarters was bombarded with gas shells. No casualties occurred.	
"	20-5-18.		Quiet day.	
"	21-5-18.		The enemy put over a terrific bombardment of Gas Shells between 11p.m.20th to about 4a.m.21st, the number of shells estimated exceeded 10,000, including 500 8". Owing to the great concentration we suffered heavy casualties i.e. 6 Officers and 134 O'Ranks of "D" and "A" Companies.	
"	22-5-18.		Owing to the depleted condition of the Brigade it was withdrawn on the 22nd inst. The Btn was relieved by the 1/4th Btn Leicester Regt and went into Rest Billets at VERQUIN and VAUDRICOURT WOOD.	O.O.62.
VERQUIN.	23-5-18.		Bathing and cleaning up. All clothing THRESHED.	
	24-5-18.		In RESERVE.	
ESSARS.	25-5-18.		The Btn relieved the 5th Btn SHERWOOD FORESTERS in the Right-Subsection of the LEFT Brigade on the night of the 25/26th, one Company of the 1/1st Btn Monmouthshire Regt being attached to this Btn.	O.O. 62A
"	26-5-18.		at 1p.m. the enemy heavily shelled the Left Support Coy Headquarters. Several direct hits were obtained, CAPTAIN F.P. SILVERS.MC. being badly wounded in the head.	
"	27-5-18.		A quiet day and night. The enemy rushed the Listening Post of 'B' Company capturing one man, killing one man and wounding one man.	
"	28-5-18.		Quiet day, Harassing fire by enemy at night. No casualties. It was announced that the Military Cross had been awarded to 1st/Lt J.B.GREGG.RC.USA.attached to this Btn(temporarily) for good work on the SOMME in MARCH 1918.	
"	29-5-18.		Btn Headquarters lightly shelled about 7-30a.m. and again at 9-30p.m. Two men were slightly wounded. The Btn was relieved by the 1/5th Btn SOUTH Staffs Regt and went into Brigade RESERVE at ESSARS. L'Cpl CONWAY A.killed in the early hours of the morning. "C" Coy slightly affected by GAS. No casualties however.	

Army Form C. 2118.

WAR DIARY
INTELLIGENCE SUMMARY.

1/6th Btn South Staffs Regt. (157).

Instructions regarding War Diaries and Intelligence Summaries are contained in F. S. Regs., Part II and the Staff Manual respectively. Title pages will be prepared in manuscript.

(Erase heading not required.)

Place	Date	Hour	Summary of Events and Information	Remarks and references to Appendices
ESSARS.	30-5-18.		News of the death of Lieut:H.SLATER as a result of the Gas attack of the 20/21st received.	
"	31-5-18.		Quiet day.	
			ooo-----------------ooo	
			Total casualties for month of MAY 1918.	
			Captain F.P. SILVERS.MC. Wounded. 26-5-18. Died 27-5-18.	
			Lieut: H.SLATER. " 22-5-18. " 28-5-18.	
			2/Lieut: E.T.GWYTHER. "	
			" A.H.KENNY. " 2-5-18. To England 9-5-18.	
			" F.C. JACKSON. " " 11-5-18.	
			" S.G. JACKSON. " 22-5-18.	
			" C.J. GUPWELL. "	
			" J.F. STRATTON. "	
			" T. BURGESS. "	
			LT COLONEL C.LISTER.MC. Wounded-2-5-18, but rejoined 6-5-18.	

OTHER RANKS.				
KILLED.	MISSING.	WOUNDED.GAS.	WOUNDED.	WOUNDED but AT DUTY.
7	1	6	32	4
		298		

DIED OF WOUNDS.
24

3rd JUNE 1918.   Chapter, Lieut:Colonel.
                   Commanding 1/6th Btn South Staffordshire Regiment.

Secret.   Operation Orders No 98.   Copy No. 13
1/6th Btn South Staffordshire Regt.
Dated 6th May 1918.

Reference:- Gorre and Lacoutre Map Sheets. 1/20,000.

1. The Btn will relieve the 1/5th Btn Leicestershire Regt in the Right Subsection of the 'Essars' Section on the night of the 6/7th May 1918.

2. On Relief Companies will be disposed as follows:-

   "A" Coy   Right Front Line. Relieves "D" Coy 5th Leicesters.
   "B" "   " Support.   "   "A" "   "   "
   "D" "   Left Front Line.   "   "C" "   "   "
   "C" "   " Support.   "   "B" "   "   "

3. Order of march:- 'HQ' "A" "D" "B" "C" Coys.
   Route:-   Verquin to X Roads E.24.d.35.15.thence along road to E.18.d.5.6.thence along Railway to F.7.b.2.8. thence to Pont Tournant Bridge(F.7.a.8.9.)where guides will be met.
   200 yards distance will be maintained between Coys to point E.18.d.5.6.thence 200 yards interval DISTANCE between Platoons.
   First COMPANY will leave Camp at 6-45p.m.tonight.

4. Lewis Guns and 24 Magazines per Gun will be picked up at F.7.a.9.4.

5. French Maps,Schemes of Defence and Work,French Stores,etc, will be taken over from Unit relieved and the usual returns will be rendered to Btn Headquarters after relief.

6. Work in progress,particularly wiring will be carried on immediately.

7. Completion of relief will be notified to Btn Headquarters by 'BAB' Code and by Runner.

8. Btn Headquarters will be situated at X.20.d.7.3.

9. Acknowledge.

                        W. S. Brand.
                                     2/Lieutenant..
   Asst/Adjutant 1/6th Btn South Staffordshire Regt.

   Copies issued to:-
       No 1. Commanding Officer.
        " 2. G.O.C. 137th I.Bde.
        " 3. O/C 1/5th Btn Leicester Regt.
        " 4. O/C "A" Company.
        " 5. " "B"   "
        " 6. " "C"   "
        " 7. " "D"   "
        " 8. " 1/5th Btn South Staffs Regt.
        " 9. " 1/6th Btn North Staffs Regt.
        " 10. Transport Officer.
        " 11. Quartermaster.
        " 12. Regt Sgt Major.
        " 13. War Diary.
        " 14. "   "   (Duplicate).
        " 15. File.
        " 16. "   (Duplicate).

SECRET.   Operation Orders No 99.   Copy No IV
                 1/6th Btn South Staffs Regiment.
Reference:- Le Hamel B Map Sheet.1/10,000.   Dated 9th MAY 1918.

1. The Btn will be relieved in the Trenches on the night of the 10/11th
   MAY 1918, by the 1/5th Btn South Staffs Regt, and on relief will go
   into Brigade Reserve at ESSARS.

2. Companies will be relieved as follows:-
   "A" Coy.1/6th Btn S.Staffs Rgt   by "A" Coy.1/5th Btn S.Staffs Rgt.
   "B"   "   "   "   "   "   "   by "B" "   "   "   "   "   "
   "C"   "   "   "   "   "   "   by "C" "   "   "   "   "   "
   "D"   "   "   "   "   "   "   by "D" "   "   "   "   "   "

3. GUIDES. 2 Guides for Btn H.Q. and one per Platoon will report to
   Headquarters,1/5th Btn S.Staffs Regt at 9p.m.tomorrow night, where
   they will receive instructions re Billets to be taken over, and will
   then guide the relieving Platoons to the Line. After Relief they
   will conduct their respective Platoons to new Billets at ESSARS.

4. Lewis Guns and Lewis Gun Magazines will be carried out by Companies.
   Baggage and Mess Kit will be carried out of the Trenches by Companies.

5. Ration Dumps for tomorrow night will be as follows:-
       Battalion Headquarters.   X.25.b.2.8.
       Support Companies("A" "C" "D") X.19.d.6.2.(Cross Roads).
       Reserve Company. ("B").   X.20.d.7.8.(Right Btn HQ).

6. The usual receipts for Trench Stores, etc, will be obtained.
   Trench Stores Lists to be sent to HQ by 2.a.m.Runner tomorrow.

7. 'Relief complete' to be wired to Btn HQ by Code-word 'FAGS' & by runner

8. Battalion Headquarters and R.A.P. after relief will be at X.25.b.2.8.
   where Companies will report their arrival in new dispositions.

9. Acknowledge.

                              W.S. Beard. 2/Lieutenant.
                              A/Adjutant 1/6th Btn South Staffordshire Regiment.

                                         (PTO).

SECRET.   Operation Orders No 39.   Copy No _____
                    1/6th Bn South Staffs Regiment.
Reference:- Le Hamel B Map sheet.1/10,000.   24th MAY 1918.

1. The Bn will be relieved on the night of the 10/11th MAY 1918 by the 1/5th South Staffs Regt on relief will go into Brigade.

2. Companies will be relieved as follows:-
   "A" Coy 1/6th Bn S.Staffs Reg. by "B" Coy 1/5th Bn S.Staffs Reg.
   "B"   "   "   "   "   "   " "D"   "   "   "   "   "   "
   "C"   "   "   "   "   "   " "A"   "   "   "   "   "   "
   "D"   "   "   "   "   "   " "C"   "   "   "   "   "   "

3. GUIDES. 2 Guides for Bn HQ and 2 per Company will report to Headquarters 1/5th Bn S.Staffs Regt at AILLY at 6 p.m tomorrow night, where they will receive instructions regarding the area to be taken over, and will then guide the relieving troops to their positions. After Relief they will conduct their respective Companies and Battalion Hqrs to BRAYES.

4. Lewis Gun Limbers and Mess Kit will be carried out of the trenches by Companies.
   Baggage and Mess Kit will be carried out of the trenches by Companies.

5. Ration Dumps for tomorrow night will be as follows:-
   Battalion Headquarters.   X.25.b.2.9.
   Support Companies("A","C","D").   X.19.c.5.2.(Cross Roads).
   Reserve Company. ("B").   X.20.c.7.8.(BLEUT Btn HQ).

6. The usual receipts for Trench Stores, &c, will be obtained. Trench Stores items to be sent to HQ by 2 a.m. under tomorrow.

7. Relief Complete' to be wired to HQ by code-word "EVAH".

8. Battalion Headquarters and R.A.P. after relief will be at X.25.b.2.9. where Companies will report their arrival in new dispositions.

9. Attention.

                                         (Signed) 2/Lieutenant.
A/Adjutant 1/6th Bn South Staffordshire Regiment.

                    (Tro).

                    Copies issued to:-
No 1.   Commanding Officer.
" 2.   HQ.137th Infantry Brigade.
" 3.   O/C 1/5th Btn South Staffs Regt.
" 4.   "   1/6th Btn North Staffs Regt.
" 5.   "   "A" Company.
" 6.   "   "B"   "
" 7.   "   "C"   "
" 8.   "   "D"   "
" 9.   Transport Officer.
" 10.   Quartermaster.
" 11.   Regtl Sgt Major.
" 12.   War Diary.
" 13.   (Duplicate)
" 14.   File.
" 15.   (Duplicate)
" 16.   O/C 1/6th Btn Sherwood Foresters.

SECRET.
Operation Orders No 100.   Copy No 12
1/6th Btn South Staffordshire Regt.
Dated 11th MAY 1918.

Reference:- Map Sheet.France 36A.SE 4.(LOCON) 1/10,000.

1. The Battalion will relieve the 1/6th Btn North Staffordshire Regt in the Left Subsection, ESSARS Sector, on the night of the 12/13th MAY 1918.

2. "A" Company.1/6th Btn S.Staffs Rgt relieves "D" Coy.1/6th N.Staffs Rgt.
   "B"   "   "   "   "   "   "   "C" "   "   "   "   "
   "C"   "   "   "   "   "   "   "B" "   "   "   "   "
   "D"   "   "   "   "   "   "   "A" "   "   "   "   "

3. Dispositions on relief will be:-
   Right Front Company. "C" Coy.   Left Front Company. "B" Coy.
   Support Company.   "D" "   Reserve Company.   "A" "

4. GUIDES.
   Five Guides each for "B" & "D" Coys and two for Btn Headquarters will report to O/C Companies and HQ respectively at 8-45p.m.
   Five Guides each for "A" & "C" Coys will report direct to these Coys.

5. 1 N.C.O. per Company will remain behind when their Companies move to the Line to show incoming Companies 'BATTLE DISPOSITIONS' in the Support Area.

6. Lewis Guns and Magazines, Mess stores, etc, will be carried to the trenches under Company arrangements.

7. Rations of "B" "C" and "D" Companies will be dumped at X.20.b.3.6. and for Btn Headquarters and "A" Company at X.19.b.95.35.

8. Trench Store Lists for the Support Area to be rendered to H.Q. by 6-0a.m.12th inst.
   Trench Store Lists and the usual returns will be rendered to Btn HQ. immediately after relief.

9. Relief complete to be wired to Btn HQ by codewords 'HAPPY HARRY' and by Runner.

10. Btn Headquarters after Relief will be at X.19.b.95.35.
    The Aid Post   after Relief will be at X.20.d.45.73.

11. ACKNOWLEDGE.

W.S. Braud 2/Lieutenant.
A/Adjutant 1/6th Btn South Staffordshire Regiment....

Copies issued to:-
No 1. Commanding Officer.
 " 2. Headquarters.137th I.Brigade.
 " 3. O/C.1/5th Btn South Staffs Rgt.
 " 4. O/C.1/6th Btn North Staffs Rgt.
 " 5. " "A" Coy.
 " 6. " "B" "
 " 7. " "C" "
 " 8. " "D" "
 " 9. Transport Officer.
 " 10. Quartermaster.
 " 11. Regtl Sgt Major.
 " 12. War Diary.
 " 13. "   "   (Duplicate).
 " 14. File.
 " 15. "   (Duplicate).

SECRET.   Operation Orders No 101.   Copy No. 10
1/6th Btn South Staffs Regiment.
Dated 13-5-1918.
Reference:- Bethune Combined Sheet and LOCON 1/10,000.

1. The 1/6th Btn South Staffs Regt will be relieved by the 1/5th Btn Sherwood Foresters(Notts and Derby Rgt)in the ESSARS Left Subsection tomorrow night 14/15th MAY 1918.
2. On completion of relief the Btn will move to rest Billets in VERQUIN area.
3. Guides,one per Platoon for incoming Battalion will report to Asst/Adjutant at PONT TOURNANT(F.7.a.8.9.)at 8-30p.m.
4. All trench maps,areoplane photos,defence schemes,etc, will be handed over.
5. Notify completion of relief by runner to Btn HQ and report arrival in Billets to Orderly Room.VERQUIN.
6. **ACKNOWLEDGE.**

                                       Captain..
       Adjutant 1/6th Btn South Staffs Regiment.
Copies issued to:-
     No 1. Commanding Officer.
     " 2. HQ.137th I.Brigade.
     " 3. O/C "A" Company.
     " 4. " "B" "
     " 5. " "C" "
     " 6. " "D" "
     " 7. Quartermaster.
     " 8. Transport Officer.
     " 9. Regtl Sgt Major.
     " 10. War Diary.
     " 11. " " (Duplicate).
     " 12. File.
     " 13. O/C.1/5th Btn Sherwood Foresters.

SECRET.	OPERATION ORDERS No 101A.	Copy No....
1/6th Btn South Staffs Regiment.
Dated 17-5-1918.

1. The Battalion will relieve the 1/5th Btn Leicester Regt in the GORRE Sector tonight the 17/18th MAY 1918.
2. On completion of relief Companies will be distributed as follows:-
   Right Front Company. "A".   Left Front Company. "D" Coy.
   Support Company.   "B"   Reserve Company.   "C"
3. Trench Store Lists and the usual returns will be rendered to Headquarters immediately after Relief.
4. Relief complete to be wired to Btn Headquarters by 'BAB' Code.

5. Battalion Headquarters will be established in GORRE CHATEAU.

6. ACKNOWLEDGE.

[signature]
Captain....
Adjutant 1/6th Btn South Staffordshire Rgt.

SECRET.   OPERATION ORDERS No 101B.   Copy No.....
                   1/6th Btn South Staffs Regiment.
                            Dated 19th MAY 1918.

1. The Battalion will be relieved in the GORRE Sector tonight the 19/20th MAY 1918 by the 1/5th Btn South Staffordshire Regt, and on relief will go into Brigade Reserve in GORRE, taking over billets as vacated by the 1/5th Btn S.Staffs Rgt.

2. Guides from Companies will report to the Adjutant at Btn HQ at 10p.m.

3. Trench Maps, details of work in progress, and Trench Stores will be handed over on relief.

4. Companies will report completion of relief by 'BAB' Code, and completion of move by 'Runner'.

5. Acknowledge.

                                            Captain......
                        Adjutant 1/6th Btn South Staffordshire Rgt.

SECRET. OPERATION. ORDERS. NO 102.   Copy No.....
          1/6 BTN SOUTH STAFFS REGIMENT.
                              DATED 22nd5.18.

1. The Battalion will be relieved by the 1/4 Leicester Regt
   in the GORRE Sector, tonight May 22/23,
2. On completion of relief Battalion will move to billets
   in VERQUIN A.B. Vaudricourt Wood.
         C & H.Q. Verquin.
3. 5. guides per Coy will report to the Adjutant at Battn
      H.Q. at 10pm.
4. One Officer per Company will remain behind at Battalion
   H.Q. for 24 hours after relief.
5. All Mess stores will be at Battalion H.Q. at 9.30.pm
6. All Lewis Guns panniers etc, will be brought to Battalion
   H.Q. on relief.
7. Report relief complete by code word "SOAK".
8. Acknowledge.

                                          Captain,.
         Adjutant 1/6 Btn South Staffs Regiment.,

SECRET.

Operation Orders No 192.A   Copy No.
1/6th Btn South Staffs Regiment.
Dated 25th MAY 1918

1. The Battalion and one Company of the 1/1st Btn Monmouthshire Rgt will relieve the 1/5th Btn Sherwood Foresters (Notts & Derby Rgt) in the Right Section ESSARS SECTOR tonight 25/26th MAY 1918.

2. Dispositions.
   Right Front Company.   "C" 1/6th S.Staffs Rgt & will relieve "A" Company 5th Sherwood Foresters.
   Left   "   "   "B" 1/6th S.Staffs Rgt. & will relieve "C" Company 5th Sherwood Foresters.
   Right support "   ½ Coy Monmouthshire Rgt & will relieve "D" Coy 5th Sherwood Foresters.
   Left   "   "   ½ Coy Monmouthshire Rgt & will relieve "B" Coy 5th Sherwood Foresters.

3. Companies will move in the order "C" "B" "Monmouths" "Headquarters". First Company to leave VERQUIN at 8-0p.m.
4. 1 Guide per platoon will be at La Motte Farm(X.26.c.55.55).
5. Companies will take over Defence Schemes, Secret Maps, Documents etc. List of French stores taken over will be forwarded to Btn Headquarters as soon as possible.
6. Report relief complete by Code-word 'Grand'.
7. Acknowledge.

                                             Captain....
                    Adjutant 1/6th Btn South Staffordshire Regt.

   Copies issued to:- No 1 Commanding Officer.
                       " 2.HQ.137th I.Brigade.
                       " 3.O/C 1/6th S.Staffs Rgt.
                       " 4. "   5th   Sherwood Foresters.
                       " 5. "   1/1st Monmouthshire Rgt.
                       " 6. "   "A" Coy.
                       " 7. "   "B" "
                       " 8. "   "C" "
                       " 9. "   "D" "
                       " 10.Transport Officer.
                       " 11.Quartermaster.
                       " 12.Regtl Sgt Major.
                       " 13.War Diary.
                       " 14. "   "   (Duplicate).
                       " 15.File.
                       " 16. "   (Duplicate).

CONFIDENTIAL.

WAR DIARY.

1/6th BTN SOUTH STAFFORDSHIRE REGIMENT.

FROM :- 1st to 30th JUNE 1918.

Pages. 158 to 160.

Army Form C. 2118.

(158).

WAR DIARY
or
INTELLIGENCE SUMMARY.
(Erase heading not required.)

1/6th Btn South Staffs Regiment.

Instructions regarding War Diaries and Intelligence Summaries are contained in F.S. Regs. Part II. and the Staff Manual respectively. Title pages will be prepared in manuscript.

Place	Date	Hour	Summary of Events and Information	Remarks and references to Appendices
VAUDRI-COURT.	1-6-1918.		Uneventful day.	
	2-6-1918.		Still quiet, except for 'Whizzbanging' at Stand-To in the morning.	
	3-6-1918.		The Battalion was relieved by the 4th Btn Leicestershire Regt, and went into RESERVE in bivouacs at VAUDRICOURT.	See O.O. No 103.
	4-6-1918.		Bathing and cleaning up.	
	5-6-1918.		Coys at disposal of Company Commanders for interior economy.	
	6-6-1918.		Inspection of Companies by the Commanding Officer.	
	7-6-1918.		The Btn relieved the 6th Btn Sherwood Foresters in the Left Sub sector of the Right Brigade Front. Rather a difficult journey up owing to gas North of the Canal.	See O.O. No 104.
	8-6-1918.		Uneventful except for mustard gas sent over by enemy, and which blew back from GORRE WOOD.	
	9-6-1918.		Quiet day.	
	10-6-1918.		A raid was carried out on enemy post by 2 parties of 15 each, under Lieut: W.M.AMES with 15 men of 'B' Coy, and 2/Lieut: F.C.BEECH with 15 men of 'A' Company. Artillery, Machine Guns and Trench Mortars co-operated. Zero hour 1a.m.11th June 1918. Lieut: Ames' Party was engaged by enemy wiring party at Zero minus 5 minutes. Lieut: Ames being wounded together with 3 men. 2/Lieut: Beech's party carried on, reached Post and found it empty, salvaged 3 loaded rifles, and 2 bags of bombs, and returned. Lieut: J.B.GREGG.RFC. USA, attached as Medical Officer, was invested with the Military Cross — an immediate award for bravery — by the G.O.C. FIRST ARMY at GOSNAY, also Coy Sgt Major G. EVANS was invested with the DISTINGUISHED CONDUCT MEDAL.	See O.O. No 105.
	11-6-1918.		Quiet day. The Battalion was relieved at night by the 1/6th Btn NORTH Staffs Regt and went into Support.	See O.O. No 106
GORRE.	12-6-1918.		Uneventful day.	
	13-6-1918.		Enemy sent over BLUE CROSS gas shells round GORRE at 3a.m. Only two casualties caused. The Btn relieved the 1/5th Btn South Staffs Regt in the GORRE Right Sub-Sector in the evening.	See O.O. No 107.
	14-6-1918.		The 3rd Division made an attack on our LEFT at 11-45p.m. Enemy artillery active on our front during the night, no damage done.	

1/6th Btn South Staffs Regiment. (159). **WAR DIARY** or **INTELLIGENCE SUMMARY** Army Form C. 2118.

Place	Date	Hour	Summary of Events and Information	Remarks and references to Appendices
GORRE.	15-6-1918.		The Battalion was relieved by the 5th Btn LINCOLNSHIRE Regt and went into Reserve, in bivouacs at VAUDRICOURT WOOD.	See O.O. No 108.
VAUDRI-COURT.	16-6-1918.		Cleaning up, bathing etc.	
"	17-6-1918.		Box Respirator Drill, and marches in Box Respirators. 6th Btn NORTH STAFFS RGT held Regimental SPORTS in the afternoon.	
"	18-6-1918.		Battalion Sports held in the afternoon in VAUDRICOURT WOOD Highly successful and greatly appreciated by all ranks.	See O.O. No 108a.
"	19-6-1918.		The Battalion relieved the 1/8th Btn SHERWOOD FORESTERS in the ESSARS SECTOR (Support).	
ESARS.	20-6-1918.		Quiet day.	
"	21-6-1918.		The Btn relieved the 1/6th Btn North Staffs Rgt in the Right ESSARS Sector. Enemy Artillery was busy on roads and tracks.	See O.O. No 109.
"	22-6-1918.		Unusually quiet day. Our Machine Guns were very active during the night.	
"	23-6-1918.		Quiet day.	
"	24-6-1918.		-do-	
"	25-6-1918.		The Btn was relieved by the 1/5th Btn SOUTH STAFFS Rgt and went into Support at ESSARS.	See O.O. No 110.
"	26-6-1918.		Quiet except for some Blue Cross Gas Shelling by enemy during the night.	
"	27-6-1918.		The Btn was relieved by the 4th Btn LEICESTERSHIRE RGT and went into RESERVE, in billets at VERQUIN.	See O.O. No 111.
VERQUIN.	28-6-1918.		Bathing and cleaning up generally.	
"	29-6-1918.		BATTALION TRANSPORT SPORTS. Highly successful and amusing.	
"	30-6-1918.		SUNDAY. Church Parades and Battalion Training.	

Army Form C. 2118.

1/6th Btn South Staffs Rgt.

(160).

WAR DIARY
or
INTELLIGENCE SUMMARY.

(Erase heading not required.)

Instructions regarding War Diaries and Intelligence Summaries are contained in F.S. Regs., Part II. and the Staff Manual respectively. Title pages will be prepared in manuscript.

Place	Date	Hour	Summary of Events and Information	Remarks and references to Appendices

			TOTAL CASUALTIES DURING MONTH OF JUNE 1918.
			++
			Lieutenant W.M.AMES, 4th Btn Black Watch(Royal Highlanders)attached WOUNDED.11-6-1918.
			
			O'RANKS. KILLED. DIED of. WOUNDED. MISSING.
			                                      WOUNDS.
			           3 7 5 —
			
			                              Christie Lieut:Colonel.
			        Commanding 1/6th Btn South Staffordshire Regiment...
			2-7-1918.	

SECRET.   Operation Orders No 103.   Copy No.....
          1/6th Btn South Staffordshire Regiment.
                    Dated 2nd ~~May~~ *June* 1918.

Reference:- VIELLE CHAPELLE-GORRE Map Sheets.

1. The Battalion will be relieved by the 1/4th Btn Leicestershire Regiment in the ESSARS Section Left Sector tomorrow night 3/4th JUNE 1918.
2. On completion of relief the Battalion will bivouac in VAUDRICOURT WOOD.
3. Route:- La MOTTE FARM - PONT TOURNANT - BROAD GAUGE RAILWAY - VERQUIN.
4. 1 Guide per Platoon and 2 for Btn Headquarters, will report to 2/Lieut: J.H.ROBINSON at LONDON BRIDGE at 9-40p.m.
5. All aeroplane photos, trench maps etc, will be handed over.
6. Report Relief complete by Code-word 'SAUCY' and arrival in billets personally.
7. <u>ACKNOWLEDGE</u>.

                                          J.F.Wood
                                          Lieutenant.-
          Acting/Adjutant 1/6th Btn South Staffs Regt.

Copies issued to:-
    No 1. Commanding Officer.
     " 2. G.O.C.137th Infantry Brigade.
     " 3/7.O/C Companies.
     " 8. "   1/4th Btn Leicestershire Rgt.
     " 9. War Diary.
     " 10. "   "   (Duplicate).

SECRET. 1/5 South Staffordshire Regt.

OPERATION ORDER No.

Reference LOCON
1/10,000.

1. 1/5 South Staffordshire Regt will raid the enemy lines at X.23.c. on the night of the 19/20th June 1918.

2. Object:- To secure prisoners or identification.

Zero hour will be notified later.

3. Lieut AMES will be in charge of the operation.
He will assemble 15 men about X.23.c.75.70 at Zero.
This party will engage any enemy attempting to retire and will cover flank and assist raid from rear if necessary.

4. Lieut BEECH will assemble in front of wire from X.23.c.70.90 to X.23.c.90.00. At Zero, party will move rapidly forward and at Zero + 2 will enter enemy post.

5. BORRE GROUP Field Artillery will barrage area round X.23.c.97.95 — X.23.c.90.00 — X.23.d.00.50 and X.23.d.10. from Zero. On "ALL CLEAR" a slow rate of fire will be maintained.

6. "C" Coy 46th M.G. Bn will barrage CSE du PAUX (X.23.a) and M.G. emplacements in the vicinity from Zero to Zero + 8, intense, and from Zero + 8 to Zero + 32, intermittently.

7. 6" NEWTON MORTAR will engage hut near house at X.23.c.70.90 from Zero till "ALL CLEAR".

8. WITHDRAWAL signal will be sounded on bugles.

9. All identifications will be removed before "STAND TO" tomorrow.

10. Watches will be synchronized at BDE. H.Q. at 6 p.m.

11. Batta H.Q. will be at X.23.a.70.60 during operation.

12. ACKNOWLEDGE.

J.F. Wood Capt.
A/Adjt. 1/5 South Staffs Regt

Issued at 12.10 p.m.

Copies to:-
1. C.O. 1/5 South Staffs Regt.
2. O.C. 137th Inf. Bde.
3. O.C. A-D Coys. 1/5 S. Staffs.
7. C.C. 1/5 S. South Staffs Regt.
8. C.O. 1/5 Leicester Regt.
9. O.C. BORRE GROUP.
10. O.C. C Coy 46th M.G. Bn.
11. O.C. Newton Mortar.
12. War Diary.

SECRET   OPERATION ORDERS No 104.   Copy No. 13
                 1/6th Btn South Staffs Regiment.
                                        Dated 7th JUNE 1918.

Reference: Map Sheet 44B. 1/10,000.

1. The Battalion will relieve the 1/6th Btn SHERWOOD FORESTERS in the GORRE LEFT-SUBSECTION tonight 7/8th JUNE 1918.

2. Companies will be disposed as follows:-
"B" Coy 1/6th S.S.Rgt will relieve "D" Coy.1/6th S.For. on the Right.
"C" "   "   "   "   "   "C"   "   "   "   "   "   Left.
"A" "   "   "   "   "   "A"   "   "   "   "   " in Support.
"D" "   "   "   "   "   "B"   "   "   "   "   " Reserve.

3. The Battalion will march by Platoons at 200 yards interval, in the following order:- "HQ" "B" "C" "A" "D".
First Platoon will pass E.28.c.1.9. at 8-40p.m.

4. ROUTE:- Speedwell Track -Broadgauge Railway-Canal Bank.

5. GUIDES. for 'A' 'B' & 'D' Companies will be at MIDLAND BRIDGE F.2.d.4.4.at 10-15p.m. (5 guides per Company).

6. Companies will take over programme of Work, Maps, Trench Stores, Aeroplane Photographs etc.
A list of Trench Stores will be sent to Orderly Room on relief.

7. The 'RELIEF COMPLETE' will be notified to Orderly Room by code-word "CREAM".

8. ACKNOWLEDGE.
                                   JPWood Lieutenant.
                Act/Adjutant 1/6th Btn South Staffordshire Rgt.

            Copies issued to:-
                 No 1. Commanding Officer.
                 " 2. Headquarters.137th Bde.
                 " 3. O/C.1/6th Btn Sherwood Foresters.
                 " 4. " 1/5th Btn South Staffs Rgt.
                 " 5. " 1/6th Btn North Staffs Rgt.
                 " 6. " "A" Coy.
                 " 7. " "B" "
                 " 8. " "C" "
                 " 9. " "D" "
                 " 10. Transport Officer.
                 " 11. Quartermaster.
                 " 12. Regtl Sgt Major.
                 " 13. War Diary.
                 " 14. "   " (Duplicate).
                 " 15. File.
                 " 16. " (Duplicate).

1/6th Btn South Staffordshire Regiment

SECRET.   OPERATION ORDERS No 106.   Copy No 6

10 June 1918.

① The Battalion will be relieved by the 1/6th North Staffs Regt in the GORRE left Sub Sector tomorrow night 11/12th June 1918.

② A Coy 1/6th N.S. Regt will relieve "B" Coy 1/6th S.S. Regt
   D "   "   "   "   "   "   C Coy "   "   "   "
   C "   "   "   "   "   "   A "   "   "   "   "
   B "   "   "   "   "   "   D "   "   "   "   "

③ On completion of relief Coys will move to Bde Reserve disposed as follows:-

   LIVERPOOL LINE   D Coy   HQ F.11 a 60.15
   WOOD SWITCH   A Coy   HQ F.10 a 60.95
   GORRE SOUTH LOCALITY   B Coy   HQ F.3 d 45.45
   LE QUESNOY   C Coy   HQ F.3 b 9.9

5 Guides per Coy will report to Bn HQ at 3.30 a.m. 11th inst.

④ Coys will hand over work in hand and proposed, Trench Maps, Aeroplane Photos, etc, to incoming Unit.

⑤ All Cooking utensils will be moved under Bn arrangements. Officers Mess Stores etc, will be moved under Coy arrangements.

⑥ Coys will report relief complete by code word Y4 received. Arrival in billets by runner.

⑦ ACKNOWLEDGE.

J F Wood
Captain &
A/Adjutant 1/6th South Staffordshire Regt

COPY No 10

SECRET   14th Btn South Staffordshire Regt
         OPERATION ORDERS No 107.   13 June 1918

① The Battn will relieve the 1/5th South Staff Regt in the GORRE right sub sector tomorrow night 13/14th June 1918.

② 'A' Coy 14 S.S. Regt will relieve 'A' Coy 1/5th S.S Regt on the right
   'D'   "   "   "   "   "   'D' "   "   "   Left
   'B'   "   "   "   "   "   'C' "   "   "   Support
   'C'   "   "   "   "   "   'B' "   "   "   Reserve

5 guides per Coy from 1/5 South Staffs Regt will report to each Coy H.Q. at dusk 13th inst.

③ All cooking utensils will be moved under Battn arrangements. Officers mess stores etc, will be moved under Coy arrangements.

④ The usual trench returns will be rendered by the 2 a.m. runner.

⑤ Coys will report relief complete by code word "STROMBOS."

⑥ ACKNOWLEDGE.

                                    Capt &
                        Adjutant 14th Btn South Staff Regt

Issued at 10 am
Copy No 1. C.O.   Copy No 7. O.C. 14th Staff
  "   " 2. G.O.C. 137 Inf Bde   "   " 8. O. " 1/5 S S&ff
  "   " 3. O.C. A Coy   "   " 9. }
  "   " 4.   "   B   "   "   " 10. } Retained
  "   " 5.   "   C   "   "   " 11. }
  "   " 6.   "   D   "

SECRET.   1/6th Bn South Staffordshire Regt.
                                              Copy No 11
         OPERATION ORDERS No 103 15 June 1918
Reference Map Bowery 1/1 1/5,000.
(1) The 1/6th Bn South Staff Regt will be relieved in
    the GORRE Right Subsector on the night of 15/16 June
    by the 5th Lincolnshire Regt.
(2) On completion of relief the Bn will move to
    rest billets in VANDRICOURT WOOD (NORTH CAMP)
(3) Trains will leave LE QUESNOY ration dump
    F3C4030 from 11 pm onwards and convey personnel
    to SPEEDWELL SDG each train holds approximately
    150.
(4) Each Coy will send 1 guide per platoon to
    Bn HQ by 3.30 am 15 June.
(5) Trench Maps details of work in progress
    trench stores will be handed over on relief
(6) All cooking utensils mess stores etc; will
    be placed in Ration Dump F3C4030 by 11.45 pm.
(7) Coys will report relief complete by
    Code Word "QUEEN'S" and on arrival in
    Billets by Runner.
(8) ACKNOWLEDGE.
                              J P Wood
                                 Capt +
Issued at 1.30 pm Adjutant 1/6th Bn South Staff Regt
Copies issued to
Copy No 1 CO   Copy No 9 GM
   "   2 137 Inf Bde   "   10 RSM
   "   3 5/Lincoln R   "   11-12 War Diary
   " 4-7 Companies   "   13-14 File
   "   8 TO

SECRET. OPERATION ORDERS No 108. Copy No 13
         1/6th BTN SOUTH STAFFORDSHIRE RGT.
                      Dated 19th JUNE 1918.

1. The Battalion will relieve the 1/8th Btn SHERWOOD
   FORESTERS in SUPPORT in the ESSARS SECTOR tonight
   the 19/20th JUNE 1918.

2. "A" Coy 1/6th S.Staffs Rgt relieves "C" Cy.1/8th Sherwoods.
                                                  in LA MOTTE.
   "B" "   "   "   "   "   " "B" " " in the CENTRE.
   "C" "   "   "   "   "   " "D" " " LE HAMEL.
   "D" "   "   "   "   "   " "A" " " LEFT.

3. Order of March:- Btn Headquarters, 'C' 'A' 'D' 'B' Coys.
4. ROUTE:- Route R4 - F.1.b.50.00 where guides will meet.
   Btn Headquarters to cross PONT TOURNANT Bridge at
   10-30p.m.
   Starting Point:- VAUDRICOURT LODGE GATES(E.28.c.15.85).
   Btn H.Q. will leave at 9-30p.m. Companies will proceed by
   platoons at 200 yards intervals.
5. Trench Maps, Aeroplane Photographs, and Schemes of Defence
   will be taken over. Lists of Trench Stores taken over
   will be forwarded to Orderly Room immediately after
   Relief.

6. 'Relief Complete' will be notified to Btn Headquarters
   by Code-Word 'RANGERS'.

7. ACKNOWLEDGE.
                                          J.R.Wood
                                          Captain....
                      Adjutant 1/6th Btn South Staffordshire Rgt.

     Copies issued to:-
            No 1. Commanding Officer.
            " 2. Headquarters,137th I.Brigade.
            " 3. O/C 1/8th Btn Sherwood Foresters
            " 4. " 1/5th Btn South Staffs Rgt.
            " 5. " 1/6th Btn North Staffs Rgt.
            " 6. " "A" Company.
            " 7. " "B"   "
            " 8. " "C"   "
            " 9. " "D"   "
            " 10. Quartermaster.
            " 11. Transport Officer.
            " 12. Regtl Sgt Major.
            " 13. War Diary.
            " 14. "   " (Duplicate).
            " 15. File.
            " 16. "   (Duplicate).

SECRET.   COPY N° 9

1/6 Bn South Staffordshire Regt.
OPERATION ORDERS N° 109.   21-6-18.

(1) The Bn will relieve the 1/6th Prince of Wales North Staffordshire Regt. in the Right ESSARS Sector tonight 21/22nd June 1918.

(2) "C" Coy 1/6 S.S.R. will relieve "B" Coy 1/6 N.S.R. on the Right
    "B"   "   "   "   "   "   "   "   "C"   "   "   "   "   " Left
    "A"   "   "   "   "   "   "   "   "D"   "   "   "   "Right Supp".
    "D"   "   "   "   "   "   "   "   "A"   "   "   "   " Left   "

(3) Guides. One guide per platoon will report at each Coy H.Q. as soon after dusk as possible.

(4) Cooking Utensils will be moved under Bn arrangements.

(5) Trench maps, aeroplane photographs etc; will be taken over lists of Trench Stores taken over will be forwarded to Orderly Room immediately after relief.

(6) Relief completed will be notified to Bn H.Q. by code word "CELTIC".

(7) ACKNOWLEDGE

                                J R Wood
                                  Capt
                    Adjt 1/6 Bn South Staffordshire Regt

Copies to.
Copy N° 1. C.O.   Copy N° 7. 16th North Staffs
  "   " 2 HQ. 137. J. Bde.   "   " 8   Q.M.
  "   " 3-6. Companies   "   " 9-10 War Diary
                               "   " 11-12 File.

SECRET.   1/6 South Staffordshire Regt   COPY N° 9
OPERATION ORDERS N° 110   24 June 1918

1. The Battn: will be relieved in the line on the night 25/26th June 1918 by the 1/5th South Staff Regt and will move into Brigade Support in ESSARS.

2. Companies will be relieved as under:-
   'C' Coy 1/6 S.S.R will be relieved by 'C' Coy 1/5 S.S.R on the Right
   'B' "   "   "   "   "   "   "   "   'B' "   "   "   "   Left
   'A' "   "   "   "   "   "   "   "   'A' "   "   "   "   Rt Support
   'D' "   "   "   "   "   "   "   "   'D' "   "   "   "   Left Support

3. GUIDES 5 guides per Coy will report to Bn. H.Q. at 2.30am. 25th inst.

4. On completion of relief Coys: will be disposed as follows:- 'A' Coy. LA. MOTTE 'B' Coy Left Coy
   'C' " LE. HAMEL 'D' " Centre

5. French Maps, aeroplane photos, and defence schemes will be handed over. Lists of French Stores handed over will be forwarded to Orderly Room immediately after relief.

6. Relief complete will be notified to Bn H.Q. by Code Word "CLYDE".

7. ACKNOWLEDGE.

                               J.P. Wood
                               /Capt &
               Adjutant 1/6 South Staff Regt
Copies to:-
   1. Commanding Officer   8. Transport Officer
   2. H.Qrs 137 Infy Bde   9-10 War Diary.
   3. O.C. 1/5 South Staff R 11-12. File
   4-7. OC A.B.C & D.Coys. 13. R.S.M.

SECRET.   COPY. No. 12

1/6 Bn South Staffordshire Regt.
Operation Orders No 111

Ref:- BEVRY. 44 B / 10,000.

1. The Battn will be relieved in Support on the night 27/28th June 1918 by the 1/4th Leicestershire Regt.

2. Companies will be relieved as under:-
   A. Coy 1/6 S.S.R will be relieved by A Coy 1/4 Leicesters on the Right.
   B. "   "   "   "   "   "   "   "   B "   "   "   "   Left.
   C. "   "   "   "   "   "   "   "   C "   "   "   "   in LE. HAMEL
   D. "   "   "   "   "   "   "   "   D "   "   "   "   in the Centre

3. On relief the Battn will move to Billets in VERQUIN and VAUDRICOURT WOOD, as under:-
   H. Qrs. A and C. Coys to VERQUIN. B and D. Coys. to VAUDRICOURT WOOD

4. ROUTE. B and D. Coys will cross the canal by the PONT TOURNANT Bridge.
   A and C. Coys will cross the AIRE-LA-BASSEE canal by MIDLAND. BRIDGE.

5. All Lewis gun material will be carried out and dumped at F.y.b.19.80. where it will be picked up by limbers, 1 man per team will be left to load up limbers.

6. Trench Maps, aeroplane photos and defence schemes will be handed over. Accurate trench store lists will reach Orderly Room by 3am 27th inst.

7. All cooking utensils, mess tins, &c will be placed on ESSARS. dump by 10 pm.

8. Relief complete will be notified by Code Word "MORTON" and arrival in billets by runner.

9. ACKNOWLEDGE.

Copies to:-
1. Commanding Officer
2. Hd Qrs 137 Inf Bde
3. O.C. 1/4 Leicester Regt
4-7 O's C. Companies
8 Transport Officer
9 Quartermaster
10 R.S.M.
11-12 War Diary
13-14 File.

J P Wood
Capt &
Adjutant 1/6th South Staff Regt.

CONFIDENTIAL.

WAR DIARY.

1/6th Btn South Staffordshire Regt.

FROM......1-7-1918.

TO........31-7-1918.

Sheets 160/162.

Army Form C. 2118.

WAR DIARY
INTELLIGENCE SUMMARY.

1/6th Btn South Staffordshire Rgt. (160).

(Erase heading not required.)

Instructions regarding War Diaries and Intelligence Summaries are contained in F.S. Regs., Part II. and the Staff Manual respectively. Title pages will be prepared in manuscript.

Place	Date	Hour	Summary of Events and Information	Remarks and references to Appendices
GORRE.	1-7-1918.		The Battalion relieved the 1/8th Btn Sherwood Foresters in the GORRE LEFT Sector.	See O.O. No 112A
"	2-7-1918.		A very quiet day.	
"	3-7-1918.		Quiet day.	
"	4-7-1918.		A very quiet day.	
"	5-7-1918.		Cpls Farmer and Blythe 'C' Coy and Pte Green 'C' Coy captured two prisoners in a daylight patrol. The Battalion was relieved by the 5th Btn South Staffs Regt and went into Brigade Support.	See O.O. No 112A
"	6-7-1918.		Enemy had a shoot on 'D' Coys Headquarters. One casualty. The Battalion relieved the 1/6th Btn North Staffs Rgt in the Right Sector.	See O.O. No 113.
"	7-7-1918.			
"	8-7-1918.		A quiet day.	
"	9-7-1918.		Quiet day. The Battalion relieved by the 1/5th Btn Leicestershire Regt, and went into Divisional Reserve in VAUDRICOURT WOOD.	See O.O. No 114
VAUDRICOURT."	10-7-1918.		Bathing and cleaning up.	
	11-7-1918.		Battalion Training on Ground near HESDIGNEUL during the morning.	
"	12-7-1918.		Battalion Training in VAUDRICOURT WOOD.	
"	13-7-1918.		Companies on Range No 14 near HESDIGNEUL during morning and afternoon.	
"	14-7-1918.		SUNDAY. Church Parade.	
"	15-7-1918.		Routine previous to the trenches. The Battalion relieved the 1/6th Btn Sherwood Foresters in the ESSARS LEFT SECTOR. A very quiet night.	See O.O. No 115.
ESSARS.	16-7-1918.		A quiet day.	
"	17-7-1918.		A little shelling round Btn Headquarters, otherwise very quiet day.	
"	18-7-1918.		Sgt Blythe, Cpl Farmer and Pte Green of 'C' Coy went out on a daylight patrol, and captured three Bosche. On returning	

1/6th Btn South Staffs Regiment.

(161).
WAR DIARY
INTELLIGENCE SUMMARY.
(Erase heading not required.)

Army Form C. 2118.

Instructions regarding War Diaries and Intelligence Summaries are contained in F.S. Regs., Part II. and the Staff Manual respectively. Title pages will be prepared in manuscript.

Place	Date	Hour	Summary of Events and Information	Remarks and references to Appendices
ESSARS.	18-7-1918.		to our line and when on the enemy side of the wire they found six Germans, who had evidently observed them before, waiting for them. Observing that there was now nine to Sgt Blythe shot the three prisoners and killed them. He then gave orders for patrol to get back, but unfortunately Cpl Farmer and Pte Green got separated from him and though he made every effort to find them he had to return to our lines without them. It is feared they were either killed or captured. During the night Sgt Blythe went out and also other patrols to try and find a trace of the two missing men, although patrols went to place where the two men were last seen by Sgt Blythe their efforts were unsuccessful. At night the Battalion moved into Support in ESSARS.	See O.O. No. 117.
"	19-7-1918.		Quiet day.	
"	20-7-1918.		The 1/5th Btn South Staffs Regt discovered on a daylight patrol a cartoon which was stuck on a post near the Bosche Line. In bad English the cartoon stated that the Germans were very glad for the two Englishmen and that they were now on their way to Germany. It is hoped that this refers to Cpl Farmer and Pte Green, reported 'Missing' on the 18-7-1918.	
GORRE.	21-7-1918.		At night the Btn was relieved by the 1/6th Btn Sherwood Foresters and went into the GORRE Right Sector, relieving the 1/4th Btn Leicestershire Regt. The 137th Bde is now termed the 'Floating Brigade of the Division'.	See O.O. No. 118.
"	22-7-1918.		Very quiet. Pte Gutteridge Killed.	
"	23-7-1918.		At night the enemy Trench Mortared Route 'A' severely, 'A' and 'D' Coys had 7 men wounded, and mine buried, the latter were not badly hurt.	
"	24-7-1918.		GORRE was rather heavily shelled from 10a.m. to 2p.m.	
"	25-7-1918.		Inter-Company relief. Front Coys shelled in the morning with 4.2". H.E. Retaliation given by Divisional Artillery.	
"	26-7-1918.		Retaliation called for by Front Line Coys for rather severe shelling of Front Lines and "Close" Support with 4.2"	

1/6th Btn South Staffordshire Regt.

Army Form C. 2118.

(162).
WAR DIARY
or
INTELLIGENCE SUMMARY.
(Erase heading not required.)

Instructions regarding War Diaries and Intelligence Summaries are contained in F. S. Regs., Part II. and the Staff Manual respectively. Title pages will be prepared in manuscript.

Place	Date	Hour	Summary of Events and Information	Remarks and references to Appendices
GORRE.	27-7-1918.		The Battalion was relieved by the 1/4th Btn Leicestershire Regiment, and moved into Divisional Reserve in VAUDRICOURT WOOD.	
VAUDRICOURT WOOD.	28-7-1918.		Bathing and cleaning up.	
"	29-7-1918.		Inspection of Companies by the Commanding Officer. Brigade Show in Vaudricourt Wood commencing 11a.m.	
"	30-7-1918.		All Companies on the Range (No 14) near HESDIGNEUL.	
"	31-7-1918.		Battalion Training and L.Gunners on Range No 214.	
			TOTAL CASUALTIES FOR THE MONTH OF JULY 1918.	
			Killed. Wounded. Wounded & Missing At Duty. Total.	
			1 27 5 2 35	
	1-8-1918.		Christie Lieut:Colonel. Commanding 1/6th Btn South Staffordshire Regiment...	

Secret.

OPERATION ORDERS No 112.   Copy No 13
1/6th BTN SOUTH STAFFORDSHIRE RGT.

Dated 1st JULY 1918.

Reference:- Map Sheet 44B.and Locon.

1. The 1/6th Btn SOUTH STAFFS RGT will relieve the 1/8th BTN SHERWOOD FORESTERS in the GORRE LEFT SECTOR tonight the 1/2nd JULY 1918.

2. DISPOSITIONS OF COMPANIES.
"B" Coy.6th S.Staffs Rgt.relieves "B" Coy, 8th S.Foresters in the Right.
"C"   "   "   "   "   "   "   "C"   " 8th S.Foresters in the Left.
"A"   "   "   "   "   "   "   "A"   " 8th S.Foresters in Support.
"D"   "   "   "   "   "   "   "D"   " 8th S.Foresters in Reserve.

3. Two trains will convey Headquarters,"A" & "D" Companies from N.27.b.1.7. to KANTARA DUMP. Trains leave at 9-0p.m. 'B' & 'C' Companies will march to trenches by Platoons first platoon will pass N.28.b.35.20. at 8-45p.m. Route:- Broadgauge Railway -Midland Bridge.

4. Mess Stores for the trenches, cooking utensils etc, will be dumped outside Orderly Room at 7-30p.m.

5. Maps, Aeroplane photos etc will be taken over. Lists of Trench Stores taken over to be sent to Btn Headquarters immediately after Relief.

6. Report 'Relief complete' by Code-word 'COX'.

7. Acknowledge.

P A Hagan 2/Lieutenant.
Asst/Adjutant 1/6th Btn South Staffs Rgt.

Copies issued to:- No 1. Commanding Officer.
" 2. H.Q.137th I.Brigade.
" 3. O/C 1/8th Btn S.Foresters.
" 4. " 1/5th Btn S.Staffs Rgt.
" 5. " 1/6th Btn N.Staffs Rgt.
" 6. " "A" Company.
" 7. " "B"   "
" 8. " "C"   "
" 9. " "D"   "
" 10. Transport Officer.
" 11. Quartermaster.
" 12. Regtl Sgt Major.
" 13. War Diary.
" 14. "   "   (Duplicate).
" 15. File.
" 16. "   (Duplicate).

SECRET.   1/6 South Staffordshire Regt   COPY. No 9
         Operation Orders No 112 A
Ref:- Maps LAWE CANAL (2) 1/20000.   4 July 1918

1. The 1/6 South Staffs Regt will be relieved by
   the 1/5 South Staffs and will go into Bde Support
   in the GORRE Sector on the night 5/6th July 1918
2. (RIGHT) B. Coy 1/6 S.S.R. will be relieved by A Coy 1/5 S.S.R
   (LEFT)   C "   "   " "   "   "   "   " B "   " " "
   (SUPPORT) A "   "   " "   "   "   "   " C "   " " "
   (RESERVE) D "   "   " "   "   "   "   " D "   " " "
3. 1 N.C.O. and 4 guides per Coy will report to
   Bn H.Q by 3-30am 5 July.
4. On being relieved Bn.H.Q will be at
   F3 C 22.25.
   A. Coy will go into WOOD SWITCH (HQ F4c 50.65)
   D "   "   "   "   LIVERPOOL LINE (HQ F4a 60.20)
   B "   "   "   "   Support GORRE SOUTH LOCALITY (HQ F3d 15.40)
   C "   "   "   "   reserve at LEQUESNOY (HQ F8b 80.90)
5. Lewis guns, panniers &c will be carried out
   by Companies.
6. Maps, aeroplane photos & work in progress will be
   handed over. Lists of French Stores will be
   sent to Bn H.Q.
7. Report relief complete by code word
   'BOX'
8. ACKNOWLEDGE.

Copies to :-
1. Commanding Officer   F.A.Morgan 2/Lt.
2. H.Q. 137. Infy Bde   A/Adjutant 1/6 South Staff R
3. O.C. 1/5 South Staff Regt   8. R.S.M.
4-7. O.C. A.B.C.D. Coys.   9-10. War Diary
                                   11-12. File.

SECRET 1/6 South Staffordshire Regiment. COPY No 9
Operation Orders. No 113.
Ref - LAWE CANAL (2) 1/20,000.   6th July 1918

1. The 1/6 South Staffs will relieve the 1/6 North Staffs Regt,
   RIGHT. BN. GORRE SECTOR on the night 7/8th July 1918.

2. (WOODSWITCH) A. Coy 1/6 S.S.R. will relieve A Coy 1/6. N.S.R.
                                        RIGHT (H.Q. X29d 8520)
   (LIVERPOOL LINE) D. Coy "   "   " relieve D. Coy 1/6 N.S.R.
                                        LEFT (H.Q. X29d 8022)
   SUPPORT   B. Coy "   "   "   relieve C Coy 1/6 N.S.R
                                        in SUPPORT (H.Q. X29d 6425)
   RESERVE   C Coy   "   "   will relieve B Coy 1/6 N.S.R
                                        in RESERVE (H.Q. F5c 1595)

   On relief Bn HQ will be at F10a y0.60

3. 1 NCO per Coy will remain behind to hand over
4. Lewis guns & panniers will be carried in by Coys.
   Cooking utensils, Mess stores will be carried in by Limplices
5. Maps, aeroplane photos &c will be handed over. Lists of
   Trench Stores to be handed over due at Bn H.Q.
   at 3.30 a.m. 7th July.
6. Work in progress will be carefully taken over
   & proceeding with immediately after relief.
7. Report relief complete by code Word 'GEORGE'
8. ACKNOWLEDGE.

                                              2/Lt.
Copies to   A/Adjutant 1/6 South Staffs R
  1. Commanding Officer   4-7. OC. Companies
  2. H.Q. 137th Inf Bde   8. R.S.M.
  3. O.C. 1/6th North Staff R 9-10 War Diary.
                               10-12 File.

SECRET.   1/6th Bn. South Staffordshire Regt.   COPY No 11
          Operation Orders No 114

Ref: / AWE CANAL (2) 1/20,000   9 July 1918

1. The 1/6th S.S.R. will be relieved in the line by
   the 5th Leicester Regt on the night 9/10th July 1918

2. RIGHT   A Coy 1/6 S.S.R will be relieved by B Coy 1/5 Leicester
   LEFT   D   "   "   "   "   "   "   C   "   "   "
   SUPPORT B   "   "   "   "   "   "   D   "   "   "
   RESERVE C   "   "   "   "   "   "   A   "   "   "

3. 4 Guides per Coy will report to Bn HQ. before 3.30am
   9 July.

4. On relief Coys will march out via STAFFORD
   BRIDGE and along road south of canal, if
   there is a train waiting for them at F3c30,25
   (SUPPORT BN DUMP) they will entrain to SPEEDWELL
   SPUR, otherwise they will proceed to MUSHROOM
   SPUR near Bde HQ (F13d 05.90) where they will
   entrain to SPEEDWELL SPUR. Thence they will
   march to bivouacs in SOUTH CAMP. VADDRICOURT.
   Coys will report to Major Frew at SUPPORT BN HQ
   DUMP.

5. Mess Stores & Cooking Utensils will be at SUPPORT
   BN HQ DUMP at 10 pm. Limbers will carry Cooks Utensils

6. Lewis Guns & Panniers will be taken on the
   train by ~~~~ Coys which entrain at
   SUPPORT BN DUMP. Coys which march to MUSHROOM
   SPUR near Bde HQ will dump them at the
   cross roads F8b 80.80 where limbers will
   meet them – 1 man per gun & 1 NCO per Coy

staying with guns.
7. Special maps, aeroplane photos, scheme of defence & work in progress will be handed over. Lists of French stores to be handed over will be in at Bn HQ by 7:30am 9th inst.
8. Report relief complete by Code Word 'CYRUS' and arrival in billets personally.
9. ACKNOWLEDGE.

Major.
1/6th Bn South Staffordshire Regt

Copies to:-
1. Commanding Officer   9. Transport Officer
2. HQ 137th Inf Bde   10. R.S.M.
3. OC 1/5th Leicestershire Regt 11&12 War Diary
4-7. OC's Companies   13&14 File
8. Quartermaster

SECRET.   OPERATION ORDERS No 115.
                        1/6th Btn South Staffordshire Regt.
                                    Dated 15th JULY 1916.
Reference:- LOOS & BEUVRY MAP SHEETS 1/10,000.
1. The 1/6th Btn South Staffs Regiment will relieve the 1/6th Btn
   SHERWOOD FORESTERS in the BOYAUS LEFT SECTOR tonight the 15/16th
   July 1916.
2. DISPOSITIONS.
   "C" Coy will relieve "D" Company.1/6th Sherwood Foresters.(RIGHT).
   "B"   "   "   "C"   "   "   "   "   (LEFT).
   "A"   "   "   "A"   "   "   "   "   (SUPPORT).
   "D"   "   "   "B"   "   "   "   "   (RESERVE).
   On relief Battalion Headquarters will be at X.19.b.95.35.
3. ROUTE.
   Companies will proceed via Route 4 to PONT TOURNANT.
   Order of March:- "C" "B" "A" "D" "HQ".
   200 yards interval will be maintained between Platoons.
   1 Platoon of "A" Coy with one Officer will proceed with "C" Coy, and
   1 Platoon of "C" Coy with one Officer will proceed with "A" Coy.
   First Platoon will leave the Lodge Gates at 8-30p.m.
   Halt at 9-15p.m. until 9-30p.m.
4. GUIDES.
   1 Guide per Platoon furnished by the Sherwood Foresters will meet
   the Battalion at PONT TOURNANT(F.7.c.75.95).
   5 Guides per Company will be waiting at SHRINE. X.20.c.60.40.
5. MESS STORES for the trenches, cooking utensils, two H.Q.Lewis Guns, and
   Reserve L.G. ammunition will be dumped outside the GUARD ROOM by 7-30p.m.
6. Lewis Guns(5 per Company) will be dumped outside the Guard Room at 7p.m.
   one man per gun to go with the limbers. Platoons will pick up their
   guns at F.7.b.20.80.
                                                              (PTO).

to be dumped outside H.Q.ness at 7p.m.
Special Msgs, aeroplane photographs,and sketches of defence,will be taken over. List of French Mores taken over to be sent to Brigade H.Q.on immediately after relief. Work will be carefully taken over and proceeded with immediately.
9. Report RMLF CUMPLETS BY COS—WORD "CELLO".
10. AMBULANCE

P.P.Moran 2/Lieutenant.
Act/Adjutant 1/6th Btn South Staffordshire Regt.

Distributed to:- No 1.Comp& Officer.
    "   "   2.B.C. 137th L.Brig.
    "   "   3.O/C 1/6th Sherwood Foresters.
    "   "   4.   " 1/5th Btn South Staffs Rgt.
    "   "   5.   " 2/6th Btn North Staffs Rgt.
    "   "   6.   " "A" Coy.
    "   "   7.   " "B" "
    "   "   8.   " "C" "
    "   "   9.   " "D" "
    "   "   10. Transport Officer.
    "   "   11. Quartermaster.
    "   "   12. Regt Sgt Major.
    "   "   13. War Diary.
    "   "   14.   "   " (Duplicate).

16th South Staffordshire Regt. Serial No. 12

Operation Orders No. 114.   17 July 1916

Ref: LOCON 7/1.000

1. The 16th South Staff Regt will be relieved in the line by the 15th South Staff Regt on the night 18/19th July to go into BRIGADE SUPPORT.

2. "C" (RIGHT) 16 S.S.Regt will be relieved by "A" Coy 15th S.S.Regt
    "B" Coy (LEFT)   "   "   "   "   "B"   "
    "A"   (SUPPORT)   "   "   "   "   "D"   "
    "D"   (RESERVE)   "   "   "   "   "C"   "

3. 4 Guides per Coy will report to B.H.Q.
    A.B.C Coys 2.30 am 18th   D Coy 5.30 pm 18th July

4. 1 N.C.O per Coy will report to B.H.Q by 2.30am 18th to take over huts.

5. 'B' Coy will provide 1 N.C.O + 3 men for each of the 4 Stragglers Posts. These to report to B.H.Q by 2.30 am 18th.

6. On relief dispositions will be:-
    'C' Coy MANCHESTER LINE. 'D' Coy CENTRE (NEWCASTLE LINE.)
    'B' " LEFT (NEWCASTLE LINE) 'A' " RESERVE (LA MOTTE)
           B.H.Q at X25a 65 40.

7. Special maps, aeroplane photos + trench stores will be handed over. Trench Store lists to be at B.H.Q by 3.30 am 18th.

8. Mess stores + cooking utensils will be carried out by Transport

9. WORK immediately after relief
    1. 'B' Coy will work on the MESPLAUX SWITCH
    2. 'D' " will work on new communication trench
    3. 'A' " will work in the vicinity of LA MOTTE under the direction of Monmouth Pol.Line
    4. 'C' Coy will report to 16 South Staff for instructions as to work
    The whole strength of Coys will work, except few Runners of B.H.Q Coys who will carry out relief guns + panniers. Work will continue till zero + Coys will report when their new lines have been occupied again after same.

10. Relief complete will be notified by Code Word SNAFFLE

11. ACKNOWLEDGE.

Copies issued to:-   F A Morgan
No.1 Commanding Officer   A/Adjutant 16th Bn South Staff Regt
 " 2 HQ 33rd Inf Bde   No.9 Quartermaster   2/Lt
 " 3 O.C 15th South Staff Regt   " 11.12 War Diary
 " 4 Y.C.C Company   " 10   R.S.M
 " 6 Transport Officer   " 13.14 File

Secret   1/6 Btn South Staffs Regt   Copy No 12

Operation Orders 118   21st July 1917

Ref Map. Vieille Chapelle –
           Givenchy 1/20,000

1. The Battalion will be relieved by the 1/6th Sherwood Foresters on night 21/22nd July in ESSARS Support and on completion of relief will relieve 4th Leicester Regt in the line Right GORRE Section.

6th South Staffs	6th Sherwoods	4 Leicester
'C' Coy will be relieved by	'B' Coy — will relieve	A Coy Reserve
'B'	'C'	D Support
'D'	'D'	B LEFT
'A'	'A'	C RIGHT

2. **Route.** On relief Companies will proceed by routes reconnoitred to-day.

3. **Guides.** 5 Guides per Coy of 4th Leicesters will be met as follows:—

   A.B.D. Coys MIDLAND BRIDGE
   C   Coy   Entrance GORRE CHATEAU } 11.45 p.m.

   4 Guides per Coy will report to BHQ at 9 p.m. 21st inst to guide 6th Sherwoods into position

   1 Officer + 1 NCO 'B' Coy will meet reliefs for STRAGGLER POSTS at LONDON BRIDGE at 5.30 p.m. See Officers will see them properly posted. Post on TURBO BRIDGE will be withdrawn + not relieved by 6th Sherwoods

4. Mess Stores, cooking utensils etc, will be stacked at ESSARS DUMP by 10 pm + will be conveyed down to KANTARA. Transplanens will carry same to cookhouses from KANTARA (1 man per Coy will accompany same)

5. Special maps, Trench Stores, aeroplane photos, and Schemes of Defence + Work, will be handed over to 6th Sherwoods + taken over from 4th Leicesters

6. Completion of first relief will be noted by code word 'GIN'.
   Completion of second — 'ITALIAN'.

7. Btn HQrs will close at ESSARS K25 a 6.6 on completion of first relief + will open at E10 a 57 7/2 immediately afterwards

8. ACKNOWLEDGE

                                              H.H. Bun   Capt & Adjutant
                                              1/6th Bn South Staffords Regt

For distribution see over.

Copies issued to :-
No 1. Commanding Officer
" 2. 139th Infy Bde H.Q.
" 3. 16th Sherwood Foresters Rgt
" 4. 14th Leicestershire Regt
" 5+6 C+D Companies

9 Transport Officer
10 Quartermaster
11. R.S.M.
12+13. War Diary
14+15. File.

WAR DIARY.

1/6th Btn South Staffordshire Regiment.

From:- 1st August 1918.
To:- 31st August 1918.

Sheets. 165 to 170.

1/6th Battalion South Staffordshire Reg. (165.)

Army Form C. 2118.

WAR DIARY
or
INTELLIGENCE SUMMARY.
(Erase heading not required.)

Instructions regarding War Diaries and Intelligence Summaries are contained in F. S. Regs., Part II. and the Staff Manual respectively. Title pages will be prepared in manuscript.

Place	Date	Hour	Summary of Events and Information	Remarks and references to Appendices
VAUDRICOURT WOOD	Aug 1st		Battalion's training during the morning. Lecture on "Aeroplanes" in the evening.	
	2nd		30 men and 2 officers were taken to the Aerodrome but weather was too bad to fly. Divisional Sports were held at "Bois-des-Dames" near Marles-les-Mines. Officers' Tug-of-war Team won for 3rd prize with O.T.C. 2nd prize was won for Battalion Transport Turnout. 1st Officers' Pony Charger, and jumping the Battalion secured 3rd prize in each. G.S. Limbered Wagons (two horses) 3rd prize. Also Rees' 1st, 2nd and a 3rd. At night the Battalion relieved the 16th Sherwood Foresters in the E-klars Support Section	See 00.121.
ESSARS	3rd to 4th		A quiet day. Enemy shelled ESSARS with 8"-guns falling very near B.H.Q. and Headquarter Details.	
	4th to 5 & 6.		Enemy shelled ESSARS and vicinity with 4.2 & 5.9 all day - about 500 rounds being sent over. At night Battalion relieved the 15th South Staffordshire Regiment in the ESSARS Right Sector.	See 00.122.

1/6th Battalion South Staffs. Regt.

Army Form C. 2118.

(16)
WAR DIARY
or
INTELLIGENCE SUMMARY.

(Erase heading not required.)

Instructions regarding War Diaries and Intelligence Summaries are contained in F.S. Regs., Part II. and the Staff Manual respectively. Title pages will be prepared in manuscript.

Place	Date	Hour	Summary of Events and Information	Remarks and references to Appendices
	Aug 6		2/Lieut" "Hussey" while out on patrol with his Sergeant in the evening was shot through the head and killed. His Sergeant tried to recover his body, but a party of seven Germans rushed out and secured it, and he was forced to come back. During the forenoon, the enemy had a shoot with 5.9" one the RIVERPOOR LINE, many direct hits were obtained.	
	7		A quiet day. The enemy retired to the left of this LAME CANAR and the 1/6th North Staffordshire Regiment was advanced their posts slightly on the night of the canal. LE CASAN was occupied.	
	8		6 prisoners of retirement were our from. The enemy was very active and alert opposite to us - patrols were out throughout the day and night, but there was no signs of his posts being vacated. Corporal Thomas of "A" Coy was wounded in attempting to enter any enemy post.	
	9		A quiet day. Patrols no contact with the enemy throughout the day. One Inter-Company relief took place at night 1st B+C Coys going in the front line.	

Army Form C. 2118.

WAR DIARY No 7.
INTELLIGENCE SUMMARY.
(Erase heading not required.)

North Staffordshire Regt.

Instructions regarding War Diaries and Intelligence Summaries are contained in F. S. Regs., Part II. and the Staff Manual respectively. Title pages will be prepared in manuscript.

Place	Date	Hour	Summary of Events and Information	Remarks and references to Appendices
ESCARS	10.8.18		A German aeroplane was driven down behind the Liverpool line in the early morning. He was however an Officer and N.C.O. sent like prisoner	
	11.8.18		In the early morning the enemy bombarded our trenches with Gas. About 10:10 Blue & Yellow X and trench Sou Shell being sent over. Casualties about 100 including 2 Officers. After a fairly quiet day the Bn who was relieved by the 10th Bn North Staff Regt, moved with Brigade Reserve the Divisional Staff Officers interested at the billowing Chaubier where every man had his clothing disinfected.	60/0125
	12.8.18		A quiet day.	
	13. 8.18		A quiet day.	
	14.8.18		A quiet day. In the evening the Bn was relieved by 1/5 Bn Sherwood Foresters moved into Divisional Reserve	

Army Form C. 2118.

WAR DIARY
or
INTELLIGENCE SUMMARY.

(Erase heading not required.)

1/6th Bn. 1/5th Staffs Regt.

Instructions regarding War Diaries and Intelligence Summaries are contained in F. S. Regs., Part II. and the Staff Manual respectively. Title pages will be prepared in manuscript.

Place	Date	Hour	Summary of Events and Information	Remarks and references to Appendices
	14.8.18		with HQ and 2 Coys in VERQUIN and 2 Coys in	See OO.
	(contd)		VAUDRICOURT WOOD	126.
VERQUIN	15.8.18		The day was spent in bathing and cleaning up.	
	16.8.18		Battalion training in vicinity of Billets. Lewis Gunners fired on Range.	
	17.8.18		Bn marched to the signal laying ground, the Divisional Demonstration Platoon gave a demonstration on the Range with Laser Bullets.	
	18.8.18		The Bn dug a line of "Retaken near GORRE" DOOR	
	19.8.18		Bn. training in vicinity of Billets. In the afternoon a tactical scheme for Officers was carried out.	
	20.8.18		The Bn relieved the 1/5th Bn Sherwood Foresters in the ESSARS left sector.	See OO. 127.
ESSARS.	21.8.18		The Bn advanced all Outposts about 300 yards. suffering a few casualties.	
	22.8.18		A quiet day. Our patrols were active.	

WAR DIARY
INTELLIGENCE SUMMARY

Army Form C. 2118.

with posts out in front keeping touch with the
enemy. At night the Bn. was relieved by the 5th Bn.
Worcestershire Regt. and moved into the bivouac
line at Bray.

Total casualties for month of August 1918.

	Officers	O/Ranks
Killed		8.
Died of wounds		1
Wounded	2	33
Wounded Gas	2	91
Missing	1	2

Charles Leup. Stoneb.
Commanding 1st Bn. Devonshire Regt.

3rd September 1918.

Secret. OPERATION ORDERS NO 121. Copy No
                1/6th Btn South Staffs Regiment.
                       Dated 1st August 1918.

Reference:- Veille Chapelle & Gorre Map Sheets.1/20,000.

1. The 1/6th Btn South Staffs Regt will relieve the 1/8th Btn
   Sherwood Foresters, in the ESSARS Support Sector on the night
   of 2/3rd August 1918.

2. Dispositions.
   "A" Company will relieve "C" Coy. 8th S.F. on Right (La Motte).
   "D"   "   "   "   "B" "   "   " in Centre (Newcastle Line).
   "B"   "   "   "   "D" "   "   " on Left.   -do-
   "C"   "   "   "   "A" "   "   " Forward. (Le Hamel).

3. ORDER OF MARCH.
   "C" "A" "B" "D" "HQ".
   First Platoon to leave North Lodge Gates at 8-30p.m.
   100 yards distance will be maintained.

4. ROUTE 4 will be used, thence to PONT TOURMENT Bridge which will
   be crossed between 9-30p.m. and 10p.m.

5. LEWIS GUNS and S.A.A. will be loaded at the Guard Room at 7p.m.
   and dumped at 'F.7.a.9.4.', where they will be picked up by
   Platoons as they pass.
   One man per gun will accompany the limbers.
   COOKING UTENSILS & OFFICERS MESS STUFF for the Line will be
   loaded at 7-0p.m. at the Guard Room.
   PACKS & OFFICERS VALISES will be loaded at the Guard Room at
   7-0p.m.

6. TAKING OVER. Companies will take over Special Maps, Aeroplane
   photos and existing schemes of Defence and work without
   alteration.
   Trench Store Lists will be forwarded to Btn Headquarters by
   2a.m. rumour.

7. STRAGGLER POSTS. 'B' Coy will relieve personnel of Sherwood
   Foresters on Straggler Posts at 7-30p.m. tomorrow.

8. Report 'Relief complete' by Code-word 'ARGYLE'.

9. Battalion Headquarters will be at 'X.25.a.65.40'.

10. Acknowledge.

                                       J.P.Wood
                                         Captain.
                   Adjutant 1/6th Btn South Staffs Regiment.

        Copies issued to:- No 1. Commanding Officer.
                           " 2. Headquarters.137th I.Brigade.
                           " 3. O/C.1/8th Sherwood Foresters.
                           " 4. " 1/5th Btn South Staffs Rgt.
                           " 5. " 1/6th Btn North Staffs Rgt.
                           " 6. " "A" Company.
                           " 7. " "B"   "
                           " 8. " "C"   "
                           " 9. " "D"   "
                           " 10. Transport Officer.
                           " 11. Quartermaster.
                           " 12. Regtl Sgt Major.
                           " 13. War Diary.
                           " 14. "   " (Duplicate).
                           " 15. File.
                           " 16. "   (Duplicate).

SECRET.   1/6th South Staffs Regt.   Copy No. 12.

Operation Orders. No. 122.   Aug. 4th 1918.

Ref. Map. 1/20,000. Loos & Neuve Chapelle.

1. The 1/6th Bn. S. Staffs Regt. will relieve 1/5 Bn. S. Staffs Regt. in the line, Right Sub-section, ESSARS Sector on the night 5/6th August.

2. Companies will be disposed as follows.
   A Coy 1/6 S.S.R. will relieve A Coy 1/5 S.S.R. on Right.
   D "   "   "   "   "   "   B "   "   "   "   Left.
   C "   "   "   "   "   "   D "   "   "   "   Rt. Support
   B "   "   "   "   "   "   C "   "   "   "   Left Support.

3. Companies will move off as soon as light permits.

4. <u>Guides</u>. One guide per platoon will report at each C.H.Q. at dusk.

5. Companies will take over special maps, aeroplane photos, and details of work.

6. Lists of Trench Stores to be handed over will be forwarded to Orderly Room by 2 a.m. inst., and stores taken over as soon as possible after relief.

7. Cooking utensils will be moved under Battn. arrangements. Mess stores under Coy arrangements.

8. Relief complete will be issued by Code Word. SUTHERLAND

9. B.H.Q. will be at X.20.d.80.40.

10. Acknowledge.

J.P. Wood
Capt.
Adjutant. 1/6th South Staffs. Regt.

<u>Distribution</u>:-
1. Commanding Officer.
2. 137th Infantry Bde.
3-6. O.C. Companies
7. Q.M.
8. O/C. 1/5. S.S.R.
9. R.S.M.
10. File
11+12. War Diary

SECRET.   1/6 South Staffordshire Regt.   Copy No. 1.
          Operation Order No 125.   10th Aug 1918.

1. The Battn: will be relieved in the line by the 1/6 North Staffs Regt on the night 11th/12th August.

2. 'B' Coy 1/6 N.S.R. will relieve 'C' 1/6 S.S. Regt in the line right.
   'C'   "   "   "   "   'B'   "   "   "   "   left.
   'D'   "   "   "   "   'A'   "   "   "   right support.
   'A'   "   "   "   "   'D'   "   "   "   left support.

3. On completion of relief the Battn will move into Bde support in ESSARS.
   'C' Coy 1/6 S.S.R. will relieve B Coy 1/6 N.S.R in LE HAMEL.
   'A'   "   "   "   "   D   "   "   " LA MOTTE.
   'D'   "   "   "   "   C   "   "   " Centre.
   'B'   "   "   "   "   A   "   "   " on the left.

4. 1 guide per platoon and 1 per Coy H.Q. will report to Battn H.Q. at dawn 11th inst.

5. Trench stores, aeroplane photos, maps and schemes of work in hand will be handed over.

6. Mess stores will be carried out by Companies. Cooking utensils will be moved under Battn: arrangements.

7. B Coy will detail 2 NCO's and 6 men for Bridge guards, the relief to be complete by 6 p.m.

8. 1st Relief complete will be wired by Code word "Bus received". 2nd relief complete by runner.

9. Battn H.Q will be at X 25 a 65.40. on completion of relief.

10. ACKNOWLEDGE.

Issued by runner.
Copy No 1. Commanding Officer.
        2. H.Q. 137 Inf Bde.
        3-6 O's C Companies
        7. QM & TO
        8. OC 1/6 North Staffs
        9. OC 1/6 South Staffs.
        10-11. War Diary
        12. File.

                              Capt & Adjt.
                              1/6 South Staffs Regt

SECRET. 1/6 South Staffordshire Regt. Copy No. 10.
                    Operation Order No. 126.
M/S. VIEILLE CHAPELLE & GORRE /20,000.   13th Aug 1918.

1. The Battn. will be relieved in the ESSARS support sector on the night 14th/15th Aug 1918, by the 1/5 Sherwood Foresters.

2. DISPOSITIONS.
'C' Coy 1/5 S.F. will relieve 'A' Coy 1/6 S.S.R. at LA MOTTE.
 A   "   "   "   "   " D "   "   "   in the CENTRE.
 B   "   "   "   "   " B "   "   "   on the LEFT.
 D   "   "   "   "   " C "   "   "   in LE HAMEL.

3. On completion of relief the Battn. will move into Divisional Reserve. H.Q., B and D Coys will proceed to billets in VERQUIN and A and C Coys to huts in VAUDRICOURT WOOD taking over billets from 1/5 Lincolnshire Regt.

4. ROUTE:- PONT TOURNANT — ROUTE 4.

5. Schemes of defence and work, maps & aeroplane photos will be handed over. French stores lists will be forwarded to Orderly Room by the 2 a.m. runner on the 14th inst.

6. Lewis Guns will be dumped at F.7.b.15.85 (where broad gauge railway crosses road) where they will be picked up by limber. 1 man per gun will accompany the limber.

7. Cooking utensils will be dumped at ESSARS ration dump under Battn. arrangements. Mess stores will be dumped at ESSARS dump at 9 p.m. under Coy arrangements. 1 man per Coy will go down on the train with the mess utensils.

8. Completion of relief will be sent by code word "B.O. received". Arrival in billets to be notified by runner.

9. ACKNOWLEDGE.

                                    J.R. Wood.
                                    Capt. & Adjt.
                                  1/6 South Staffs Regt.

Issued by runner:-
Copy No. 1. Officer Commanding.
       2. H.Q. 137 Inf Bde.
       3-6. O's C Coys.
       7. Quartermaster.
       8. Transport Officer.
       9. O.C. 1/5 Sherwood Foresters.
       10-11. War Diary.
       12. File.

SECRET.
OPERATION ORDERS No 124.
1/6th Btn South Staffs Regiment.
Dated 20th August 1918.

Copy No.

Reference:- Map Sheets. LOCON 1/20,000. BETHUNE COMBINED 1/40,000.

1. The Battalion will relieve the 1/5th Btn Sherwood Foresters in the ESSARS Left Sector, tonight the 20/21st August 1918.

2. Dispositions after Relief will be:-
   'C' Company. 1/6th S.S.R. relieve 'A' Coy. S. Foresters on the Right.
   'B'   "   "   "   "   'B' "   "   "   " Left.
   'A'   "   "   "   "   'D' "   "   "   in Support.
   'D'   "   "   "   "   'C' "   "   "   Reserve.
   One Platoon of 'D' Coy will report to O/C 'C' Coy, prior to proceeding to line, for duty with 'C' Company.

3. Order of March:- 'B' 'C' 'A' 'D' 'HQ'.
   Route 4 will be used to PONT TOURNANT. First Platoon will not cross the Bridge before 8-30p.m.
   Companies will pass E.29.c.00.60., commencing with 'B' Company at 7-30p.m.
   200 yards interval will be maintained between Platoons.

4. Guides will meet Companies (5 per Company) at X.30.c.20.30.

5. Trench Maps, Schemes of Defence, Work, etc, will be taken over from the relieved Battalion. All work taken over will be proceeded with without delay.

6. Lewis Guns (Company) will be loaded at the Transport Lines at 6-0p.m. and will be dumped at F.7.b.10.70. where they will be picked up by Platoons as they pass. One man per gun will proceed with the Limbers.
   Headquarter Lewis Guns will be loaded at the Quartermaster's Stores at 6-30p.m. One man per gun to report with the Guns.

7. COOKING UTENSILS and OFFICERS' MESS STUFF for the trenches will be loaded at 6-30p.m. at the Quartermaster's Stores. Two men per Company to go with same.
   Packs will be collected at 4-0p.m. and Officers' Valises at 5-00p.m.

8. Report 'RELIEF COMPLETE' by Code-word 'KILMARNOCK'.

9. ACKNOWLEDGE.

                                           W E Beard   2/Lieutenant.
                                       A/Adjutant 1/6th Btn South Staffordshire Regt.

Copies issued to:-   No 1. Commanding Officer,
                       " 2. Headquarters. 137th I. Brigade.
                       " 3. O/C. 1/5th Btn Sherwood Foresters.
                       " 4. " 1/5th Btn South Staffs Regt.
                       " 5. " 1/6th Btn North Staffs Regt.
                       " 6. " 'A' Company.
                       " 7. " 'B'   "
                       " 8. " 'C'   "
                       " 9. " 'D'   "
                       " 10. Quartermaster.
                       " 11. Transport Officer.
                       " 12. Regtl Sgt Major.
                       " 13. War Diary.
                       " 14. "   "   (Duplicate).
                       " 15. File.
                       " 16. "   (Duplicate).

           oOo------------------------------------oOo

SECRET   1/6th Bn. South Staffs Regt.   Copy No 11.
Ref: Locan 1/10.000.   Operation Order No 128   25th Aug 1918

1. The Battn will be relieved in the line by 1/6th North Staffs Regt on the night of 26th/27th August 1918 and upon completion of relief will go into Brigade support in the ESSARS sub-sector.

2. DISPOSITIONS

'D' Coy 1/6 SSR will be relieved by 'B' Coy 1/6th N.S.R in the line RIGHT
'A' Coy   "   "   "   'C' Coy   "   LEFT
'B' Coy   "   "   "   'D' Coy   "   SUPPORT
'C' Coy   "   "   "   'A' Coy   "   RESERVE

Dispositions of Companies after relief will be as follows.

'A' Coy 1/6 SSR   LA MOTTE   Coy. H.Q. at X.26.C.75-60
'B'   "   (RIGHT) LIVERPOOL LINE   "   "   "   X.27.a.80.80.
'C'   "   (LEFT)   "   "   "   "   "   X.20.b.30.60.
'D'   "   NEWCASTLE LINE   "   "   "   X.25.b.05.80.

Battn H.Q. will be at X.25.a.65-40.
Regt. Aid Post   "   "   X.25.C.95-85.

3. GUIDES

2 Guides per platoon and 1 per Coy H.Q. for each of A & D Coys will report at B.H.Q. at 5 a.m. 26th inst. 1 Guide per platoon & 1 per Coy H.Q. for each of B & C Coy will report at the relieving Coy H.Q. at 6 p.m. 26th inst.

4. Cooking utensils will be moved under Battn. arrangements, Mess Stores &c will be moved under Coy. arrangements.

5. Schemes of defence and work in progress, maps, aeroplane photos and trench stores will be handed over.

6. List of trench stores to be handed over to reach Battn. H.Q. by 2 p.m. 26th inst.

7. Completion of relief to be notified by CODE WORD "TEA UP" and arrival in new dispositions by runner.

8. ACKNOWLEDGE.

                     W S Braund 2/Lt.
Issued by runner   A/Adjt 1/6th South Staffs Regt.
Copy No 1   to   Commanding Officer
     2   H.Q. 137 Inf. Bde.
     3-6   O.C. Companies
     7   Q.M.
     8   O.C. 1/6 North Staffs Regt.
     9 & 10   File
     11 & 12   War Diary

1/6th BTN SOUTH STAFFORDSHIRE REGT.

Army Form C. 2118.

(183).

WAR DIARY
or
INTELLIGENCE SUMMARY.
(Erase heading not required.)

Instructions regarding War Diaries and Intelligence Summaries are contained in F.S. Regs., Part II. and the Staff Manual respectively. Title pages will be prepared in manuscript.

Place	Date	Hour	Summary of Events and Information	Remarks and references to Appendices
ESSARS.	1-9-1918.		Quiet day. In the afternoon the Battalion vacated the NEWCASTLE LINE and marched to Reserve Billets in VAUDRICOURT WOOD.	See O.O. No R.M.
VAUDRICOURT WOOD.	2-9-1918.		Day was spent in Cleaning up and Bathing etc.	
"	3-9-1918.		Battalion Training in vicinity of Camp.	
"	4-9-1918.		-ditto-	
"	5-9-1918.		-ditto- The Battalion marched to ALLOUAGNE and billeted there.	See O.O. No
ALLOUAGNE.	6-9-1918.		Battalion Training. The Btn paraded for a Medal Presentation by the "Corps Commander."	
"	7-9-1918.		-ditto-	
"	8-9-1918.		-ditto-	
"	9-9-1918.		The Btn paraded and formed an Escort at the funeral of the late Brigadier General EAST, CMG, DSO.	
"	9-9-1918.		Battalion Training.	
"	10-9-1918.		-ditto-	
"	11-9-1918.		-ditto-	
"	12-9-1918.		The Battalion entrained at LILLERS STATION.	See O.O No 132.
NEILLY.	13-9-1918.		The Battalion detrained at NEILLY and occupied billets there.	
"	14-9-1918.		Battalion Training.	
"	15-9-1918.		The Btn paraded for Divine Service. Officers Compass Scheme.	
"	16-9-1918.		The Btn paraded for a Route March and Attack Scheme.	

1/6th BTN SOUTH STAFFORDSHIRE RGT.

(184).

WAR DIARY
INTELLIGENCE SUMMARY.
(Erase heading not required.)

Army Form C. 2118.

Instructions regarding War Diaries and Intelligence Summaries are contained in F. S. Regs., Part II. and the Staff Manual respectively. Title pages will be prepared in manuscript.

Place	Date	Hour	Summary of Events and Information	Remarks and references to Appendices
HEILLY.	17-9-1918.		Battalion Training.	
"	18-9-1918.		Brigade Tactical Scheme.	See O.O. No 133.
"	19-9-1918.		The Battalion embussed at 4-0p.m. and proceeded to VRAIGNES and TERTRY.	
VRAIGNES.	20-9-1918.		Battalion Training.	
"	21-9-1918.		The Battalion moved into Reserve Brigade Area, (LEVERGUIER).	See O.O. No 134
LEVERGUIER	22-9-1918.		Quiet day.	
"	23-9-1918.		The Battalion relieved the 1/5th Btn Leicestershire Regt in SUPPORT.	See O.O. No 135
"	24-9-1918.		The 138th Infantry Brigade attacked the Village of PONTRUET and gained a footing in it.	
"	25-9-1918.		The enemy put down a Barrage on our Line inflicting some Casualties. In the evening the Btn moved back into Brigade Support in LE VERGUIER.	
JEANCOURT.	25-9-1918.		In Brigade Support.	
JEANCOURT.	26-9-1918.		" "	See OO. No 136.
"	27-9-1918.		The Battalion relieved the 1/5th Btn Leicestershire Regt in the Line.	
"	28-9-1918.		The Btn moved in the evening into ASSEMBLY POSITIONS prior to an Attack on the ST QUENTIN CANAL and BELLENGLISE.	
"	29-9-1918.		At 5-50a.m. under a Heavy Artillery and Machine Gun Barrage the Battalion as part of the 137th Infantry Brigade crossed the ST QUENTIN CANAL and captured the HINDENBURG LINE and the Village of BELLENGLISE.	See O.O No 137.
BELLENGLISE	30-9-1918.		The day was spent in consolidating our new positions.	

Army Form C. 2118.

WAR DIARY
or
INTELLIGENCE SUMMARY.

(185).

1/6th BTN SOUTH STAFFORDSHIRE REGT.

(Erase heading not required)

Instructions regarding War Diaries and Intelligence Summaries are contained in F. S. Regs., Part II. and the Staff Manual respectively. Title pages will be prepared in manuscript.

Place	Date	Hour	Summary of Events and Information	Remarks and references to Appendices
			TOTAL CASUALTIES FOR THE MONTH OF SEPTEMBER 1918.	
			OFFICERS.	
			KILLED. WOUNDED. DIED OF WOUNDS. MISSING. TOTAL.	
			2/Lieut:E.RILEY. Captain G.L.B.Evans. Major E.Lewis. --------- TWELVE.	
			2/Lieut:S.L.Banks.	
			" C.W.Briand.	
			" R.Smith.	
			" P.W.Burgess.MC.MM.	
			" J.H.Robinson.	
			Major. J.M.Frew.MC.	
			" E.Lewis.	
			2/Lieut:H.W.Wootton.	
			" H.Watts.DCM.	
			Captain.A.P.Buswell.	
			O'RANKS.	
			KILLED. WOUNDED. DIED OF WOUNDS. MISSING. TOTAL.	
			23 175 3 12 213	
	6-10-1918.		*Charles* Lieut:Colonel, Commanding 1/6th Btn South Staffordshire Regiment............	

SECRET

REF MAP.
GORRE 1/20.000

1/6th South Staffs Regt.
Operation Order No 131

Copy No.
1st Sept 1918.

1. The Battn. will march to reserve billets in VAUDRICOURT WOOD this evening and take over from 1/5th Leicester Regt.

2. Companies will march by platoons. 200 yards interval between platoons.
1st Platoon of A Coy will pass Shrine (F.1.b.60-10) at 7-5 pm.
Headquarters will pass ESSARS CHURCH at 7 pm.
1st Platoon of
    D Coy   "   "   "   " 7-5 pm
    C Coy.   "   "   "   " 7-10 "
    B Coy   "   "   "   " 7-20 "

3. ROUTE:- PONT TOURNANT - Track No.4.

4. All Lewis Guns and ammunition for B C & D Coys will be stacked at B.H.Q at 6-45 pm. and those of A Coy at shrine at same time.
Cooking utensils will be stacked at B.H.Q. at 5 pm. those of A Coy at Shrine at same time.
Mess stores to be at B.H.Q. by 6-45 pm. A Coy's at shrine by same time.

5. ACKNOWLEDGE

Issued by Runner.

J. Wood
Capt.
Adjt. 1/6th South Staffs Regt.

Copies to:-
    No 1.   Commdg. Officer.
    2   H.Q. 137 Inf. Bde.
    3/6.   O.C. Coys
    7   Q.M.
    8   T.O
    9   R.S.M.
    10   Signals
    11.   File
    12+13.   War diary.

SECRET.   OPERATION ORDER NO. 132   Copy No. 13
          1/6th Bn. South Staffordshire Regiment.
Ref. Map FRANCE 36B 1/40,000.   Dated 10th Sept.1916.

1. The Battalion will move tomorrow 11th inst. to another area, entraining at LILLERS station.

2. The Battalion less "B" Company will parade at 10.30.p.m. Head of column at D.2.a.50/20. facing S.W.

3. Order of March:- Drums, Headquarters, "A"."C" & "D" Coys. 100 yards interval will be maintained between Coys.

4. Dress:- Field Service Marching Order.

5. "B" Company will parade at same place at 4.30.a.m. 12th inst.

6. All Transport less "B" Coy's cooker & team and O.C.Coys horse will be at LILLERS Station at 10.40.p.m. Watercarts will travel filled

7. "B" Coy's cooker and team and O.C.Coys horse will be at LILLERS Station at 4.40.a.m. 12th inst.

   Rations for the 12th inst will be carried on the man.

9. Lieut.Walker M.C. & 1 N.C.O. per Coy will report at Orderly Room at 8.30.p.m. 11th to proceed to LILLERS station to assist R.T.O. in entraining.
   Capt P.H.Highfield Jones M.C. & 1 N.C.O. per Coy & 1 N.C.O. to represent Q.M. & T.O. will report to Orderly Room at 4.30.p.m. 11th inst proceed in advance as billeting party.

10. Entraining States will be in Orderly Room by 4.0.p.m. 11th inst.

11. ACKNOWLEDGE.

                                                J.K.Wood
                                                Capt & Adj
                    1/6th Bn. South Staffs.Regt.
Issued by Runner at 9.30.p.m.
   Copy to:-
     No 1. Commanding Officer.
         2. H.Q. 137th Inf. Bde.
       3-6. O'sC. Companies.
         7. Quartermaster.
         8. Transport Officer.
         9. Medical Officer.
        10. R.S.M.
        11. File.
        12. "
        13. War Diary.
        14. "   ".

SECRET.

OPERATION ORDER No 134.   Copy No.
1/6th Bn South Staffordshire Regiment.
Dated 30th September 1918.

1. The Battalion will move into Reserve Brigade Area tomorrow,
and occupy Trenches in B.4.

The Battalion will parade in Field Sortie Marching Order,
Battalion Parade Ground at 8-0a.m. tomorrow, and move
off Platoons at 100 yards interval, via FOUILLY - ELMGHIN-
VENDHUILE.

Order of march :- Headquarters, 'A', 'B', 'C', 'D', Coys.

Arrival at Destination will be reported to Bn Headquarters
by runner.

J.W.Lord
Captain.
Adjutant 1/6th Bn South Staffs Regiment.

SECRET.   Copy No 1.
                  Operation Order No 135.
              1/6 South Staffordshire Regt.
Ref MASSEMY SHEET 1/20000   23.9.18.
1. The Battn will relieve the 1/5th Bn
   Leicestershire Regt in Support to night.
2. Dispositions after relief will be
   right to left A, B, C, D Coys. HQ &
   RAP will remain in present positions.
3. 1 guide per Coy will meet Coys at
   road junction L.34 b 60.99. at following
   times A Coy 10 pm. B Coy 10.5 pm. C Coy
   10.10 pm. D Coy 10.15 pm. One guide per
   platoon will meet platoons at Coy HQ.
4. Rations & water for 24th inst will be
   carried on the man.
5. Dress Fighting Order plus great coats
   1 NCO & 2 men per platoon will be left
   on present line to look after packs &c
6. Relief complete will be reported to
   Bn HQ by runner.
7. ACKNOWLEDGE.
                                J.P. Wood
                                Capt & Adjt
                              1/6 South Staffs Regt.
Copies to No 1 Commanding Officer.
          2   HQ 137 Inf Bde
       3-6. O.C. Companies.
          7. File
       8 & 9. War Diary.

SECRET   OPERATION ORDER No 136   Copy No /.

1/6th. South Staffordshire Regt.

MAPS REF. 62c N.E. MAISEMY.   27th Sept. 1918.

1. The Battn. will relieve the 1/5th. Lincolnshire Regt. in the line to-night:- 27th/28th inst.

2. The Battn. will move by platoons at 100 yards interval, in the following order, A. B. C. D Coys. Companies will move at 15 minutes interval. 1st platoon will leave at 8 PM
Dress as laid down at conference.
Route:- At Company Commanders discretion.

3. <u>Guides</u>:- 1 guide per platoon will be met at L.35.d.00.90.

4. A. Coy. 1/6. S.S.R. will relieve 'C' Coy. 1/5 Lincs. and a portion of 'D' Coy. 1/5 Lincs. in the front line.
B. Coy. 1/6. S.S.R. will relieve 'A' Coy. 1/5th Lincs. in Support.
C " " " " " " 'B' " " " " "
D " " " " " occupy DRAGOON POST vicinity.
Reconnaissance of Areas will be carried out by 1 Officer per Coy. during the day.

5. BN. HD. QRS. will be at ~~HOOK POST~~ HUDSON POST R.6.a.7.5. ~~G.31.d.~~

6. Regt. Aid Post will be at M.26.90.90.

7. ACKNOWLEDGE.

J H Wood
Capt. & Adjt.
1/6th. South Staffordshire Regt.

Issued by runner.
Copies to:- No 1. Commanding Officer.
    2. H.Q. 137 Infy. Bde.
    3-6 O.C. Companies
    7. O.C. 1/5th. Lincolns Regt.
    8. Transport Officer.
    9. R.S.M.
    10. File
    11 & 12. War Diary.

SECRET.   OPERATION ORDERS No 137.   Copy No. 9
                    1/6th Btn South Staffordshire Regt.
                                        Dated 27th September 1918
Reference:- Map Sheet 1/10,000. BELLICOURT WEST.

1. At an hour and date to be notified later the Battalion
   will as part of the 137th Infantry Brigade, advance
   under a barrage, cross the ST QUENTIN CANAL between
   G.34.b.6.0.and G.34.b.90.75., capture the HINDENBURG
   LINE (BLUE LINE) and the BROWN LINE (shown on maps issued
   to O/C. Companies.

2. No troops are attacking on the Right flank of the Btn;
   the 1/5th Btn South Staffs Regt are attacking on the
   Left flank and the 1/6th Btn North Staffs Regt on the
   Left of the 1/5th Btn South Staffs Regt.
   The 1st Division will form a defensive flank in G.34.c.

3. The Battalion will be formed up in depth of four Coys
   each company with four platoons in two lines at 30 yards
   distance.
   Distance between front lines of Companies 100 yards.
   Order of forming up:-   'A' 'B' 'C' 'D'.

4. The frontage of the Battalion Attack will be:-
   (a) Forming up lines to be notified later.
   (b) ST QUENTIN CANAL G.34.b.6.0. to G.34.b.90.75.
   (c) BLUE LINE.   G.34.d.6.5. to G.35.a.55.55.
   (d) BROWN LINE.   M.5.a.00.95.to G.35.b.60.35.

5. When the BROWN LINE is established the 139th Infantry
   Brigade will pass through the Battalion and continue
   the attack. The 32nd Division will in turn pass
   through them.

6. After the troops continuing the attack have passed
   through the Battalion will organize the defences of the
   bridge-heads gained.

7. Battalion Headquarters will be in the HINDENBURG
   Outpost Line at a place to be notified later.
8. Detailed instructions will be issued later.
9. ACKNOWLEDGE.
                                        J F Woods
                                           Captain.
                    Adjutant 1/6th Btn South Staffs Regt..
        Copies issued to:- No 1 Commanding Officer.
                           " 2. Headquarters.137th I.Bde.
                           " 3. O/C 1/5th South Staffs Regt.
                           " 4. "   1/6th North Staffs Regt.
                           " 5/8.O/C Companies.
                           " 9. War Diary.
                           " 10. "   " (Duplicate).
                           " 11. File.
                           " 12. " (Duplicate).

Army Form C. 2118.

WAR DIARY
INTELLIGENCE-SUMMARY.
(Erase heading not required.)

1/6th Bn. South Staffordshire Regiment.
OCTOBER 1st. to OCTOBER 31st 1918.

Place	Date	Hour	Summary of Events and Information	Remarks and references to Appendices
	Oct 1st.		The Battalion spent the day in trenches round BELLENGLISE. Capt A.P. Buswell was wounded.	
	" 2nd.		The Battalion received orders at 10.P.M. to be in position for an attack by 05.00 the next day. The Battalion moved off from BELLENGLISE AT 02.00 (3rd inst)	
	" 3rd.		The Battalion was in position by 05.00. Zero hour was 06.05. The attalion was on the right of the attack, the 32nd Division taking SEQUEHART on our right flank. 'C' and 'D' Companies were in the first wave, 'A' and 'B' Companies in the second wave. The battalion met with very strong opposition from the enemy, his machine gunners being especially troublesome. After some very hard fighting during which many of the enemy were killed and many captured, the attalion reached its objective by about 08.00. Outposts were pushed forward on to MANNEQUIN HILL but later had to be withdrawn owing to the intense enfilade machine gun fire. Unsuccessful counter-attacks on both flanks were made by the enemy. Shelling and machine gun fire was severe throughout the day. 2/Lt C.P.H.Sylvester and 2/Lt G.Evans were killed and 2/Lt S.Walters severely wounded. Capt P.H.Teeton and Capt N Dickson were also wounded.	
	" 4th.		Enemy shelling and machine gun fire was rather severe throughout the day. There was no change in the situation. At night the Battalion was relieved by the 1st Gloucestershire Regt. (1st Div) and went back to billets in MAGNY LA FOSSE.	
	" 5th.		The Battalion moved back to near ASCENSION FARM. Bivouacs were erected and quarters made as comfortable as possible.	
	" 6th.		Company training was carried out and hastily improvised baths were used.	
	" 7th.		Further company training was carried out.	
	" 8th.		The attali-n moved to the old front line before Spt. 29th and rested there the night.	
	" 9th.		At 05.00 the attalion took the road for LEVERGIES and reached there by about 07.00. On arrival the news came through that the enemy had retired from FRESNOY LE GRAND. At night the Battalion moved to and occupied the sunken road on MANNEQUIN HILL.	
	" 10th.		In the morning the Battal on moved on to FRESNOY LE GRAND AND WERE BILLETED in the village for the night.	
	" 11th.		The Battalion moved off very early along the main road to BOHAIN and relieved the 1/4th Bn. Leicester Regt in support in front of RIQUEVAL WOOD.	

Army Form C. 2118.

WAR DIARY
or
INTELLIGENCE SUMMARY.
(Erase heading not required.)

Instructions regarding War Diaries and Intelligence Summaries are contained in F. S. Regs., Part II. and the Staff Manual respectively. Title pages will be prepared in manuscript.

Place	Date	Hour	Summary of Events and Information	Remarks and references to Appendices
	Oct 12th.		At 12.00 the 1/5th South Staffordshire Regt who were holding the front line made an attack on RIQUEVAL WOOD with this Battalion in Support. On the right the 1/5th South Staffs Regt supported by our 'B' Company made good progress into the wood. They were forced to retire owing to an extremely heavy barrage of all calibre shells and heavy trench mortars.	
	" 13th.		A fairly quiet day, the enemy showed little activity.	
	" 14th.		The Battalion relieved the 1/5th Bn. South Staffs Regt in the line.	
	" 15th.		The battalion was relieved at night by the 1/6th Bn. North Staffs. Regt. and moved into billets in BOHAIN.	
	" 16th.		Companies under Company Commanders during the morning - in the afternoon companies bathed at FRESNOY LE GRAND.	
	" 17th.		Before Zero hour the Battalion moved into position in rear of the BOHAIN - FRESNOY railway. The Battalion was in Divisional Reserve. The attack was successful and the Battalion was able to return to BOHAIN by mid-day. There was slight shelling of BOHAIN By an H.V. gun during the morning.	
	" 18th.		The Battalion moved off at 11.00. to relieve the 1/4th Bn. Leicester Regt. in the front line in front of ANDIGNY LES FERMES. The Battalion started retiring at mid-day so the battalion remained 'liasing' with the 1st Division on the left and with the French on the right. 1 other rank was the only casualty. The Battalion was BOHAIN and FRESNOY were slightly shelled with H.V. gun during the morning. The Battalion was relieved and returned to billets at 00.30 in BOHAIN.	
	" 19th.			
	" 20th.		There was a Church Parade for 200 men from each battalion in the Division at FRESNOY LE GRAND in the morning. The remainder of the Battalion attended Church Parade with our own Chaplains. Bathing was continued at FRESNOY.	
	" 21st.		Training was carried out during the morning.	
	" 22nd.		Company trainings under Company Commanders and musketry on the range.	
	" 23rd.		Training in the morning and recreation in the afternoon.	
	" 24th.		At mid-day the Battalion moved to MONTBREHAIN and was billeted there.	
	" 25th.		Companies under Company Commanders for training during the day.	
	" 26th.		200 men from each battalion in the Division attended a parade for presentation of medals awarded by the French Government and presented by a French General.	
	" 27th.		Training was continued for the next four days.	
	" 30th.		Bathing for the whole of the Battalion.	
	" 31st.		The Battalion moved to BOHAIN and was billeted there.	

10..11..18.

Major.
Commanding 1/6th Bn. South Staffordshire Regt.

WAR DIARY or INTELLIGENCE SUMMARY

Army Form C. 2118.

Place	Date	Hour	Summary of Events and Information	Remarks and references to Appendices
BOHAIN.	Nov 1st.		**1/6th Bn. South Staffordshire Regiment.** **NOVEMBER 1st 1918 to NOVEMBER 30th. 1918.** Training was carried out in BOHAIN.	
	2nd.		The Battalion paraded at 11.00 and carried out a practice attack	
	3rd.		In the evening the Battalion moved to VAUX ANDIGNY and took over billets occupied by the 1st Division (1st. N.Hants)	
	4th.		The Battalion moved off from billets at 05.40 and proceeded to ST MARTIN RIVIERE. The day was spent at ST. MARTIN. In the evening orders were received to move to LA LOUVIERE, arriving there at 21.30.	
	5th.		The Battalion left LA LOUVIERE at 05.45 and moved to BOIS DE L'ABBAYE. From there the Unit moved at mid-day to LE SART where billets were occupied for the night. On entering LE SART the Battalion was shelled and 'C' Company suffered four casualties.(1 killed and 3 wounded) There was slight shelling during the night.	
	6th.		At 07.30 this Battalion on the left and the 1/6th North Staffs Regt on the right advanced with very little opposition. By 10.00 PRECHES was occupied and our final objective, CARTIGNIES, was reached by mid-day. Practically no opposition was met with on our front. Civilians who were repatriated by our advance gave the troops a great welcome. There was only one casualty throughout the day. Machine gun fire was met with on the outskirts of CARTIGNIES. Two companies were billeted in CARTIGNIES in reserve and two companies held the front line. There was slight shelling of CARTIGNIES during the night.	
	7th.		At 07.30 the 1/5th Leicestershire Regt(138th Inf.Bde) went through the two companies in the front line and advanced towards AVESNES. The Battalion remained in billets in CARTIGNIES and the day was spent in cleaning up. There was slight shelling of the outskirts of CARTIGNIES during the night.	
	8th.		The Battalion remained in CARTIGNIES and carried on with general cleaning up and refitting.	

Army Form C. 2118.

WAR DIARY
or
INTELLIGENCE SUMMARY.
(Erase heading not required.)

(185)

Instructions regarding War Diaries and Intelligence Summaries are contained in F. S. Regs., Part II. and the Staff Manual respectively. Title pages will be prepared in manuscript.

1/5th Staffs

Vol 46

Q46

Place	Date	Hour	Summary of Events and Information	Remarks and references to Appendices
	Nov. 9th.		The Battalion left CARTIGNIES at 08.00 to relieve the 1/4th Leicester Regt. On the way to the front line these orders were cancelled and the 137th Inf. Bde. proceeded to ZOREES (SOUTH EAST of AVESNES) The enemy was reported to be in full retreat. In the afternoon the 138th Inf. Bde. pushed through this Brigade to gain touch with the enemy.	
	" 10th.		The Battalion remained in billets in ZOREES for the night. Before Church Parade in the morning Brigadier General J.V. Campbell V.C., C.M.G., D.S.O. spoke to the Battalion and told us he was leaving the Brigade to take command of a Brigade of Guards. Everybody was exceedingly sorry to lose a General who was so much liked, admired and respected. In the afternoon the Major General presented Military Medals gained by the men of the Brigade on the 29th September, 3rd of October and 10th October.	
	" 11th.		Early in the morning the news was received that the Armistice conditions had been accepted and signed by the Germans.	
	" 12th.		The Battalion carried on training and sports.	
	" 13th.		The Battalion moved at mid-day to AVESNES and was billeted there for the night.	
	" 14th.		The Battalion moved off at 07.40 - practically the whole Division was on the line of march. The Battalion arrived at PREUX AU BOIS after a march of 24 kilometres, at 15.00 and was billeted there.	
PREUX AU BOIS. Nov. 15th.			Companies were under Company Commanders for physical training and interior economy.	
"	16th.		Companies were at the disposal of Company Commanders for general military training.	
"	17th.		In the morning there was a Divisional Parade Service. Lieutenant.Colonel J.E. Blackwall D.S.O., T.D. took over the Command of the Battalion.	
"	18th.		Companies were at the disposal of Company Commanders for physical training and kit inspection.	

Army Form C. 2118.

WAR DIARY
or
INTELLIGENCE-SUMMARY.
(Erase heading not required)

(185)

Instructions regarding War Diaries and Intelligence Summaries are contained in F. S. Regs., Part II. and the Staff Manual respectively. Title pages will be prepared in manuscript.

Place	Date	Hour	Summary of Events and Information	Remarks and references to Appendices
PREUX AU BOIS.	Nov. 19th.		The Battalion commenced salvage work in the vicinity of the Forest of MORMAL. Three companies per day were engaged in salvage work and one company continued training.	
"	20th.		Salvage work was continued and an Educational Scheme was started. A lecture on 'DEMOBILISATION & RECONSTRUCTION' was delivered by Capt. A.P. Whitehead, M.C.	
"	21st.		In the morning salvage was continued and inter-company football matches were played in the afternoon.	
"	22nd & 23rd.		Salvage work and training was continued.	
"	24th.		The Battalion attended Church Parade.	
"	25th.		The Major General inspected the Transport and billets.	
"	26th.		One company used the Rifle Range for Musketry and the other three companies continued salvage work.	
"	27th.		The Commanding Officer inpsected "B" Company and the other companies continued salvage work.	
"	28th.		Training and salvage work was continued. Lectures were also continued in connection with the Educational Scheme.	
"	29th.		In the morning training and salvage; in the afternoon bathing and football was continued.	
"	30th.		The Commanding Officer inspected "C" Company. Three companies were engaged in salvage work.	

4.。12..18.

J.R.Whitehall

Lieut. Colonel.

Commanding 1/6th Bn. South Staffordshire Regiment..Q

Army Form C. 2118.

WAR DIARY
or
INTELLIGENCE SUMMARY.
(Erase heading not required.)

1/6th The South Staffordshire Regiment.

Summary of Events and Information

1st DECEMBER 1918 TO 31st DECEMBER 1918.

Place	Date	Hour	Summary of Events and Information	Remarks
PREUX AU BOIS.	Dec. 1st.		The Battalion attended Divine Service in the morning and afterwards marched to LANDRECIES to see His Majesty the King pass through the town.	
	2nd		The Battalion continued salvage work in the morning and recreation in the afternoon.	
	3rd		At 12.15 His Majesty the King passed through the outskirts of PREUX AU BOIS. The Battalion lined the roads and His Majesty alighted from his car and spoke to the troops. Great enthusiasm was displayed by the troops and they were much cheered. The usual routine work was carried out. Educational and vocational training was also continued.	
	4th 6 a.m.		The Battalion marched to BUSIGNY arriving in billets at 04.30.	
BUSIGNY.	9th-10th		After a nights rest at BUSIGNY the Battalion marched to FRESNOY- LE-GRAND. arriving at FRESNOY about 13.00.	
	11th 4:00 6 16 a.		The billets at FRESNOY were found in bad condition and the following	

Army Form C. 2118.

WAR DIARY
or
INTELLIGENCE SUMMARY.
(Erase heading not required.)

Place	Date	Hour	Summary of Events and Information	Remarks and references to Appendices
FRESNOY LE GRAND	DEC. 16th to 24th		16th was spent in observing billets. The Battalion commenced holding 25th in the vicinity of FRESNOY LE GRAND. Each company was billeted in one and all company dumps were formed. Good bathing accommodation was made.	
	25th		Before Christmas Day the billets had been made very comfortable, tables and stoves had been made and each Platoon had a comfortable mess room in which to spend Christmas Day. Although our a less certain the Battalion was able to celebrate Christmas Day in the old English way. Boxing Day was also kept as a holiday.	
	26th			
	27th to 31st		The remainder of the month was spent in salvaging, recreational and educational training.	
	6.1.19.			

H. Stockwell Lieut. Colonel
Commanding 1/5th Bn. South Staffs Regt.

1/6 S Staff

9827 48

Q48

WAR DIARY
or
INTELLIGENCE SUMMARY.

(Erase heading not required.)

Army Form C. 2118.

Instructions regarding War Diaries and Intelligence Summaries are contained in F. S. Regs., Part II. and the Staff Manual respectively. Title pages will be prepared in manuscript.

Place	Date	Hour	Summary of Events and Information	Remarks and references to Appendices
FRESNOY-le-Grand	Jan 1st to 3rd.		The Battalion continued with the usual salvage work. Educational and Recreational work still carried on.	
"	Jan 4th		The Battalion attended Divine Service as usual.	
"	" 5th		This day was mixxixxx occupied in Salvaging in the FRESNOY area.	
"	" 6th		The day was allotted to bathing. The M.O. held a Scabies inspection after the Companies had finished bathing.	
"	" 7th to 9th		The Battalion continued Salvaging.	
"	"10th		The Battalion Paraded for Ceremonial Drill	
"	"11th		The Battalion attended Divine Service as usual.	
"	"12th		The day was allotted for bathing and scabies inspection.	
"	"13th		The Battalion continued Salvaging in the FRESNOY Area.	
"	"14th		Salvaging was continued. One Company commenced the New Area. (LEVERGIES) leaving FRESNOY at 09.00 hours and returning at 16.30. The Cooker accompanied this Company.	
"	"15th to 19th		Salvaging still continued, companies taking turns in going out to the New Area for the day. Educational & Recreational Work still carried on.	
"	"20th		The day was allotted to bathing and scabies inspection.	

Army Form C. 2118.

WAR DIARY
or
INTELLIGENCE SUMMARY.
(Erase heading not required.)

Instructions regarding War Diaries and Intelligence Summaries are contained in F. S. Regs., Part II. and the Staff Manual respectively. Title pages will be prepared in manuscript.

Place	Date	Hour	Summary of Events and Information	Remarks and references to Appendices
FRESNOY	Jan 21st		A route march was held by one Company, the remaining companies continued Salvaging.	
"	" 22nd		The Battalion continued Salvaging.	
"	" 25th to 26th		The day was allotted to bathing and scabies inspection.	
"	" 27th to 31st		The remainder of the month was spent in Salvaging, Recreational, and Educational Training.	

A.P.Nathur. Capt. for Lieut: Colonel.

Commanding 1/6th Btn South Staffordshire Regiment.

Army Form C. 2118.

WAR DIARY
or
INTELLIGENCE SUMMARY.
(Erase heading not required.)

1/6 S. Staff Regt
Vol 49

Q49

Place	Date	Hour	Summary of Events and Information	Remarks and references to Appendices
Fauquemberg	Feb. 1		The Battn continued salvage work, paying special attention to villages.	Miss Wells
Lignerolles	2		The Battn attended Divine Service, & usual.	
	3		The Battn continued Salvage work. Educational work resumed.	
	4		Major Symes, Lt. Boyd E.C. R.M.C., 2/Lt D.G.W. Rowlett, 2/Lt S. Coleman D.C.M. joined with 4 O.R's. 2/Lt Rowlett, the Batn handed as strong as possible to witness the presentation, the Major Symes afterwards entertained the Dining Hall & Divisions. The remainder of the day was devoted to bathing, Lieutenant & Recreational work.	
	6 & 7			
	8		Salvage, Educational & Recreational work was carried on. Companies were at the disposal of Company Commanders.	
	9		Divine Service was attended as usual.	
	10		Companies were at the disposal of Company Commanders. Football Match:- Officers versus Sgts. Result:- Officers 2 goals, Sgts 2 goals.	
	11		The day was devoted to Bathing & Public Inspection and held afterwards.	
12 to 15			Companies were as the disposal of Company Commanders.	
	16.		Divine Service was attended as usual.	

Army Form C. 2118.

WAR DIARY
or
INTELLIGENCE SUMMARY.
(Erase heading not required.)

Instructions regarding War Diaries and Intelligence Summaries are contained in F. S. Regs., Part II. and the Staff Manual respectively. Title pages will be prepared in manuscript.

Place	Date	Hour	Summary of Events and Information	Remarks and references to Appendices
Iudiampoli	1/20 19.		Companies less Educational Students, were at the disposal of Company Commanders	
	20.		The day was allotted for bathing.	
	21.		Companies were at the disposal of Company Commanders.	
	22.		During the morning, Companies were at the disposal of Company Commanders. In the afternoon, all men not available for Demobilization, were transferred to the 1/6th L.I.R. together with a number of Officers, and all the men of the 1/5th L.I.R. available for Demobilization were transferred to this Battn.	
	23.		The Battn paraded for Divine Service, as usual.	
	24.		What men were available carried on with Salvage work on the Training Area.	
	25.		The day was allotted for bathing. Educational Class carried on.	
	26 to 27		Companies were at the disposal of Company Commanders. The Headquarters Guard was disbanded with.	

Chute Lieut-Colonel
Commanding 1/6 th Non South Staff Regiment.

192

Army Form C. 2118.

1/6 S Staff Bn 50

Q 50

WAR DIARY
or
INTELLIGENCE SUMMARY.
(Erase heading not required.)

Instructions regarding War Diaries and Intelligence Summaries are contained in F. S. Regs., Part II. and the Staff Manual respectively. Title pages will be prepared in manuscript.

Place	Date	Hour	Summary of Events and Information	Remarks and references to Appendices
FRESNOY-LE-GRAND.	March 1		Summer time was brought into force. Companies were at the disposal of Company Commanders.	
	2.		There was no Battalion Parade for Divine Service, but Voluntary Services were held as usual.	
	3 & 4		Companies were at the disposal of Company Commanders.	
	5.		The Battalion moved to TROISVILLES, leaving FRESNOY-LE-GRAND at 09.30 hours and marching via BOHAIN - BUSIGNY - HONNECHY - RUEMONT - TROISVILLES. Arrived at Billets in TROISVILLES at 15.00	
TROISVILLES.	6.		A Muster Parade was held at 10.00 hours. All W.Os. N.C.Os. and men attended. The remainder of the day was devoted to improving Billets etc.	
	7.		Companies were again at the disposal of Company Commanders.	
	8.		All available men paraded at the Q.M.Stores for fatigue.	
	9.		There was no Parade Service, but Voluntary Services were held in the Church Army Building.	
	10 & 11.		All available men paraded at the Q.M.Stores for fatigue.	
	12.		All available men reported to the Transport Officer, but there was some difficulty in finding sufficient men.	
	13 to 15.		All available men again paraded at the Q.M.Stores for fatigue.	
	16.		There was no Parade Service, but Voluntary Services were held in the Church Army Building.	
	17.		During the morning all men were again at the Q.M.Stores. In the afternoon the major part of the Battalion -- 37 other ranks,-- and nearly all the Officers, went to VALENCIENNES to see a performance by the 1st Army Concert Party "The Rouges et Noirs".	

Army Form C. 2118.

WAR DIARY
or
INTELLIGENCE SUMMARY.
(Erase heading not required)

Instructions regarding War Diaries and Intelligence Summaries are contained in F. S. Regs., Part II. and the Staff Manual respectively. Title pages will be prepared in manuscript.

Place: TROISVILLES.

Date	Hour	Summary of Events and Information	Remarks and references to Appendices
March 18 & 19.		All available men paraded at the Q.M.Stores.	
20.		At 09.45 the battalion paraded for the purpose of saying good-bye to the G.O.C. 46th N.M.Division Major General G.F.Boyd, C.B. C.M.G. D.S.O. D.C.M.	
21 & 22.		All available men paraded at the Q.M.Stores.	
23.		There was no parade Service, but Voluntary Services were held in the Church Army Building.	
24 & 25.		All available men again paraded at the Q.M.Stores.	
26.		The Battalion bathed during the morning. In the afternoon a party went to VALENCIENNES to see a performance by the "Rouge et Noirs".	
27.to 29.		All available men again paraded at the Q.M.Stores.	
30.		The Battalion paraded for Roll Call and Rifle Inspection. There was no parade Service, but a Voluntary Service was held in the Church Army Building.	
31.		The Battalion paraded for fatigue at the Q.M.Stores, and afterwards for Roll Call.	

J. Robertson Captain for
Lieutenant-Colonel.
Commanding 1/6th Battalion South Staffordshire Regiment.

WAR DIARY
or
INTELLIGENCE SUMMARY.

Army Form C. 2118.

(Erase heading not required.)

Instructions regarding War Diaries and Intelligence Summaries are contained in F. S. Regs., Part II. and the Staff Manual respectively. Title pages will be prepared in manuscript.

Place	Date	Hour	Summary of Events and Information	Remarks and references to Appendices
TROISVILLES	April 1.		All men who were available paraded at the Q.M.Stores for fatigue.	
	2.		All available men again paraded at the Q.M.Stores in the morning, and also bathed.	
	3.		All men paraded at the Q.M.Stores as before. A stables inspection was held during the morning.	
	4.		All available men paraded at the Q.M.Stores for fatigue.	
	5.			
	6.		The was no parade Service, but a Voluntary combined Service was held in the French Schools near the Mairie.	
	7.		All available men paraded at the Q.M.Stores for Salvage Work.	
	8.			
	9.			
	10.		All available men paraded at the Q.M.Stores for fatigue.	
	11.		All available men again paraded at the Q.M.Stores for fatigue. All men bathed during the morning.	
	12.		The Roman Catholic Padre saw all Roman Catholics in the Church TROISVILLES in the evening.	
	13.		All available men again paraded for fatigue at the Q.M.Stores.	
	14.		There was no parade Service, but a Voluntary Service was held in the old Church Army Building during the morning.	
	15.			
	16.			
	17.			
	18.			
	19.		All available men paraded at the Q.M.Stores for fatigue.	
	20.		All men paraded for Divine Service with the exception of a party at work at CAUDRY.	
	21.		The fatigue party for cleaning limbers at Caudry paraded as before.	
	22.		All available men again paraded at the Q.M.Stores.	
	23.		All men paraded at the Battalion Orderly Room.	
	24.			
	25.		All available men again paraded at the Q.M.Stores.	
	26.		The Battalion paraded for Roll Call on the Football Field near the crucifix.	
	27.		Sunday. No Voluntary Service or a Parade Service.	
	28.			
	to 30		All available men again paraded at the Q.M.Stores.	

S. R. Rickerford, Captain & Adjutant
for Lieutenant-Colonel
Commanding 1/6th Battalion South Staffordshire Regiment.

Army Form C. 2118.

WAR DIARY
or
INTELLIGENCE SUMMARY.

(Erase heading not required.)

Instructions regarding War Diaries and Intelligence Summaries are contained in F. S. Regs., Part II. and the Staff Manual respectively. Title pages will be prepared in manuscript.

Place	Date	Hour	Summary of Events and Information	Remarks and references to Appendices
	May 1st to May 31st		Cadre Battalion. 6 of this Battalion awaiting instructions to enroll.	

3rd June 1919.

Lieutenant-Colonel.
Commanding 1/6th Battalion South Staffordshire Regiment.

www.ingramcontent.com/pod-product-compliance
Lightning Source LLC
Chambersburg PA
CBHW080812010526
44111CB00015B/2547